Rand McNally
Historical Atlas of the
WORLD

⊕ Rand McNally
Historical Atlas of the
WORLD

Rand McNally & Company
CHICAGO   NEW YORK   SAN FRANCISCO

General editor
R. I. Moore   *University of Sheffield*

Associate editors
Mark Greengrass   *University of Sheffield*
Bernard Wasserstein   *University of Sheffield*

Contributors
Graeme Barker   *University of Sheffield*
Julian Birch   *University of Sheffield*
J. G. de Casparis   *University of Leiden*
Gordon Daniels   *University of Sheffield*
J. F. Drinkwater   *University of Sheffield*
Mark Elvin   *St Antony's College, Oxford*
Richard Fletcher   *University of York*
Bernard Hamilton   *University of Nottingham*
Peter Hardy   *S.O.A.S., University of London*
Robert Irwin   *Formerly of St Andrew's University*
Colin Jones   *University of Exeter*
Edmund King   *University of Sheffield*
D. O. Morgan   *S.O.A.S., University of London*
T. A. Reuter   *University of Exeter*
Francis Robinson   *Royal Holloway College,*
   University of London
J. Roy   *University of Sheffield*
John Stevenson   *University of Sheffield*
David Turley   *University of Kent*
A. Wasserstein   *University of Jerusalem*
Henry S. Wilson   *University of York*
John Woodward   *University of Sheffield*

Rand McNally
Historical Atlas of the World

Original edition published under the title of the Hamlyn
Historical Atlas, by the Hamlyn Publishing Group
Limited.

Text © The Hamlyn Publishing Group Limited 1981
Maps © The Hamlyn Publishing Group Limited and
Creative Cartography Limited 1981, except maps and text
appearing in the United States Historical Map Section,
pages 167 through 182 which are copyright by Rand
McNally & Company.

SBN 528-83124-0
Library of Congress Catalog Card Number: 81-51409

Cartography by Creative Cartography Limited: Nicholas
Skelton and Terry Allen. Color origination by Grantown
Graphics, London, except for maps appearing in the
United States Historical Map Section, pages 167 through
182, which were created by Rand McNally & Company.

Printed in the United States of America

Contents

The age of European supremacy

I Europe and a wider world   page 72

II Colonies and commerce   page 77

III The Eurasian land empires   page 81

IV Europe divided   page 89

V The ancien régime   page 97

VI The age of revolutions   page 105

VII The Industrial Revolution   page 109

VIII Liberalism and nationalism   page 115

IX The age of imperialism   page 123

The emergence of the modern world

United States Historical Maps

Survey of maps by date and region

This chart shows the rough chronological span of each map, and serves as a guide to the coverage of each region's history in this Atlas. As well as the maps indicated for each specific region, information about that region may also be found on the maps of the relevant continent, and on the world maps.

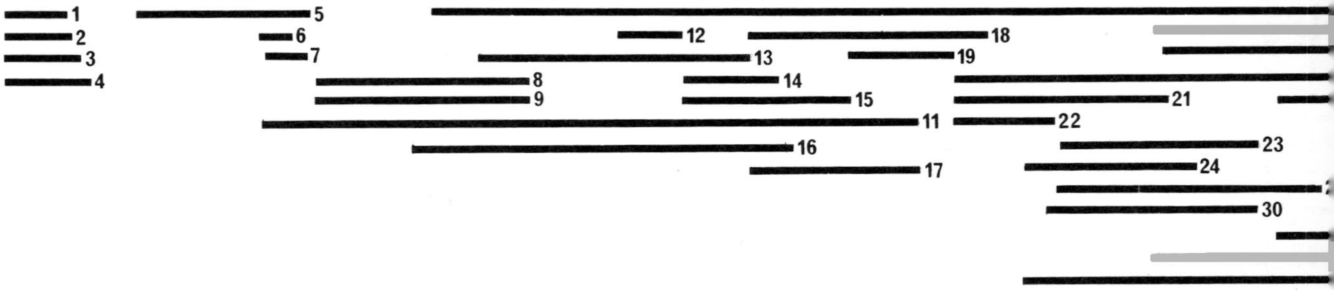

	up to 1000 BC	1000-500 BC	500-250 BC	250-1 BC	AD 1-250	250-500	500-750	750-1000	1000-1150	1150-1300
The World	1 2 3									
THE AMERICAS										
NORTH AMERICA										
SOUTH AMERICA										
EUROPE				8 11	12	14	17		20	28
Scandinavia									24	
Germany & Central Europe									23	
WESTERN EUROPE										25
France & the Low Countries								22		
British Isles									24	25
Spain & Portugal										
Italy										
THE MEDITERRANEAN		5		8	12	14	17 19		27	
Eastern Mediterranean	4						18			26
Greece & the Balkans	4	5	7				18	21		
AFRICA				11					20	
NORTH AFRICA	3						19		27	
EURASIA				11					20	
Russia								21		
Persia & Asia Minor	3	6		9		15	19		27	
INDIA	3				16					
THE FAR EAST				11					20	
China					10	13			30	
Japan										
AUSTRALASIA	1									
	up to 1000 BC	1000-500 BC	500-250 BC	250-1 BC	AD 1-250	250-500	500-750	750-1000	1000-1150	1150-1300

Timeline chart (numbers 10, 25, 74, 37, 38, 60, 61, 75, 20, 39, 62, 28, 40, 63, 29, 41, 64, 34, 47, 65, 35, 52, 66, 76, 36, 50, 67, 42, 51, 77, 31, 53, 78, 32, 45, 54, 79, 33, 46, 80, 43, 55, 56, 81, 44, 57, 48, 58, 82, 83, 49, 59, 84, 68, 85, 69, 86, 70, 71, 87, 72, 73, 88)

0-1400	1400-1500	1500-1600	1600-1700	1700-1800	1800-1850	1850-1900	1900-1925	1925-1950	1950-1980	
	36		50			58	67		83 84 88	**The World**
				51					85	**THE AMERICAS**
			38	53	68	69		78		NORTH AMERICA
			37	59						SOUTH AMERICA
	35	45	52		55 60	57	75	78 80 81	82	**EUROPE**
			48							Scandinavia
34		44	47		61		76	77		Germany & Central Europe
		44 46								WESTERN EUROPE
			49	54						France & the Low Countries
				56						British Isles
33										Spain & Portugal
32						62				Italy
								81		THE MEDITERRANEAN
	42								87	Eastern Mediterranean
						63				Greece & the Balkans
			50		66		74			**AFRICA**
								81	87	NORTH AFRICA
31										**EURASIA**
	43				70		71 76			Russia
									87	Persia & Asia Minor
29			41			65			86	**INDIA**
			39			64	73	79	86	**THE FAR EAST**
			40							China
						72				Japan
			50			67			83 88	**AUSTRALASIA**

| 0-1400 | 1400-1500 | 1500-1600 | 1600-1700 | 1700-1800 | 1800-1850 | 1850-1900 | 1900-1925 | 1925-1950 | 1950-1980 | |

9

Introduction

"SHOW ME THE MAP OF A REGION," a great French geographer used to say, "and I will tell you its history." Since Herodotus, 5th century historian, other historians have appreciated the influence of environment on human development. They have known that the outcome of a battle—even of an entire war—has often been determined by the lay of the land. Climate, topography, natural resources, and lines of communication have shaped the more enduring aspects of civilization, influencing even the religious and political life of a people. As a way of understanding history, maps have proved as valuable as written records.

Thus, the first aim of an historical atlas is to show, through the combined use of maps and text, the development of human society in its physical setting. This means describing not only boundaries, military conquests, and trade routes but the climate, terrain, soils, and vegetation of the world, both as they are today and as they were at various times in the past. The reader—whether a serious student of history or a curious layperson—will be able to see more clearly the connection between geography and the historical development of a region—between, say, the annual flooding of the Nile river and the rise of Egypt as a major world center. While detailed geographical information is not always available, we believe this Atlas presents a vivid account of the world's environment at different periods in history.

The maps in this volume are designed to be clear and attractive, encouraging readers to linger over detail, stirring their imagination and curiosity, and reminding them of the real world in which historical conflicts and controversies have taken place. We have included full-page or double-page maps of as many areas as possible, preferring to show one or two points of their history in detail rather than many points superficially. Also, we have avoided using multiple inset maps whose information would be barely visible to the naked eye. Instead, the maps have been selected to present highlights of historical periods and to give the reader a broad view of human history as a whole.

The text complements the maps by discussing some of the larger historical themes and questions, and by providing a context for various groups of maps. For example, the complex illustrations of Italian city-states are more meaningful when the reader understands the political, religious, and cultural background of that time. Like the maps, the text is selective and compressed, often covering several hundred years in one stroke and touching on only the most decisive events influencing a region's history. In addition, captions summarize the basic points illustrated by individual maps. Only in the special section of United States historical maps is each period of history treated in greater detail.

The theme we offer in this Atlas is simple and straightforward: humanity's gradual progress from isolated societies to a world that is rapidly becoming a single global community. More than in any other period of history people today are bound together in their political destinies and connected in an expanding network of communication. Distances between people have been bridged by the expansion of communities, by exploration and trade, and by the search for land and riches. Differences among people have been broken down by conquest, cooperation, the spread of universal religious and political ideals, and the rise of dominant civilizations. One has only to compare the maps of early scattered settlements with the maps of industrialized nations to see a graphic illustration of our basic theme.

The foundations of the world community taking shape today are rooted in Europe's recent expansion, imperialism, technical innovations, and industrial development. While Europeans no longer claim the lion's share of history as confidently as they used to, their impact on the world has been profound. Compared to many parts of the world, European and North American societies have been remarkably diverse and subject to rapid change. These factors account for the Western orientation of this volume. Yet to gain a balanced view of world history, we must also look at the emergence of cultures in the Middle East, Asia, and Africa. The level of international tension existing today makes it imperative that we acquire a better understanding of world history. Conflicts among nations are often born of their ignorance about the way ancient differences of circumstance and culture have molded each other's values and conventions. Without an appreciation of one another's historical development, countries often become locked into patterns of old antagonisms and prejudices. Thus, the idea that the study of history must be "relevant"—that is, limited solely to the immediate past of one's *own* immediate region—is not only foolish but dangerous.

This Atlas, with its portrayal of world history and geography, will help the reader gain a stronger grasp of historical events and their impact on the world we live in today.

Preface

THE 23 CONTRIBUTORS to this Atlas have benefited from the help and advice of several times that number of friends and colleagues in many academic fields, including the staffs of many libraries, and they have relied on the tolerance and encouragement of many wives and families, whom it is impossible to list by name

The editor's debts are enormous; foremost to the contributors, whose willingness to undertake a novel and difficult task in a short time, many of them at the request of a stranger, has been equalled by the patience with which they have dealt with his questions and quibbles since. To say that responsibility for all errors rests with the editor alone is no mere formality, for among his many debts to the contributors not the least is for the forebearance with which they have accepted his suggestions and submitted to his judgements.

The associate editors have performed a thankless task with inexhaustible grace and good humor. Without their knowledge and judgement and their readiness to undertake the execution of a very large proportion of the maps and text, the editor's task would have been quite impossible; they are responsible for many of the Atlas's virtues and none of its defects.

I cannot sufficiently express my personal gratitude to all those who have made it possible for me to complete it, and especially, for everything they have put up with, to my wife and daughter.

R. I. Moore

The ancient world I

The beginnings of civilisation

FOSSIL REMAINS of primitive forms of man have been discovered from sites in Africa dating to the beginnings of the Pleistocene Era (the first Ice Age), at least two or three million years ago, such as Lake Turkhana and Olduvai Gorge (*see Map 1*), but the process of anatomical development leading up to these 'hominids' can be traced back much further, to at least fifteen million years ago.

The earliest true member of our genus, called *homo erectus*, belongs to the Middle Pleistocene period, roughly half a million years ago. Like the ancestral hominids, *homo erectus* was confined to Africa and the frost-free zones of Europe and Asia.

From about 100,000 years ago Neanderthal Man (now commonly regarded as a member of the species *homo sapiens* rather than as a divergent species) occupied much the same area of world. He was replaced about 40,000 years ago by fully modern man, *homo sapiens sapiens*. Like the earlier forms of man *homo sapiens sapiens* was a hunter-gatherer, but culturally he was more advanced – at what is termed the Upper Palaeolithic stage. He was equipped with a stone and bone technology much more sophisticated than those of earlier hunters, as well as a conceptual repertoire that included systematic burial of the dead and adornment of the living and a fertility ideology best known from the so-called 'Venus figurines' and painted caves such as Lascaux in France and Altamira in Spain.

Modern man spread rapidly over the globe. He probably reached North America about 20,000 years ago, by means of a land bridge that existed then between Siberia and Alaska (the plain of Beringia, where the Bering Straits are now) and a corridor between the northern ice sheets of Canada and Alaska. To reach Australia by about 35,000 years ago he must have used sea-going craft of some sophistication, for no land bridge existed across the Wallace Line. All the more remarkable, the rapid expansion of modern man over the world took place at the climax of the Ice Age, when many parts of the world were ice-covered and when the temperate regions of today were extremely inhospitable. Yet, well-adapted to these severe conditions, man the hunter had colonised nearly all the ice-free parts of the globe by the end of the second Ice Age, 12,000 years ago.

Gordon Childe's use of the term revolution to describe the beginnings of agriculture has been criticised because we now know that agriculture took many thousands of years to evolve in different parts of the world. Nevertheless the development of food production remains the most revolutionary advance in prehistoric subsistence technique. The origins of agriculture probably lie in the highly specialised forms of hunting and plant collecting that had developed amongst many Palaeolithic societies by the end of the Ice Age 12,000 years ago. Three or four thousand years later there is clear evidence for farming communities in the hills of Palestine, Turkey, Iraq and Iran and in surrounding areas such as Greece and Crete, perhaps in Egypt, and in Turkmenia (*Map 2*). These regions are thought to have been the natural habitats of the wild ancestors of domesticated wheat, barley, sheep and goats – the staple crops and stock of the first farmers here. Although research has tended to concentrate in the Near East (because very early farming was expected here, given the development of the Sumerian and Egyptian civilisations by 3000 BC), current work in the Americas, the Far East and South-East Asia indicates that agricultural systems using different crops and animals may well

have developed at similarly early dates, within three or four millennia of the end of the Pleistocene Era.

In the Americas, domesticated animals were by and large unimportant. Instead a wide range of plants was taken into cultivation in different areas, including avocado pears, beans, peppers, pumpkins, squashes, and maize which eventually became the major staple. In China pigs and millet were the staple resources of the first farmers, and people in New Guinea kept domesticated pigs and grew yams and taro. Later on rice became the staple crop in the Far East, and the first agriculture in sub-Saharan Africa was based mainly on cattle and millet.

Between 3000 BC, when urban life was beginning in Mesopotamia and Egypt, and the time of Christ, farming spread over the most accessible parts of the world. Many regions beyond these areas of early farming were still occupied by hunting and gathering societies, some of which have survived to modern times, such as the Aborigines of Australia and Bushmen of southern Africa. Within the farming world, also, some societies continued with the hunting and gathering way of life and others practised both types of subsistence. On the fringes of the farming world there have always been other societies practising 'intermediate' economies like the reindeer herders of Lapland and Siberia, or the Bedouin camel herders of the Arabian and Saharan deserts.

In Europe the spread of agriculture from the south-east to the north-west between 6000 and 3000 BC has long been regarded as accompanying the movement of new people – the first farmers – into a sparsely inhabited environment. In recent years, however, it has become increasingly clear that a vigorous hunter-gatherer population was living in most parts of Europe, and that the development of prehistoric agriculture in Europe has to be understood as much in terms of the adaptation of existing people to new resources (for cereals and sheep and goats must have been introduced to temperate Europe from the eastern Mediterranean) as in terms of the arrival of colonist farmers. Similarly, the beginnings of farming in other parts of the Eurasian and African continents used to be regarded as the result of the diffusion of ideas or people or both from the 'hearth area' of early agriculture in the Near East, but the variation we now see between early farming peoples across the world – different crops and animals, different farming techniques, different timescales of development – makes it clear that many prehistoric societies in different parts of the world developed agricultural systems in the millennia following the end of the Ice Age without any major stimulus from each other.

Dry farming (that is, farming without irrigation) had developed in the hills of Mesopotamia by 6000 BC. In the next two thousand years, population pressure in these hills seems to have forced the colonisation of the Tigris and Euphrates plains below, where rainfall was insufficient for dry farming (*Map 3*). To survive, the new villages had to develop simple irrigation systems to farm the land of the Twin Rivers. The new technology both demanded higher levels of social and economic complexity and in turn allowed much higher levels of population than were possible in the hills. By 3500 BC the Sumerian civilisation had evolved in lower Mesopotamia: it consisted of a collection of a dozen or so cities and their territories. The cities were dominated by temple complexes housing priestly elites who controlled a large part

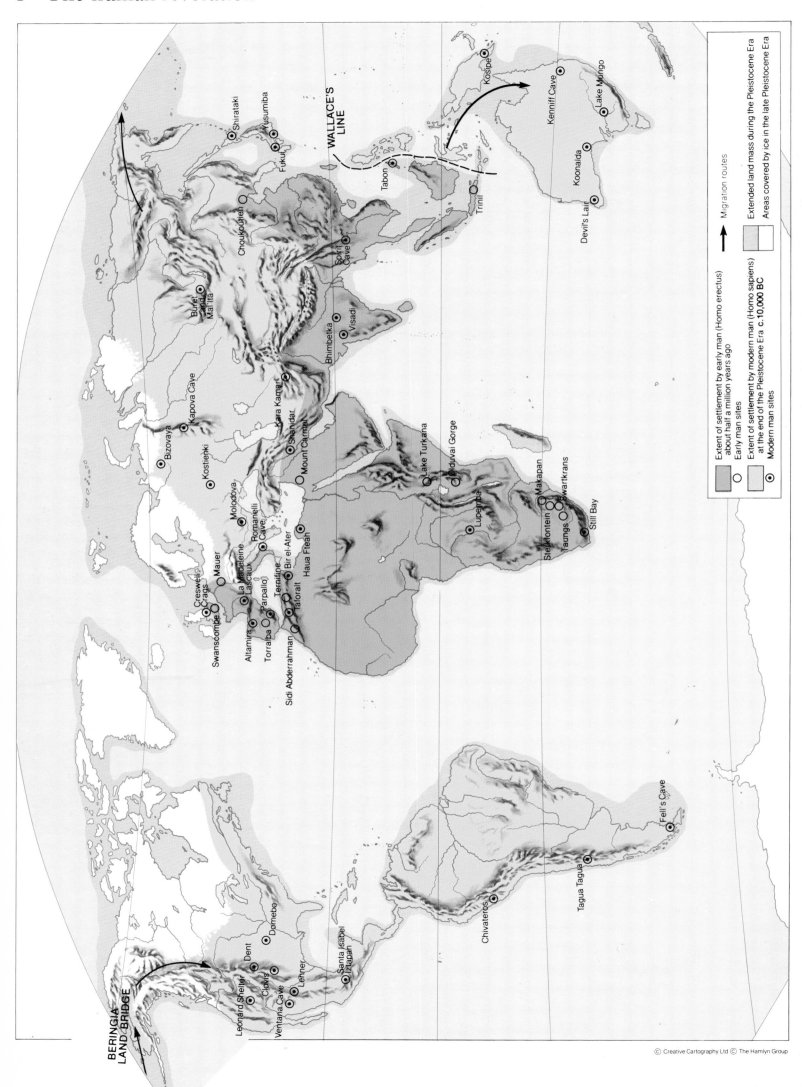

BERINGIA
LAND BRIDGE

Leonard Shelter
Dent
Clovis
Ventana Cave
Lehner
Santa Isabel
Iztapan
Domebo

Chivateros
Tagua Tagua
Fell's Cave

Swanscombe
Creswell Crags
Mauer
La Madeleine
Lascaux
Altamira
Torralba
Parpallo
Terrifine
Taforalt
Sidi Abderrahman
Bir el-Ater
Haua Fteah
Romanelli Cave
Molodova
Kostienki
Bizovaya
Kapova Cave
Buret
Mal'ita
Kara Kamar
Shanidar
Mount Carmel

Still Bay
Makapan
Swartkrans
Sterkfontein
Taungs
Lupemba
Olduvai Gorge
Lake Turkana

Bhimbetka
Visadi
Spirit Cave
Choukoutien
Fukui
Yusumiba
Shirataki

WALLACE'S
LINE

Tabon
Trinil

Kosipe
Kenniff Cave
Lake Mungo
Koonalda
Devil's Lair

Legend:

Extent of settlement by early man (Homo erectus) about half a million years ago
○ Early man sites

Extent of settlement by modern man (Homo sapiens) at the end of the Pleistocene Era c. **10,000 BC**
◉ Modern man sites

→ Migration routes

Extended land mass during the Pleistocene Era

Areas covered by ice in the late Pleistocene Era

1 The human revolution
The earliest members of our *genus* were confined to Africa and the frost-free zones of Europe and Asia. About 40,000 years ago they were succeeded by *homo sapiens sapiens*, who spread across the world.

2 The Neolithic revolution
The great pre-historian Gordon Childe coined the term 'Neolithic revolution' to describe the transformation in prehistoric society represented by the beginning of agriculture: it was to be the springboard for early civilisations in several parts of the world.

3 The urban revolution
Childe described the next major stage in the evolution of prehistoric societies as the 'Urban revolution'. He referred mainly to the earliest civilisations of Mesopotamia, Egypt and the Indus valley, but the same revolutionary process also took place in other parts of the world.

of the social, economic and ritual life of the city state. Writing systems were developed for accounting purposes, and craft technology attained a very high level of sophistication.

By 3000 BC a very different civilisation was established in Egypt. There was a single state rather than a series of small city states, geared to the exploitation of the Nile valley by highly organised irrigation systems, controlled by a single ruler (the pharoah) and his regional governors. By 2500 BC a third – as different – civilisation emerged in the Indus Valley, the Harappan. The nature of the leadership is not clear, but the cities were carefully planned on a grid system (quite unlike the Sumerian and Egyptian cities) with artisans' quarters and residential areas, well provided with drains and fresh water supplies, and with massively defended citadels containing public buildings.

These civilisations are so different from each other that the Egyptian and Indus cities must almost certainly be thought of as independent in origin rather than as the result of diffusion from Sumeria, although there is considerable evidence for systematic trade between Sumeria and both Egypt and the Indus valley. Civilisation continued virtually uninterrupted in Mesopotamia and Egypt for thousands of years, up to the classical period, but the Indus state collapsed after only a few centuries, in about 1700 BC. The state system here depended on intensive irrigation agriculture, and over-exploitation of the valley may have led to soil deterioration, erosion and flooding, until the weakened state fell prey to outside attack.

The second millennium BC saw the emergence and florescence of complex state societies in Crete, mainland Greece and central Turkey (*Map 4*). In China, proto-urban societies may have developed by c.2500 BC, but the first dynasty recorded in the Chinese annals to be identified by archaeology is that of the Shang (traditionally dated 1523-1027 BC). Shang society, according to both documentary records and excavation, was extremely hierarchical and warlike. Subsistence was still based on millet and pigs rather than rice (irrigation was very limited), but craft techniques were highly sophisticated, particularly bronze casting, jade carving, pottery and silk weaving.

In the New World, complex societies emerged in Mesoamerica and Peru at the end of the first millennium BC. The Maya civilisation in Mesoamerica (Guatemala, Yucatan and Belize) achieved its climax between AD 300 and 900. Massive ceremonial centres were constructed in the rain forests by a stone-age society for a priestly élite which seems to have owed much of its power to its control of the ceremonial calendar and its ability to predict astronomical events. The centres were not cities,

for the ordinary people were dispersed throughout the countryside. In Peru the ceremonial centres began in the first millennium BC, but the Moche and Nazca states flourished at the same time as the Maya. Like the Maya they were founded on maize cultivation and were dominated by huge ceremonial centres, but on the other hand the Andean cultures were technologically more advanced, practising irrigation and bronze smithing.

By the beginning of the second millennium AD these early states had been replaced by the major imperial civilisations, the Aztecs in Mesomaerica and the Incas in Peru (*see also Map 36*). The fundamentals of these civilisations were much as before – monumental centres, obsessive and savage religions, all-powerful élite groups and relatively primitive technologies. Unlike the Maya, the Aztecs built true residential cities and intensive irrigation systems in the arid highlands of Mexico. Both Aztecs and Incas controlled large imperial domains, exacting tribute from subject states, but neither was able to organise effective resistance when the Spaniards invaded and their empires were swiftly dismembered, the Aztec in 1519-1521 and the Inca in 1527-1532.

In sub-Saharan Africa, two notable prehistoric states flourished between about AD 1000 and 1500, roughly contemporary with the Aztec and Inca civilisations. In Nigeria, stimulated by Arab caravan trade across the Sahara for gold, ivory and slaves (*Map 27*), complex hierarchial societies (like the Yoruba) developed in the savannah zone between the desert and coastal west Africa, best known today from the fine bronze heads of Ife made by the *cire perdue* technique of casting, a skill acquired from the Arab traders. In central southern Africa, the *zimbabwe* states developed c.1200-1600 out of the preceding simple agricultural societies of the African Early Iron Age, in Rhodesia and (only recently discovered) in Mozambique. Cattle were a major source of wealth for the *zimbabwe* rulers, who traded with Arab and then Portuguese communities on the east coast for Arabian, Persian and Indian glass beads (and occasionally even Chinese porcelain) in exchange for gold, iron and ivory. Like the American civilisations the African states were unable to withstand European technology and military organisation, although their destruction was less cataclysmic.

Further reading: D. and R. Whitehouse, *An Archaeological Atlas of the World* (Thames & Hudson, 1977); V. Gordon Childe, *The Dawn of European Civilisation* (Routledge, 1957; Paladin, 1973); J. G. D. Clarke, *World Prehistory in New Perspective* (Cambridge University Press, 1977); G. Daniel, *The First Civilisations* (Thames & Hudson, 1968); Jacquetta Hawkes, *The First Great Civilisations* (Hutchinson, 1973; Penguin, 1977).

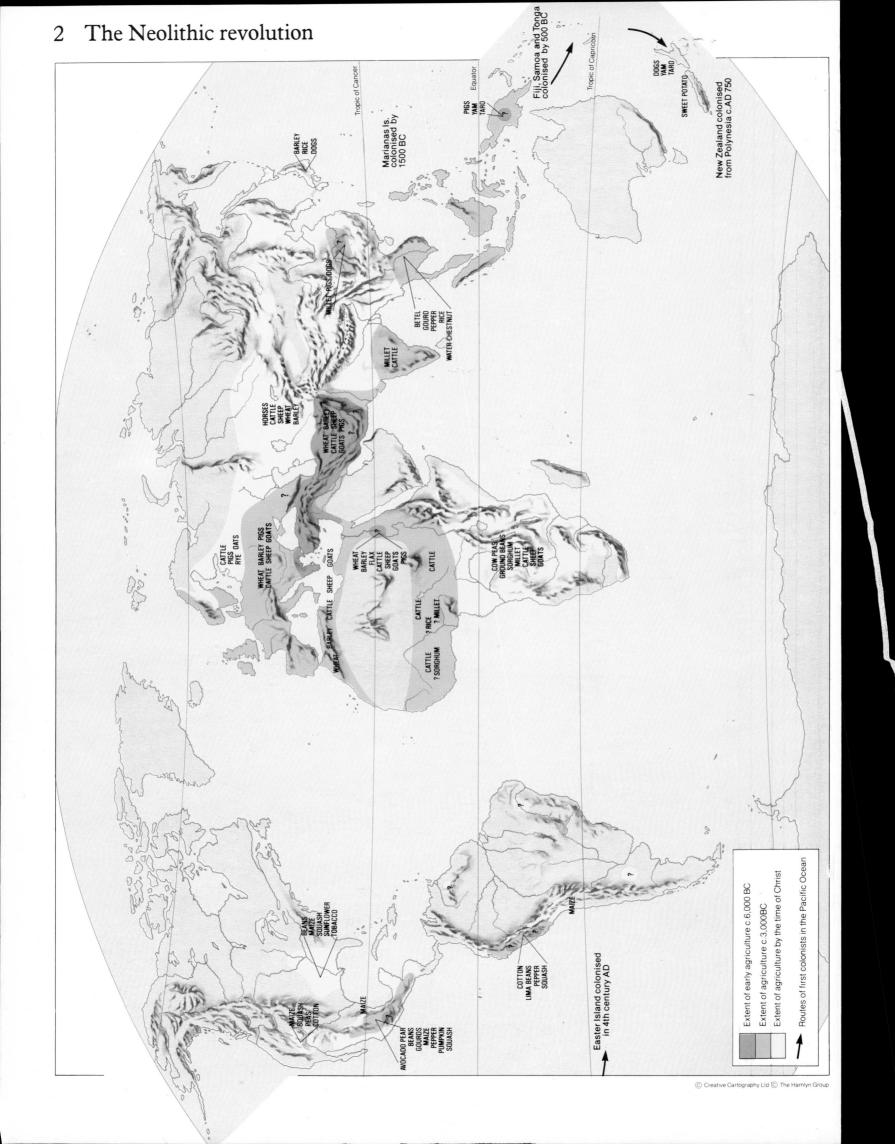

BARLEY
RICE
DOGS

Marianas Is.
colonised by
1500 BC

PIGS
YAM
TARO

Fiji, Samoa and Tonga
colonised by 500 BC

DOGS
YAM
TARO

SWEET POTATO

New Zealand colonised
from Polynesia c.AD 750

MILLET PIGS DOGS

BETEL
GOURD
PEPPER
RICE
WATER CHESTNUT

MILLET
CATTLE

HORSES
CATTLE
SHEEP
WHEAT
BARLEY

WHEAT BARLEY
CATTLE SHEEP
GOATS PIGS

CATTLE
PIGS
RYE OATS

WHEAT BARLEY PIGS
CATTLE SHEEP GOATS

WHEAT BARLEY CATTLE SHEEP GOATS

WHEAT
BARLEY
FLAX
CATTLE
SHEEP
GOATS
PIGS

CATTLE

CATTLE
? RICE
? MILLET

COW PEAS
GROUND BEANS
SORGHUM
MILLET
CATTLE
SHEEP
GOATS

CATTLE
? SORGHUM

BEANS
MAIZE
SQUASH
SUNFLOWER
TOBACCO

MAIZE

COTTON
LIMA BEANS
PEPPER
SQUASH

MAIZE
SQUASH
PEAS
COTTON

MAIZE

AVOCADO PEAR
BEANS
GOURDS
MAIZE
PEPPER
PUMPKIN
SQUASH

Easter Island colonised
in 4th century AD

Tropic of Cancer

Equator

Tropic of Capricorn

Extent of early agriculture c.6,000 BC
Extent of agriculture c.3,000BC
Extent of agriculture by the time of Christ

Routes of first colonists in the Pacific Ocean

© Creative Cartography Ltd © The Hamlyn Group

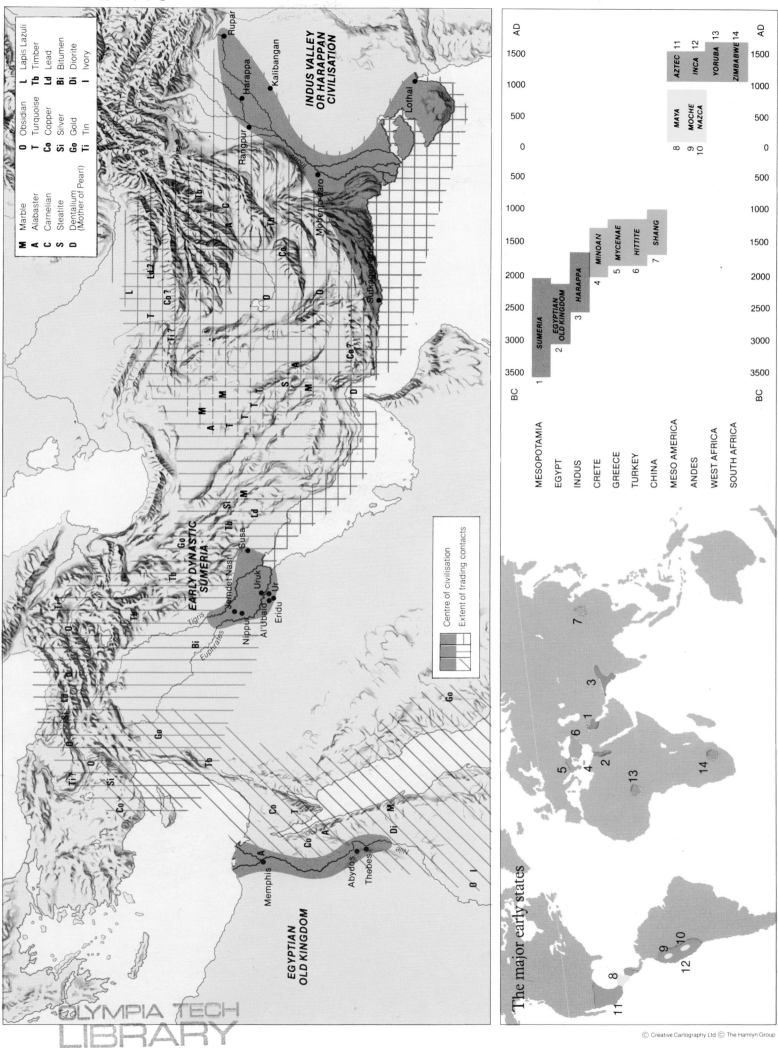

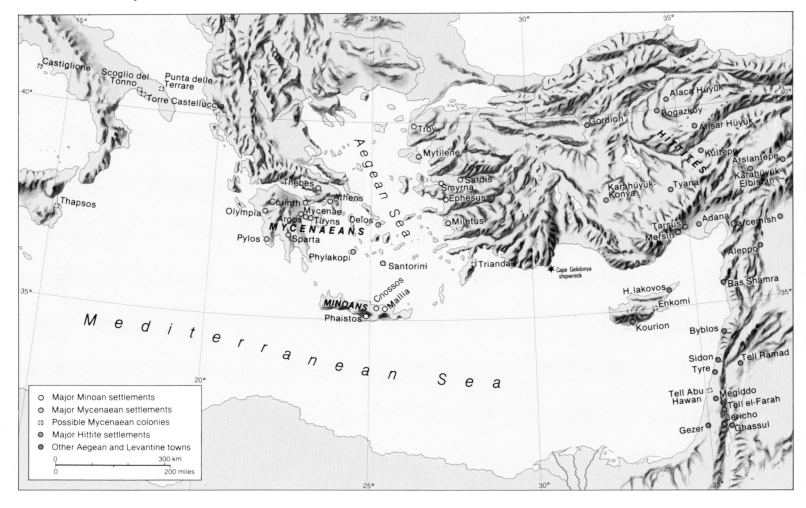

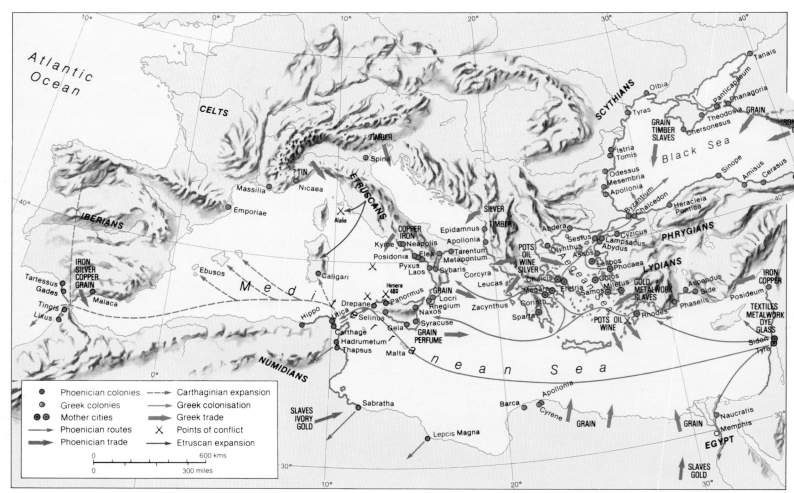

The ancient world II

The ancient Mediterranean

4 Minoans, Mycenaeans and Hittites; and
5 Phoenicians and Greeks
After about 2000 BC the shores and islands of the Mediterranean were gradually colonised by a succession of enterprising peoples who laid the foundations of the cultural and commercial unity upon which classical civilisation was based.

AFTER SOME three thousand years of prehistoric settlement the Minoan civilisation emerged in Crete around 2000 BC. The island was controlled by a series of palaces, of which the best known are Knossos, Phaistos and Mallia (*see Map 4*). Each palace, which was undefended, had a large courtyard at its focus, surrounded by elegant monumental buildings, often decorated with highly coloured frescoes. The palaces also housed workshops for craftsmen, who were especially skilled in the working of precious metals and stones, and substantial storerooms. The palaces were primarily administrative centres. Their officials organised agricultural production in the surrounding countryside, (particularly of sheep for wool, and cereals, olives and vines), the collection and storage of foodstuffs, the distribution of rations to craftsmen and agricultural workers, and trade with the outside world. The Minoan script, 'Linear A', still undeciphered, was presumably developed for the complex accounting which this 'palace economy' required.

In about 1450 BC, perhaps in the wake of a volcanic eruption on Santorini (Thera), Crete seems to have fallen under the control of the Mycenaeans, who had established themselves in mainland Greece at about 1700. Their palace architecture, craft skills and decorative arts were very similar to those of Minoan Crete. The Mycenaean script, 'Linear B', is an early form of Greek. It was also primarily an accounting device, for the administrative centres of Greece operated much the same sort of economy as those of Crete. However the Mycenaean centres were usually much smaller and closer together than the Minoan and had massive defences.

In their heyday the Mycenaeans not only controlled Crete and the Cyclades, but traded throughout the eastern Mediterranean, mainly in wine and olive oil. They set up colonies in Italy, Cyprus and the Levant. Some of the most remarkable evidence for their trade comes from a Mycenaean shipwreck with 'ox-hide ingots' (copper weights of a standard measure) discovered off Cape Gelidonya in southern Turkey. The wealth and power of the Mycenaean lords in life is spectacularly illustrated by the fabulous metalwork placed with them in death in the Shaft Graves of Mycenae.

Urban life in Anatolia began on a significant scale with the emergence of the Hittite state after 2000 BC. There had probably been petty chiefdoms in the area before that, for the treasures of the 'royal tombs' of Alaca Hüyük and Troy, dating from about 2500 BC, provide clear evidence of concentrated wealth, advanced craft skills and social hierarchy. However the process of social stratification in Anatolia was apparently accelerated by contact with the established civilisation of Mesopotamia. The region was drawn into the trading networks of the higher cultures to the south-east. Shortly after 2000 BC an Assyrian colony was established outside the town of Kültepe (Hittite Kadesh) to organise the export of metal, particularly copper, back to Mesopotamia. The Hittites built a great capital city at Bogazköy (Hattusha), with massive defensive walls four miles in circumference. Perhaps their most significant achievement was their mastery of iron production, which gave them military supremacy in their time. They were far more warlike and expansionist than the Minoans and Mycenaeans, and at the height of their power sacked Babylon (destroying the Babylonian first dynasty) and defeated an Egyptian army near Kadesh.

The Minoan, Mycenaean and Hittite civilisations all collapsed in about 1200 BC, and in Egypt the system of government of the Pharaohs crumbled temporarily. The immediate cause in every region seems to have been military attack, but such raids should be regarded more as symptoms of internal disintegration than as a fundamental cause of collapse. Social and economic failure, compounded by natural disasters such as drought and disease, opened the way for the invaders. In addition, the fact that iron making had become very widely diffused in Anatolia and Asia Minor by 1000 BC not only contributed to the confusion of the following centuries, as one people after another bid for supremacy, but suggests that the loss of the Hittite monopoly of ironworking was one reason for their decline. Advanced civilisation had lost its technological lead over its barbarian neighbours.

Whatever its cause, the collapse of 1200 BC inaugurated a long period of obscurity and confusion from whose debris the continuous history of western civilisation begins to emerge. By around 500 BC, the Eurasian landbridge of the Middle East and Anatolia had been subjected to a unified political domination which stretched to the edges of desert, sea and steppe, while the shores of the Mediterranean had been settled by colonists from the Levant and the Aegean (*Maps 5 and 6*). This contrast between the two great homes of classical civilisation was not only geographical: the words 'Persian' and 'Greek' already stood, as they would continue to do, for 'despotism' and 'democracy'.

The Assyrian empire, which controlled the trade routes between Mesopotamia and the Mediterranean from the time of Ashur-narsi-Pal (*r.*883-859 BC) and conquered Egypt in that of Essarhaddon (*r.*680-669), provided the most centralised and the most brutal government that man had yet seen. Its populations were subjugated by mass murder, deportation and enslavement on a huge scale. Assyrian governors, supported by a professional and internationally recruited army, imposed a single code of law and administration. Even more than the Medes who overthrew them, destroying their capital of Ninevah in 612, the Assyrians were the precursors of the more enduring despotism of the Persian empire.

The Achaemenids had ruled Persia as tributaries since about 700 BC. Cyrus I (*r.*559-29) rebelled against the Medes, capturing their capital at Ecbatana in 550. He extended his rule to the banks of the Jaxartes and, with the seizure of the Lydian kingdom and the exaction of tribute from the Greek cities of the Ionian coast, to the shores of the Aegean. The conquests of Darius I (*r.*521-486) completed the empire (*Map 6*). He established a system of imperial government which gave a common institutional and cultural heritage to the whole region. Both from the administrative districts (satrapies) of the directly ruled empire and from his subject kings he demanded a fixed annual tax. A complex bureaucracy maintained a standing army and labour forces to construct vast temples and cities, extensive irrigation works, a common coinage and the system of royal roads—the most famous running from Sardis to Susa—which both symbolised and permitted a new degree of unity and coherence. The wealth and power of the king of kings were reflected in the magnificence of his palace, the elaboration of his court ceremonials, his proclamation as immortal by his subjects, (who prostrated themselves before him in the gesture which the Greeks would long regard with contempt as the supreme expression of

19

The ancient Mediterranean

oriental servility), and the proliferation of harems and later of the palace eunuchs whose sinister influence would play behind the thrones of this region for the next two thousand years and more.

Oriental despotism was founded upon the physical domination of those who cultivated the land through the ruthless and large-scale centralisation which was necessary to create and maintain the vital irrigation systems. The bare, steep and deeply indented shores of the Mediterranean did not require irrigation on so large a scale nor did they permit the easy expansion of communities across large areas of land. The peoples who lodged around it were compelled to independence by their isolation from each other, and to inter-dependence by the constant need to exchange men and goods across the sea.

By comparison with these fundamental bonds, the larger political structures which the wealth of the Mediterranean basin periodically called into being were ephemeral. When the Roman Empire collapsed it became apparent that, among the components into which it crumbled, those which had been created by Greek colonisation between 750 and 550 BC (*Map 5*) still remained distinct. They persisted, politically and culturally vital, for another thousand years (*see Maps 17 and 21*).

The Greeks believed that the maritime expansion of the Phoenician cities – Aradus, Byblus, Berytus, Sidon and, greatest of all, Tyre (*Maps 5 and 9*) – preceded their own. In fact there is no evidence that anyone traded between Greece and the Phoenician coast until the Greeks themselves founded a colony at Al Minah in the eighth century BC, or that the Greek colonies in Sicily displaced Phoenician ones. The early Phoenicians seems to have been content to trade where 'civilised' peoples had already settled, for example at Cyprus, Rhodes and Crete. The first proven colonies appeared after about 750 BC (probably following Assyrian attacks on the mother cities) in Sardinia, Sicily, Africa and Spain; those at Leptis Magna, Utica, Hadrumetum and Gades were among the first. And Gades, with its proximity to the Guadalquivir river and the metal deposits of Spain, suggests the motive. In a pattern that would appear again (*compare Map 27*) the Phoenicians exchanged for raw materials – slaves, ivory and above all metals – the fripperies of civilisation such as metal ornaments, glassware, and the legendary purple cloth of Tyre. Phoenician colonisation, in short, began at much the same time as Greek, and in much the same way, developing in response to pressures on the mother cities some time after a pattern of irregular trading had been established. Phoenician colonies, unlike those of the Greeks, were tied to their founders by an obligation to pay tribute. Carthage (traditionally founded in 814) became the effective leader of the western colonies when Tyre fell to the Assyrians in the eighth century; it then founded an empire of its own with the planting of a colony at Ibiza in 654-53 (*see Map 8*).

The extension of the Hellenic world to Sicily and the shores of the Black Sea was intimately bound up with the evolution of cultural unity and a measure of political co-operation among the Greeks. During the dark age around 1200, when the Dorian Greeks apparently moved southwards into Thessaly, Boeotia, Achaea, the Peloponnese and some of the islands, settlement apparently continued at some Mycenaean centres, including Crete and Athens

(*Map 7*). According to tradition the re-occupation of the Ionian coast and islands was organised from Athens around 1000. The story may reflect a preponderance which Athens had already attained, for it was the first centre of iron-age culture in Greece.

Expansion beyond the Aegean basin followed in Mycenaean footsteps. From about 700 BC eastern goods, designs and ideas were brought from the Levant by the Euboeans. A little later they planted the first western colony at Cumae (Kyme). Others followed rapidly; the fact that Reggio and Messina were among the earliest, though not the most fertile or convenient spots available, suggests that securing supplies of metal from Etruria was an immediate objective. The unending search for metal took the Greeks to the Rhône delta, the Spanish coast and the shores of the Black Sea in the next century. Nevertheless trade was not the most important reason for their expansion. If there was a prime cause, over-population is the most likely. The severe limit which the poor soils, narrow plains and inhospitable hills of the Aegean basin set upon natural increase was perfectly clear to its inhabitants, and simple overcrowding as well as political dispute compelled many of the early colonists to leave their native cities.

Emigration produced a measure of co-operation among the Aegean communities. The colonies were founded by a relatively small number of cities. Samos, Phocaea and Miletus founded many settlements along the Black Sea and in the west, as did Chalcis and Eretria of Euboea, and Megara on the mainland. Corinth and Achaea contributed most of the colonies in Sicily and the toe and instep of Italy. Since it would be absurd to suppose that all the colonists came from these few places, they must be regarded as organisers and initiators of colonising activity on the part of others.

Westward expansion was checked by an alliance of the Etruscans and Carthaginians at Alalia, *c*.540, a battle which marks the appearance of new powers in the western Mediterranean. Both would be succeeded in their turn by the Romans (*Map 8*). Commerce continued, however, and in return for their metals the Etruscans had already acquired, though they had not absorbed, a substantial inheritance of Greek culture in the form of metalwork, pottery and fresco painting far more advanced than they could have attempted themselves. This was what the Greeks had to exchange (in addition to their wine and olive oil, which were highly valued) for the extensive variety of goods which they imported.

The colonies not only provided the cities of Aegean Greece with an outlet for their surplus population but enabled them to support a greater one themselves, particularly as the great granaries of Sicily and Southern Italy, Egypt (through Naucratis) and the northern shores of the Black Sea were opened up. Rapidly increasing population provided the foundation for the achievements which ensured that the cultural influence of the Greeks would always surpass the limits of their political power.

Further reading: P. Warren, *Aegean Civilisation* (Elsevier-Phaidon, 1975); D. B. Harden, *The Phoenicians* (Thames & Hudson, 1971); J. Boardman, *The Greeks Overseas* (Penguin, 1964); R. J. Hopper, *Trade and Industry in Classical Greece* (Thames & Hudson, 1979); D. Strong, *The Early Etruscans* (Evans, 1968).

6 The Achaemenid Empire in Persia
The Achaemenids set up the Persian empire, established common legal and administrative arrangements, and a common currency and built a system of royal roads linking the earliest centres of civilisation.

7 The Greeks in the Aegean
'We sit around our sea like frogs around their pond', Socrates said of the Greeks. The people of the cities of island and mainland Greece began to come together for games and religious worship, united by a common culture and institutions rather than by political union.

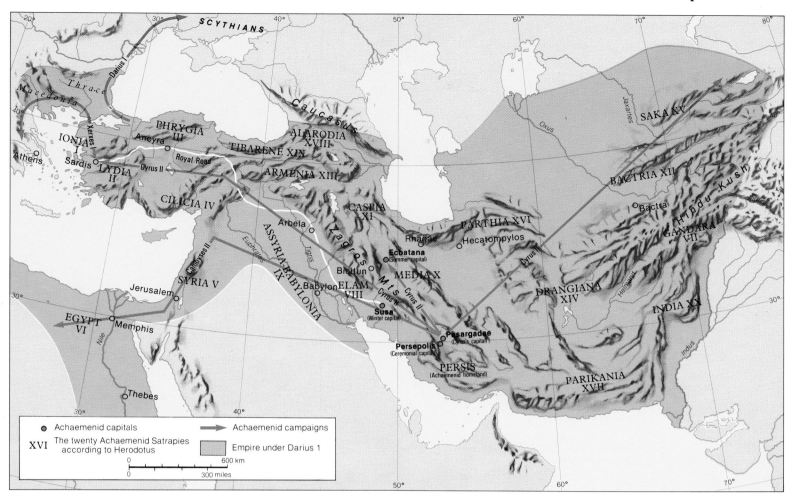

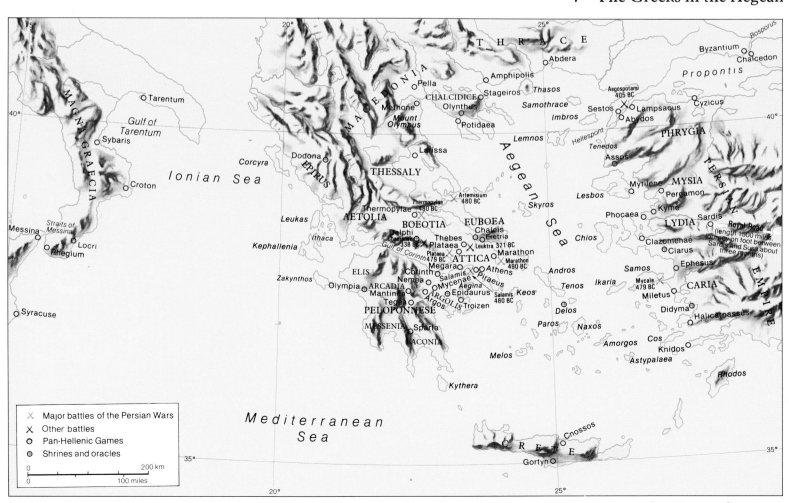

© Creative Cartography Ltd © The Hamlyn Group

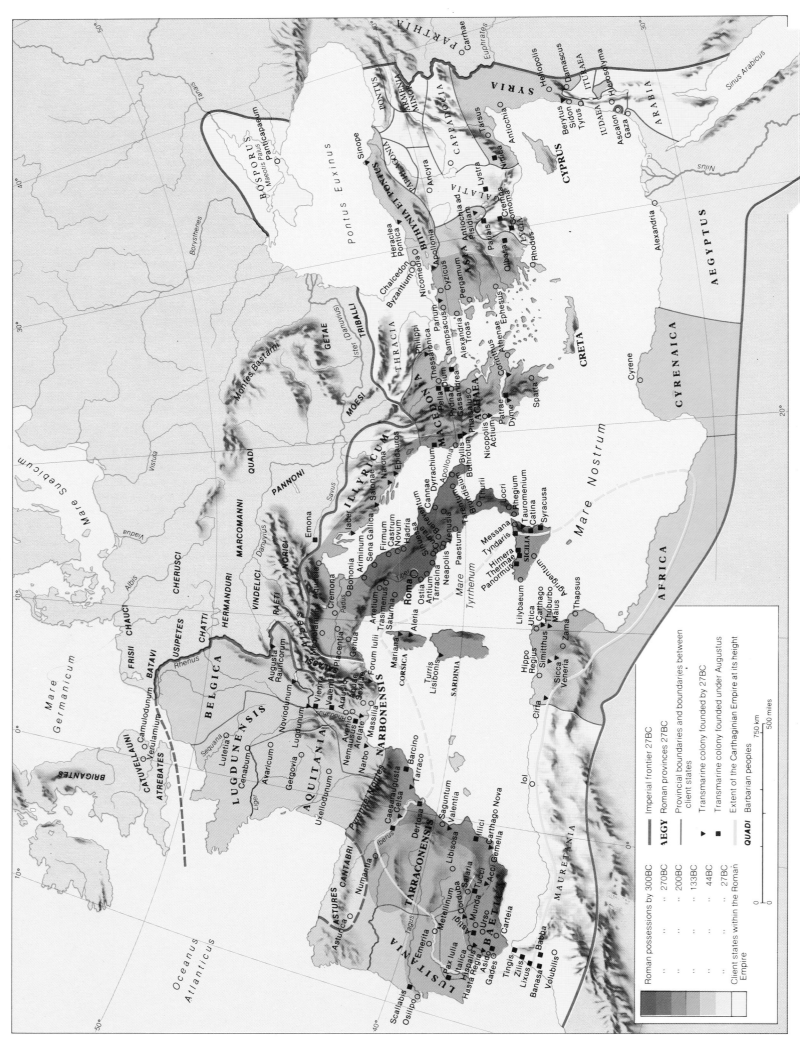

Key

Roman possessions by 300BC

" " 270BC

" " 200BC

" " 133BC

" " 44BC

" " 27BC

Client states within the Roman Empire

—— Imperial frontier 27BC

AEGY Roman provinces 27BC

—— Provincial boundaries and boundaries between client states

▼ Transmarine colony founded by 27BC

■ Transmarine colony founded under Augustus

—— Extent of the Carthaginian Empire at its height

QUADI Barbarian peoples

750 km
500 miles

© Creative Cartography Ltd © The Hamlyn Group

8 The rise of Rome
Three centuries of almost continuous warfare made Rome the first and last power to unite the shores of the Mediterranean under a single regime, overthrowing the empires of Carthage (destroyed 146 BC), the Seleucids (64 BC) and the Ptolemies (30 BC) and, especially in the west, garrisoning the conquered territories with colonies of Roman citizens.

9 The Hellenistic world
In the footsteps of Alexander the Great, the Greeks founded scores of cities in the old Persian empire, and absorbed others at economically and strategically vital points. They created a network which connected all the known civilisations of the world, and which was completed when the Chinese opened the silk route c. 112 BC.

THE BELIEF of the Greeks that they inhabited an island of freedom in a sea of despotism was well founded. By 500 BC the monarchies and aristocracies of heroic Greece had faded away in most places, to leave a world comparatively little marked by variations of wealth and privilege. Its free citizens were accustomed to ruling their own lives, and, except in Sparta, many slaves differed little from them in the pattern of their everyday lives, the structure of their families and the range of their occupations. The Greeks began to express a sense of community when they came together for festivals of games and music—the Olympiads were reckoned from 776 BC—and at the shrines of the most famous oracles (Map 7); and many of them joined together, under the leadership of Sparta and Athens, to reject Persia's demand for a general submission after the brutal suppression of the revolt of the Ionian cities (499-94), and to win the ensuing war.

The plays, the histories, the philosophy of the golden age which followed are marked by an intense curiosity about the nature of man as a social animal, possessed of the power to shape his destiny and thereby obliged to define and seek 'the good'. 'We Athenians, in our own persons, take our decisions on policy and submit them to proper discussion' Pericles, the greatest of their leaders, told his fellow citizens. 'We give our obedience to those whom we ourselves put in positions of authority.' The quest for the highest good, to which the actions of free men should be directed, is ideally depicted in the dialogues of Plato (428-347), while the results of calm enquiry into the nature of the visible world are triumphantly set out in the writings of his pupil Aristotle of Stagira (384-22). Aristotle's works, surviving in effect as lecture notes collected by his pupils, lack the charm and grace of Plato's, but they cover every branch of the knowledge of his time, from aesthetics and politics to botany and physics. Their conclusions dominated western thought for more than 2000 years and their method still does. If we fail to be startled by Aristotle's close and dispassionate observations of diligently collected facts, from which conclusions are drawn with scrupulous attention to the soundness of argument and the legitimacy of deduction, or to be astounded by the absence of any appeal to the supernatural to resolve the mysteries of nature, it is because the 'father of reason' has taught us to take reason for granted. Nor did this reason defeat itself by resting on instinct. Its basis in the nature of language and knowledge themselves was examined and set forth in the logical works which remain the foundation of all rational thought.

The conquests of Aristotle's pupil Alexander of Macedon (Map 9) constitute another remarkable monument to the curiosity of the Greeks. Beyond destroying a Persian empire already in decay they had little political purpose or importance. After Alexander's death in 322 his empire fragmented into a shifting assortment of successor (diadochi) states ruled by his generals and their descendants, of which the most important were those of Egypt under the Ptolemies and Syria-Iran under the Seleucids. But Alexander's journey represented an extension of Greek civilisation from the Nile to the Indus. The Achaemenids had already done much to unite this area (Map 6). Although the Ptolemies adopted a lighter coinage which ran through the Nile valley and the southern and western Mediterranean—the Phoenician world—there was a great expansion in the volume and regularity of the exchange of goods across this great common market, now settled by

Greek communities linked to one another by the ties of language and culture (see Map 9).

Some of the new cities were only glorified fortresses. In many others the Greeks (who, despite some intermarriage with the existing populations, remained socially and culturally dominant) built temples, gymnasia and theatres, educated their children in Greek schools and settled their disputes before Greek judges according to Greek law. The universality of their influence is attested by the foundation of the two greatest libraries of antiquity, at (Egyptian) Alexandria and Pergamum, or by the inscription which records the arrival at the frontier city of Ai Khanum, in modern Afghanistan, of a visiting lecturer from mainland Greece.

The wealth and sophistication of the Hellenistic world are most familiar today through its dynamic and often tortuous sculpture, the Venus of Milo or the Laocoön, and its mechanical ingenuities such as the lighthouse at Alexandria, the screw of Archimedes, the steam engine invented by Hero of Syracuse or the water organs and animated dolls which amused the court of the Ptolemies. But failure to develop equal skill in metallurgy prevented most of these devices from becoming more than playthings, and the lasting achievements were still in the area of theory, especially in mathematics and physics. The work of Euclid (c.300 BC) and Archimedes (c.287-212 BC) in these fields was not surpassed until the age of Descartes and Newton.

The diffusion of Greek culture in the Hellenistic age multiplied the manuscripts in which it was preserved. Many of them were copied by the technique invented at Pergamum of writing on animal skins—parchment, much more durable than papyrus—which made it possible for their contents to survive the vicissitudes of a thousand years and be taken up again by the Arabs.

The Jews, whose kingdom had been founded about 1000 BC under David, split by rival claimants, crushed by the Babylonian captivity (586-538 BC) and revived under the protection of the Achaemenids, flourished in this age of cultural exchange. The destruction of Jerusalem by Nebuchadnezzar in 587 began the dispersal (diaspora) which became the continuous experience of the Jews (see Map 11). It also gave rise to the practice of regular collective reading of the scriptures and insistence upon close observance of the Law—for the Destruction was interpreted as divine punishment for its neglect—which have contributed so much to Jewish survival. In the Hellenistic age, according to the Jewish historian Josephus, 'countless myriads whose numbers cannot be ascertained' spread through Syria and Asia Minor to Armenia and the Crimea, and around the Mediterranean. The great Jewish community at Alexandria produced many distinguished philosophers and the first Greek translation of the Old Testament. This meeting of Jewish and Greek culture created the essential context, socially and intellectually, for the appearance and early development of Christianity.

Some time before the rise of the Achaemenids a new religion appeared among the peoples of the Iranian plateau. Its prophet, Zoroaster, is one of the most shadowy of religious leaders, every detail of his life and teaching being open to radically differing interpretations. Probably he preached in eastern Iran in the first half of the sixth century BC. His principal innovations were the monotheism which denounced the many gods of Iranian paganism in favour of Ahuru-Mazda, the creator, and the

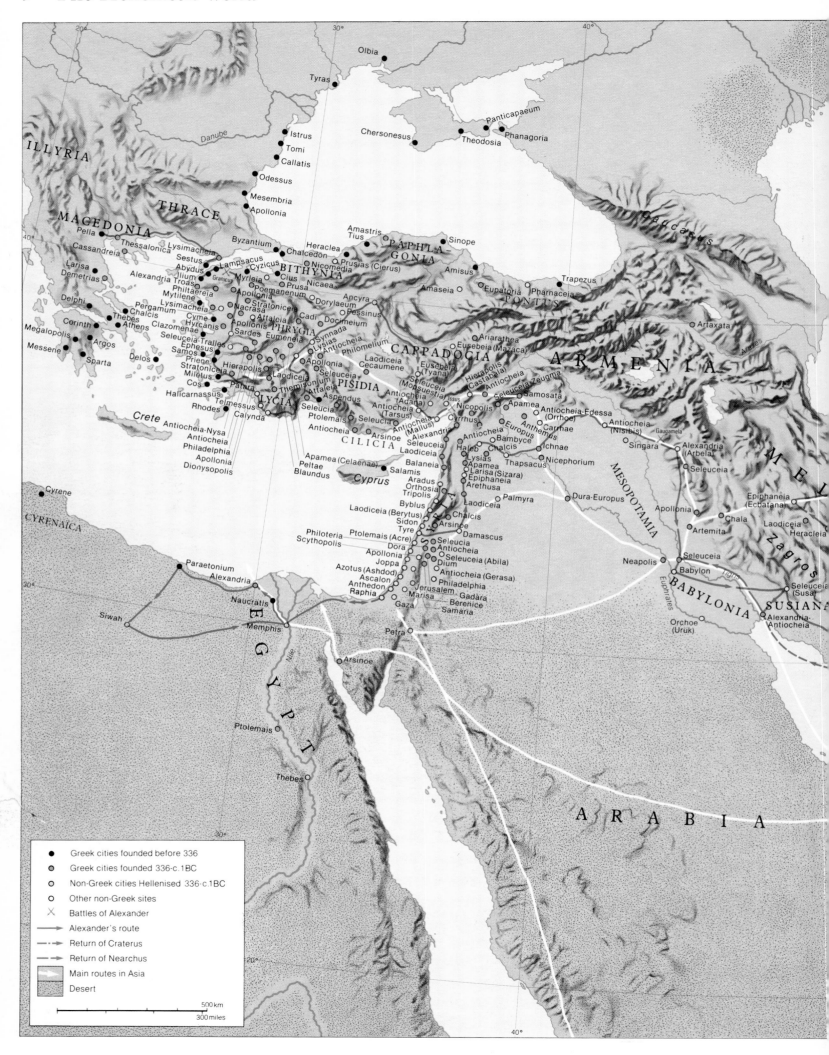

ILLYRIA

THRACE

MACEDONIA
Pella
Cassandreia
Thessalonica
Lysimacheia
Larisa
Demetrias
Sestus
Abydus
Lampsacus
Alexandria Troas
Philtaereia
Ilium
Granicus
Myrleia
Cyzicus
Cius
Delphi
Mytilene
Pergamum
Lysimacheia
Apollonia
Poemanenum
Cyme
Nacrasa
Stratonicea
Chalcis
Thebes
Clazomenae
Hyrcanis
Attalea
Cadi
Corinth
Athens
Seleuceia-Tralles
Apollonis
PHRYGIA
Megalopolis
Argos
Ephesus
Sardes
Eumeneia
Synnada
Messene
Sparta
Samos
Priene
Hierapolis
Antiocheia
Docimeium
Philomelium
Delos
Stratonicea
Laodicea
Apollonia
Lysias
Miletus
Cos
Patara
Themisonium
Attaleia
Aspendus
Halicarnassus
Telmessus
Calynda
Rhodes
Antiocheia-Nysa
Antiocheia
Philadelphia
Apollonia
Dionysopolis
Apamea (Celaenae)
Peltae
Blaundus

Cyrene

CYRENAÏCA

Paraetonium
Alexandria
Siwah
Naucratis
Memphis
EGYPT
Nile
Arsinoe
Ptolemais
Thebes

Olbia
Tyras
Istrus
Tomi
Callatis
Odessus
Mesembria
Apollonia
Byzantium
Chalcedon
Heraclea
Nicomedia
Prusias (Cierus)
BITHYNIA
Nicaea
Prusa
Dorylaeum
Pessinus
Ancyra
PAPHLAGONIA
Chersonesus
Sinope
Amastris
Tius
Amisus
Amaseia
PONTUS
Eupatoria
Pharnaceia
Trapezus
Panticapaeum
Theodosia
Phanagoria
Caucasus

Ariarathea
Eusebeia (Mazaca)
CAPPADOCIA
Laodicea
Cecaumene
Eusebeia (Tyana)
Seleuceia (Mopsuestia)
Antiocheia (Adana)
Antiocheia (Tarsus)
PISIDIA
Seleucia
Ptolemais
Seleucia
Arsinoe
Antiocheia
CILICIA
Antiocheia (Mallus)
Alexandria
Issus
Cyrrhus
Nicopolis
Hierapolis (Castabala)
Antiocheia
Seleuceia Zeugma
Samosata
Apamea
Antiocheia-Edessa (Orrhoe)
Carrhae
Anthemus
Bambyce
Ichnae
Nicephorium
Europus
Chalcis
Haleb
Lysias
Apamea
Larisa (Sizara)
Epiphaneia
Arethusa
Thapsacus
Dura-Europus
Palmyra
MESOPOTAMIA
Antiocheia (Nisibis)
Gaugamela
Singara
Alexandria (Arbela)
Seleuceia
ME[...]
Epiphaneia (Ecbatana)
Apollonia
Artemita
Chala
Laodiceia
Heracleia
Zagros
Seleuceia (Susa)
SUSIANA
Alexandria-Antiocheia

ARMENIA
Artaxata
Araxes

Cyprus
Salamis
Aradus
Orthosia
Tripolis
Byblus
Laodiceia
Balanaia
Laodiceia (Berytus)
Sidon
Tyre
Arsinoe
Damascus
Chalcis
Philoteria
Scythopolis
Ptolemais (Acre)
Dora
Apollonia
Joppa
Azotus (Ashdod)
Ascalon
Anthedon
Raphia
Gaza
Marisa
Jerusalem
Gadara
Samaria
Berenice
Petra
Seleucia
Antiocheia
Seleuceia (Abila)
Dium
Antiocheia (Gerasa)
Philadelphia

Laodiceia
Neapolis
Babylon
BABYLONIA
Tigris
Euphrates
Orchoe (Uruk)

ARABIA

Crete

Legend:
- ● Greek cities founded before 336
- ◐ Greek cities founded 336-c.1BC
- ○ Non-Greek cities Hellenised 336-c.1BC
- ○ Other non-Greek sites
- × Battles of Alexander
- → Alexander's route
- –·→ Return of Craterus
- – –→ Return of Nearchus
- Main routes in Asia
- Desert

500 km
300 miles

60°   70°   80°

Jaxartes

Tien Shan

40°

○ Alexandria Eschate

S O G D I A N A

Oxus

Pamirs

Ai Khanum ○

Indus

Antiochela ●
(Merv)

Bactra-
Zariaspa

B A C T R I A *Kush*

Hindu

Khawak
Pass

Himalayas

—z Mts.

Hecatompylus ○

A R I A

Alexandria-ad-
Caucasum

opus
agae ○

Apamea ○

Alexandria
(Herat)

D R A N G I A N A

Taxila ○

Caspian
Gates

P A R T H I A

Alexandria
(Ghazni)

Nicaea ○ Bucephala
○ Euthydemeia
(Sagala)

Hydaspes

Acesines

Hypnasis
(Beas)

Demetrias ○

Hydraotes

Zaradrus

Mts

Methone

P E R S I S

Alexandria in Arachosia
(Kandahar) ○

30°

Pasargadae ○

Propthasia ○

Helmund

Persepolis ○

C A R M A N I A

A R A C H O S I A

Bolan
Pass

○ Alexandria

Alexandria ○

Mulla
Pass

G E D R O S I A

Indus

Patala ●

20°

I N D I A

errha

60°   70°

© Creative Cartography Ltd © The Hamlyn Group

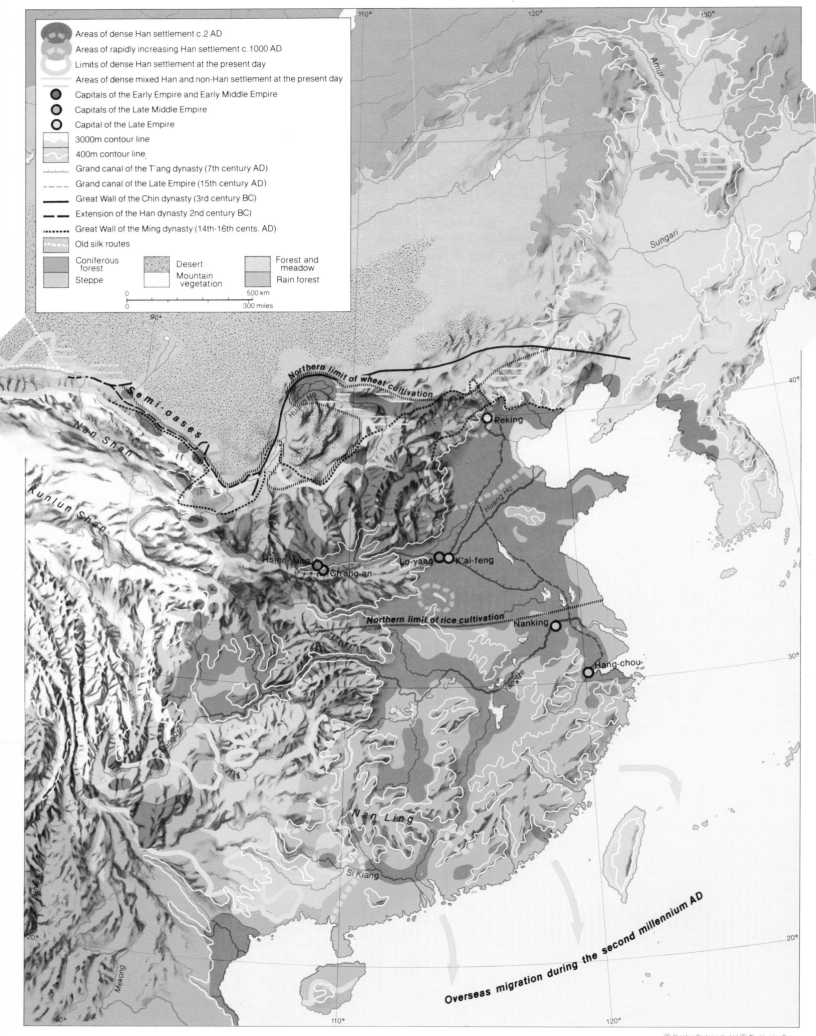

Areas of dense Han settlement c.2 AD
Areas of rapidly increasing Han settlement c.1000 AD
Limits of dense Han settlement at the present day
Areas of dense mixed Han and non-Han settlement at the present day
Capitals of the Early Empire and Early Middle Empire
Capitals of the Late Middle Empire
Capital of the Late Empire
3000m contour line
400m contour line
Grand canal of the T'ang dynasty (7th century AD)
Grand canal of the Late Empire (15th century AD)
Great Wall of the Chin dynasty (3rd century BC)
Extension of the Han dynasty 2nd century BC)
Great Wall of the Ming dynasty (14th-16th cents. AD)
Old silk routes

Coniferous forest
Steppe
Desert
Mountain vegetation
Forest and meadow
Rain forest

0   500 km
0   300 miles

Amur
Sungari
Nan Shan
Semi-oases
Kunlun Shan
Huang Ho
Northern limit of wheat cultivation
Peking
Huang Ho
Hsien-yang
Ch'ang-an
Lo-yang
K'ai-feng
Northern limit of rice cultivation
Nanking
Hang-chou
Yangtze
Yangtze
Nan Ling
Si Kiang
Mekong

Overseas migration during the second millennium AD

© Creative Cartography Ltd © The Hamlyn Group

10 The expansion of Han Chinese settlement
Beginning in the first millennium BC, the expansion of the Han Chinese people and of Chinese culture from the central river valleys has been continuous for more than two thousand years. It has been closely related to the ability of the Chinese to control and exploit an extremely varied natural environment.

11 The appearance of the world religions
Between about 1000 BC and AD 500 all the formative religions and philosophies of the world except Islam established themselves as the bases of the great civilisations. Here short-term fluctuations in their influence are ignored to show the relationship between the areas in which they began and those over which they exercised permanent influence.

stark and uncompromising confrontation which he proclaimed between those who followed his teaching – the Truth – and adherents of the old cults – the Lie, perhaps reflecting the bitter hostility in eastern Iran in his time between the settled farmers of the plateau and the nomads of the steppes to whose depredations they were constantly exposed.

Zoroaster preached a universal faith commending good thoughts, good words, good deeds' (including either opposition to or great moderation of animal sacrifice) and offering eternal peace to the blessed and the torments of the damned to the wicked. There is little doubt that the Achaemenid kings from Darius I onwards accepted it as a religion of state, though its hostility to the older cults was considerably softened by the readmission of the worship of gods other than Ahuru-Mazda, in a subordinate position. Other religions were still tolerated, and this, together with the great extent of the Achaemenid empire, gave Zoroastrianism an influence on many other faiths, including both Judaism and Hinduism, and later Christianity and Buddhism (*see Map 11*). Its close association with the Persian empire persisted, and during the Sassanid revival (*Map 15*) it flourished again, championed from the time of Bahram I (*c.* AD 273-6) by savage persecution of the religious minorities which abounded in the Persian world. It was apparently during this second period of prosperity that Zoroastrianism, in common with Manicheeism (which under Shapur I (*d.* 273) had almost supplanted it as the official religion and spread widely through the late antique world in spite of universal persecution) developed its prophet's delineation of the war between good and evil into a theological dualism which divided creation between the realms of Light and Dark, Spirit and Flesh, inspiring a radical asceticism which left its mark on most of the world religions.

The origins of Hinduism are lost in obscurity. It grew slowly from the Vedic religions of the Aryan peoples who conquered the Indus valley about 1000 BC, and did not attain a single coherent theology until, perhaps, about AD 500, but hints of its unique institution, the system of caste, have been found in the Harappan as well as the Aryan civilisation. As Hinduism expanded it absorbed the cults of many gods and many styles of religious life. But its essential character derived from caste, the belief that men are divided into self-contained and sealed groups, or castes. Into one of them each man is born, within it he will marry and die, living his life in accordance with its particular rules, prohibitions and customs, to be rewarded if merit and fortune permit by reincarnation in a higher caste. The original groups were occupational – warriors (*kshatriyas*), priests (*brahmans*), cultivators (*vaishyas*) – and among them the brahmans quickly took over the first place by proclaiming the divine origin of kingly authority. A fourth caste, those of non-Aryan origin – *shudras* – appeared very early, and beneath these four a network of subcastes was elaborated, defined by occupation and, increasingly with time and Aryan expansion, by race. Essentially a device to preserve the racial purity of the Aryan conquerors by allowing them to absorb but not to mix with the conquered peoples, caste has remained until the present day the framework of Indian social and political life.

Resentment of brahman dominance first appeared among the *shudras* and the *vaishyas*, whose importance as landowners and as the leaders of an increasingly farflung

trade conflicted with their low caste. The principles of Jainism appeared perhaps a century before the birth (*c.*540 BC) of its effective prophet, Mahavira, who won a substantial following in the Ganges valley. The core of his teaching was the renunciation of killing, upon which he insisted so absolutely that his followers not only refused to eat meat but wore muslin masks over their mouths to avoid inhaling insects. It was not a creed to appeal to farmers, but it attracted, and still retains, considerable support in the merchant community.

The teaching of Gautama Buddha (born *c.*566 BC, the son of a *kshatriya* prince) was also based on the renunciation of desire. The Buddha's path, however, was not that of bodily asceticism – which he tried and found wanting – but of meditation, directed to a balanced and moderate life, cleansed of the passions which were the cause of suffering. Salvation lay in *nirvana* (extinction), freedom from the cycle of suffering, death and rebirth. Buddhism rejected caste and the idea of a personal God. It was disseminated by monks who wandered from place to place begging for alms. The universality of its appeal was expressed in its repudiation of social and even sexual distinctions (which the brahmans were emphasising increasingly) in the egalitarian organisation of Buddhist monasteries and nunneries.

The decision to undertake systematic proselytisation, which eventually made Buddhism the religion of east and south-east Asia was taken at a great council at Pataliputra in 250 BC, shortly after the conversion of Ashoka, ruler of the Maurya empire from about 272 to 231. Ashoka was converted through revulsion from the bloodshed of the wars he himself had waged to gain control of the trade routes to the south. He distinguished clearly between his personal conviction and his imperial duty, as he saw it, to treat all religions with impartial respect. Nevertheless the association between the evolution of the world religions and the appearance of great political structures is more than coincidence. Between the accession of Chandragupta Maurya in 321 BC and the death of Ashoka, the Mauryan emperors used their control of the Ganges and Indus valleys to bring under their sway an area which stretched from territory beyond the Indus, recovered from the Seleucids, to the far south of the sub-continent. The rock and pillar inscriptions of Ashoka not only show the extent of his influence (*Map 16*) but illustrate the spirit in which it was exercised. In several languages, including Greek, they command religious tolerance, respect for human dignity and gratitude for the benevolence of a paternal ruler. His messages were designed to promote unity in a heterogeneous kingdom hastily assembled, but ruled with a sophistication which stretched from collecting taxes and maintaining communications to creating an imperial espionage service and planting banyan trees along the road to give shade to travellers. This degree of political evolution, common to the cradles of all the great religions, not only created conditions in which they could spread and flourish, but rested on a degree of homogeneity among those who made the systems of government work, and their ability to express and share values which were necessarily more abstract and reflective than the blood-stained cults of warrior kings.

Chinese civilisation too began to assume its familiar aspect during the first millennium BC. The Chou dynasty, which replaced the Shang probably in 1027, presided over a world effectively ruled by a nobility which gave it

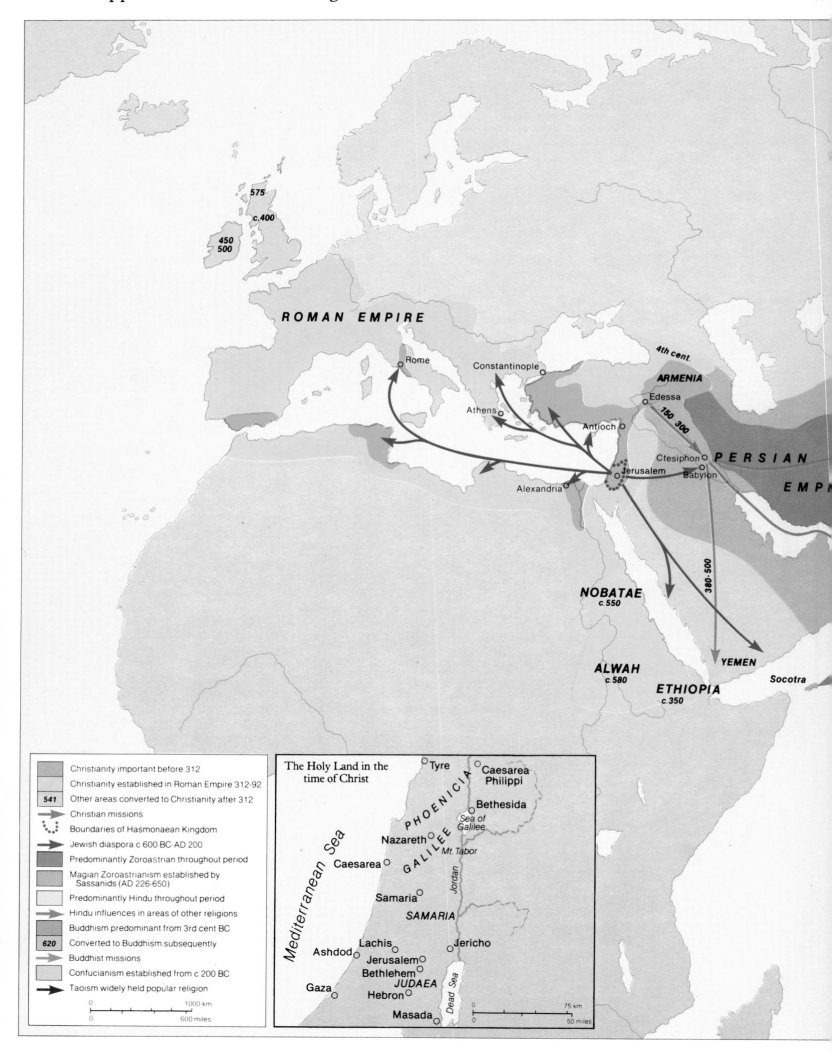

ROMAN EMPIRE

575
c.400
450
500

Rome

Constantinople

4th cent.

ARMENIA

Edessa

150-300

Athens

Antioch

PERSIAN

Ctesiphon

Jerusalem   Babylon

Alexandria

EMP

NOBATAE
c.550

380-500

ALWAH
c.580

YEMEN

Socotra

ETHIOPIA
c.350

Christianity important before 312

Christianity established in Roman Empire 312-92

541 Other areas converted to Christianity after 312

Christian missions

Boundaries of Hasmonaean Kingdom

Jewish diaspora c 600 BC–AD 200

Predominantly Zoroastrian throughout period

Magian Zoroastrianism established by
  Sassanids (AD 226-650)

Predominantly Hindu throughout period

Hindu influences in areas of other religions

Buddhism predominant from 3rd cent BC

620 Converted to Buddhism subsequently

Buddhist missions

Confucianism established from c 200 BC

Taoism widely held popular religion

0   1000 km
0   600 miles

The Holy Land in the
time of Christ

Tyre   Caesarea
             Philippi

PHOENICIA

Bethesida

Sea of
Galilee

Nazareth

GALILEE

Mt. Tabor

Caesarea

Samaria

SAMARIA

Lachis   Jericho

Ashdod

Jerusalem

Bethlehem
           JUDAEA

Gaza   Hebron

Masada

Mediterranean Sea

Jordan

Dead Sea

0   75 km
0   50 miles

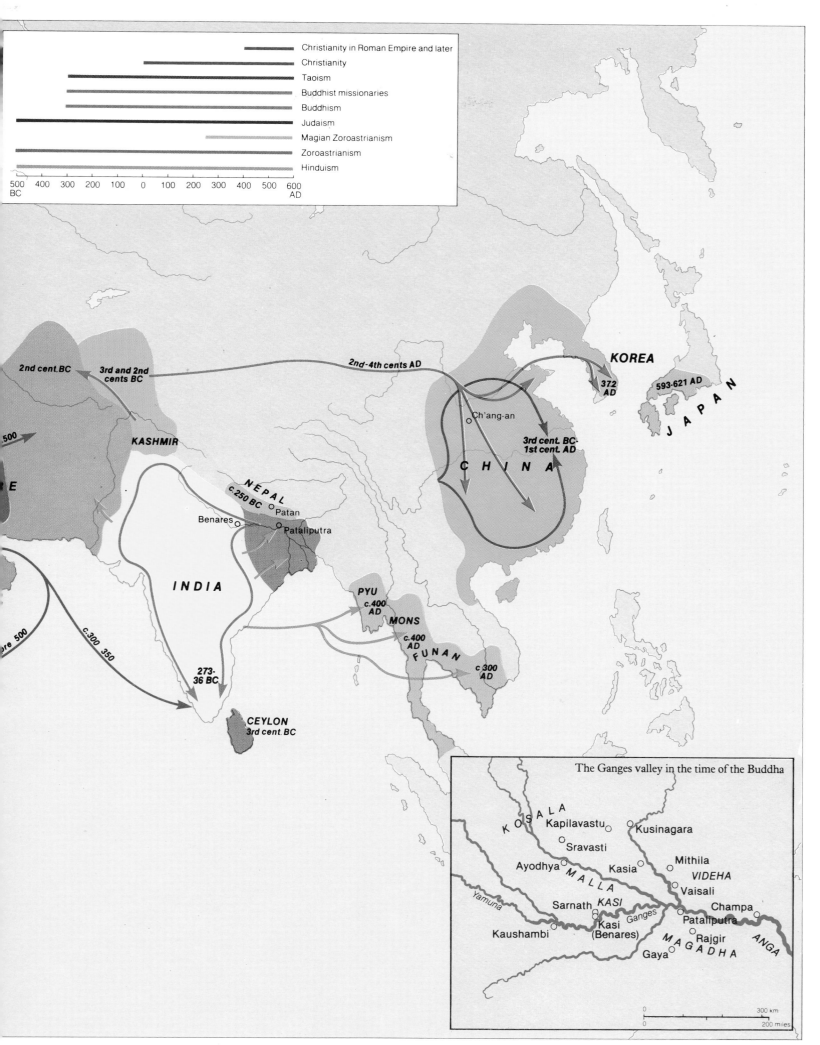

Christianity in Roman Empire and later
Christianity
Taoism
Buddhist missionaries
Buddhism
Judaism
Magian Zoroastrianism
Zoroastrianism
Hinduism

500 400 300 200 100 0 100 200 300 400 500 600
BC   AD

2nd cent. BC   3rd and 2nd cents BC

2nd-4th cents AD

KOREA

372 AD

593-621 AD

JAPAN

Ch'ang-an

KASHMIR

3rd cent. BC-1st cent. AD

CHINA

c.250 BC

NEPAL

Patan

Benares

Pataliputra

INDIA

PYU
c.400
AD

MONS
c.400
AD

FUNAN

c.300
AD

c.300-350

273-36 BC

CEYLON
3rd cent. BC

The Ganges valley in the time of the Buddha

K O S A L A

Kapilavastu

Kusinagara

Sravasti

Ayodhya   Kasia

Mithila

VIDEHA

M A L L A

Vaisali

Yamuna

Sarnath   KASI

Champa

Kaushambi

Kasi
(Benares)

Ganges

Pataliputra

ANGA

M A G A D H A   Rajgir

Gaya

0   300 km
0   200 miles

© Creative Cartography Ltd © The Hamlyn Group

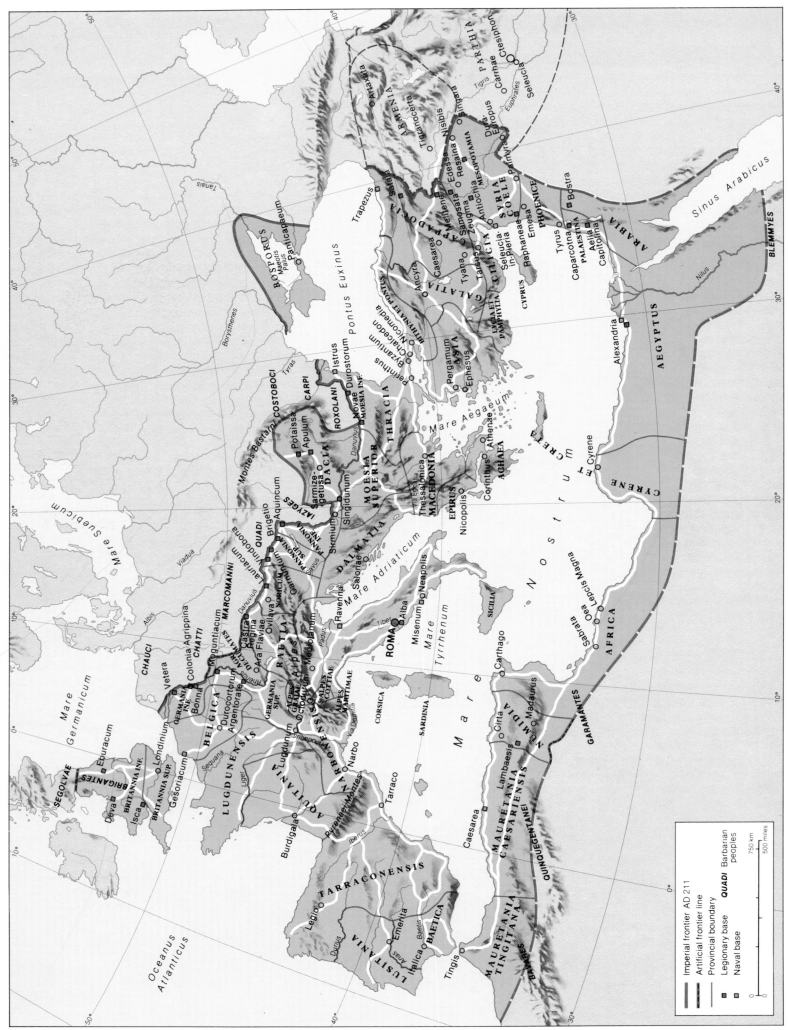

BRITANNIA INF.
SEGOLVAE
BRIGANTES
Eburacum
Deva Isca
BRITANNIA SUP.
Gesoriacum
Londinium

Mare Germanicum
Oceanus Atlanticus

CHAUCI
CHATTI
Vetera
Colonia Agrippina
Bonna
Moguntiacum
GERMANIA INF.
GERMANIA SUP.
BELGICA
Durocortorum
Argentorate
Castra Regina
Ara Flaviae
Lauriacum
Vindobona
Brigetio
Aquincum
MARCOMANNI
QUADI
IAZYGES
DACIA
Sarmizegetusa
Apulum
Potaissa
COSTOBOCI
CARPI
ROXOLANI

Mare Suebicum
Albis
Viadua

LUGDUNENSIS
Lugdunum
AQUITANIA
Burdigala
NARBONENSIS
Narbo
ALPES GRAIAE
ALPES COTTIAE
ALPES MARITIMAE
RAETIA
NORICUM
PANNONIA SUP.
PANNONIA INF.
Carnuntum
Singidunum
Sirmium
MOESIA SUPERIOR
MOESIA INF.
Novae
Durostorum
Istrus

Tarraco
TARRACONENSIS
LUSITANIA
Emerita
Italica
BAETICA
Tingis
MAURETANIA TINGITANA
BAQUATES
QUINQUEGENTIANEI
MAURETANIA CAESARIENSIS
Caesarea
Lambaesis
Madaurus
Cirta
NUMIDIA
Carthago
AFRICA
GARAMANTES
Sabata
Oea Lepcis Magna

Ravenna
Mediolanum
ROMA
Alba
Misenum Neapolis
CORSICA
SARDINIA
SICILIA
Carthago
Mare Tyrrhenum
Mare Internum
Mare Nostrum
Mare Adriaticum

DALMATIA
Salonae
THRACIA
Byzantium
Chalcedon
Nicomedia
BITHYNIA ET PONTUS
Perinthus
MACEDONIA
Thessalonica
EPIRUS
Nicopolis
ACHAEA
Corinthus
Athenae
Mare Aegaeum
CRETA ET CYRENE
Cyrene
CYRENE

BOSPORUS
Panticapaeum
Maeotis Palus
Borysthenes
Tanais
Pontus Euxinus
Trapezus
Satala
ARMENIA
Artaxata
Tigranocerta
CAPPADOCIA
Caesarea
Ancyra
GALATIA
ASIA
Pergamum
Ephesus
LYCIA ET PAMPHYLIA
CILICIA
Tarsus
Tyana
Melitene
Samosata
Zeugma
Seleucia-in-Pieria
Antiochia
SYRIA COELE
Raphaneae
Emesa
PHOENICE
Tyrus
PALAESTINA
Aelia Capitolina
Caparcotna
ARABIA
Bostra
Edessa
Resaena
MESOPOTAMIA
Nisibis
Singara
Duva
Europus
Palmyra
PARTHIA
Carrhae Ctesiphon
Seleucia
Tigris
Euphrates

AEGYPTUS
Alexandria
Nilus
Sinus Arabicus
BLEMMYES

Monte Bastarnic
Tyras
Danuvius
Rhenus
Rhodanus
Sequana
Liger
Garumna
Durius
Iberus
Baetis
Anas
Pyrenaei Montes
Legio
Padus
Tiber

© Creative Cartography Ltd © The Hamlyn Group

Imperial frontier AD 211
Artificial frontier line
Provincial boundary
Legionary base
Naval base
QUADI Barbarian peoples
750 km
500 miles

12 The Roman Empire at its height
By AD 211 the Roman Empire had expanded to fill its natural frontiers, completed where necessary by man-made barriers. Within them the whole empire was now subjected to a uniform system of administration whose important centres were connected by a network of roads radiating from Rome.

formal allegiance. Traditionally the nobles owed their lands to the king and gave him military service in return. The very emptiness of his power in practice suggests that it was some sense of community among the Chinese that led them to acknowledge his rule. This allegiance remained a fiction until the Age of the Warring States (481-221 BC) ended when the warrior state of Ch'in swallowed all the rest, to be replaced after only fourteen years by the real founders of imperial China, the Han (*Map 13*).

Behind these events the permanent features of Chinese society were already evident. The expansion of civilisation which has been the central thread of 2000 years' development (*see Map 10*) was already in progress. Increasing activity in the Huang-ho valley by the seventh century BC was quickly followed by the first stages of the conquest of the south. The wealth of this warlike and sophisticated world was produced by a vast peasant labour force – this was already the world's most populous region – tied to the land in subjection to the nobles. To judge from the beauty of their pottery, painting and bronzes (the art of bronze-casting had been inherited from the Shang) and from the importance which they attached to literacy, this nobility was already more than a simple warrior caste. By 800 BC it had assumed the twin responsibilities of organising government and conducting the worship of its ancestors according to the traditional rites. In consequence China had no need of, and never developed, a specialised priestly class.

The preoccupations of the nobility shaped its philosophies. By around 500 BC three attitudes to the relations between the individuals and the state had become apparent: henceforth they would compete for influence over the government of China. Rejection was represented by the Taoists who, inspired by the fifth-century teacher Lao-tze, advocated complete withdrawal from worldly affairs to submit, in contemplative calm, to the Way (*Tao*), the cosmic principle that sustained the harmony of the universe. Lao-tze said that his disciple should know of the existence of villages beyond his own – he would hear their cocks crow in the morning.

The Taoists in a sense sidestepped the great debate of the Age of Warring States. The Legalists sought order through a universal system of law to which all men should be held subject by the authority of a powerful, centralised state. On these principles the Ch'in dynasty (221-206 BC) made a determined assault upon the fragmentation which was blamed for the years of war. The old kingdoms were broken up and replaced by administrative districts with different boundaries; the nobles were transported and the peasants upon whom their power had rested were freed. To destroy local customs and loyalties all libraries in private hands were ordered to be destroyed. Uniform weights and measures were introduced, the script (which, by denoting ideas rather than sounds has enabled Chinese of different regions to communicate freely without being able to understand one another's dialect) was simplified and standardised, and the first Great Wall was completed to keep out the barbarian horsemen (*Map 10*).

The death of Shih Huang Ti, the First Emperor – as he justly called himself – in 209 BC was followed by rebellion and the fall of his dynasty, but he had already laid the foundations of the unity which the Han achieved. They adopted the principles of Kung Fu-tzu – Confucius (551-479 BC) – who had looked not to the force of law, but to the power and example of tradition, enshrined in scrupulous adherence to precedent and diligent observance of ritual. Confucius and his followers put their trust in the disinterested skills of bureaucrats, honest and modest in their conduct, and carefully inculcated with the values of loyalty and justice through the study of the literary classics. 'Documents, conduct, loyalty, faithfulness' were their watchwords. Under the Han classical works were recovered and recopied, and a new literature created whose leading achievement was the inauguration of the series of official dynastic histories. By recording in detail the wise acts of successful emperors and officials, and the errors of foolish ones – as the Confucian historians saw them – these embodied the code of the official class and became the repositaries of a tradition of government which lasted until this century. Local officials were carefully trained, and though most were still appointed on the recommendation of nobles and other officials, recruitment by public examinations, perhaps China's most remarkable gift to the modern world, was begun.

The Confucian tradition, elaborated by generations of disciples (among whom Mencius, in the fourth century BC, emphasised that the welfare of all mankind must be the goal of good government) has been almost as much the formative thread of Chinese as Hinduism has of Indian history. In sharp contrast Confucianism has no interest in the supernatural. Even the worship of the ancestors is explicitly recommended as reinforcing the values of the ruling class, and of the here and now.

Confucianism and Legalism both took for granted what was already the most remarkable thing about China, the idea that the cultural unity of this vast area, with its great variety of soils and terrains, its extremes of climate and profusion of peoples, was more important than the political powers which rose and fell upon it. The Chinese, like the Greeks, defined barbarians as those who did not speak their language. Unlike the Greeks they were isolated from other advanced peoples by distance and the immense physical barriers which surrounded them. By the time their isolation was breached they were secure in the conviction of their superiority to the rest of mankind. This belief remained unshaken by the occasional necessity to submit to barbarian power until Chinese culture could absorb it. When the Chinese entered into contact with the European powers in the nineteenth century it was to accept not diplomatic relations, but tribute.

Further reading: A. Andrewes, *The Greeks* (Hutchinson, 1967: Penguin as *Greek Society*, 1971); R. Lane Fox, *Alexander the Great* (Allen Lane, 1973; Omega Books, 1975); Aristotle, *Politics* (trans. T. A. Sinclair, Penguin, 1962); R. Thapar, *Asoka and the Decline of the Mauryas* (Oxford University Press, 1961); Confucius, *The Analects* (trans. D. C. Lau, Penguin, 1979).

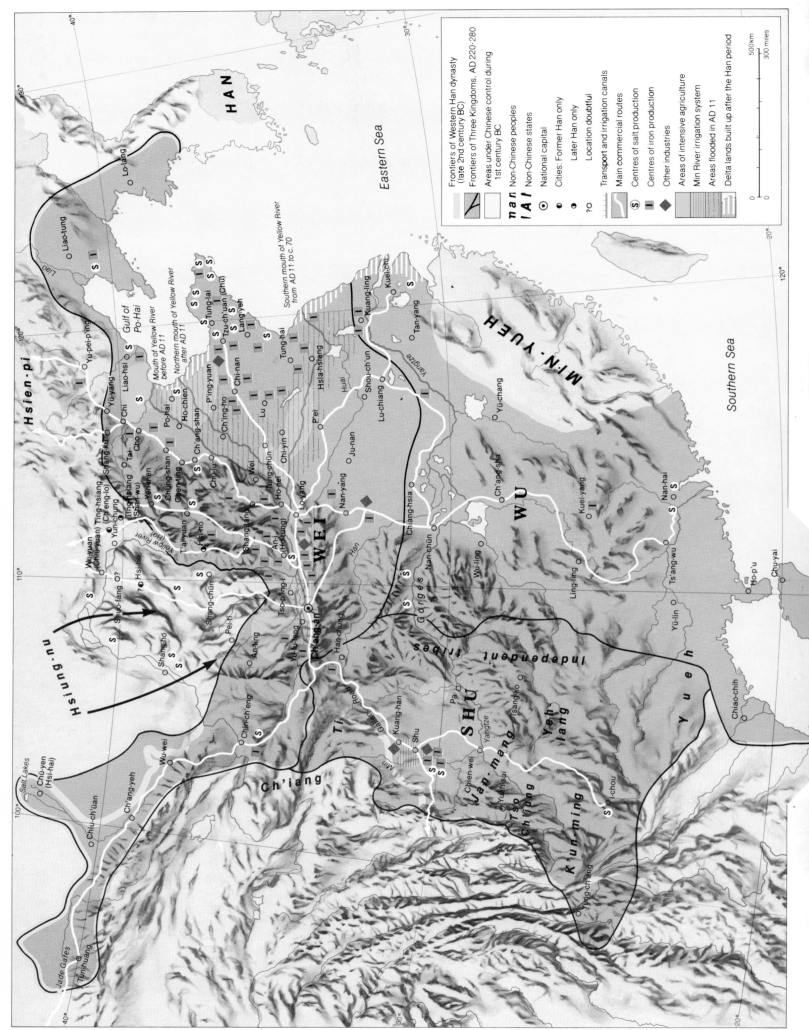

Eastern Sea

Southern Sea

HAN

WEI

WU

SHU

MIN-YUEH

Hsien-pi

Hsiung-nu

Ch'iang

Yueh

K'un-ming

Yeh-lang

Tien

Independent tribes

Gorges

Yangtze

Yellow River (Ho)

Han

Huai

Tibetan Road

Gulf of Po-Hai

Liao

Southern mouth of Yellow River from AD 11 to c. 70

Mouth of Yellow River before AD 11

Northern mouth of Yellow River after AD 11

Ch'ang-an

Lo-yang

Salt Lakes

Jade Gates

Tun-huang

Legend:

Frontiers of Western Han dynasty (late 2nd century BC)
Frontiers of Three Kingdoms, AD 220–280
Areas under Chinese control during 1st century BC
Non-Chinese peoples — n a n
Non-Chinese states — l A l
National capital
Cities: Former Han only
Later Han only
Location doubtful
Transport and irrigation canals
Main commercial routes
Centres of salt production — S
Centres of iron production
Other industries
Areas of intensive agriculture
Min River irrigation system
Areas flooded in AD 11
Delta lands built up after the Han period

500 km
300 miles

13 China under the Early Empire
Under its longest-lived dynasty, the Han (206 BC-AD 9, AD 25-220), the economic, administrative and cultural foundations of Chinese unity were laid securely enough for it to survive the fragmentation of the 3rd century and re-emerge under the leadership of the highly developed north.

BY THE LAST centuries BC the political systems of the regions of the most ancient civilisations (*see Map 3*) had proved able to survive their creators by absorbing conquerors: Iran was ruled by Greeks (under the Seleucids) and Parthians (from 247 BC to AD 227) much as it had been by the Achaemenids, whose tax-gathering system and claim to divinity were taken over with equal nonchalance. The shores of the Mediterranean and the banks of the Ganges and the Yellow River now became in their turn the seats of empires which future rulers in those regions would strive to imitate and aspire to restore.

From 206 BC to AD 9 and from AD 25 to 220 the Han—the longest-lived of China's dynasties and the only one to regain power—extended the reach of imperial government southward to control the coast as far as the Gulf of Tonkin, introduced Chinese civilisation to Korea, and drove the nomads of the steppes back beyond the Gobi desert to take control of the caravan routes which brought China for the first time into contact with the west (*Map 13*). Political unity and improving communications—road and canal systems had been developing for centuries, more often for military and political than for commercial reasons, and had been greatly extended and systematised by the first Ch'in emperor shortly before 200 BC—stimulated trade, and created a cash economy and a wealthy merchant class. The Emperor Wu (*r*.140-86 BC) made minting and the distribution of salt state monopolies, and made part of the land tax payable in grain which could be stored for redistribution in times of famine, offsetting one of the commonest causes of revolt.

The vision of empire had been left to India by the Mauryas in the third century BC. It was most nearly realised by Candra Gupta (*c*.AD 320-35) and his successors. The Guptas ruled the densely populated Ganges valley directly, but their influence over much of the rest of the subcontinent was expressed through a network of tributaries and alliances reminiscent of the relations of the Chinese and Roman empires with the barbarian peoples beyond their boundaries (*see Map 16*). The ensuing stability contributed to a marked increase in the prosperity of the privileged classes, and with it an opulent flowering of sculpture, building and literature which made the fourth and fifth centuries AD the golden age of Hindu culture.

The drama of the rise and fall of empires tends to obscure their nature, which is more truthfully shown by their internal than by their external frontiers. *Map 10* shows how the Han Chinese people, who carried Chinese culture with them as they spread from their homeland in the Yellow River basin, advanced gradually through the most fertile and accessible country, while above them on the mountains and beyond them in the rain forests of the tropical south lived peoples who were very slowly—or never—assimilated into Chinese civilisation. In India disease exacerbated and caste acknowledged the same failure of conquest to eradicate multiplicity, and in Europe the spectacular expansion of the Roman empire along its roads and through its cities conceals the reality of peoples of mountain and forest remaining effectively untouched by the march of Roman civilisation.

The great empires rested on the ability to exploit the process of colonisation, the formation of settlements to become agricultural centres. The expansion of the Han Chinese is paralleled by that of the Romans, who conquered the neighbourhood of Latium in 498-93 BC. Their progress was temporarily checked when the Celts sacked the city in 387 BC, but after regrouping their allies they launched the series of wars that made them masters of Italy south of the Po by 272 BC, and then of the Mediterranean and of western Europe (*see Map 8*). At each victory the Romans annexed territory and peopled it with colonists, at first as individual settlers and later in heavily fortfied self-governing towns with the right to control the land (*territorium*) around them. Thus they provided land for Roman citizens, defence of the conquered territories, and bases for further expansion.

The process of conquest transformed the conquerors. The very precariousness of Rome's early existence helped to shape a society for which warfare was not an occasional expedient but a normal, even necessary, part of its life. Expansion confirmed the pattern. There were perhaps only four or five years in which Rome was not at war between 327 and 241 BC, and perhaps ten in the next century and a half. This was too great a burden for a peasant economy to bear. In the prolonged absence of their proprietors, small farms went unworked. The ruin of many was completed by the devastation of southern Italy in the war of 218-201 BC against Hannibal and perpetuated when expansion in the wake of that victory took Roman armies ever further from home and for ever longer periods (*see Map 8*). In the second century BC periods of conscription of ten to sixteen years were normal, to support an army which has been estimated at about one-eighth of all citizens, one of the highest proportions ever known.

The victories which ruined the peasantry brought immense gains to the generals. Vast fortunes were created by the spoils of war and the pillaging of the provinces which followed. Much of the loot was invested in land which the peasantry was being forced to abandon. It was stocked instead with slaves, of whom the wars created a plentiful supply; great factory farms (*latifundia*) were built up, producing specialised crops and large profits, owned by syndicates of shareholders who probably never set eyes on them. Such holdings soon dominated the agriculture of southern Italy and Sicily and became widespread throughout the western empire.

The republican constitution of early Rome could not stand the strain. The dispossessed drifted into the city to live off the public dole of corn, and provide in the mob a reservoir of discontent and instability. The professionalisation of the army followed the destruction of its citizen base—the property qualification for military service was abolished in 107 BC—and this created an even more tempting instrument for the ambitious. The immense fortunes of the few, renewed by conquest and dissipated in display and competition for office, fuelled political jobbery on a dizzying scale. The restoration of the peasantry through redistribution of land was the only solution, as Tiberius and Gaius Gracchus saw; their deaths, in 123 and 121 BC, showed that the oligarchy would not accept it. A century of bloody warfare across the Roman world followed, as the generals bid in turn for supreme power. It ended only with the overthrow of the republic, the brief dictatorship of Caesar, and the inauguration of the Empire and reorganisation of its government during the long reign of Augustus (*r*.27 BC-AD 14).

The burden of military service affected the Chinese peasantry in much the same way as the Roman. The cost of raising and supplying huge armies precipitated the

The great empires of antiquity

revolts and civil war in which the Ch'in dynasty failed. The defence of the great walls was a heavy drain on manpower, and the maintenance of the growing administration drained the taxes. The free peasant economy gave way to *latifundia*—in effect—in which merchants and officials invested their profits. The Emperor Wu, though, unlike the Gracchi, was strong enough to carry out extensive confiscations of land. These weakened the princes and created a reserve of land for granting to small proprietors, though in practice they were more often used to reward favourites and hangers-on. But Wu's northward expansion against the barbarian threat produced, as he feared, just the consequences that his land policy was designed to avert. By AD 9 famine, peasant revolt and aristocratic turbulence brought his dynasty down. It was restored, in AD 25, by a coalition of magnates, and under the Later Han the growth of great estates and the reduction of the peasantry to personal dependence on the proprietors again continued unchecked.

From the borders of Scotland to the Sinai desert, from Tangier to the Black Sea, the physical remains of the Roman Empire are more numerous, more massive and more durable by far than those of any other civilisation. Their roads still carry traffic, their aqueducts water, their drains sewage. These are the visible fruits of the Augustan Peace and the end of the long struggle of the Romans to win their empire, and among them to control it. The piecemeal structure which left each province as it was won to be looted by its governor was replaced by a unitary administration (*compare Maps 8 and 12*). Cities were planted over the western Empire of a new size and sophistication, with water supplies, baths, theatres and markets. Superb communications and internal order—the Mediterranean was freer of piracy in the first two centuries AD than it would be again before the nineteenth century—permitted a wide circulation of goods within the empire. International trade was swollen as Rome exchanged its wines and pottery, its glass and precious metals, for the furs and amber of the northern barbarians, the spices, jewels, textiles and dancing girls of India, and, at times, the silks of China.

Since their imposing and intricately decorated buildings were of wood and their finest paintings on silk the physical remains of the Han are less imposing, although nothing Roman matched the magnificence of the Han tombs and their contents. In China too restoration was immediately successful. The Later Han recovered control of the northern frontier and the central Asian territories and routes, resumed the colonisation of the south, and presided over an epoch of commercial expansion and cultural brilliance. In AD 166 the Emperor received men who claimed to be envoys of the western ruler An Tun (Marcus Aurelius Antoninus), though he suspected that they were only merchants trying to smooth their path.

At that moment it seemed that both empires had attained a secure height of splendid achievement. But their problems had been evaded, not solved. The maintenance of armies, the defence of the walls and the support of the bureaucracy still, in both empires, laid an insupportable burden on the peasantry. In both, land and power accumulated in the hands of magnates increasingly able to evade imperial control and taxation, thus transferring these burdens ever more relentlessly to the shoulders of the primary producers. The pressure of barbarians on the frontiers hastened the process of internal dissolution.

By the time a real envoy from Rome reached China in AD 226 the Han empire had fallen apart, prey to the now-familiar combination of peasant revolts, ambitious princes and invading barbarians. The permanence of Rome was also illusory. Expansion of the frontiers did not end with Augustus, as he had intended. There were still client states to be reduced, restless neighbours and outsiders to be subdued. The victories of Trajan (*r.*98-117) were as spectacular as those of any of his predecessors, and it took his successors another century to bring the frontier to natural limits and consolidate control within them in the fortress-empire of Septimius Severus (*Map 12*). In 212, the year after his death, all free inhabitants of the empire were granted citizenship. But in 251 the Emperor Decius was killed by Goths who had crossed the Danube, and in the next two decades every frontier collapsed, Persia under the newly established Sassanid dynasty again became a formidable threat (*see Map 15*), and raiders on sea and land penetrated the heart of the Empire. Rome was saved by military takeover. A succession of common soldiers culminating with Diocletian (*r.*284-305) seized the throne, excluded the aristocracy from military command, doubled the size of the army (to some 600,000 men), imposed a rigid and detailed direction of labour, and radically decentralised the government of the Empire (*Map 14*). These measures gained for it another century of life, one of the most brilliant and fascinating in its history, though increasingly based on the wealthier and more populous eastern part of the Empire and its new capital at Constantinople. But the fundamental problems were aggravated, especially in the west, where population declined, land went out of cultivation, trade declined and cities shrank. The empire had not changed its nature, or made life bearable for those who bore it on their backs, and they showed no inclination to save it by resisting new invasions. 'What are kingdoms if not great robberies?' asked Augustine of Hippo, one of the ornaments of late antique culture. Writing a few years after the Visigoths had sacked Rome in AD 410, he knew that the answer was nothing.

Further reading: W. V. Harris, *War and Imperialism in Republican Rome* (Oxford University Press, 1979); R. Syme, *The Roman Revolution* (Oxford University Press, 1939; p.b.); F. Millar, *The Roman Empire and its Neighbours* (Weidenfeld and Nicolson, 1962); C. P. Fitzgerald, *Ancient China* (Phaidon, 1978); G. Herrmann, *The Iranian Revival* (Phaidon, 1977).

14 The later Roman Empire
The Emperors Diocletian (*r.*284-305) and Constantine (*r.*312-337) overhauled the administration, and divided the Empire between East and West, but failed to make it either strong enough to prevent the entry of the peoples who lived beyond its frontiers or flexible enough to absorb them.

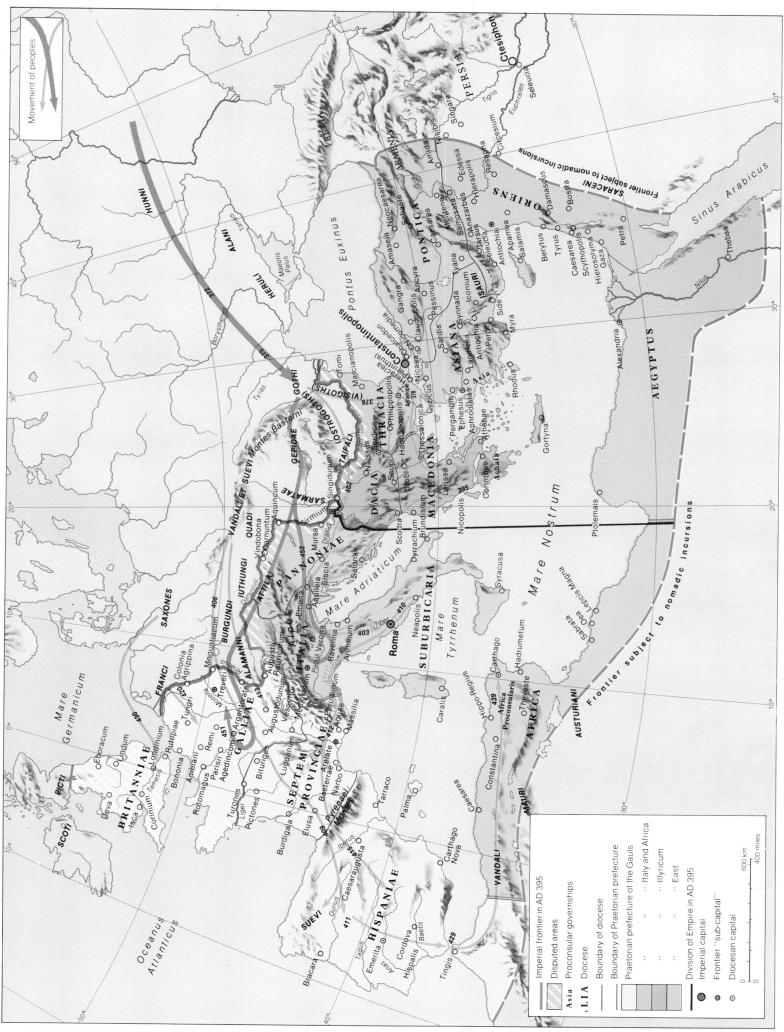

Movement of peoples

HUNNI

ALANI

HERULI

SAXONES

FRANCI

PICTI

SCOTI

BRITANNIAE

Oceanus
Atlanticus

Mare
Germanicum

Eboracum
Lindum
Londinium
Isca
Corinium   Tamesis
Deva
Rutupiae
Bononia
Ambiani
Remi
Rotomagus
Parisii
Turones
Ligeri
Pictones
Bituriges
Burdigala
Elusa
Pyrenaei Montes
Caesaraugusta
Iberus
Bracara
Durius
Emerita
Anas
Cordova
Hispalis
Baetis
Tagus
Carthago Nova
Palma
Tarraco
Narbo
Baeterrae
Arelate
Aquae
Massilia
Tolosa

HISPANIAE
SUEVI
411
409
429
Tingis
MAURI
VANDALI

SEPTEM
PROVINCIAE
GALLIAE
Lugdunum
Vesontio
Augustodunum
Agedincum
Treveri
Mosella
Moguntiacum
406
Colonia
Agrippina
Rhenus
Argentorate
413
Augusta
Raurica
Vienna
451
400
407
BURGUNDI
ALAMANNI
UTHUNGI
QUADI
Vindobona
Carnuntum
Aquincum
Dravus
Siscia
Sirmium
Singidunum
402
Mursa
Savonae
Sala
Aquileia
Emona
Verona
Padus
Mediolanum
Ravenna
Ariminum
403
Roma
410
Neapolis

ITALIA
Alpes

PANNONIAE
SARMATAE
TAIFALI
GEPIDAE
(VISIGOTHS)
VISIGOTHI
OSTROGOTHI
GOTHI
376
375
Tyras
Borysthenes
Montes Bastarni
VANDALI ET SUEVI
Maeotis
Palus

DACIA
Naissus
Serdica
Scupi
Stobi
Ophthiopolis
452
Singidunum
Scodra
Dyrrachium
Brundisium
Nicopolis
Actium
Corinthus
Achaia
Athenae
Sparta

MACEDONIA
Thessalonica
Hadrianopolis
378
Philippopolis
Marcianopolis
Tomi

THRACIA
Perinthus
Heraclea
Constantinopolis
Chalcedon
Nicomedia
Nicaea
Claudiopolis
Ancyra
Pessinus
Gangra

PONTICA
Amasea
Neocaesarea
Sebaste
Sinope
Caesarea

Pontus Euxinus

Sardis
Ephesus
Pergamum
Aphrodisias
Cibyra
Laodicea
Side
Perge
Myra
Rhodus

ASIANA
Asia
Synnada
Iconium
Tyana
Tarsus
Antiochia

ISAURI

ARMENIA
Nisibis
Singara
Amida
Edessa
Hierapolis
Resaena
Circesium
Seleucia
Ctesiphon
Tigris
Euphrates

PERSIA

ORIENS
Melitene
Samosata
Onazarbus
Seleucia
Apamea
Antiochia
Salamis
Berytus
Tyrus
Damascus
Bostra
Caesarea
Scythopolis
Hierosolyma
Gaza
Petra

SARACENI
Frontier subject to nomadic incursions

Sinus Arabicus
Thebae
Nilus

AEGYPTUS
Alexandria
Ptolemais

Mare Nostrum
395

Mare Adriaticum

SUBURBICARIA

Mare
Tyrrhenum
Syracusa
Caralis

AFRICA
PROCONSULARIS
Carthago
Hippo-Regius
Caesarea
Constantina
Theveste
Hadrumetum
439
Sufetula
Lepcis Magna
Sabrata
Oea

AUSTURIANI
Frontier subject to nomadic incursions

MAURI
Africa
Proconsularis

Gortyna

© Creative Cartography Ltd   © The Hamlyn Group

Imperial frontier in AD 395
Disputed areas
Asia   Proconsular governships
ALIA   Diocese
Boundary of diocese
Boundary of Praetorian prefecture
Praetorian prefecture of the Gauls
"   "   Italy and Africa
"   "   Illyricum
"   "   East
Division of Empire in AD 395
Imperial capital
Imperial "sub-capital"
Diocesan capital

0   600 km
0   400 miles

15 The Sassanid Empire in Persia

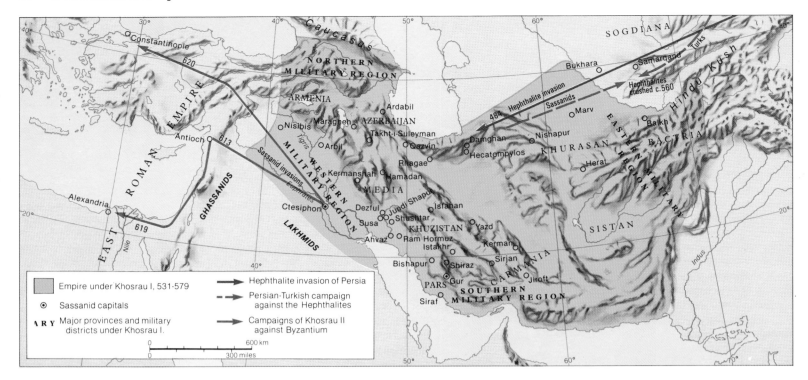

Empire under Khosrau I, 531-579

⊙ Sassanid capitals

ARY Major provinces and military districts under Khosrau I.

→ Hephthalite invasion of Persia

--→ Persian-Turkish campaign against the Hephthalites

→ Campaigns of Khosrau II against Byzantium

0 — 600 km
0 — 300 miles

16 The Empire of the Guptas in India

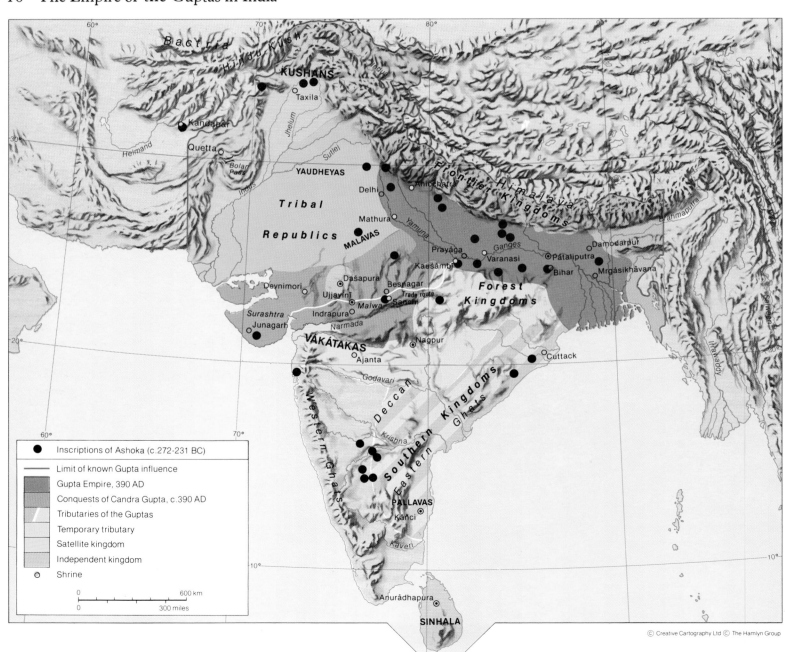

● Inscriptions of Ashoka (c.272-231 BC)

— Limit of known Gupta influence

Gupta Empire, 390 AD

Conquests of Candra Gupta, c.390 AD

Tributaries of the Guptas

Temporary tributary

Satellite kingdom

Independent kingdom

⊙ Shrine

0 — 600 km
0 — 300 miles

© Creative Cartography Ltd © The Hamlyn Group

15 The Sassanid empire in Persia
The Sassanid revolution against the Parthian kings in AD 224 brought to power a dynasty which, seeing itself as successor to the Achaemenids, created a powerful and highly centralised state in Persia. It expanded to take over the Kushan empire to the east and present a growing threat to Rome in the west, especially after its reorganisation by Khosrau I. The Hephthalites or White Huns were nomad invaders from the steppes.

16 The empire of the Guptas in India
The Gupta empire was the first native state to establish itself since the fall of the Mauryas—the extent of whose empire is indicated by the inscriptions of Ashoka—in 180 BC. It based its power on the Ganges valley and at its height exercised a hegemony over much of the sub-continent, through a variety of links of which few were permanent.

17 The world of late antiquity
The distribution of population—though the figures given are highly conjectural—reflects a lasting division between the Greek, Roman and barbarian worlds which reappeared as the Roman empire disintegrated and the struggle for political and cultural leadership intensified. The 'frontier of literacy' shows the northern limit in Gaul of inscriptions and other indications of secular literacy.

THE OTTOMAN conquest of the Byzantine Empire in the fifteenth century and the Manchu of Ming China in the seventeenth (*Maps 39 and 42*) were the last of the barbarian invasions. Since then the backward peoples of the world have retreated before the advanced. Formerly, though the frontiers of civilisation always tended to expand in the long run, they were always liable to collapse before the invader, and known to be so by those who lived within them. The decline of the great empires of antiquity was one of the most momentous and has remained one of the most discussed of these collapses. In AD 316 northern China was overrun by the Hsiung-nu, who divided it into several kingdoms. Between 375 and about 410 several peoples crossed the Roman frontiers, this time to stay (*see Maps 14 and 17*). Throughout the fifth century the Hephthalites (misleadingly called White Huns) launched campaigns against Bactria which eventually forced the reorganisation of the Sassanid empire on a strictly military footing under Khosrau I (*Map 15*) and they are often credited with the collapse of the Indian empire of the Guptas.

It is easy to exaggerate. The Gupta emperors, whose influence outside the Ganges and Indus valleys was so indeterminate that its decline hardly requires explanation (*Map 16*), were already facing disaffection among their underlings, and had been forced to debase their coinage before the attacks became serious in the middle of the fifth century AD. The Sassanid empire, after spectacular expansion in the two centuries after its foundation in AD 226, was riven by disputed succession, aristocratic faction, bitter social division and religious animosity (*compare Map 11*). The fragmentation of northern China reflected Chinese social divisions as well as the rivalries of the barbarian tribes, who were thoroughly sinicised by contact and often by inclination. When one of them, the Toba, became strong enough to reunite the region and found the Northern Wei dynasty (439-535) they adopted Chinese ways in agriculture and administration, manners and dress, made Chinese the language of their court and moved their capital to Lo-yang (*see Map 13*). Throughout this period traditional education, literature and the arts flourished in China, as they did in India and Persia. Only in the western Roman world did the end of a political regime threaten that of the culture which had accompanied it.

The western barbarians admired the Romans. The Goths adopted the Arian form of Christianity, for example, not because it was anti-Roman but, on the contrary, because when their apostle Ulfilas was consecrated in 341 Arian teaching was that commended by the court and bishops of Constantinople. Later the Romans used the 'heresy' of the barbarians as a rationalisation of the same aloofness that made them refuse to receive ambassadors from the Visigoths before the battle of Adrianople in 379 at which the Emperor Valens was killed, or to discuss food supplies with them outside the walls of Rome in 410 before the city was sacked. The barbarians set up their own kingdoms inside the western empire during the fifth century not from choice, but because they were denied assimilation.

When Justinian became emperor in Constantinople in 527 the west was the most hopeful spot on his horizon.

Theodoric the Ostrogoth had ruled Italy as an imperial nominee from 493 to 526 in the spirit of his famous saying that 'Every Goth wants to be a Roman; only a poor Roman would want to be a Goth.' Gaul was dominated by the sons of Clovis, who had accepted baptism from the Catholic bishops and a consular robe from the Emperor Anastasius (*see Map 17*). By contrast the Danube frontier was heavily pressed by Avars and Slavs and war had just broken out with the old enemy, Persia, formidably strong again under Khosrau I. Worst of all, generations of imperial incompetence had allowed great stretches of territory to fall under the unfettered domination of noble families, and through conceding or selling to the magnates the right to make appointments (the *suffragium*), seen the imperial bureaucracy itself become simply an expensive extension of their privilege.

Justinian's claim to greatness is that he tried to dismantle that privilege, his misfortune that his propaganda still disguises it. His quaestor Tribonian renewed the basis of imperial authority with a new, and as it turned out definitive, codification of Roman law, the *Corpus Juris Civilis*. His praetorian prefect, John the Cappadocian, overhauled the administration: his enemies said that he kept a torture chamber beneath the palace, to make the rich pay their taxes. His general, Belisarius, sustained imperial prestige and won rich rewards at little cost by reconquering the provinces of Africa (533-4) and Italy (535-40). It was a bold strategy which nearly worked. But in 540 Khosrau I attacked, breaking the 'eternal peace' for which he had been handsomely paid in 532, and the Slavs took the opportunity to cross the Danube. In 542 plague killed perhaps a quarter of the population of the Empire, and, recurring every few years, left armies devastated, land uncultivated and taxes unpayable. The struggle for survival destroyed Justinian's policy. While vast sums were raised to man and fortify the Persian and Danube frontiers the reconquered provinces rebelled and Italy became the Vietnam of the age; Slav incursions became ever deeper and more frequent, the Persian threat more ominous; and to resist them posts and power were once more mortgaged to the magnates, this time irredeemably.

Like many radical reformers Justinian pretended only devotion to the past, seeking the loyalty of his subjects by proclaiming his intention to restore the Roman Empire, and that of the bishops by professing a fervent concern for Catholic unity. In fact what he conquered was the old Greek world, soon to shrink almost to its ancient extent (*compare Maps 17, 5 and 20*). He gave it a law, a tradition of imperial absolutism in church and state, and, through the public and religious buildings which he everywhere erected or inspired, a uniform and magnificent art. He failed to rescue it from the rapacity of its aristocracy.

Further reading: E. Gibbon, *The Decline and Fall of the Roman Empire* (1776-88, ed. J. B. Bury, 1909-13; avoid abridgements); F. Lot, *The End of the Ancient World and the Beginning of the Middle Ages* (Routledge and Kegan Paul, 1931; Harper, 1961); Peter Brown, *The World of Late Antiquity* (Thames & Hudson, 1971; p.b.); M. Elvin, *Patterns of the Chinese Past* (Eyre Methuen, 1973; p.b.).

Atlantic
Ocean

PICTS

Iona
Devenish
Lindisfarne
Armagh
Kells
Clonard
Whithorn
NORTHUMBRIANS
MERCIANS
EAST
ANGLIANS
St. Davids
West
Saxons
KENT
Canterbury
Tintagel

North Sea

Baltic

c. 540-
560
c. 460

KINGDOM
OF THE FRANKS
(481)

Cologne
c. 511-48
Trier
Rouen
Soissons
Reims
486
Paris
Faremoutiers
Sens
Le Mans
486
Orléans
Auxerre
Luxeuil
c. 511-48
Tours
Bourges
Besançon
St. Gall
Bregenz
Poitiers
Nevers
553-4
Chur
Vouillé
Clermont
Burgundian
507
Limoges
Lyons
Kingdom
Cahors
Vienne
(443-534)
Monza
537
Milan
Bobbio
511
Toulouse
Valence
Narbonne
Arles
Avignon
Pavia
Verona
Genoa
Marseille
Lérins
Luna

ALEMANIA

Rhine
Elbe
Oder
Danube

LOMB
568

The Alps

Dol
Rennes

Bay of
Biscay

Pyrenees

KINGDOM
OF
THE SUEVI
(464-585)

Oviedo
Leon
Braga
Palencia
Pamplona
Burgos
Ebro

VISIGOTHIC
KINGDOM
(455-711)

Saragossa
Tortosa
Tarragona
Gerona
Reccopolis
Toledo
Merida

Valencia
Ibiza
Seville
Cadiz
Cartagena
Tingis
Septem

Balearic Is.

Corsica
Ajaccio

Sardinia
Forum Trajani
Cagliari

KINGDOM OF THE
OSTROGOTHIS
(489-555)

Aquileia
Grado
Parenzo
Pola
Ravenna
Rimini
Ancona
Auximum
Salona
Perugia
Sublaco
Rome
Lucera
Monte Cassino
Capua
Naples
Salerno
Brindisi
Taranto
Otranto
Cosenza
Croton
Vivarium
Palermo
Messina
Reggio
Agrigento
Sicily
Syracuse

K   I   N   G   D   O   M

Atlas Mts.

Pomaria
Caesarea
Sitifis
Timgad

O   F   T   H   E

MAURETANIA

VANDALS
(442-534)

Hippo Regius
Cirta
NUMIDIA
Thelepte
BYZACENA
Tacape

PROCONSULARIS
Carthage
Thagaste
Grasse
Hadrumetum
Caput Vada

Sabrata
Leptis Magna

TRIPOLITANIA

Medit

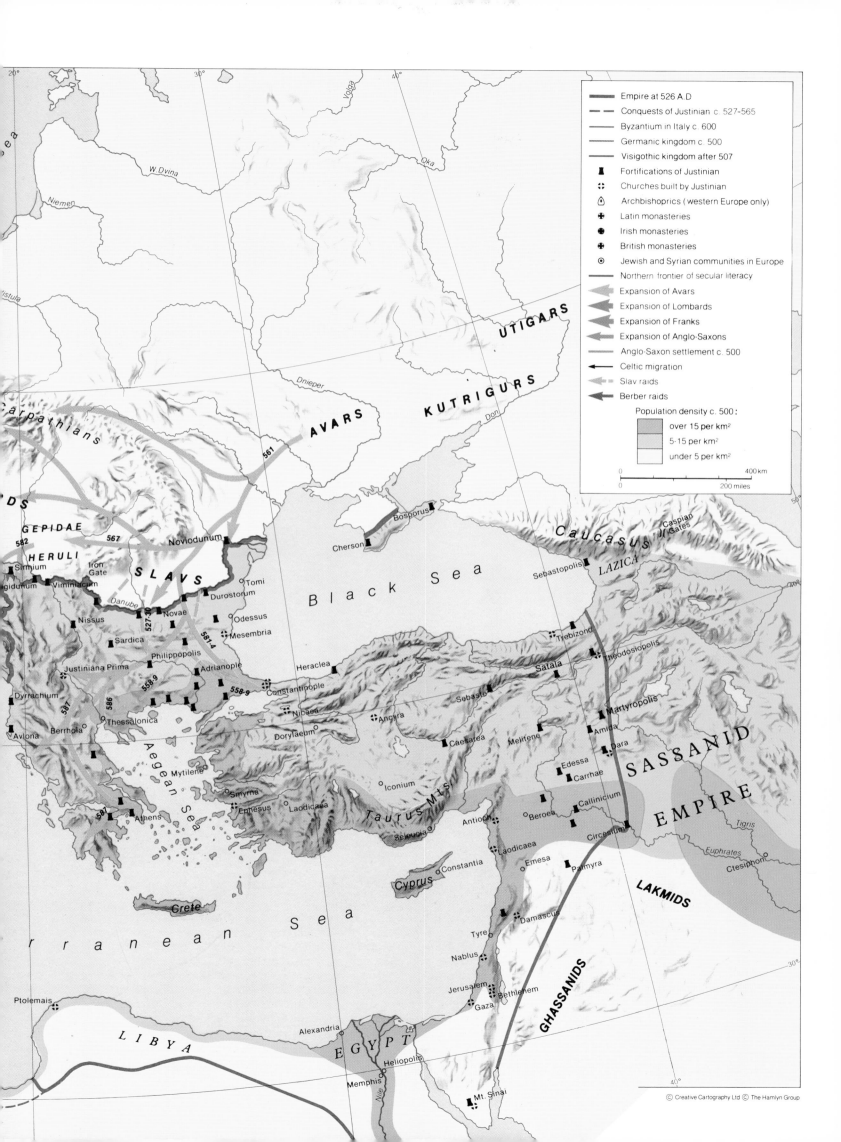

Legend:

Empire at 526 A.D
Conquests of Justinian c. 527–565
Byzantium in Italy c. 600
Germanic kingdom c. 500
Visigothic kingdom after 507
Fortifications of Justinian
Churches built by Justinian
Archbishoprics (western Europe only)
Latin monasteries
Irish monasteries
British monasteries
Jewish and Syrian communities in Europe
Northern frontier of secular literacy
Expansion of Avars
Expansion of Lombards
Expansion of Franks
Expansion of Anglo-Saxons
Anglo-Saxon settlement c. 500
Celtic migration
Slav raids
Berber raids

Population density c. 500:
over 15 per km²
5-15 per km²
under 5 per km²

0   400 km
0   200 miles

UTIGARS

AVARS   KUTRIGURS

Carpathians

GEPIDAE
582   567
HERULI
Sirmium   Iron
Gate   Noviodunum
DS
igidunum   Viminiacum   SLAVS
Nissus   527-30   Novae   Tomi
Sardica   Durostorum
Justiniana Prima   Philippopolis   Odessus
581-4
Dyrrachium   558-9   Mesembria
Adrianople
586   558-9
587   Berrhoia   Thessalonica   Heraclea
Avlona   Constantinople

Danube

Cherson   Bosporus   Caucasus
Caspian
Gates
Sebastopolis   LAZICA

Black   Sea   Trebizond
Theodosiopolis
Satala
Sebaste
Martyropolis
Ancyra   Amida
Nicaea   Dara
Caesarea   Melitene
Dorylaeum   SASSANID
Edessa
Iconium   Carrhae
587   Callinicium   EMPIRE
Athens   Smyrna   Beroea
Aegean   Ephesus   Laodicaea   Antioch   Circesium   Tigris
Sea   Mytilene   Seleucia   Euphrates
Laodicaea   Ctesiphon
Emesa   Palmyra
Cyprus   Constantia   LAKMIDS
Damascus
Crete   Tyre
rranean   Sea   Nablus   GHASSANIDS
Jerusalem   Bethlehem
Ptolemais   Gaza
Alexandria
LIBYA   EGYPT
Heliopolis
Memphis   Nile   Mt. Sinai

Taurus Mts.

W. Dvina
Niemen
Vistula
Volga
Oka
Dnieper
Don
561

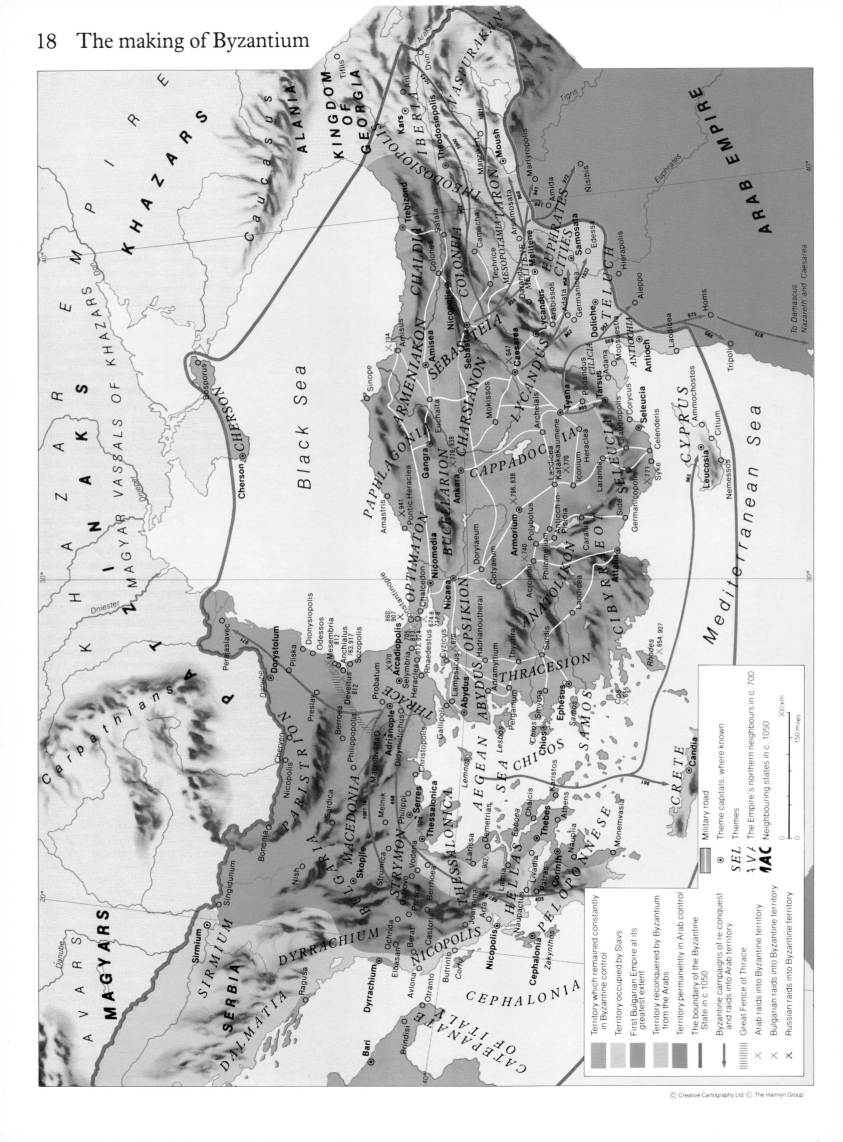

ARAB EMPIRE

KHAZARS

EMPIRE

ALANIA

KINGDOM OF GEORGIA

IBERIA

VASPURAKAN

Tiflis

Kars ⊙
Ani

Theodosiopolis

Dvin

Manzikert

Moush ⦿

Arsamosata
Amida
Melitene

EUPHRATES CITIES

Edessa
Hierapolis
Aleppo

Homs ⦿

To Damascus
Nazareth and Caesarea

Caucasus

Black Sea

Trebizond ⦿

CHALDIA

COLONEIA

Satala
Colonea
Camacha

Tephrice

MESOPOTAMIA

TARON

Germanicea

Samosata

TELUCH

Doliche ⦿

Laodicea

Tripoli

MAGYAR VASSALS OF KHAZARS

Bosporus

Cherson ⦿ CHERSON

Dnieper

Amisus

×194

ARMENIAKON

Sinope

Amastris

PAPHLAGONIA

Pontic Heraclea
×941

Gangra ⦿

Ankara ⦿

BUCELLARION

SEBASTEIA

Sebastea ⦿
CHARSIANON

×776,838
Euchaita
Mokissos

Nicopolis ⦿

Caesarea ⦿
×647

×796,838

CAPPADOCIA

×770

LYCANDUS

Lycandus
Arabissos
Adata

CILICIA

Pedandus
Mopsuestia
Adana
Tarsus ⦿
Corycus

ANTIOCHIA

Antioch ⦿

Seleucia ⦿
SELEUCIA
Celenderis
Syke

CYPRUS

Leucosia ⦿

Ammochostos
Citium
Nemessos

Mediterranean Sea

KHAZARS

Dniester

Dnieper

Archelais
Tyana ⦿
×965
Heraclea
Iconium
Laranda
Claudiopolis
Germanicopolis
Side

SAMOS

Dristra

OPTIMATON

Nicomedia ⦿
Nicaea ⦿

Chalcedon

Constantinople

Doryaeum

OPSIKION

Cotyaeum

Cyzicus

ABYDUS

Abydus ⦿

THRACESION

Pergamum

Smyrna

Ephesus ⦿

Chios
CHIOS

AEGEAN SEA

Lemnos
Lesbos

ANATOLIKON

Philomelium
Amorium ⦿ ×740
Polybotus
Antioch-in Pisidia
Sardis
Thyatira
Adramyttium
Laodicea
Attalia ⦿
CIBYRRHEOT

Rhodes
×654,907

×196

CRETE

Candia ⦿

MAGYARS

AVARS

Carpathians

Danube

Singidunum

Sirmium ⦿ SIRMIUM

SERBIA

DALMATIA

Ragusa

Avlona

DYRRACHIUM

Dyrrachium ⦿

Elbasan
Berat

Ochrida

NICOPOLIS

CEPHALONIA

Corfu
Butrinto
Otranto

CATEPANATE OF ITALY

Bari ⦿
Brindisi

Pereiaslavec
×148

PARISTRION

Dorystolum ⦿

Danube
Preslav

Pliska

Dionysiopolis
Odessos

Mesembria
Anchialus
Sozopolis

BULGARIA

Cheven

Nicopolis
Sardica

Presipa

Berrhoea
Philippopolis

Develtus

THRACE

Arcadiopolis ⦿

Selymbria
Heraclea

Probatum

Didymoteichus
Christopolis

MACEDONIA

Skopje ⦿

Melnik

Serres ⦿
Philippi

STRYMON

Vodena
Berrhoea

THESSALONICA

Thessalonica ⦿

Lemnos

Berrhoea

Larissa
Demetrias

HELLAS

Livadia
Thebes ⦿
Athens

PELOPONNESE

Corinth ⦿
Patras
Monemvasia
Nauplia

Nish

Bononia

Nicopolis ⦿

Joannina

Naupactus

Cephalonia ⦿

Zakynthos

Carpathians

Legend:

Military road

SEL Theme capitals, where known

SEL Themes

↑↗ The Empire's northern neighbours in c. 700

MAC Neighbouring states in c. 1050

Territory which remained constantly in Byzantine control

Territory occupied by Slavs

First Bulgarian Empire at its greatest extent

Territory reconquered by Byzantium from the Arabs

Territory permanently in Arab control

The boundary of the Byzantine State in c. 1050

Byzantine campaigns of re-conquest and raids into Arab territory

Great Fence of Thrace

Arab raids into Byzantine territory

Bulgarian raids into Byzantine territory

Russian raids into Byzantine territory

300 km

150 miles

© Creative Cartography Ltd © The Hamlyn Group

Heirs to the ancient world I

Religions and civilisations

18 The making of Byzantium
After administrative and military reorganisation, Constantinople (*Byzantium*) and its hinterland, to which the Eastern Roman Empire was reduced by the invasions of Slavs and Arabs in the 7th century, became the centre of fresh expansion and a vigorous civilisation in the 8th and 9th centuries.

THE BLOODY rivalry between Persia and Byzantium which had continued since the end of Justinian's reign in 565 was rudely interrupted when Arab armies seized the Byzantine provinces of Syria in AD 635, Palestine in 638 and Egypt in 642, and took the Persian capital of Ctesiphon in 636. In those years the ancient world gave way to the modern. The conquests of Islam, which continued only slightly less rapidly until its armies seized Toledo, Samarqand and Multan in 711-13 (*see Map 19*), changed the course of world history. The Mediterranean basin, upon whose commercial and cultural unity classical civilisation had been built, was divided for ever. The fragmentation of the Roman world which had become increasingly obvious in the preceding centuries (*Maps 14, 17*) now became permanent, and each part was sent on its own distinctive path (*Maps 18, 21 and 22*). The world of Islam became a vast market linking all the economies of the known world to support a civilisation of opulent splendour, whose hunger for manpower and raw materials stimulated the opening up of the forests and plains of central Europe and initiated the systematic plundering of Africa that has sustained the development of advanced economies ever since (*Map 27*). The pattern of the great religions of the world, and its principal cultural and political divisions, was completed (*Maps 11 and 20*).

The Arabian peninsula in the time of Muhammad (traditionally, *b*.570) combined violence with sophistication. Its rugged desert terrain, occupied by nomadic Bedouin, kept conquerors at bay while its cities prospered on the trade between the Red Sea, the Persian Gulf and the Indian Ocean, and on the fabled spices and perfumes of Arabia, cultivated and manufactured in the Yemen. Competition and warfare were constant between the merchant dynasties of the cities and the Bedouin, and within each of these groups. Muhammad's power was rooted in diplomacy. The *Koran*, revealed to him in a series of visions from about 610 onwards, contained the basis upon which, as his followers said, 'Allah has sent us a prophet who will make peace between us'; the message was largely one of repudiating the network of family obligation and social custom of traditional Arab society, with its ever-violent code of manliness, honour and revenge, in favour of a stark confrontation between the believer and his God, whose inexorable judgement, would ask only whether the precepts of the *Koran* had been unflinchingly observed, regardless of worldly connection and reputation. Muhammad unified the peninsula by diplomacy, aided when necessary by the doctrine of holy war – 'It was not you who slew them, but Allah who slew them', as the prophet assured his followers when the slaughter of a Meccan caravan seemed momentarily to have flouted the *Koran*'s prohibition of violence. He was planning the conquest of Syria when he died in 632.

His work was continued by the Caliphs (successors) Abu Bakr (*r*.632-4) and Omar (*r*.634-44). Their decree that the land of those who surrendered would remain inviolate while that of any who had actually to be conquered would be forfeit to the state, to be merely leased again to its former owners, facilitated the advance. It was a prudent policy, for the Arab armies, with no advantages save the great speed of movement that their camels gave them and remarkable confidence in their own destiny, could probably not have overcome sustained resistance, despite their spectacular victories over numerically superior forces at Yarmuk (636) and Qadesiya (637). But

the Roman hold on Africa and the Middle East was tenuous in the extreme, and the Sassanid Empire on the point of collapse. These two powers had recently waged savage wars in which they alternately committed the most brutal atrocities upon the subject populations of the Middle East who repeatedly passed from the control of one to the other, with religious minorities, Christian and Jewish, suffering particularly heavily, being constantly vulnerable to accusations of treason and collaboration. These wars simply emphasised the weakness and the unpopularity of both their rules. The new Islamic masters demanded more modest taxes and services, and did not even inconvenience their new subjects to the extent of living in their towns, preferring to build new ones for themselves nearby; inevitably they were readily welcomed by exhausted and long-tyrannised communities. Like the fall of the Roman Empire in the west, the collapse of so much of the Eastern Roman Empire and of its Persian counterpart rid their former lands of an expensive, cumbersome and blood-stained rule that had long outlived its vitality and its usefulness.

The established world religions also underwent fundamental changes in the early centuries of the Christian era. Hinduism now assumed greater coherence by concentrating its literature and religious activity upon three of the many gods whose worship the Vedic religion had embraced, Brahma (the creator), Vishna (the preserver) and Shiva (the destroyer of the corrupt world). The myth and ceremony associated with the last two in particular, together with the Sanskrit language, were deliberately employed by various dynasties to disseminate Aryan culture from its strongholds in the north of the subcontinent. Hinduism, however, was not a missionary religion. To an even greater extent than Judaism, which was disseminated widely in the west through the travels of the Jews, but did not usually attempt to convert outsiders (*see Map 11*), Hinduism spread with but not beyond those who were born into it. Birth was indeed the only means of entry, and the absorption of new peoples by the creation of sub-castes – a technique which could not be applied to individuals – was necessarily a slow business. The process of rapid evangelisation in India was left to the Jains and to Buddhism, which, like Christianity in the west, was a religion of personal conviction and conversion.

The teaching of the Buddha was not written down for several centuries after his time, with the result that a large number of sects offered competing versions of it. Some held, despite his warning that he was not to be deified, that the historical Buddha was only one of a series of incarnations in which the divine being appeared, sacrificing the *nirvana* which he had earned by his perfection to secure the redemption of others through his own suffering. As such he could be represented and worshipped in the *bodhisattvas*, the idealised stone images which now proliferated in the great monuments of Buddhist art. Early in the second century AD, those who held this belief, together with others who wished to incorporate new practices and philosophies into their faith, separated to follow their 'Greater Vehicle' (*Mahayana*) from those who clung to the 'Lesser Vehicle' (*Hinayana*) of the teaching of the historical Buddha, literally observed. As Buddhism spread the Mahayana system became predominant in China, Japan, Korea and Vietnam, while the Hinayana prevailed in Burma, Thailand, Cambodia and Ceylon.

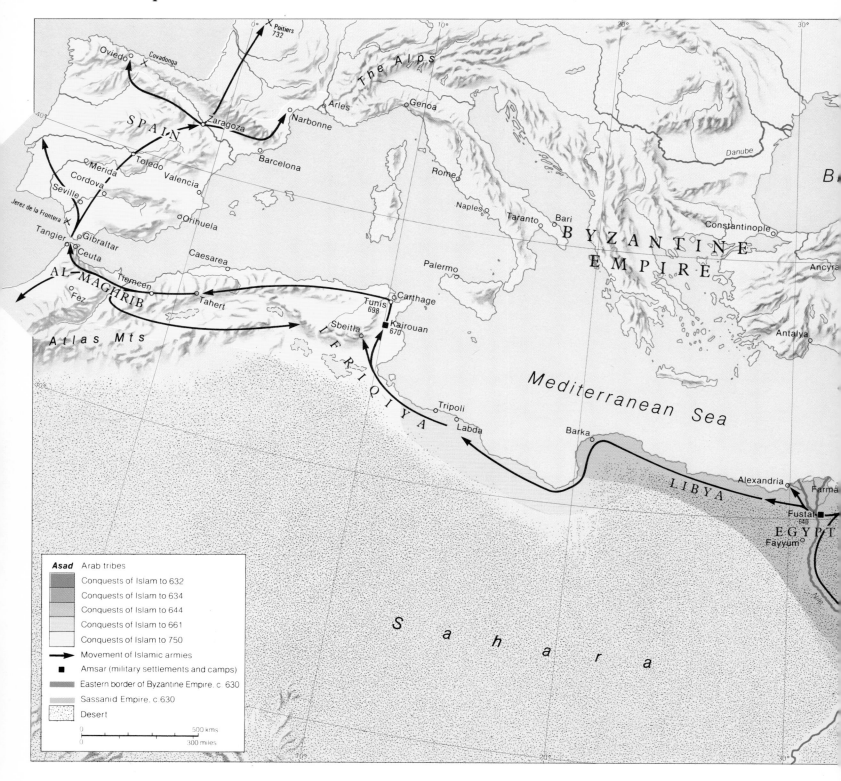

Legend:
Asad Arab tribes
Conquests of Islam to 632
Conquests of Islam to 634
Conquests of Islam to 644
Conquests of Islam to 661
Conquests of Islam to 750
→ Movement of Islamic armies
■ Amsar (military settlements and camps)
Eastern border of Byzantine Empire. c. 630
Sassanid Empire. c. 630
Desert

500 kms
300 miles

Buddhism probably reached China along the central Asian trade routes in the early years of the Later Han dynasty; the traditional date is AD 65. Its early development there was slow, hindered both by philosophical difficulties—such as the flat contradiction between the Chinese veneration of family and the Buddhist renunciation of all family ties—and by practical ones such as the difficulty of translating the Sanskrit scriptures—which reached China haphazardly and piecemeal. The work was done by Chinese monks who made a number of pilgrimages to India for the purpose. By the fourth century, however, China was ruled by barbarians. The foreignness of Buddhism became a positive attraction, and many of the rulers adopted Buddhist monks as political advisers to offset the influence of the Confucian Chinese around them. The favour of the courts and the lavish patronage

of the powerful stimulated the spread of Buddhism in northern China in the fourth and fifth centuries, accompanied by magnificent temples and sculptures. At the same time the noble Chinese families who had migrated to the south in large numbers found the Buddhist custom of withdrawal an attractive expedient in troubled times, and chose to make the monasteries, which they founded in large numbers, centres for the preservation of their own cultural traditions. Hence Buddhism contrived to appeal both to the Taoist aspiration of withdrawal from the world, and to the Confucian veneration of tradition and scholarship, while in the north it won great influence among the non-Chinese. In consequence although it was occasionally subjected to persecution Buddhism became the third of China's religions. Conversely it is a notable proof of the essential stability and sophistication of

19 The conquests of Islam
Within ten years of the death of Muhammad in 632 the armies of Islam had conquered most of the old Roman empire and occupied the Persian capital; within 70 they commanded territories stretching over 5000 miles, of which only Spain and Portugal are no longer predominantly Muslim.

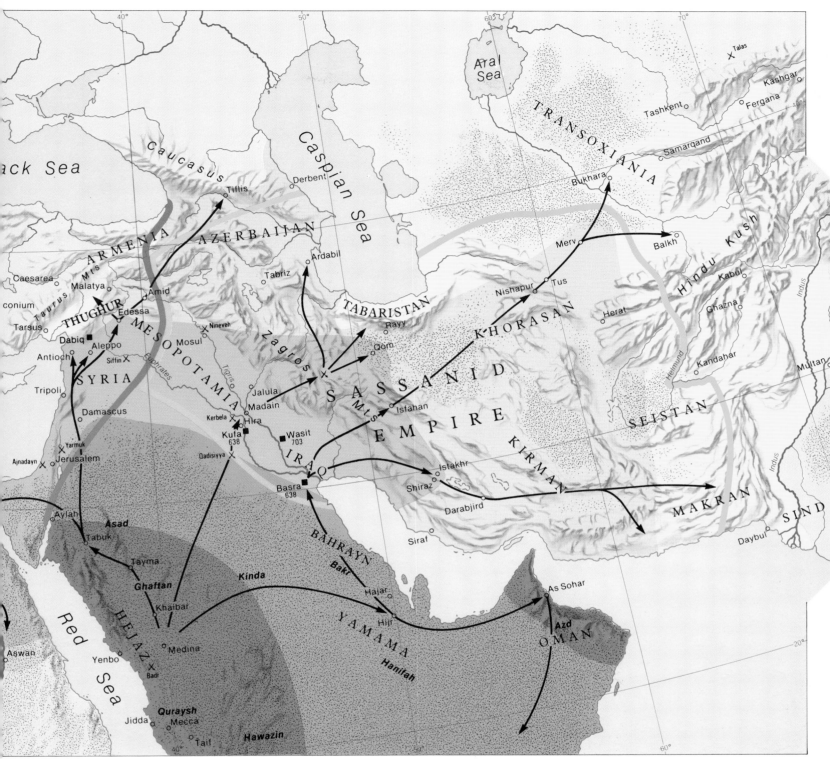

© Creative Cartography Ltd © The Hamlyn Group

20 Religions of the medieval world
Between the 8th and 15th centuries, four universal religions (all with internal sects and divisions which are not shown here) came to dominate the civilised world, eradicating paganism from most areas. The social and cultural patterns which they created or reflected have endured.

Chinese culture that it was, until comparatively recent times, the only one in the civilised world which did not require to be underpinned by religious monopoly.

The early history of Christianity had a great deal in common with that of Buddhism. It too was founded essentially as a movement of reform within an older religion, by comparison with which it stressed personal spirituality rather than formal adherence to law, charity rather than ascetic prohibitions. It too repudiated political structures, social distinctions and, implicitly, the priority of kinship loyalties, renouncing violence and emphasising the brotherhood of mankind. Like the Buddha, Christ was regarded by his followers as a perfect being who redeemed the sins of mankind through his own suffering. In his case too the absence of a strictly contemporary record of his teaching encouraged the

multiplication of sects among his devotees, most of whom came to attribute to him a divinity which he had not explicitly claimed. They drew upon the philosophical and cultural traditions of their time to evolve a universal theology to support their cult. Particularly important was the reconciliation of Christian theology with the neoplatonist system of philosophy, based on the idea of the unity of creation, which also provided an idealist foundation for the pagan cults of the third and fourth centuries AD. Finally, like Buddhism, Christianity was assisted in its diffusion by the regular and far-flung communications of a great empire (*see Map 11*), but attained real social power and political influence by exploiting its decline.

The Christians of the Roman Empire were conceded freedom of worship by Constantine in 313, and the

43

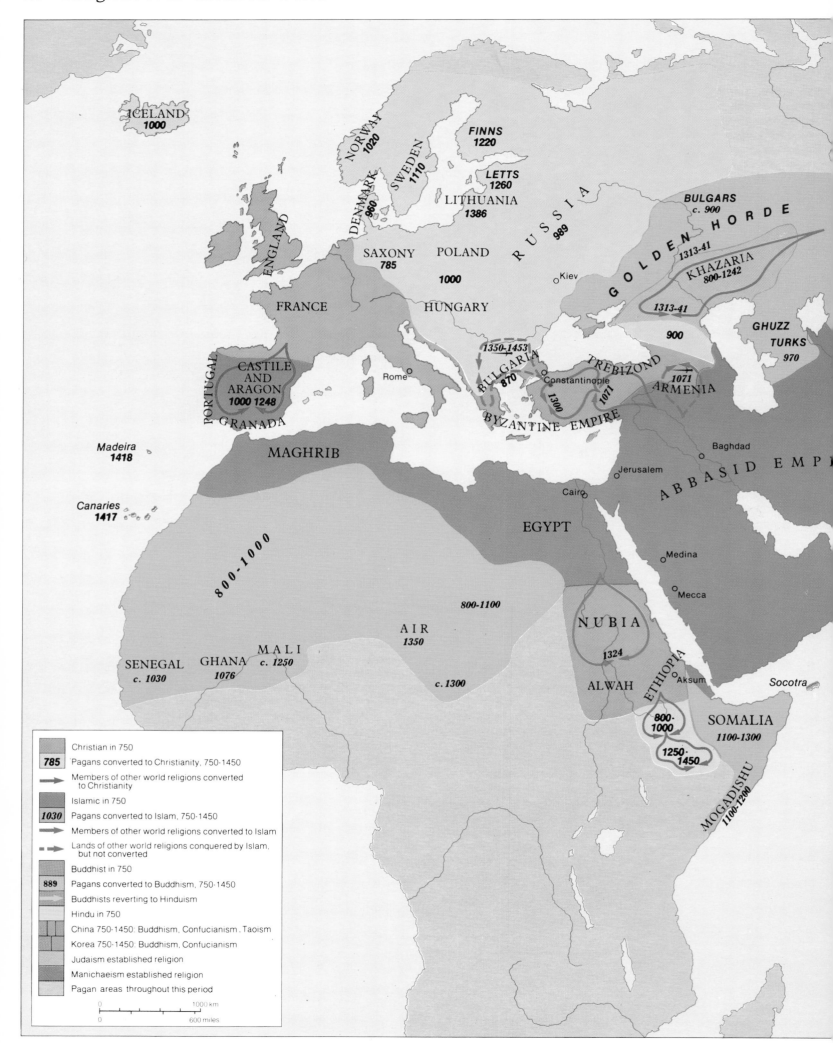

ICELAND
1000

NORWAY
1020

FINNS
1220

DENMARK
960

SWEDEN
1110

LETTS
1260

LITHUANIA
1386

ENGLAND

SAXONY
785

POLAND
1000

RUSSIA

Kiev

BULGARS
c. 900

GOLDEN HORDE

1313-41

KHAZARIA
800-1242

1313-41

FRANCE

HUNGARY

900

GHUZZ
TURKS
970

PORTUGAL

CASTILE
AND
ARAGON
1000 1248

GRANADA

Rome

1350-1453

BULGARIA
870

TREBIZOND

Constantinople

1300

1071

1071

ARMENIA

1071

BYZANTINE EMPIRE

Baghdad

Madeira
1418

MAGHRIB

Jerusalem

Cairo

ABBASID EMPI

Canaries
1417

800-1000

EGYPT

Medina

Mecca

800-1100

NUBIA

1324

AIR
1350

Socotra

MALI
c. 1250

ETHIOPIA

Aksum

SENEGAL
c. 1030

GHANA
1076

c. 1300

ALWAH

800-
1000

SOMALIA
1100-1300

1250-
1450

MOGADISHU
1100-1200

	Christian in 750
785	Pagans converted to Christianity, 750-1450
→	Members of other world religions converted to Christianity
	Islamic in 750
1030	Pagans converted to Islam, 750-1450
→	Members of other world religions converted to Islam
⇢	Lands of other world religions conquered by Islam, but not converted
	Buddhist in 750
889	Pagans converted to Buddhism, 750-1450
→	Buddhists reverting to Hinduism
	Hindu in 750
	China 750-1450: Buddhism, Confucianism, Taoism
	Korea 750-1450: Buddhism, Confucianism
	Judaism established religion
	Manichaeism established religion
	Pagan areas throughout this period

0   1000 km
0   600 miles

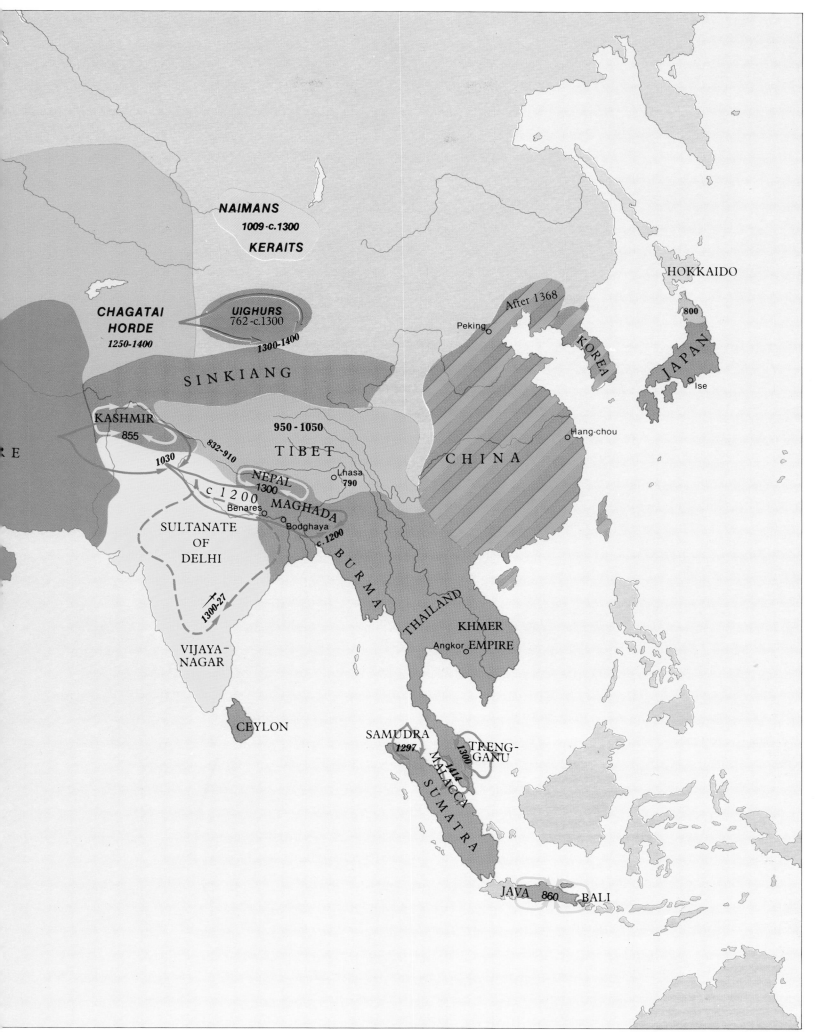

NAIMANS
1009 -c.1300

KERAITS

HOKKAIDO

After 1368

800

CHAGATAI
HORDE
1250-1400

UIGHURS
762 -c.1300

KOREA

Peking

JAPAN

1300-1400

S I N K I A N G

Ise

KASHMIR
855

950 - 1050

Hang-chou

832-910

TIBET

C H I N A

1030

Lhasa
790

NEPAL
1300

c 1200

MAGHADA

Benares
Bodghaya

SULTANATE
OF
DELHI

c. 1200

B U R M A

1300-27

THAILAND

KHMER

Angkor EMPIRE

VIJAYA-
NAGAR

CEYLON

SAMUDRA
1297

TRENG-
GANU

1300

1414

M A L A C C A

S U M A T R A

JAVA 860 BALI

Religions and civilisations

communities which were now found in most parts of the Roman world could come into the open. Christianity did not, however, immediately become the dominant religion of the Roman world. During the fourth century the legal disabilities which it had suffered were gradually transferred, by imperial decree, to the traditional pagan cults. In the east, where the cities in which Christianity flourished were most populous and the pagan aristocracy least influential, the order to close the temples and the prohibition of pagan worship in public were taken as licence for successful persecution. Monks and holy men from the deserts of Egypt and the mountains of Syria led bloodthirsty mobs in a reign of terror which destroyed the fabric of pagan life and culture. The worst excesses were the destruction of the shrine of Serapion at Alexandria, and with it the greatest library of antiquity, in 391 and in 415 the lynching of Hypatia, the virgin queen of the neoplatonist schools.

In the west, social leadership and public office remained in the hands of the Roman aristocracy. To its members paganism, which was now heavily impregnated with neoplatonist idealism, expressed the values and enshrined the traditions of their class, much as Confucianism did in China. The aristocracy did not hurry to implement the anti-pagan decrees of the upstart emperors they despised, and they were under little popular pressure to do so. A pagan attempt to recapture the Western Empire failed only through the chance of battle (or, as the winners said, a miracle) as late as 394. Christianity triumphed only when the Roman aristocracy came to see it as the means of preserving their culture from the collapse of the empire, and the church as the vehicle through which, under traditional leadership, Rome would recover its ancient pre-eminence. As the empire dissolved, the scions of the Roman aristocracy adopted episcopal mitres to resume the leadership that their forefathers had exercised in senatorial purple. They copied the manuscripts which contained their culture and collected them in monasteries, where literacy might, however precariously, be preserved. When these men

began to come to terms with the invaders the foundations of a new age were laid. In Gaul Clovis, king of the Merovingian Franks, was converted in c.500, and made them the guides and mentors of a dynasty which brought Gaul under a single, if rapidly enfeebled, rule and inaugurated Europe's most important Catholic regime (*see Map 17*).

Thomas Hobbes described the Roman Church as 'the ghost of the Roman Empire sitting crowned upon the grave thereof.' So it was elsewhere. The world religions neither replaced nor transformed the ancient civilisations. They were the means by which the civilisations survived the ruin of their original political structures. Even Islam, the starkest and most uncompromising of the new faiths, was no different. The Abbasid revolution began in Khorasan in 750 to restore the fundamentals of Islam. The Umayyad dynasty which it replaced had treated conquest as a means of enriching the Arab aristocracy, and was led by the very families which had once driven the Prophet from Mecca. Under their rule Christian Arabs enjoyed high office, and the capital was moved from Medina to the Roman city of Damascus, where, like the Dome of the Rock in Jerusalem, the Great Mosque was decorated by Byzantine craftsmen, in Byzantine style. The Abbasid regime turned its back on the corrupting shores of the Mediterranean, to rule from Iran a central Asian empire of great wealth and magnificence. Its caliphs claimed over their subjects absolute powers which they exercised ruthlessly with the help of Persian officials. Their splendid courts observed the etiquette and ceremonial of the Sassanids, whose literature and art now experienced a revival. Their new capital was at Baghdad, 35 miles from the ruins of Ctesiphon.

Further reading: B. Lewis, *The Arabs in History* (Hutchinson, 1950; p.b.); F. Gabrieli, *Muhammed and the Conquests of Islam* (Weidenfeld and Nicolson, 1968; p.b.); C. P. Fitzgerald, *A Concise History of East Asia* (Penguin, 1966); R. Thapar, *A History of India*, Vol. 1 (Penguin, 1966); H. Chadwick, *The Early Church* (Penguin, 1968); Peter Brown, *Religion and Society in the Age of St. Augustine* (Faber & Faber, 1972).

21 The Byzantine commonwealth
The Slavs were converted to Christianity in the 9th century by Saints Cyril and Methodius. Although their work was largely destroyed within a century by Magyar invasions, the Orthodox Church, represented by Byzantine artists and builders as well as missionaries and monks, remained the greatest formative influence on eastern Europe.

VIATKA

L. Ladoga

Birka
Reval
Ladoga
1167
Beloozero
Khlynov

LETTS

NOVGOROD
c.1000
Novgorod the Great

Izborsk
Pskov
Kholm
Yaroslav
Rostov
1040
Volga
Nishni
Novgorod

Grobina
Riga
1201
Apuole

LITHUANIANS

Tver
SUZDAL
Suzdal
Vladimir
1198

Dmitrov
Moscow
Murom
1090
Bukhara

TEUTONIC ORDER
Koenigsberg
1254
PRUSSIANS

Wolin
c.1140
Elbing
1237
Polotsk
1105
SMOLENSK
Kolomna
Ryazan
c.1200
RYAZAN

BULGARS

WESTERN
Magdeburg
962
Gneizno
c.1100
Poznan
968
Thorn
1234
Plock
c.1075

Cherven

Smolensk
c.1136
Bryansk
CHERNIGOV
Starodub
Trubchevsk
Novogorod
Sevirsky
Kursk

EMPIRE

Breslau
c.1000

KINGDOM OF
POLAND

Pinsk
VOLHYNIA
Turov
c.1120
Chernigov
c.1066
Great Bulgar

Saracen Route

Prague
975
BOHEMIA
Cracow
c.1000
KIEV
Vladimir-
in-Volhynia
1090
PEREJASLAV
c.1040

Olmutz
1069
MORAVIA
Przemysl
Galich
c.1160
Kiev
989
Perejaslav
c.1000

Salzburg
Danube
KINGDOM OF
HUNGARY
GALICIA
Belgorod
c.989
Dnieper
Route
989
Donets
Volga
Bukhara

The Alps
Aquileia
Esztergom
Carpathians
CUMANS
Dniester
Sarkel
Itil
Baghdad

Venice
11th-12th
centuries
Pazin
Zagreb
1092
Kolocsa
c.1135
1091-1240
Don
KHAZARS

G
Rijeka
G
G
KNG
Seni
CROATIA
Sirmium
c.1252
Singidunum
Alba Julia
c.1106
Belgorod
PATZINAKS
895-1091
Sea of Azov
Bosporos
ALANIA

STATES OF
Ancona
Zadar
Sibenik
Spalato
Hvar
G
Milisevo
1230
Studenica
1200
Danube
Cherven
Pliska
Cherson
CHERSON
Cherson
c.900
Caucasus
KINGDOM OF
GEORGIA
Tiflis

THE CHURCH
Ragusa
Pec
c.1200
Sopocani
1203-5
SERBIA
Nerizi
1164
Turnovo
1204
Preslav
BULGARIA
Mesembria
870
Black Sea

Rome
Grottaferrata
Monte Cassino
1057-86
Dyrrachium
Veles
Ochrida 1037-56
Kurbinovo
1150
Rila
Sardica
Philippopolis
Armenia

Capua
Melfi
Bari
Prespa
Thessalonica
Adrianople
ARMENIA
Echmiadzin

Naples
Amalfi
Salerno
Taranto
Brindisi
Lecce
Rossano
1282-9
Arta
Larissa
Constantinople
Trajanopolis
Nicaea
11th cent
Claudiopolis
Neocaesarea
Coloneia
Trebizond
c.1250

NORMAN KINGDOM
OF SICILY
Palermo
1132-43
Cefalù
1148
Mileto
Messina
Troina
Syracuse
Aegean
Sea
Hosias
Lucas
Nea Moni
Daphne
11th cent
Athens
11th cent
Patmos
Patras
Lesbos
Chios
1042-54
Mitylene
Smyrna
Ephesus
Laodicea
Cotyaeum
Ankara
Sebastea
Antioch
Rock monasteries
of Cappadocia
c.850-1200
Iconium
Caesarea
Camacha
Melitene
Taurus Mts

Monreale
1184-92
Malta
Side
Seleucia
Myra
Rhodes
Black
Mountain
Antioch
Euphrates
Tigris

Candia
Crete
Koutzivendi
1164
Constantia
Cyprus
ABBASID
CALIPHATE

Tyre

Alexandria
Nile
Jerusalem
1048, 1170
Bethlehem
c.1167
St. Saba

Sinai
Mount Sinai

Legend:

Orthodox Christendom (Greek rite)
Orthodox Christendom (Slavonic rite)
Orthodox Christendom (Georgian rite)
Latin Christendom

Patriarchal sees
Metropolitan sees and archbishoprics*
Bishoprics*
Latin archdioceses and dioceses in which Glagolitic rite was used
Orthodox monasteries (Greek rite)
Orthodox monasteries (Slavonic rite)
Orthodox monasteries (Georgian rite)
Greek monasteries of the Latin obedience
Strongholds of the Teutonic Knights
187   Centres of Byzantine artistic activity with dates of prominence
Boundary of Byzantine Empire at its greatest extent c.1045
Boundary of the Norman Kingdom of Sicily
Creation of new provinces in the Orthodox Church
Creation of new provinces in the Latin Church
R E J   Principalities of Kievan Russia on the eve of the Mongol invasions
Main Viking routes
*Where appropriate, approximate dates of foundation are given

0   500 km
0   300 miles

© Creative Cartography Ltd   © The Hamlyn Group

Heirs to the ancient world II

Land and power

THE DIFFERENCES between the eastern and western parts of the Roman Empire, still clearly visible in the modern world (*compare Maps 14 and 84*), were greatly accentuated when the Roman state itself, having disappeared from the west, emerged from its difficulties in the east with even more comprehensive pretensions than it had had before. The Byzantine Empire came very close to destruction at the beginning of the seventh century. Persian armies reached the Nile and the Bosphorus for the first time since the Achaemenids (*Map 15*). The Slavs overran the Balkan peninsula and laid siege to Constantinople. When Heraklius became emperor in 610, he considered abandoning the city and setting up his capital at Carthage. Yet by 629 his armies had recaptured Jerusalem, and their approach to Ctesiphon had provoked a coup d'état there. The conquests of Heraklius were immediately nullified by those of Islam, which threw Byzantium desperately on the defensive again. In preparing for them, however, he renewed the foundations of a Byzantine state which re-established itself as the dominant power in the Balkans, the bulwark of Christendom against Islam and the peoples of Asia (*see Map 18*), and the evangelist of the Slavonic peoples (*Maps 20 and 21*).

Heraklius broke the sequence which led from military expansion to swollen bureaucracy and heavy taxation, the ruin of the peasantry and reliance on mercenary armies, and which had brought down the great empires of antiquity. Ordinary soldiers were given land in frontier regions in return for military service; otherwise they were exempt from taxation. Their sons inherited the obligation. The provinces were reorganised into *themes* (*see Map 18*) under the command of generals to whom the civilian administration was subordinated. Thus a cheap and effective defence force was created, needing neither complex administration nor long lines of supply, and the peasant class, the source of future recruitment, was strengthened. And these soldiers were not only less expensive than mercenaries but could be better trained, enabling the empire to recover military superiority over its barbarian neighbours. In the long run the creation of provincial strongholds for military dynasties would inevitably cause trouble, but, until that happened, after the death of Basil II in 1025, the system of Heraklius sustained the most successful and creative period of Byzantium's history.

The Byzantine theme system has been compared with that which enabled the Sui (589-617) and T'ang (618-906) dynasties to reunify China and carry out governmental reform and territorial expansion. In 590 Emperor Wu of the Sui dynasty decreed that old soldiers were to be given land; it was distributed both to veterans and to those who remained as guards in frontier regions. As in Byzantium this created a trained peasant militia and strengthened the class from which professional soldiers were recruited, permitting significant advances in training and technique. At the same time a network of canals was built, using forced labour on a huge scale. Its masterpiece, the Grand Canal—forty paces wide—joined the north of China to the Yangtze basin, the most productive agricultural region (*Map 10*). This facilitated the supply of the armies, and permitted taxes in grain to be collected and redistributed more efficiently, an important insurance against famine and rebellion. The principle of recruitment to the imperial bureaucracy by examination was revived, and gradually became the sole means of entry. In these respects the reunified China

repeated, more systematically and on a larger scale, the policies of the early emperors.

In the seventh and eighth centuries the T'ang emperors presided over one of the greatest periods of Chinese civilisation. It was exceptionally open to contact with the west, welcoming missionaries of the Nestorians and the Manichees (*Map 20*), and giving refuge to the last Sassanid emperor, who died an exile in Chang-an. But the immense extension of the empire which stimulated these contacts required the creation of professional armies which, operating on distant frontiers, became effectively independent powers and the source of the revolts in which the dynasty failed.

Byzantine influence was extended in a different way. The churches of Rome and Constantinople, already growing apart in doctrinal emphases, were further separated by the Lombard invasion of Italy in 568 (*Map 17*). Islam engulfed the patriarchal sees of Jerusalem, Antioch and Alexandria. Constantinople remained as the unchallenged arbiter of eastern Christendom. As its missionaries spread their faith in Asia Minor and among the Slavs (*see Map 20*) they disseminated the influence of the Byzantine state of which their church was, in effect, an arm, for it was under direct imperial control. Monks, scholars and artists carried Byzantine civilisation in the wake of the missionaries, to form the culture and shape the destinies of the Slavonic peoples (*see Map 21*).

The Byzantine and Chinese empires were revived by vigorous assertion of the power of the state. The Carolingian empire was the product of its decay. As the Roman world declined its trade diminished, its cities shrank, its roads fell out of use and its institutions ceased to operate. Power resided exclusively in the possession of land. This meant that sooner or later power in Europe would move to the north, whose deep and rich soils were potentially far more fertile than those of the Mediterranean regions. The revolution began in the eighth century. With the assistance of the 'heavy' plough, whose mould-board turned the soil over instead of simply scratching its surface, land in the middle Rhine region, where it seems to have been introduced, began to be cleared and population to grow. The Carolingian family which controlled Austrasia seized the opportunity to endow an army of mounted warriors. Charles Martel conquered northern Gaul, vindicating his claim to supremacy by defeating an Arab army at Poitiers in 732. His son Pepin III overthrew the last Merovingian in 751, and got the Pope to legitimise his coup in return for support against the Lombards. Pepin's son Charlemagne (*r.768-814*) brought the emerging society of western Europe under a single rule for the first time (*Map 22*), and entered legend when Pope Leo III crowned him emperor at St Peter's in Rome on 25th December 800.

The coronation of Charlemagne was an echo of the past. In reality he was already spending most of his winters at his 'new Rome', Aachen, in the region which had already become, as it remains, the cockpit of Europe (*Map 22 inset; compare Map 57 and Map 75 inset*). The shift of wealth and power was clearly displayed by the appearance of new centres of population (*portus*) where merchants stopped along the Rhine and its tributaries, while the Roman cities of the Mediterranean languished, and by the establishment of most of the *scriptoria* (writing offices) on what in the sixth century had been the barbarian side of the northern limit of surviving indications of literacy (*compare Maps 17 and 22*). By the middle

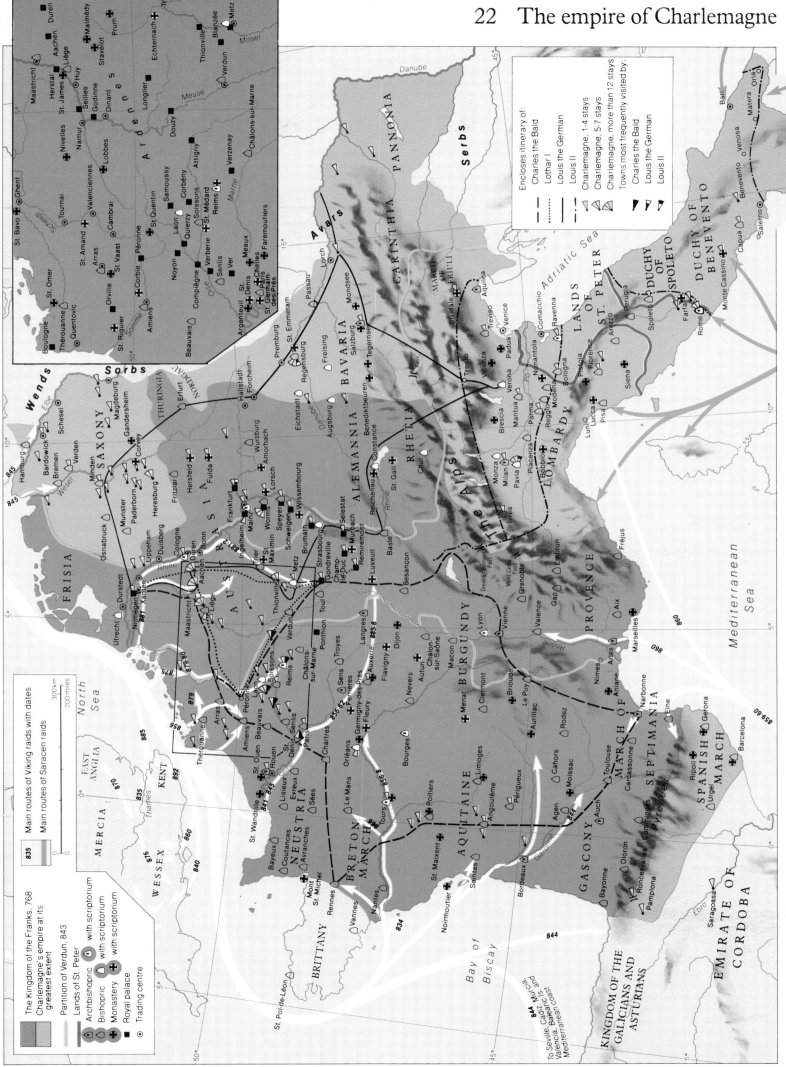

Legend

- ▬ Boundaries of Empire. c. 1050
- — Other boundaries
- — Frontier between Romance and Germanic languages
- Uncertain or disputed frontier
- Lands lost to Empire after 983
- Concentrations of royal lands in early eleventh century
- Concentrations of royal lands in late twelfth century
- □ Palace
- ◆ Fortification
- Ⓐ Archbishopric with date of foundation
- △ Bishopric with date of foundation, date from which permanently established
- ✠ Monastery with date of foundation
- ✠ Centre of monastic reform with date of foundation

- **I T C** Country or German duchy
- **H E S** Main new territorial centre in late twelfth century
- **M E I** Lesser territorial division
- **O B O** Slav and Magyar peoples
- *M a g* Slav and Magyar tribes
- Surrounds places visited more than four times by Otto I, 936-973
- Surrounds places visited more than four times by Henry IV
- Surrounds places visited more than four times by Frederick I, 1152-90

Scale: 0 — 150 km / 0 — 100 miles

Regions and peoples

DENMARK, PRUSSIANS, POMERANIANS, CUJAVIA, POLES, POLAND, SILESIANS, GREAT POLAND, SILESIA, SORBS, LAUSITZ MARCH, MEISSEN MARCH, BILLUNG MARCH, NORTH MARCH, WILZI, OBODRITES, HOLSTEIN, BRUNSWICK, FRISIA, SAXONY, BRANDENBURG, Hevelli, MERSE BURG MARCH, ZEITZ MARCH, Milzeni, THURINGIA, WESTFALIA, HESSE, BRABANT, LUXEMBURG, (LOWER) LOTHARINGIA, (UPPER), FRANCONIA, PALATINATE, WÜRZBURG, NORDGAU, BOHEMIA, CZECHS, MORAVIA, MORAVIANS, EAST MARCH, AUSTRIA, MAGYARS, Kabars, HUNGARY, Horka, Botond, SUABIA, BAVARIA, CARINTHIAN MARCH, STYRIA, CARINTHIANS, CARINTHIA, KRAIN MARCH, CROATS, CROATIA, DUCHY OF BURGUNDY, FRANCHE-COMTÉ, ZÄHRINGER, WELFS, BURGUNDY, SAVOY, The Alps, TIROL, TRENTO, AQUILEIA, VERONA, ITALY, TURIN, Adriatic Sea, Baltic Sea

Places

Schleswig 948, Lübeck 968, 1149, Ratzeburg 1149, Schwerin 1062, 1167, Kolberg c1000, Kammin 1140, 1176, Włocławek c1066, Płock c1000, Bremen, Verden, Havelberg 948, 1149, Brandenburg 948, 1157, Lebus 11th cent., Poznán 968, Gniezno c1000, Osnabrück, Minden, Hildesheim, Magdeburg 968, Münster, Corvey, Gandersheim, Halberstadt, Goslar, Merseburg 1004, Meissen 968, Naumburg 968, 1029, Breslau 966, Crakow c1000, Utrecht, Nijmegen, Werden, Paderborn, Fritzlar, Hersfeld, Erfurt, Prague 973, Sázawa 1035, Olomouc 960, 1063, Cologne, Siegburg 1068, Fulda, Liège, Aachen, Gembloux, Stavelot, Prüm, Frankfurt, Bamberg 1007, Würzburg, Ingelheim, Mainz, Trebur, Worms, Lorsch, Speyer, Nuremberg, Regensburg, Eichstätt, Windberg 1126, Niederaltaich, Melk, Prémontré 1120, Reims, Verdun, Metz, Gorze, Toul, Hirsau, Passau, Heiligenkreuz 1136, Nitra 1034, Esztergom 1000, Vác 1055, Győr 1009, Citeaux 1098, Strasbourg, Augsburg, Freising, Salzburg, Admont 1074, Veszprém 1009, Colmar, SUABIA, Rottenbuch 1074, Tegernsee, Gurk 1072, Horka, Kalocsa, Reichenau, Constance, St. Blasien 1065, Basel, St. Gallen, Brenner Pass, Brixen 967, Pécs 1009, Cluny 909, Besançon, Chur, Carinthia, Zagreb 1093, Dijon, Lausanne, L. Geneva, Sion, Simplon Pass, Trent, Aquileia 1042, Grado, Trieste, Lyon, Genève, Great St. Bernard Pass, Little St. Bernard Pass, Bergamo, Brescia, Verona, Padua, Venice, Vienne, Mont Cenis Pass, Frottuaria 1027, Turin, Vercelli, Milan, Lodi, Cremona, Mantua, Pavia, Piacenza, Payerne 961

Rivers: Elbe, Oder, Vistula, Weser, Rhine, Main, Mosel, Danube, Drava, Sava, Po, L. Geneva

© Creative Cartography Ltd © The Hamlyn Group

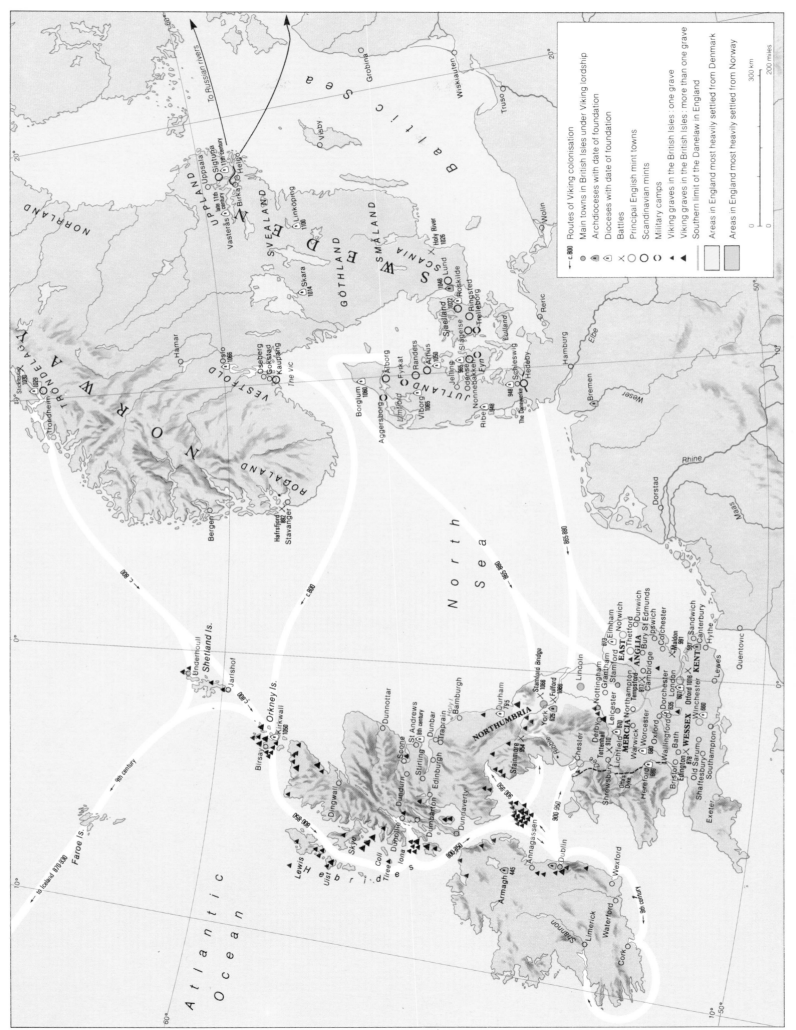

NORRLAND

Baltic Sea

To Russian rivers

Grobina

Wiskiauten

20°

UPPLAND
Uppsala
Sigtuna late 11th century
Vasterås 11th century
Birka Helgö

SVEALAND

Linköping 1100

Visby

GÖTHLAND

WEST GÖTHLAND

SMÅLAND

SCANIA

Truso

Skara 1014

Wolin

Holy River 1025

Lund 1048

Reric

50°

Roskilde 1022

Ringsted
Trelleborg

Sjaelland

Slagelse

NORWAY
TRØNDELAG
VESTFOLD
ROGALAND

Hamar
Oslo 1066

Oseberg
Gokstad
Kaupang 1066

The vic

Aggersborg
Fyrkat
Viborg 1065

Ålborg
Randers
Århus 1050

JUTLAND

Jelling 960
Odense 965
Nonnebakken

Fyn

Schleswig
Hedeby

Hamburg

Elbe

Stiklestad 1030
1029

Trondheim

Bergen

Hafrsfjord 892
Stavanger

Limfjord
Borglum 1060

Ribe
Nonnebakken

The Danewerke 948
948

Bremen

Weser

Dorstad

Rhine

Maas

North Sea

885-880

885-880

Faroe Is.

to Iceland 870/930

9th century

c. 900 ?

c. 800

c. 800

c. 800 ?

Atlantic Ocean

10°

Shetland Is.
Underhoull
Jarlshof

Orkney Is.
Birsay
Kirkwall 1050

Hebrides
Lewis
Uist
Skye
Coll
Tiree
Iona

Dingwall
Dunollie

Dunnottar

Dunadd
Dumbarton

St Andrews 8th century
Scone
Stirling
Edinburgh
Dunbar
Traprain
Dunaverty

800-850

800-850

900-950

900-950

900-950

Holy I.
Bamburgh
Durham 995

NORTHHUMBRIA

Stainmore 954

York 625 867
Fulford 1066
Stamford Bridge 1066

Lincoln

Elmham 673
Norwich
Thetford
EAST ANGLIA
Dunwich
Bury St Edmunds
Ipswich
Colchester
Maldon 991
Sandwich
KENT Canterbury 597
Hythe

Chester

Ribble

Nottingham
Derby
Grantham
Stamford
MERCIA Northampton
Tattenhall 910
Leicester
Tempsford
Cambridge
Lichfield 670
Warwick
Worcester 680
Oxford
London
Dorchester 635
Wallingford
Bath
Hereford 680
Bristol
Edington 878
WESSEX
Winchester 660
Shrewsbury
Offa's Dyke
Old Sarum
Shaftesbury
Exeter
Otford 1016
Lewes
Quentovic

NORTHUMBRIA

Annagassen

Armagh 445

Dublin

Wexford

Waterford

Limerick

Cork

Shannon

Munster

9th century

© Creative Cartography Ltd © The Hamlyn Group

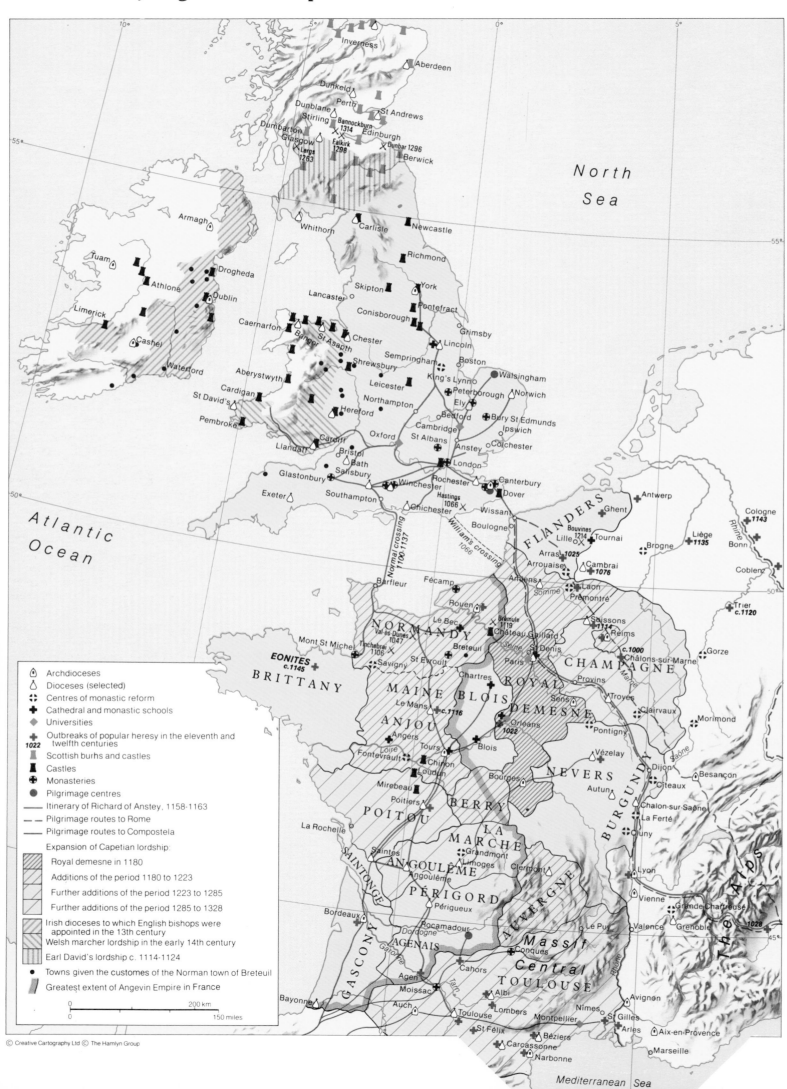

North Sea

Atlantic Ocean

Inverness
Aberdeen
Dunkeld
Perth
Dunblane St Andrews
Stirling
Dumbarton Bannockburn 1314
Glasgow Edinburgh
Largs Falkirk Dunbar 1296
1263 1298 Berwick

Armagh
Whithorn Carlisle Newcastle
Tuam Richmond
Drogheda
Athlone Skipton York
Dublin Lancaster Conisborough Grimsby
Limerick Caernarfon Chester Sempringham Boston
Cashel Bangor St Asaph Lincoln
Shrewsbury Leicester King's Lynn Walsingham
Waterford Aberystwyth Northampton Peterborough Norwich
Cardigan Hereford Ely
St David's Cambridge Bury St Edmunds
Pembroke Cardiff Oxford St Albans Ipswich
Llandaff Bristol Anstey Colchester
Bath London
Glastonbury Salisbury Rochester Canterbury
Exeter Winchester Dover
Southampton Hastings 1066 Wissant
Chichester Boulogne

FLANDERS Antwerp Cologne 1143
Ghent
Normal crossing 1100-1137 Bouvines 1214 Tournai Brogne Liège 1135 Bonn
William's crossing 1066 Lille
Arras 1025 Cambrai 1076 Coblenz
Arrouaise
Amiens Laon Trier c.1120
Somme Prémontré
Barfleur Fécamp Rouen Reims
Fécamp Brémule 1119 Soissons 1114 Gorze
Mont St Michel NORMANDY Château Gaillard c.1000
Val ès-Dunes 1047 Seine St Denis CHAMPAGNE
Tinchebrai 1106 Breteuil Paris Châlons-sur-Marne
EONITES Savigny Provins
c.1145 St Evroult Chartres ROYAL Sens Troyes Clairvaux
BRITTANY MAINE BLOIS DEMESNE Clairvaux Morimond
Le Mans c.1116 Orléans 1022 Pontigny
ANJOU Vézelay Dijon
Angers Tours Blois NEVERS Cîteaux Besançon
Loire Chinon Bourges Autun Chalon-sur-Saône
Fontevrault Loudun La Ferté
Mirebeau BERRY BURGUNDY Cluny
Poitiers Lyon
POITOU LA Grandmont
MARCHE Limoges Clermont
La Rochelle Vienne
SAINTONGE ANGOULÊME Grande Chartreuse
Saintes Angoulême PÉRIGORD AUVERGNE Valence Grenoble c.1028
Périgueux Le Puy The Alps
Bordeaux Rocamadour Massif
AGENAIS Dordogne Central
GASCONY Garonne Cahors TOULOUSE Avignon
Agen Conques
Moissac Albi St Gilles
Bayonne Auch Lombers Nîmes
Toulouse Montpellier Arles
St Félix Aix-en-Provence
Béziers
Carcassonne Marseille
Narbonne

Mediterranean Sea

Legend:
- Archdioceses
- Dioceses (selected)
- Centres of monastic reform
- Cathedral and monastic schools
- Universities
- Outbreaks of popular heresy in the eleventh and twelfth centuries
- 1022
- Scottish burhs and castles
- Castles
- Monasteries
- Pilgrimage centres
- Itinerary of Richard of Anstey, 1158-1163
- Pilgrimage routes to Rome
- Pilgrimage routes to Compostela

Expansion of Capetian lordship:
- Royal demesne in 1180
- Additions of the period 1180 to 1223
- Further additions of the period 1223 to 1285
- Further additions of the period 1285 to 1328
- Irish dioceses to which English bishops were appointed in the 13th century
- Welsh marcher lordship in the early 14th century
- Earl David's lordship c. 1114-1124
- Towns given the customes of the Norman town of Breteuil
- Greatest extent of Angevin Empire in France

0   200 km
0   150 miles

25 Normans, Angevins and Capetians
The Norman kingdom and its successor the Angevin empire dominated western Europe in the 12th century, to be ousted by Capetian France in the 13th. The power of both monarchies rested on their control of castles, towns and the church, and on the exploitation and extension of their rights of justice over their subjects.

of the ninth century the growing importance of the strongholds on the eastern frontier foreshadowed the rise of the Saxon empire when Otto I in his turn inaugurated a dynasty, secured a papal coronation at Rome in 962, and, succeeding where the Carolingians had failed, founded an enduring empire (*Map 23*).

The Carolingians conceived the responsibilities of kingship more broadly than their predecessors had. Charlemagne attempted, persistently and often successfully, to provide protection through his courts for *miserabiles personae* – the weak – against the tyrannies of the powerful, and, in a measure which led directly to the appearance of universities in the twelfth century, he commanded every bishop to provide elementary education in his diocese for those who could benefit from it. His enthusiasm for learning and patronage of scholars stimulated a renaissance in art and literature. So many of the earliest surviving manuscripts of classical works are written in the script invented by Carolingian scribes that Italian Renaissance scholars mistakenly dubbed it 'Roman', as we still do.

The Carolingian Empire was ruined by the force which raised it. Charlemagne's government barely extended beyond his personal presence, except so far as his will was understood and respected by the counts and bishops who governed the empire in his name. As a result, on Maps 22 and 23, his itinerary and those of his successors display the extent of their power more truthfully than largely notional boundaries. But just as, with literacy confined to a very few, there was no way to govern the empire except through the nobility, in a natural economy there was no way to reward them except by granting them benefices (presents) of land. This equation of landholding with service, the classic definition of feudalism, became effectively, though not yet legally, universal in Charlemagne's reign. It wrote the death warrant of his empire. Land was power; once transferred it might not easily be recovered. For a time the system had worked well. Charles Martel and Pepin III entrusted the government of their growing kingdom to fellow-members of the Austrasian nobility from which they sprang. Charlemagne tried to maintain the coherence of this ruling group by bringing up their sons at his court. But by the end of his reign corruption and rebellion already made it plain that control was gone. The feudatories took advantage of the rivalries of his successors to tear the empire apart, and the Vikings – though not strong enough to destroy well-governed kingdoms as the Muslims in Spain and Alfred in Wessex (*d*.899) showed – took advantage of the disorder to plunder the towns and monasteries, spreading terror wherever they appeared.

The Merovingian kings had regarded public rights and duties as private property which might be given to favoured subjects, and especially to the Church. A grant of 'immunity' from taxation to a landlord entitled him to raise the taxes from the land involved for his own benefit, and by extension to demand the services which had formerly gone to the state, to do justice and keep for himself its considerable profits. As the Carolingian Empire disintegrated, the counts, most of whom already

had immunities of this kind, kept for themselves the public rights which their office had conferred on them. Collectively referred to as the *ban* – the right to compel – these rights were exercised over all free men, and were therefore much more extensive, and potentially more lucrative, than those of landlordship. But by about 1000 the counts had suffered at the hands of their own retainers the usurpation which they had inflicted on the kings. Effective power was exercised from the castles which had appeared everywhere, over such an area as one man and his retinue could control by direct force. And over that area the castellan, unchecked by any superior power, claimed the *ban* for himself, and with it whatever 'customary' rights and payments he chose to demand. The powers that had once been the state's were now indistinguishable from those conferred by the ownership of private property.

This ruthless consolidation of seigneurial power was one consequence of the impoverishment suffered by the nobility in the tenth century. Another was the rush to bring new land into cultivation during the eleventh, increasing the revenues of its owners as well as supporting a rapid growth of population. It was caused not only by the extravagant lifestyle which included, for example, the foundation of splendid monasteries, but especially by the custom of dividing land between all the children of each generation. To preserve the integrity of the inheritance, male primogeniture was now introduced in northern France. This change produced the most characteristic figure of European medieval society, the younger son who, as the mounted knight bound to his aristocratic relations by a common code of chivalry, and condemned to wander far and wide until by his wits and his sword he could win a rich wife, or her price in combat. Political power would lie with whoever could assert control over his feudatories and attract these adventurers to his banner. The Duchy of Normandy, itself probably founded by some such process (although the Normans disguised it with a splendid tale that they were descended from Viking pirates who had been confirmed in the duchy by a Carolingian king), showed the way. Its younger sons and dispossessed wandered over Europe to play prominent parts in the reconquest of Spain, the foundation of the Kingdom of Sicily and the crusades (*Maps 21, 26 and 33*). Meanwhile its Duke William I (*r*.1033-87) subdued his inheritance and won himself a kingdom in England, which his successors plundered with ruthless brilliance to create an empire which dominated western Europe in the twelfth century (*see Map 25*). It was broken only by even greater exponents of feudal power, their rivals of the French royal house of Capet.

Further reading: J. M. Hussey, *The Byzantine World* (Hutchinson, 1957; p.b.); D. Obolensky, *The Byzantine Commonwealth* (Weidenfeld and Nicolson, 1971. Cardinal); G. Duby, *The Early Growth of the European Economy* (Weidenfeld and Nicolson, 1974); F. L. Ganshof, *Feudalism* (Longmans, 1952; p.b.); M. Bloch, *Feudal Society* (Routledge, 1961; p.b. 2 vols.); R. H. C. Davis, *The Normans and their Myth* (Thames & Hudson, 1976; p.b.).

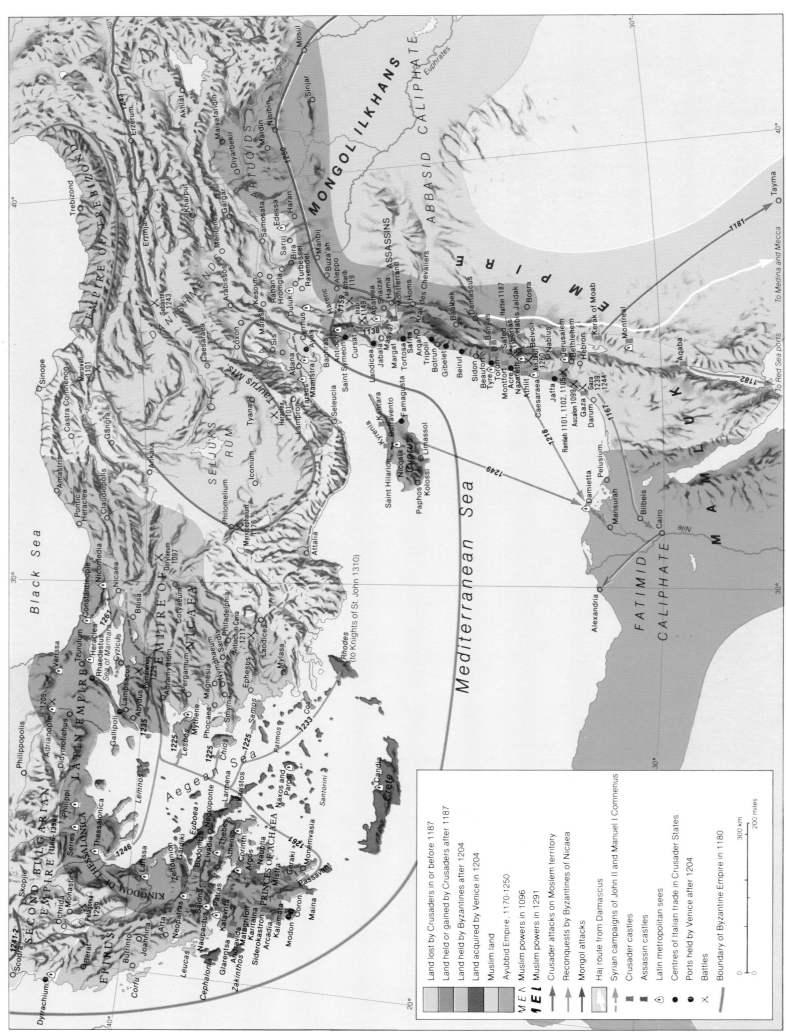

Mosul

Sinjar

Nisibin

MONGOL ILKHANS

Euphrates

ABBASID CALIPHATE

Tayma

To Medina and Mecca

1181

EMPIRE OF TREBIZOND

Erzerum

Akhlāt

Maiyafariqin

Mardin

Diyarbekir

ARTUQIDS

Kharput

Gargar

Melitene

Samosata

Edessa

Haran

Trebizond

Erzinjan

Sebastea
1243

Coxon

Albistan

Maraš

Kesoun

Raban

Hromgla

Saruj

Bira

Turbessel

Ravendel

ASSASSINS

Buza'ah

Manbij

Aleppo

al-Atharib
1119

Harenc

1260

SELJUKS OF RŪM

Tarsus
1101

Adana

Mamistra

Sis

Cursat

Ayas

Bagras

Antioch

Saint Symeon

1138

Inab
1149

Apamea

Shaizar

Hama

Masyaf

Montferrand

Homs

Damascus

Krak des Chevaliers

Baalbek

E M P I R E

Krak of Moab

Montreal

Aqaba

To Red Sea ports

1182

1181

Caesaraea

Heraclea
Mersivan

Amasia

Gangra

Ankara

Tyana

Heraclea
1101

Philomelium
1176

Iconium

Attalia

Seleucia

Lampron

Laodicea

Jabala

Margat

Tortosa

Arqa

Tripoli

Gibelet

Beirut

Sidon

Tyre

Acre

Toron

Athlit

Caesaraea

Jaffa

Ascalon 1099

Darum

Gaza
1239,
1244

Ramleh 1101, 1102, 1105

1228

1260

Safita

Banyas

Safed

Tiberias

Hattin 1187

Bosra

Beaufort

Belvoir

Nazareth

Ain Jalut

Nablus

Jerusalem

Bethlehem

Hebron

M A M L U K

1167

Castra Comnenon

Sinope

Amastris

Pontic
Heraclea

Claudiopolis

Black Sea

Nicomedia

Nicaea

Brusa

Cotyaeum

EMPIRE OF NICAEA

Dorylaeum
1097

Constantinople
1261

Myriocephalum
1176

Rhaedestus

Heraclea

Izurulum
1261

Rhodes
(to Knights of St. John 1310)

Saint Hilarion

Kantara

Kyrenia

Buffavento

Nicosia

Cyprus

Famagusta

Limassol

Paphos

Kolossi

Mediterranean Sea

Damietta

Pelusium

Mansurah

Bilbeis

Cairo

Alexandria

Nile

FATIMID CALIPHATE

1249

SECOND BULGARIAN EMPIRE (1186-1396)

Philippopolis

Skopje

Adrianople
1205

Didymotichus

Cyzicus

Sea of Marmara

Abydus
1205

Pegae
1225

Lampsacus
1225

Gallipoli

Lemnos

Adramyttium
1225

Pergamum
1225

Magnesia

Philadelphia
1211

Sardis

Antioch in Caria
1211

Laodicea
1211

Ephesus

Smyrna

Phocaea

Chios

Lesbos

Mytilene

LATIN EMPIRE

Samos

Patmos

Myiasa

Cos

1233

Naxos and Paros

Santorini

Candia

Crete

Ochrida

Monastir

Pelagonia
1259

Berat

1241-2

Scodra

Dyrrachium

Durazzo

EPIRUS

Joannina

Arta

Buthrotum

Leucas

Cephalonia

Zakinthos

Corfu

Skopje

Verissa

Serres

Philippi

Philip

Thessalonica

1246

Larissa

Zeitounion

Gardiki

Neopatras

Naupactus

KINGDOM OF THESSALONICA

Lamia

Salona

Livadia

Thebes

Negroponte

Euboea

Athens

Corinth

Argos

Nauplia

PRINCES OF ACHAEA

Mistra

Geraki
1261

Monemvasia

Passavant

Maina

Modon

Coron

Kalamata

Arcadia

Karitaina

Siderokastron

Matagrifon

Andravida

Glarentsa

Patras

Kalavrita

Vostitsa

Aegean Sea

Aca

Legend:

MEN Muslim land

AMEL Ayubbid Empire, 1170-1250

Muslim powers in 1096

Muslim powers in 1291

Crusader attacks on Moslem territory

Reconquests by Byzantines of Nicaea

Mongol attacks

Hajj route from Damascus

Syrian campaigns of John II and Manuel I Comnenus

Crusader castles

Assassin castles

Latin metropolitan sees

Centres of Italian trade in Crusader States

Ports held by Venice after 1204

Battles

Boundary of Byzantine Empire in 1180

Land lost by Crusaders in or before 1187

Land held or gained by Crusaders after 1187

Land held by Byzantines after 1204

Land acquired by Venice in 1204

Muslim land

300 km

200 miles

Trade and aggression

26 The world of the Crusaders
Between the invasions of the Seljuk Turks in the 11th century and the Mongols in the 13th the Byzantine and Arab worlds were subjected to successive attacks from both western Europe and central Asia. The Latins lost Constantinople in 1261 and Acre in 1291, but the empire of the Turkish Mamluks, like that of Byzantium, survived until the Ottoman conquests.

THE POLITICS and culture of the medieval civilisations deliberately imitated or unconsciously perpetuated those of the ancient world. It was not in the first instance their achievements in those fields, impressive as they were, that enabled these civilisations to break out of the rhythms which had governed the rise and fall of civilisations for millennia. The crucial achievement both of China and western Europe was to transform economic life sufficiently to produce a sustained population growth which, although it was liable to prolonged recession such as that associated with the epidemics of the later middle ages (*see Map 35*) was, in the long run, irreversible. Recent estimates put the population of Europe at about 36 million in AD 1000, 79 million in 1300, and 81 million in 1500; of China at 66 million, 86 million and 110 million at the same dates; and of the Indian sub-continent at 79 million, 91 million, and 105 million. By contrast such evidence as there is – usually very little – suggests that the population of most other parts of the world remained stagnant. That of the world of Islam reached a peak during its golden age, between about 800 and 1000, and was somewhat in decline thereafter.

The agricultural advances of the early middle ages which sustained this growth were very similar in China and in Europe. The heavy plough was widely used in both regions by about 1000, and was increasingly assisted by other technical advances. In Europe there were iron tools, efficient harnessing for animals and wind- and water-mills, and similarly in China dams, dykes, waterwheels and other aids to irrigation. As Europe had an eastward frontier region, in addition to its great expanses of forest and marsh, so China had the rice-growing region of the south to invite steady expansion and continuous growth over a very long period (*Maps 10, 23 and 34*). Finally, in large parts of both regions the partial freeing of slaves since ancient times combined with the gradual enserfment of free men by coercion had produced a manorial organisation which could permit the direction of labour and the investment of capital in such land and tools as large projects might require.

To sustain their growth, however, agricultural communities needed markets to reward them for producing beyond their immediate needs, and cities to drain off their surplus population and encourage its rapid replacement. The second part of the medieval economic revolution was the creation of world-wide markets, exchanging goods and services more regularly and in greater volume, across greater distances, and in particular providing a growing demand for manufactured goods.

The conquests of Islam united the economies of the Persian and much of the Roman worlds, between which there had previously been little exchange. They also implanted a way of life which demanded the creation of a massive international trade. The conquerors did not expect to demean their hands with labour, and were inhibited in the exploitation of their new subjects by the readiness of most of them to convert to Islam. They expected to live in cities – Baghdad was the largest city in the world, two million in population, within half a century of its foundation in 762 – and to enjoy the enormous variety of goods which could be collected from across their vast territories. Yet those territories, the home of the most ancient civilisations, were near exhaustion, their soils poor, their forests stripped bare, their population very low. So the world of Islam became a trading empire on a scale never seen before (*see Map 27*).

At first the imports were paid for largely with the silver of the fabled mines of the Hindu Kush, inherited from the Sassanids, but after the Abbasid revolution the migration of Arabs and other dissidents from Persia began to open up the Islamic west: North Africa was brought more firmly under control, and ports were established on the Nile and new towns on the desert caravan routes to bring gold and ivory, as well as slaves, from the African interior, both east and west.

The needs of Islam had momentous consequences for Europe. In Carolingian times Metz and Verdun, junctions between the German interior and the routes to Spain and Africa (*via* Marseilles), were important slave markets, and Muslim wealth was a major, if distant, stimulus of the traffic along the Rhine and its tributaries (*Map 22*). Later the riches of the forests beyond the Elbe and in Bohemia and Carinthia made the more easterly route down the Adriatic the main thoroughfare to the Mediterranean, leading to the rise of Venice, its mistress, and the Po valley, its link with western Europe. The revenue gained from those flows of Muslim wealth not only gave Otto I the basis of an empire in the north, but drew him and his successors continually both eastwards and southwards (*Maps 23 and 32*).

The great pioneers of trade between the north and the advanced world were the Vikings. By the ninth century they were in touch with Muslim traders along the Volga, whose upper waters were easily accessible from the Baltic (*see Map 21*). For a century Persian silver poured into Scandinavian hoards (*Map 24*): more than sixty thousand Muslim coins have been found there, and as many more in northern Russia, Poland and Pomerania. By the end of the tenth century, when trade with Islam began to fall away, the Vikings – known as Varangians to the Greeks – had also reached the Black Sea by way of the Dnieper, down which the Rus people of Kiev had long brought their furs, honey and wax to Byzantium.

Along the rivers of Russia the Vikings forged permanent links between northern and eastern Europe (*compare Map 28*). Their voyages into the Atlantic, leading to the colonisation of Iceland and settlement in Greenland and somewhere on the North American coast at Vinland, constituted the first extension of the known world since ancient times and, after their own conversion, a major expansion of Christendom (*see Map 20*).

Within the huge area which their remarkable ships and nautical talents opened to them the Vikings settled in many places, though seldom (most scholars now think) in large numbers. Colonies appeared in the ninth century at the mouths of many of the rivers along which they raided, including the Elbe and the Weser, the Rhine, the Seine and the Loire, but the most important were on the islands of the North Sea and around the British Isles, the nucleus of a great seaborne empire in the time of Cnut (*r*.1014-35), and still a region of distinctive cultural and political traditions (*Map 24*).

The history of the Vikings is a reminder that piracy is never far from trade, or trade from colonisation. The raids on the accumulated treasures of the monasteries of Francia and England – almost the only respect in which their activity differed from that of the warring nobles of Christian Europe – have given them the fearsome reputation of legend and exaggerated the importance of their destructive activity. Their voyages mark the beginning of the maritime unity of Europe, joining the coastal traffic of the Channel and the North Sea to that of the Atlantic

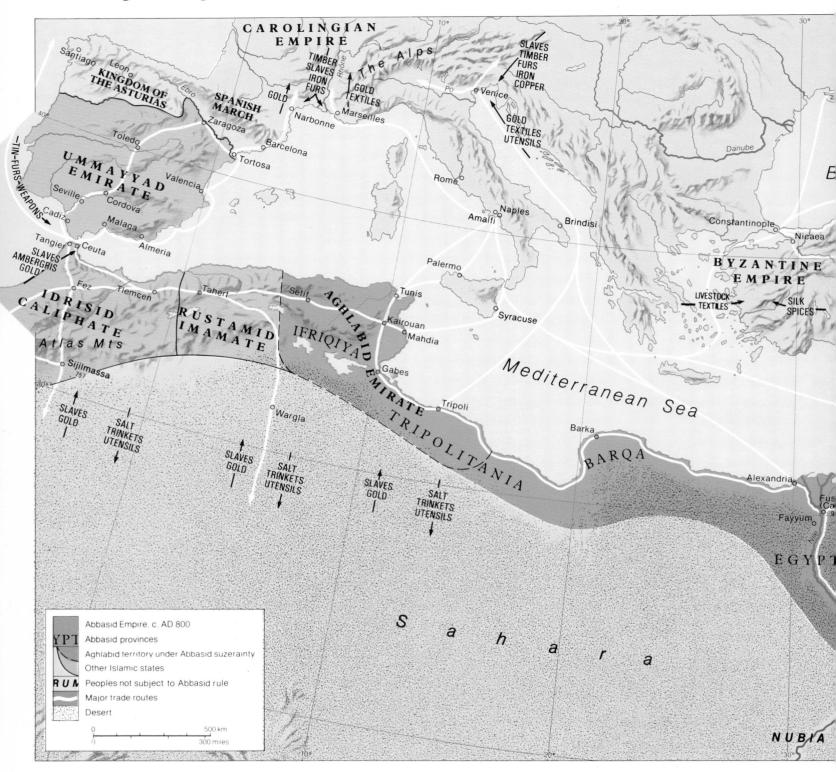

and Mediterranean seaboards for the first time. Little of the tribute which they collected from the Franks and English found its way back to the Scandinavian hoards. It was most probably used to buy land for settlement, or to be recirculated as part of the trade which in their hands so clearly foreshadowed the medieval economy at its height (*see Map 28*).

Rather as the Vikings benefitted from the disintegration of the Carolingian empire Europe as a whole profitted from the decline of Islam and Byzantium. The political unity of the Caliphate ended after the Abbasid revolution, when the leaders of provincial armies–emirs –became increasingly inclined to declare themselves independent of Baghdad. The process was accelerated by the growing habit of granting them the farm of taxes and revenues of the state in place of payment for their troops,

and completed when Baghdad itself was seized by a Persian prince in 945, leaving the Caliph as a spiritual figurehead, bereft of real power. In the eleventh century the precipitous decline of its external trade, a series of rebellions and civil wars among the Muslim peoples, which saw the creation of a Berber empire in Africa and Spain, and the devastation of Libya and Tunisia by Bedouin tribesmen (it was now that the ancient agricultural prosperity of the region was destroyed), and, most important, the advance of the Seljuk Turks from central Asia (*Map 26*), all laid the Muslim world open to Christian attack.

The dissolution of the Caliphate of Cordoba in Spain in 1010 provided the Christian kings of León and Castile with an opportunity to enlarge their territories and to launch the *reconquista* which was to be the theme of

27 The golden age of Islam
The conquests of Islam joined the markets and trade routes of the known world. The wealth of its aristocracy stimulated a vast and varied trade which supported a brilliant civilisation, although political fragmentation had already begun by the 9th century.

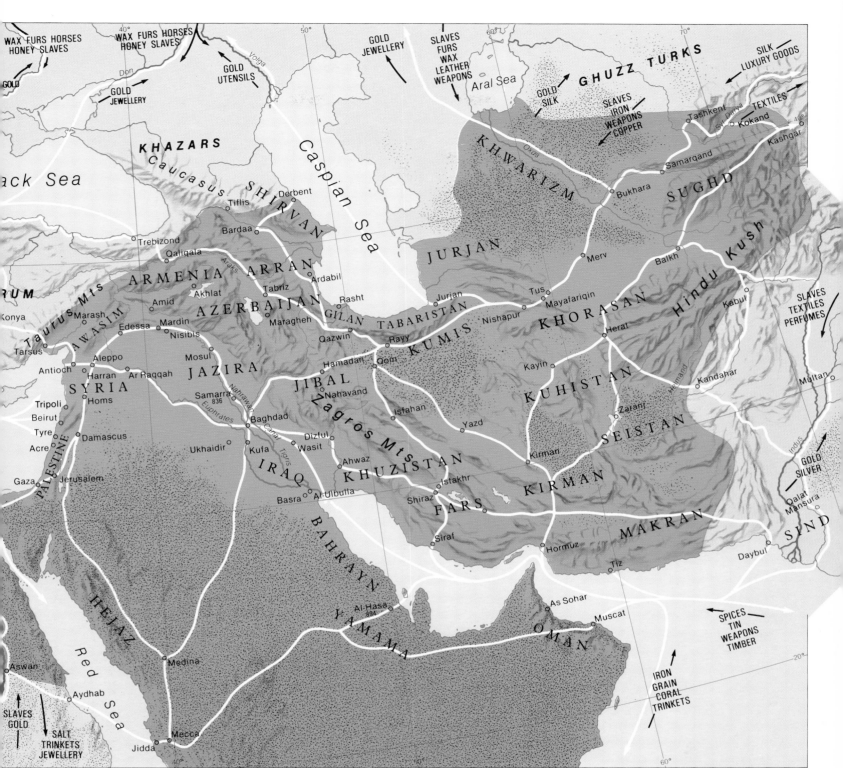

WAX FURS HORSES
HONEY SLAVES

GOLD

WAX FURS HORSES
HONEY SLAVES

40°

GOLD
UTENSILS

Don

Volga

GOLD
JEWELLERY

GOLD
JEWELLERY

50°

SLAVES
FURS
WAX
LEATHER
WEAPONS

Aral Sea

60°

GOLD
SILK

GHUZZ TURKS

SLAVES
IRON
WEAPONS
COPPER

SILK
LUXURY GOODS

70°

Tashkent

TEXTILES

Kokand

KHAZARS

Caspian Sea

Oxus

KHWARIZM

Syr Darya

Kashgar

ck Sea

Caucasus

SHIRVAN

Derbent

Tiflis

Bardaa

Trebizond

Qaliqala

40°

ARMENIA **ARRAN**

Ardabil

Araks

Akhlat

Tabriz

JURJAN

Samarqand

Bukhara

40°

SUGHD

Merv

Balkh

Hindu Kush

Kabul

UM

Amid

AZERBAIJAN

Maragheh

Rasht

Jurjan

GILAN **TABARISTAN**

KUMIS

Tus

Nishapur

Mayafariqin

KHORASAN

Herat

SLAVES
TEXTILES
PERFUMES

Konya

Marash

AWASIM

Edessa

Mardin

Qazwin

Rayy

Qom

Kayin

Kandahar

Multan

Tarsus

Nisibis

Hamadan

JIBAL

Nahavand

KUHISTAN

Antioch

Aleppo

Ar Raqqah

Mosul

JAZIRA

Zaranj

Indus

SYRIA

Harran

Samarra
836

Nahrawan

Isfahan

Yazd

Kirman

SEISTAN

GOLD
SILVER

Tripoli

Homs

Euphrates

Baghdad

Canal

Dizful

Wasit

Beirut

Damascus

Ukhaidir

Kufa

Tigris

Ahwaz

KHUZISTAN

Istakhr

KIRMAN

Qalat
Mansura

Tyre

Acre

Zagros Mts

Shiraz

FARS

MAKRAN

SIND

Gaza

Jerusalem

PALESTINE

Basra

Al-Ubulla

IRAQ

Siraf

Hormuz

Daybul

Tiz

BAHRAYN

As Sohar

Muscat

SPICES
TIN
WEAPONS
TIMBER

20°

HEJAZ

YAMAMA

Al-Hasa
894

OMAN

IRON
GRAIN
CORAL
TRINKETS

Aswan

Red Sea

Medina

SLAVES
GOLD

Aydhab

SALT
TRINKETS
JEWELLERY

Mecca

Jidda

40°

50°

60°

© Creative Cartography Ltd © The Hamlyn Group

28 The medieval economy at its height

By the 13th century the traders and trade routes of Europe were well enough established to encourage increasing economic specialisation, and the growing cities–though still very small by world standards–provided markets for luxuries from far afield as well as for the products of their own hinterlands.

Spanish medieval history (*see Map 33*). It rapidly became a European enterprise as the prospect of land and booty attracted knights from far and wide, and the monastic orders came behind them to bring spiritual comforts and Christian services in return for a handsome share of the spoils. Still richer pickings in southern Italy were available to the followers of the Norman adventurers who by 1048 had conquered most of Apulia and Calabria from the Byzantine Empire (*see Map 21*). They forced the Pope to recognise their conquests in 1059, and turned against Islam in 1072 when they captured Palermo, which their descendants would make the capital of the wealthiest and most sophisticated kingdom in the twelfth-century west.

The death of the Byzantine emperor Basil II in 1025 was followed by a period of prolonged conflict between

the military dynasties of the provinces and the civilian aristocracy of Constantinople, during which the state was permanently weakened by the farming out of revenues and offices in bids for political support. Basil's annexation of Bulgaria and Armenia (which was implemented after his death, in 1043) removed what had been in effect buffer states against the Asiatic nomads. In 1065 Armenia fell to the Seljuk Turks and in 1071 they defeated the Emperor at Manzikert to take Anatolia, as the Arabs had never done. In the same year Bari, his last stronghold in Italy, fell to the Normans.

The assault of Christian Europe on the Middle East and the Balkans (*Map 26*) was conducted, in principle, not by wandering adventurers but by its anointed leaders. The Pope issued the summons to the First Crusade at the Council of Clermont in 1095, and his successors always

North Sea

Baltic

Atlantic Ocean

Bay of Biscay

Mediterranean

Adriatic Sea

The Alps

Pyrenees

Atlas Mts.

COPPER
IRON
Fulun
Stockholm
Visby
Bergen

Dublin
COAL
Chester
Hull
WOOL
Boston
Norwich
Ipswich
WOOL
Bristol
London
Southampton
TIN
Bruges
Ypres
St Omer
Lille
Ghent
Antwerp
Louvain
Brussels
Arras
Tournai
Douai
Liège
WOAD
Péronne
Rouen
Reims
Seine
Paris
Lagny
Provins
Metz
Troyes
Tours
Bar-sur-Aube
Strasbourg
Loire
Bourges
Dijon
Besançon
Poitiers
La Rochelle
Bordeaux
Garonne
Bayonne
IRON
Albi
Toulouse
Nîmes
Montpellier
Béziers
Aigues Mortes
Arles
Avignon
Marseilles
Perpignan

Utrecht
Brunswick
Magdeburg
Frankfurt an der Oder
Duisberg
COPPER
IRON
SILVER
Harz Mts.
Elbe
Lübeck
Rostock
Danzig
Thorn
Oder
COAL
IRON
Cologne
Erfurt
TIN
IRON
Wrocław
IRON
Frankfurt am Main
Erzberg Mts.
Mainz
Prague
Worms
Nuremberg
Strasbourg
Regensburg
Rhine
Augsburg
Vienna
Danube
St. Gotthard
Inn
Brenner
Lyon
St. Bernard
Mt. Cenis
Rhône
Milan
Brescia
Verona
Padua
Pavia
Mantua
Venice
Piacenza
Parma
Modena
Bologna
WOAD
Genoa
Lucca
Pistoia
Forlì
Po
Pontebba
Drava
Zara
Ancona
Pisa
Florence
Siena
Volterra
Orvieto
Viterbo
Rome
Dubrovnik

Valladolid
Medina del Campo
Douro
Tagus
Lisbon
Setúbal
Guadiana
Badajoz
Saragossa
Ebro
Toledo
Barcelona
Córdoba
Guadalquivir
Seville
Jaén
Valencia
Palma
Ibiza
Murcia
Granada
Almería
Jerez
Cádiz
Málaga
Salé
Casablanca
Honein
Bougie
Bône
Tunis
Djerba I.
Tripoli
Cagliari
Trapani
Palermo
Messina
Catania
Syracuse
Gaeta
Naples
Salerno
Barietta

20°
10°
50°
40°
30°
0°

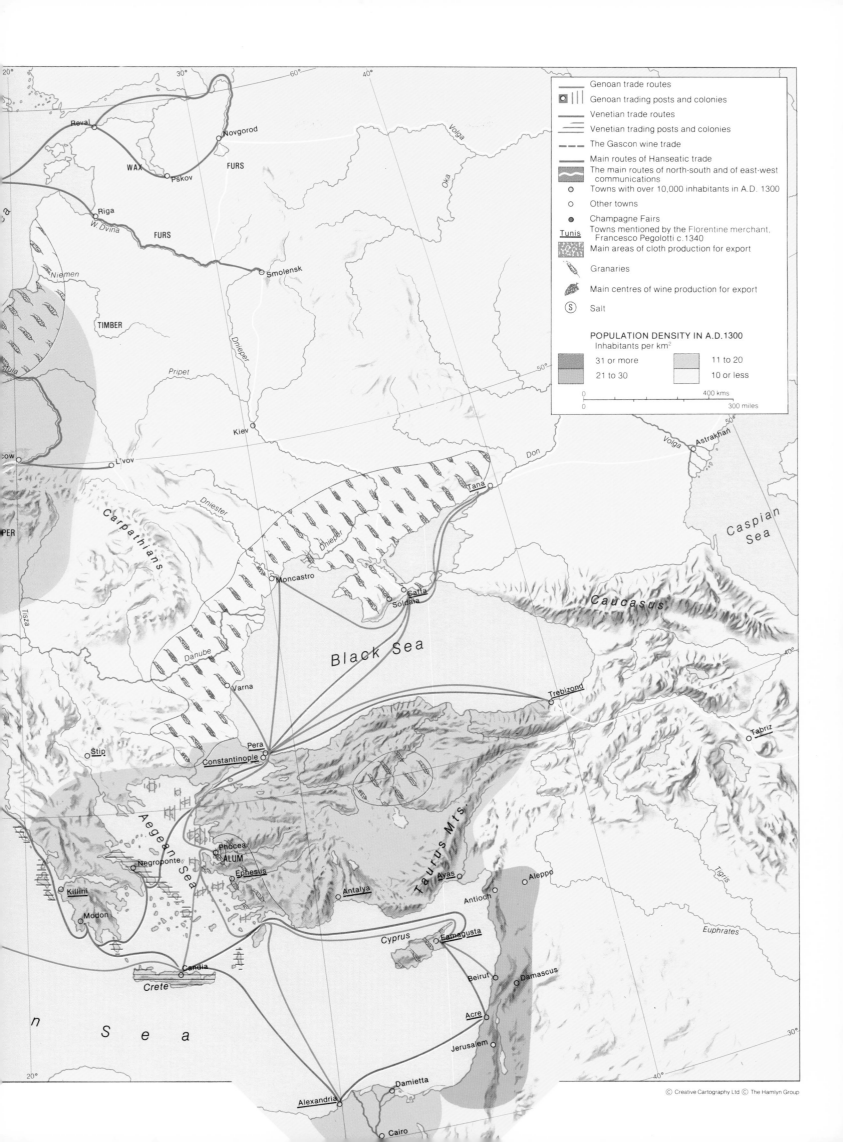

Legend

Genoan trade routes
Genoan trading posts and colonies
Venetian trade routes
Venetian trading posts and colonies
The Gascon wine trade
Main routes of Hanseatic trade
The main routes of north-south and of east-west communications
○ Towns with over 10,000 inhabitants in A.D. 1300
○ Other towns
● Champagne Fairs
Tunis Towns mentioned by the Florentine merchant, Francesco Pegolotti c.1340
Main areas of cloth production for export
Granaries
Main centres of wine production for export
Ⓢ Salt

POPULATION DENSITY IN A.D.1300
Inhabitants per km²

31 or more
21 to 30
11 to 20
10 or less

0   400 kms
0   300 miles

Reval
Novgorod
WAX
FURS
Pskov
Riga
W. Dvina
FURS
Niemen
TIMBER
Smolensk
Pripet
Dnieper
Kiev
Volga
Oka
Astrakhan
cow
L'vov
Carpathians
Dniester
Dnieper
Tana
Don
Volga
Caspian Sea
PER
Tisza
Danube
Moncastro
Caffa
Soldaia
Caucasus
Varna
Black Sea
Trebizond
Tabriz
Stip
Pera
Constantinople
Taurus Mts.
Aegean Sea
Phocea
ALUM
Ephesus
Ayas
Aleppo
Negroponte
Antioch
Kilini
Antalya
Tigris
Modon
Euphrates
Cyprus
Famagusta
Candia
Beirut
Damascus
Crete
Acre
n   S   e   a
Jerusalem
Damietta
Alexandria
Cairo

Trade and aggression

took the lead in marshalling the resources of the feudal west for future crusades. The Second Crusade (1147-49), preached by the spiritual leader of Christendom in his time, St Bernard of Clairvaux, was led by the Holy Roman Emperor and the King of France; the Third (1189-92) by the Kings of France and England. The ostensible origin of the crusading movement was the request of the Byzantine Emperor Alexius I for western mercenaries to help against the Turks; its ostensible goal the defence of the Holy Places against the infidel. Jerusalem was indeed taken in 1099 and held until 1187, and western feudal kingdoms were constructed in the Holy Land. But its most important consequence was the sack of Constantinople by crusaders in 1204 and the dismemberment of the Byzantine Empire.

The crusades are often described as part of the expansion of feudal Europe. But the fleets of the First Crusade were provided by the Genoans and the Pisans, and the Fourth Crusade was directed to Constantinople by its Venetian paymasters, whose interests in the Balkans had expanded rapidly since Alexius I had bought naval assistance from them in return for extensive trading privileges throughout his Empire. Genoa and Pisa had begun their rise to power late in the tenth century, on the profits of piracy upon Muslim vessels in the Mediterranean; Venice by exporting slaves to Egypt. Throughout the period of the crusades the Italian cities were the main paymasters and the chief beneficiaries. The fortunes of the crusading states fluctuated far more according to the extent to which Italian trading interests were threatened than with the attitudes of the feudal monarchs. Unlike the knights and their clerical brothers who devoted much energy (and much sincerity) to convincing themselves of the righteousness of the holy war, the cities felt no need to disguise their interest, and no ideology inhibited their pursuit of profit. 'The Venetians, the Genoese and the Pisans bring into Egypt choice products of the west, especially arms and war materials' wrote Saladin, the greatest of the Muslim leaders. 'This constitutes an advantage for Islam and an injury to Christianity.' In return for those goods, they brought to the west, which now offered a rapidly expanding market for luxuries, the spices, silks and perfumes of the Orient. Networks of trading posts were established and continued to flourish long after the crusading kingdoms had died (*Maps 26 and 28*)—as they did after the Mongol conquests diverted the Far Eastern trade routes towards the Black Sea ports (*see Map 31*), so that there was no longer any need for the Venetians and their compatriots to maintain outposts in the Holy Land.

The clash of values between the merchants and the knights which the crusades revealed so clearly was already transforming European society. Around 1000 society could be described as consisting of 'those who fight, those who pray and those who work (*agricultores*)'. The growth of population and diversification of economic activity brought new classes into being. Cities grew rapidly in what had been a wholly rural world (*see Map 28*). Their inhabitants clashed bitterly with each other as sharp divisions of wealth and power appeared between the weavers or seamen, often wretchedly poor, and the patricians, rapidly forming their own dynasties, who employed them; the cities themselves clashed with the secular and ecclesiastical aristocracy as they sought freedom to conduct their own affairs, protect their own interests, and eventually dominate the countryside around them (*see Map 32*). New tensions produced new institutions, new mentalities and a new culture, often sharply opposed to the chivalrous code of the aristocracy and the hierarchical conservatism of the church. The contrast was observed with distaste, but not with contempt, by Otto of Freising when he described the expedition of his nephew the Emperor Frederick Barbarossa to Italy in 1154. 'That they may not lack the means of subduing their neighbours' he wrote of the Milanese, 'they do not disdain to give the girdle of knighthood to young men of inferior status, and even some workers of the vile mechanical arts whom other peoples bar like the plague from respected and honourable pursuits. From this it has resulted that they surpass all other states of the world in wealth and power.'

Further reading: M. Lombard, *The Golden Age of Islam* (North Holland Publishing Co., 1975); A. Murray, *Reason and Society in the Middle Ages* (Oxford University Press, 1978); H. Pirenne, *Medieval Cities* (Princeton University Press, 1925; p.b.); P. H. Sawyer, *The Age of the Vikings* (Edward Arnold, 1962; p.b.); S. Runciman, *A History of the Crusades* (3 vols, Cambridge; 1951-4, Penguin, 1971).

29 India under Muslim domination
The Sultanate of Delhi, founded in 1211 by Turks from Afghanistan, was the principal centre of Muslim power in India; but the fortunes of both Muslim and Hindu kingdoms fluctuated with the loyalties of the chiefs and officials commanding the military strongpoints which controlled the trade routes and the countryside. The invasions of Timur destroyed the hegemony of Delhi, and independent sultanates emerged in several regions.

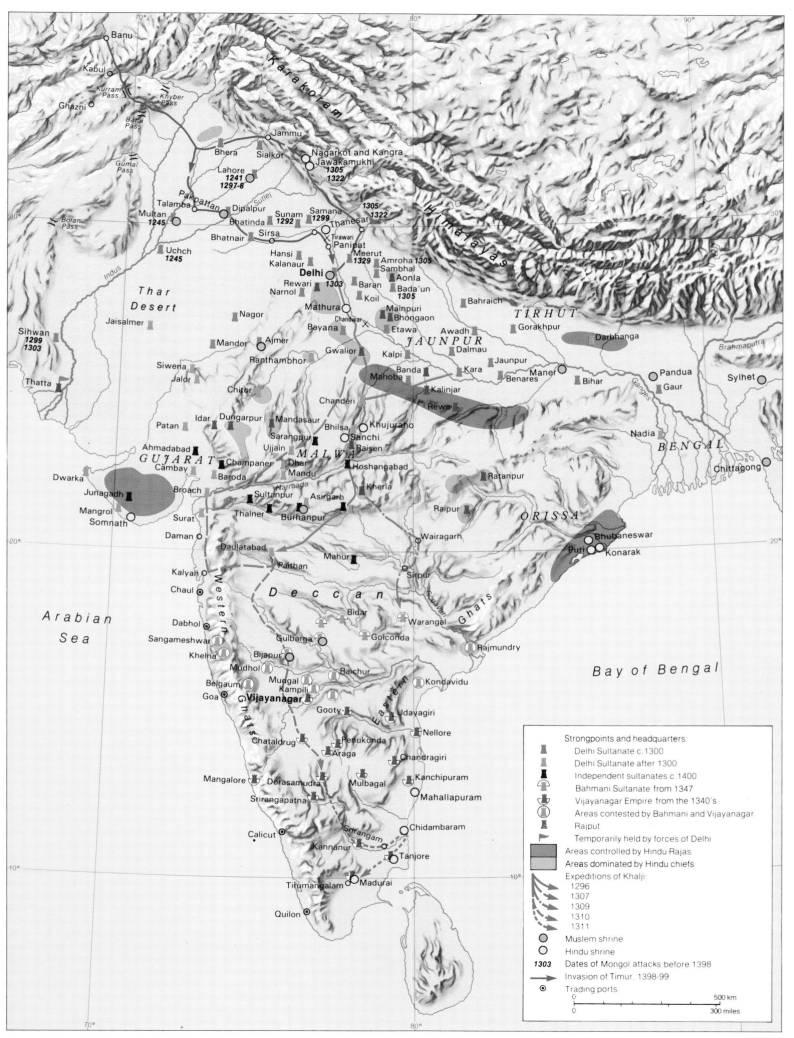

Banu
Kabul
Ghazni
Kurram Pass
Khyber Pass
Bara Pass
Gumal Pass
Bolan Pass
Karakoram
Jammu
Bhera
Sialkot
Nagarkot and Kangra
Jawakamukhi
1305
1322
Lahore
1241
1297-8
Talamba
Multan
1245
Pakpattan
Dipalpur
Bhatinda
Sunam
1292
Samana
1299
1305
1322
Thanesar
Sutlej
Himalayas
Sirsa
Bhatnair
Tirawari
Panipat
Hansi
Kalanaur
Meerut
1329
Amroha *1305*
Sambhal
Aonla
Bada'un
1305
Bahraich
TIRHUT
Gorakhpur
Darbhanga
Brahmaputra
Delhi *1303*
Rewari
Narnol
Baran
Koil
Mainpuri
Bhongaon
Etawa
AWADH
Mathura
Nagor
Chandwar
Bayana
JAUNPUR
Kalpi
Dalmau
Jaunpur
Maner
Pandua
Sylhet
Jaisalmer
Thar Desert
Ajmer
Gwalior
Banda
Kara
Benares
Bihar
Gaur
Siwena
Mandor
Ranthambhor
Mahoba
Kalinjar
Nadia
BENGAL
Jalor
Chitor
Chanderi
Rewa
Indus
Sihwan
1299
1303
Thatta
Idar
Dungarpur
Mandasaur
Bhilsa
Khujuraho
Sanchi
Chittagong
Patan
Sarangpur
Ujjain
Raisen
Ahmadabad
Champaner
MALWA
Dhar
Mandu
Hoshangabad
Cambay
Baroda
ORISSA
Dwarka
Broach
Narmada
Kherla
Ratanpur
Junagadh
Sultanpur
Asirgarh
Raipur
Mangrol
Somnath
Surat
Thalner
Burhanpur
Wairagarh
Bhubaneswar
Daman
Mahur
Puri
Konarak
Daulatabad
Paithan
Mahur
Sirpur
Kalyan
Deccan
Western
Ghats
Eastern
Ghats
Godavari
Warangal
Chaul
Bidar
Golconda
Rajmundry
Dabhol
Gulbarga
Sangameshwar
Bijapur
Raichur
Kondavidu
Khelna
Mudhol
Mudgal
Kampili
Belgaum
Goa
Vijayanagar
Gooty
Udayagiri
Nellore
Chataldrug
Penukonda
Chandragiri
Araga
Kanchipuram
Mangalore
Dorasamudra
Mulbagal
Srirangapatna
Mahallapuram
Calicut
Srirangam
Chidambaram
Kannanur
Tanjore
Tirumangalam
Madurai
Quilon

Arabian Sea
Bay of Bengal

GUJARAT

Strongpoints and headquarters:
Delhi Sultanate c.1300
Delhi Sultanate after 1300
Independent sultanates c.1400
Bahmani Sultanate from 1347
Vijayanagar Empire from the 1340's
Areas contested by Bahmani and Vijayanagar
Rajput
Temporarily held by forces of Delhi
Areas controlled by Hindu Rajas
Areas dominated by Hindu chiefs
Expeditions of Khalji:
1296
1307
1309
1310
1311
Muslim shrine
Hindu shrine
1303 Dates of Mongol attacks before 1398
Invasion of Timur, 1398-99
Trading ports

0   500 km
0   300 miles

© Creative Cartography Ltd © The Hamlyn Group

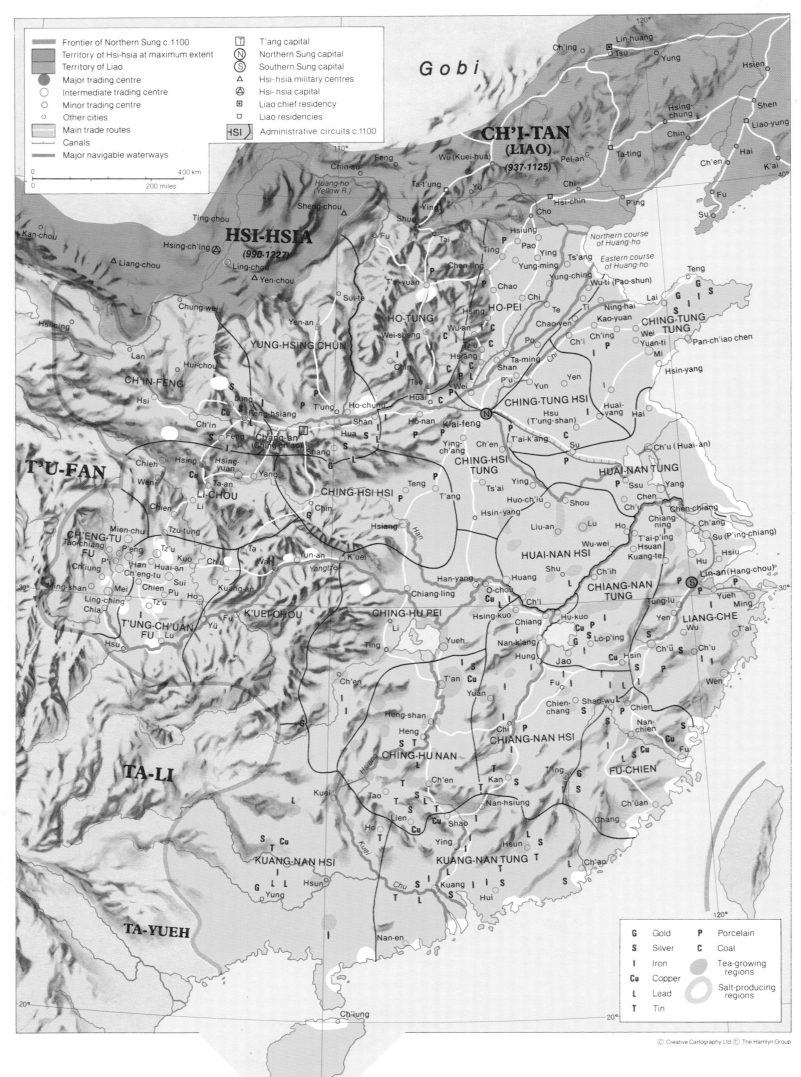

Legend:

- Frontier of Northern Sung c.1100
- Territory of Hsi-hsia at maximum extent
- Territory of Liao
- Major trading centre
- Intermediate trading centre
- Minor trading centre
- Other cities
- Main trade routes
- Canals
- Major navigable waterways

- T'ang capital
- Northern Sung capital
- Southern Sung capital
- Hsi-hsia military centres
- Hsi-hsia capital
- Liao chief residency
- Liao residencies
- HSI Administrative circuits c.1100

0 ___ 400 km
0 ___ 200 miles

Gobi

CH'I-TAN
(LIAO)
(937-1125)

HSI-HSIA
(990-1327)

Huang-ho (Yellow R.)

Northern course of Huang-ho
Eastern course of Huang-ho

T'U-FAN

TA-LI

TA-YUEH

HO-TUNG

HO-PEI

YUNG-HSING CHÜN

CH'IN-FENG

CHING-TUNG TUNG

CHING-TUNG HSI

LI-CHOU

CHING-HSI HSI

CHING-HSI TUNG

HUAI-NAN TUNG

HUAI-NAN HSI

CH'ENG-TU FU

K'UEI-CHOU

T'UNG-CH'UAN FU

CHING-HU PEI

CHIANG-NAN TUNG

LIANG-CHE

CHIANG-NAN HSI

FU-CHIEN

CHING-HU NAN

KUANG-NAN HSI

KUANG-NAN TUNG

Resources legend:

G	Gold	P	Porcelain
S	Silver	C	Coal
I	Iron		Tea-growing regions
Cu	Copper		
L	Lead		Salt-producing regions
T	Tin		

© Creative Cartography Ltd © The Hamlyn Group

Tradition and innovation

30 The China of the Northern Sung
About 1100 China probably excelled the rest of the world in economic development, literacy and numeracy. A far-flung trade and the presence on its boundaries of the relatively settled and civilised states of the Hsi-Hsia and the Liao made it more nearly part of a system of international relations than was the case under the Han or the Manchu.

31 The Mongols
The unification of the Mongol tribes under Chingiz Khan paved the way for the destruction of states and kingdoms throughout central Asia and eastern Europe, culminating in the conquest of China and the creation of the greatest land empire in history. It disintegrated rapidly, but Timur (r. 1360-1405), a descendant of Chingiz, threatened to renew it, and was planning to attack China at the time of his death.

THE CONQUESTS of Islam which had halted at the Indus in the eighth century (*see Map 19*) were carried into India by Mahmud of Ghazni (*r.*999-1030), whose west-Asian empire was based on Afghanistan, and more permanently by Muhammed Ghuri, who conquered the kingdom of Delhi in 1192. His successors failed to create an Indian empire but the Sultanate of Delhi became the dominant political power of northern and central India, and the principal force in the establishment of Islam and its culture in the sub-continent (*see Map 29*).

Throughout the Islamic world conquest made a clear break with the past. The adoption of a new religion which accompanied it involved the explicit repudiation of the old cultures and traditions, even if in practice they remained deeply influential, and their literature and thought provided the foundation for the brilliant civilisation of Islam's golden age. In Christendom and in China, on the other hand, the classical past and its traditions and values were cherished, and played a formative role in the civilisations' development. In both civilisations respect for tradition, as might be expected, acted as an inhibiting force, but by the end of the fifteenth century it was clear that the difference in the ways in which it had done so was to have momentous consequences.

By about 1100 the economic revolution had produced in China many of the features of an industrial society (*see Map 30*). Coal and iron were mined on a large scale, and the iron put to a great variety of uses–for nails and chains and currency, in bridges and in buildings, for machinery, for the textile industries and agricultural tools, which were probably more widely available to the peasantry at this time than in the early twentieth century. Most of it, however, went to the state armaments factories, which every year turned out arrowheads by the million, swords and suits of armour by the tens of thousands, even armoured vehicles for use against cavalry. Other major industries included salt-processing, ship-building and printing, for a population in which both literacy and numeracy were widely diffused. Networks of roads and canals built and maintained by the state and elaborate arrangements for credit, including a paper currency, sustained a thriving internal trade. Ships with watertight bulkheads–unknown to Europeans until the nineteenth century–exchanged silk and porcelain for the luxuries of the civilised world in the Pacific, the Indian Ocean and the Persian Gulf.

If the wealth of the Northern Sung period (960-1126) enabled China to sustain tremendous military strength it also made it an ever more tempting prey to its barbarian neighbours. The Liao and the Hsi-Hsia were relatively civilised states with which the Chinese had regular if not invariably cordial diplomatic and trading relations. But in 1125 the Liao fell to invaders, the Chin Tartars from Mongolia who went on to occupy much of northern China, including the capital Kai-feng. The immediate consequences were not catastrophic. The industrial north was lost but the Southern Sung dynasty retained the regions where agricultural wealth had been increasing rapidly and overseas trade was most naturally based. The new capital at Hang-chou soon became the largest city in the world, the centre of a wealthy, sophisticated, more urban, and in many ways more ostentatious society than its predecessor.

In the long run the fall of Liao had graver consequences. The Chin state became a conduit through which

Chinese iron weapons passed to the Mongols beyond, to provide–quite literally–the sharp edge of the most horrific and most dramatically successful of all the barbarian invasions. Temujin was declared Supreme Monarch–Chingiz Khan–of the Mongol tribes in 1206 after he had unified them in years of bitter warfare. By simple military superiority–they were usually greatly outnumbered by their civilised opponents–and unexampled ferocity, his armies conquered the greatest empire in history. *Map 31* suggests that their raids were designed to prepare the way, by systematically eliminating every possibility of rivalry elsewhere, for the invasion of China, the traditional objective of the inhabitants of the Mongolian steppes. Chingiz died in 1227, while completing his second and permanent occupation of the Hsi-Hsia. The subjugation of China (which required the Mongols to learn new techniques of waterborne and siege warfare), as well as that of Russia and parts of the Middle East, was completed by his successors. They divided his empire between them, but always recognised the ruler of China as the Great Khan to whom the others remained subordinate in theory, and for some time in practice.

The Mongols drew a line across the history of Asia. Their savagery, no doubt exaggerated by legend, was quickly moderated as they realised the value of prosperous subjects. The Mongols lived on tribute and quickly saw how they could profit from trade, which they always encouraged. Italian merchants were prominent beneficiaries. Their bases in the Crimea and on the Black Sea became the great terminals of the overland trade which flourished as the routes to China and Qaraqorum became safer, and busier, than ever before. Correspondingly, the one successful defence against the Mongols, that of Egypt by its Mamluk rulers, severed Africa once again from the Middle East and made Mesopotamia a southern backwater of the empire of the steppes (*compare Maps 31 and 27*).

The political consequences of the Mongol conquests were less beneficient. Unlike most previous conquerors they did not govern their empire through existing administrations. They appointed in each region governors from some other part of the empire, or outside it altogether, whose sole function was to see that their tribute was paid and their dictates respected. The Venetian Marco Polo ruled a Chinese province for them for several years without knowing a word of Chinese. This system not only made Mongol rule detested but left a brutal and absolutist legacy. The Russian principalities, for example, which had emerged from the disintegration of the Kievan state (*Map 21*), had retained from their Byzantine inheritance a tradition that the ruler should consult the interests of his subjects and respect the restraints of Christian conduct. Their successor when the Mongol empire began to disintegrate was the Duchy of Moscow, whose effective founder Ivan I (*r.*1328-40) secured his position by receiving from the Khan, for himself and his descendants, the right to collect the tribute in return for guaranteeing its payment (*see Map 43*). He got with it the right to exercise the Khan's absolute power over his new subjects. It was the beginning of a very different political tradition.

The Mongol conquest of north China was carried out with appalling ferocity. When it was completed the Chinese were treated as a subject people for the first time in their history. This followed the fall of a dynasty which

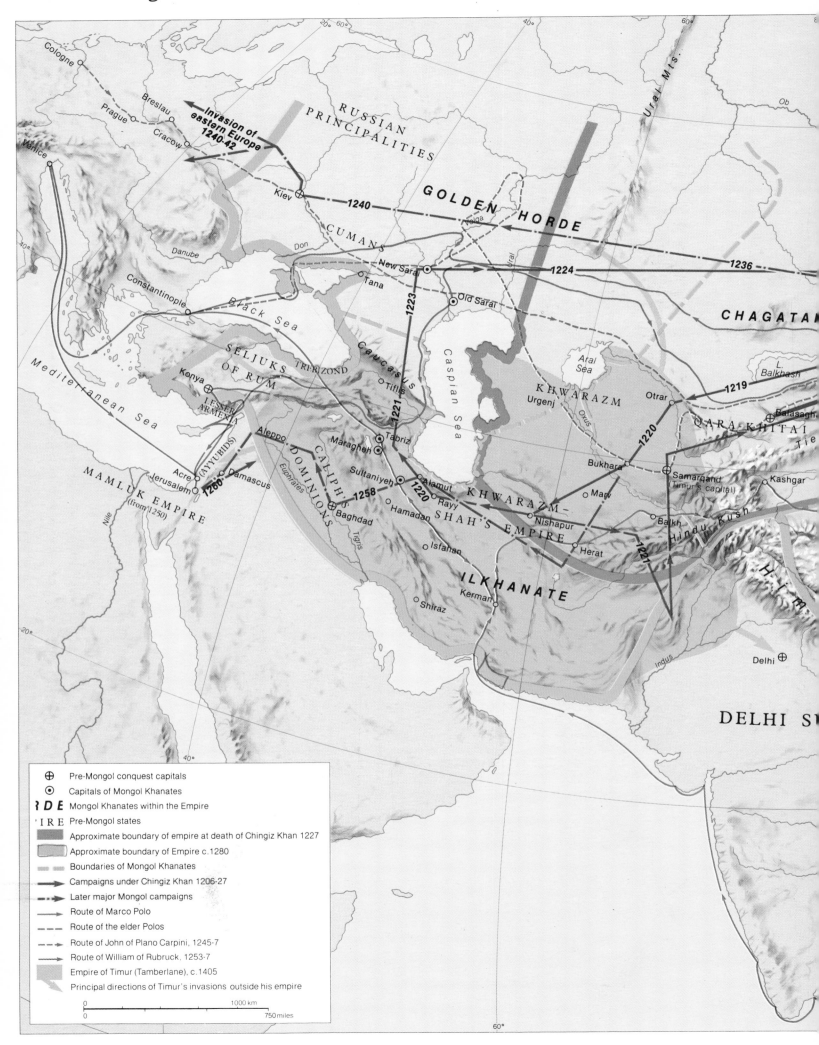

Cologne

Breslau
Prague
Cracow

Invasion of eastern Europe 1240-42

Venice

RUSSIAN PRINCIPALITIES

GOLDEN HORDE

Ural Mts.

Ob

Kiev **1240**

CUMANS

Volga

New Sarai

Tana

Old Sarai

1224

1236

CHAGATAI

Danube

Don

Constantinople

Black Sea

Mediterranean Sea

SELJUKS OF RUM

TREBIZOND

Konya

LESSER ARMENIA

Aleppo

Acre
Jerusalem
(AYYUBIDS)
Damascus

1260

MAMLUK EMPIRE
(from 1250)

Nile

CALIPH'S DOMINIONS

Baghdad

Euphrates

Sultaniyeh
1258

Alamut
Rayy
Hamadan
KHWARAZM-SHAH'S EMPIRE

Isfahan

1220

Caucasus

1221

1223

Tiflis

Tabriz
Maragheh

Caspian Sea

KHWARAZM

Aral Sea

Urgenj
Oxus

Bukhara

Marv

Nishapur

Balkh

Herat

Hindu Kush

Otrar

1219

L. Balkhash

Samarqand
(Timur's capital)

Kashgar

QARA-KHITAI

Balasagh

Tien

1227

ILKHANATE

Kerman

Shiraz

Tigris

Indus

Delhi

HIM

DELHI SU

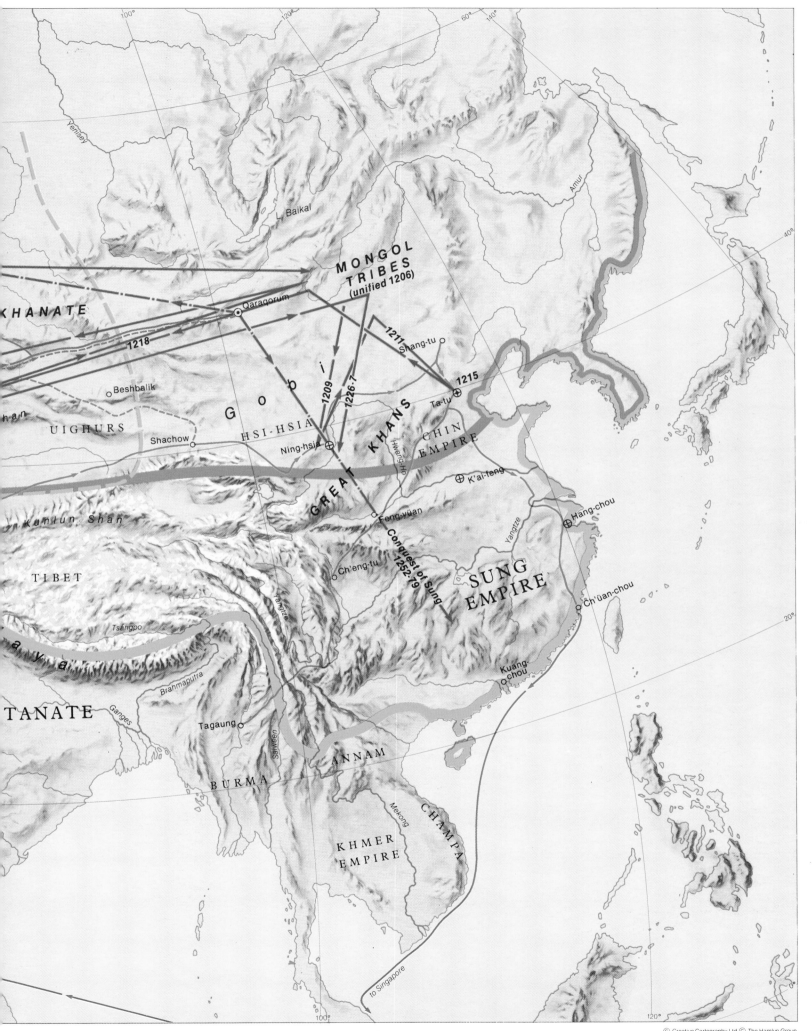

MONGOL
TRIBES
(unified 1206)

KHANATE

Qaraqorum

1218

1211
Shang-tu

Beshbalik

1209

1226-7

1215
Ta-tu

han

UIGHURS

Shachow

HSI-HSIA

G o b i

GREAT KHANS

CHIN
EMPIRE

Ning-hsia

Hwang-Ho

K'ai-feng

Kunlun Shan

Feng-yüan

Hang-chou

TIBET

Ch'eng-tu

SUNG
EMPIRE

Conquest of Sung
1252-79

Yangtze

Tsangpo

Ch'üan-chou

a y a

Brahmaputra

Yangtze

TANATE

Ganges

Kuang-
chou

Tagaung

Salween

ANNAM

BURMA

CHAMPA

Mekong

KHMER
EMPIRE

To Singapore

L. Baikal

Yenisey

Amur

had presided over unequalled peace and prosperity. The lesson was not lost. Chu Yuan-chang, the founder of Ming dynasty (1368-1644) left on his grave the words 'Rule like the T'ang and the Sung'. Action was suited to the words with a devotion that was, in the long run, self-defeating. The examination for the imperial bureaucracy, brought to a peak of scrupulous impartiality by the Sung (under whom scripts were recopied to protect the anonymity of the candidates) was restored. But its syllabus now demanded not only a minute knowledge of the great commentators on Confucius of the Sung period, but unquestioning adherence to their precepts. Even the form in which essays were to be written was soon exactly prescribed. The Sung had fallen not through any difficulty in maintaining their armies and military expenditures, such as had brought down their predecessors, but because Chinese weapons, knowledge and materials had been exported to the barbarians. The conquest had been assisted, perhaps decisively, by Chinese advisers. The Ming régime drew itself apart from the outer world. In spite of some notable achievements like the voyages of Cheng Ho to the African coast and East Indies between 1405 and 1433 the navy was run down, and trade and cultural contacts with outsiders increasingly discouraged. The accumulated wisdom and governmental expertise of the Chinese past was applied with devoted skill to the maintenance of the agricultural wealth of the interior and the development of internal trade and communications to produce a self-sufficient economy, maintaining relative prosperity and an advanced culture, without resort to the world beyond. It did so at the price of stagnation.

Compared with the territories which the Mongols ruled, western Europe was remarkably diverse in its economy and culture. This was due partly to its range of climate and terrain, and partly to the variety of influences to which it had been subjected. That it exhibited, nevertheless, a common culture and common attitudes and assumptions was the work of the Catholic Church. Ever since Pope Gregory I had organised the conversion of England just before 600, it had assumed responsibility for bringing new peoples within the orbit of civilisation—with which indeed Christianity was synonymous among the western as it was among the eastern successors of the Roman Empire (see Map 20). In the middle of the eleventh century the Papacy began to shake the Church away from lay control, beginning a conflict with the German emperors which dominated European politics for centuries. The church gradually secured its freedom to elect its own popes, appoint its own bishops and other officers, and subject its clergy to its own (canon) law and machinery of government, centred on Rome, rather than those of the secular powers. In 1215 the Fourth Lateran Council, attended by more than 400 bishops from all over Europe, endorsed a programme of doctrinal, ritual and moral precepts to be observed by the faithful and administered and enforced by a clergy which was now clearly distinguished from the laity in dress, conduct (quite often in practice as well as in theory) and allegiance.

The clergy was Europe's equivalent to China's mandarins. No prince or magnate was without his clerical advisers, who often had very great influence. Since the clergy had a monopoly of literacy, except perhaps in Italy, from the ninth to the thirteenth centuries, the operations of government were necessarily in their

hands. Great advances in administration were made in the twelfth century, through written instruments, the keeping of records and accounts, the making of surveys of land and resources (of which the English Domesday in 1087 was the most remarkable example); these were carried out by clerks (clerici) under the supervision of the bishops and abbots who were the monarch's closest advisers. While the clerks contributed indispensably to the development of royal power they also strove, with a good measure of success, to set limits to its use. Charlemagne had been encouraged, as a Christian prince, to conquer Saxony, but his clerical adviser Alcuin rebuked him for massacring its pagan inhabitants. The men who staffed the Treasury and Chancery which gave Angevin England the most powerful grip over its subjects of any government in the Latin world (see Map 25) wrote 'mirrors for princes' which portrayed royal virtue as lying in moderation, compassion for the weak and respect for the rights and interests of their subjects. And when the barons of England decided, in 1215, to protect their rights and interests by rebellion, the archbishop of Canterbury helped them to write their manifesto, which became Magna Carta.

Like the mandarins, the European clergy derived their own common standards and culture from the intensive study of a body of venerated writings and commentaries on them. Like the mandarins they strove in their best moments to preserve their caste from becoming a closed one, notably (from the eleventh century) by insisting on celibacy, so that it could not be hereditary. But here the analogy, however loose, breaks down. The clerks were too various a class, serving too many masters with an insufficiently sophisticated bureaucratic apparatus either to maintain the same degree of conformity among themselves as the mandarins could, or the same degree of control over the world around them. On the contrary, the relative autonomy of the European intelligentsia from the structures of both church and state was its most distinctive characteristic. It stemmed directly from the collapse of the Roman state in the west, which compelled the guardians of learning and culture to develop their own institutions (at first in the monasteries), find patrons and protectors wherever they could, and in doing so acquire a measure of independence which they never entirely lost.

The tremendous advance of thought and learning in the twelfth-century West both owed and contributed much to this independence. It was largely a by-product of the assault on Islam, and in the first place of the Spanish reconquest. Islamic civilisation far excelled that of Europe; when the largest libraries of the West contained four or five hundred volumes that at Cordoba had four hundred thousand. Among them were the works of the Greek and Hellenistic philosophers and scientists, translated into Arabic after the conquests of Syria and Egypt, but for the most part unknown to readers of Latin. Now they were translated with the help of Christian Arabs and of the Jews who were well established all over Spain (see Map 33). Later Norman Sicily, the crusading kingdoms and Constantinople became centres of translation directly from the Greek. The flood of new material, rising fast from about 1140 onwards, transformed every branch of knowledge and teaching. At the same time the transformation of Europe into an urban and bureaucratic society was creating an immense demand for education. In consequence the teachers in the great cities were able to establish their right to decide who should be of their

32 Italy in the middle ages
The cities of northern Italy used their early prosperity to establish their independence as self-governing communes and their control over the countryside around them. By the end of the 13th century they were beginning to surrender to despotism. Their population is shown here on the eve of the Black Death, c. 1340.

33 Spain in the middle ages
The gradual 'reconquest' of Spain by Christians—by no means an exclusively military process—left Muslim and Jewish communities in the Christian kingdoms. Their co-existence produced the most distinctive characteristics of Iberian history, providing the main channel through which Greek and Arabic philosophy and science reached the West in the 12th century, and, later, a bitter legacy of intolerance and persecution.

34 Germany and Central Europe in the later middle ages
The expansion of German settlement in central Europe continued until the 14th century. It provided the chief stimulus to economic and commercial development and assisted the continuing consolidation of the territorial principalities in the Empire and in the kingdoms of Poland, Bohemia and Hungary.

Roads
Battles
Archdioceses
Principal monasteries
Principal universities
Guelf alliance in Tuscany
Ghibelline alliance in Tuscany
Early communes
Town/city population over 50,000
"   "   "   c.50,000
"   "   "   20,000–40,000
"   "   "   c.10,000
Areas dominated by Rome, Milan, Genoa, Florence and Venice c.1100
Boundary of lordship 1450
Milan Centre of lordship 1450

0   200 km
0   150 miles

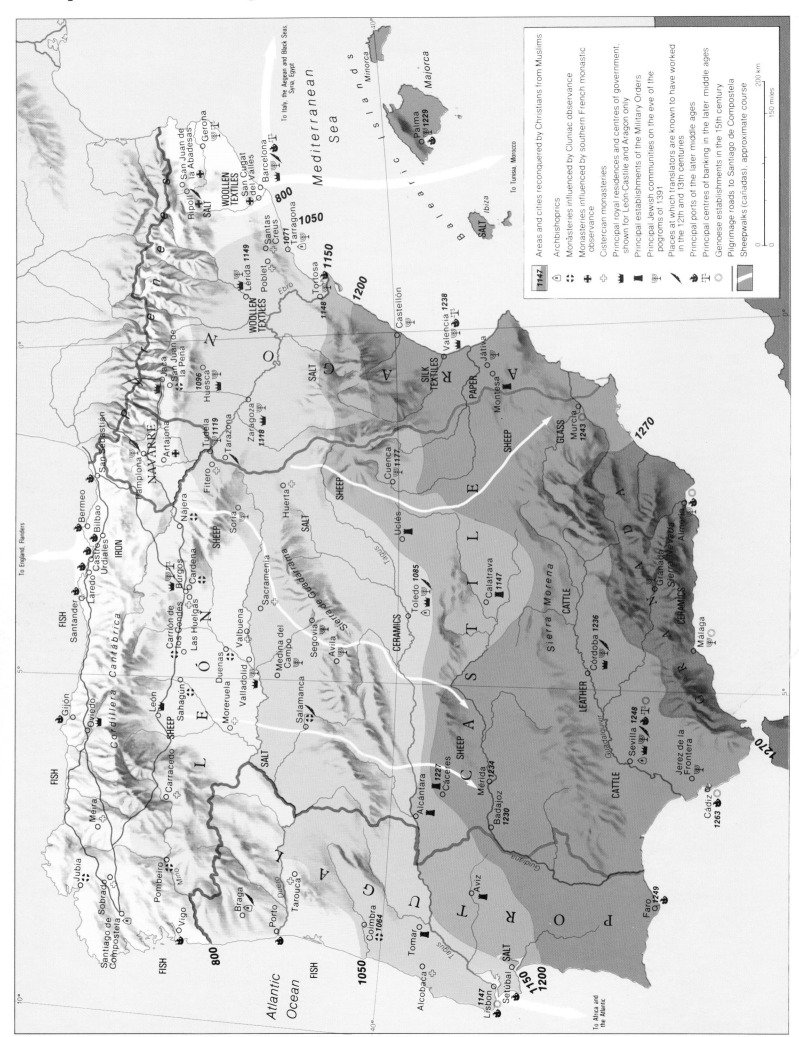

Mediterranean Sea

Islands

Minorca

Palma *1229*
Maiorca

Ibiza

SALT

To Italy, the Aegean and Black Seas, Syria, Egypt

To Tunisia, Morocco

San Juan de la Abadesas
Gerona
Ripoll
WOOLLEN TEXTILES
SALT
San Cugat del Vallés
Barcelona
800
Santas Creus
Poblet
1071
Tarragona
1050
Lérida *1149*
WOOLLEN TEXTILES
Ebro
Tortosa
1150
1148
1200
Castellón
Valencia *1238*
Játiva
SILK TEXTILES
PAPER
Montesa
GLASS
Murcia *1243*
1270

Areas and cities reconquered by Christians from Muslims
Archbishoprics
Monasteries influenced by Cluniac observance
Monasteries influenced by southern French monastic observance
Cistercian monasteries
Principal royal residences and centres of government, shown for León-Castile and Aragon only
Principal establishments of the Military Orders
Principal Jewish communities on the eve of the pogroms of 1391
Places at which translators are known to have worked in the 12th and 13th centuries
Principal ports of the later middle ages
Principal centres of banking in the later middle ages
Genoese establishments in the 15th century
Pilgrimage roads to Santiago de Compostela
Sheepwalks (cañadas), approximate course

1147

200 km
150 miles

P y r e n e e s

Jaca
San Juan de la Peña
Huesca *1096*
Artajona
Pamplona
NAVARRE
Tudela *1119*
Tarazona
Zaragoza *1118*
Fitero
Huerta
SALT
SHEEP
Soria
Sacramenia
Cuenca *1177*
SHEEP
Uclés
Toledo *1085*
Calatrava *1147*
CERAMICS

To England, Flanders
Bermeo
Bilbao
Castro Urdiales
San Sebastián
IRON
Laredo
Santander
FISH
Gijón
Oviedo
Cordillera Cantábrica
FISH
Nájera
Carrión de los Condes
Cardeña
Burgos
SHEEP
Las Huelgas
Sahagún
León
SHEEP
Carracedo
Duenas
Valbuena
Moreruela
Valladolid
Medina del Campo
Segovia
Ávila
Salamanca
Sierra de Guadarrama
CERAMICS
Tagus
C A S T I L E
Sierra Morena
CATTLE
Córdoba *1236*
LEATHER
Sevilla *1248*
CATTLE
Guadalquivir
Jerez de la Frontera
Granada
Sierra Nevada
CERAMICS
Málaga
Almería
1270

A R A G O N
V A L E N C I A
A N D A L U C I A
G R A N A D A

L E Ó N

Méira
FISH
Jubia
Sobrado
Pombeiro
Santiago de Compostela
Vigo
Braga
Porto
Tarouca
Coimbra *1064*
Tomar
800
Miño
Douro
G A L I C I A
1050
P O R T U G A L
Aviz
Alcántara *1227*
Cáceres
Mérida *1234*
Badajoz *1230*
Guadiana
Cádiz *1263*
Faro *1249*
1200

Atlantic Ocean
FISH
FISH
Alcobaça
Lisbon *1147*
Setúbal
SALT
1150
1200
To Africa and the Atlantic

© Creative Cartography Ltd © The Hamlyn Group

Legend:

- ▫ Town of over 20,000 population
- △ Town of 10-20,000 population
- ○ Town of under 10,000 population
- ♠ ♠ Archbishopric / bishopric with important territory
- ♠ Archbishopric (with date of foundation)
- ♠ Bishopric (with date of foundation)
- ♦ University
- ▪ Member of Hanseatic League
- **MAI** Electoral territory
- GELD Important territory
- ▬▬ Boundaries of Empire in 1378
- ── Boundaries of lands of Teutonic Order in 1378
- ── Other boundaries
- ▨ Important trade routes
- ═ Alpine passes
- ▨ Hapsburg lands in 1378
- ▨ Wittelsbach lands in 1378
- ▨ Luxemburg lands in 1378
- ▨ Lands of Swiss Confederation in 1378
- ▨ Areas of German settlement
- ▨ Areas of extensive use of German town law

150 km / 100 miles

Baltic Sea

North Sea

DENMARK

HOLSTEIN

Schleswig
Lübeck
Ratzeburg
Hamburg
Lüneburg
BREMEN
VERDEN
BRAUNSCHWEIG
Minden
Braunschweig
OSNABRÜCK
MÜNSTER
PADERBORN
HILDESHEIM
Goslar
Halberstadt
MAGDEBURG
SAXONY
Merseburg
Naumburg
Erfurt
THURINGIA
FULDA
HESSE
WESTFALIA
BERG
Dortmund
Soest
Cologne
COLOGNE
Aachen
Maastricht
JÜLICH
NASSAU
TRIER
Trier
LUXEMBURG
MAINZ
Mainz
Worms
Speyer
PALATINATE
Heidelberg
WÜRZBURG
Frankfurt
BAMBERG
UPPER PALATINATE
Nuremberg
Eichstatt
Regensburg
Nördlingen
Augsburg
Freising
WÜRTTEMBERG
Tübingen
Ulm
Munich
BAVARIA
Chiemsee 1216
Passau
AUSTRIA
Vienna 1468
Wiener Neustadt 1468
Freising

MECKLENBURG
Rostock
Schwerin
Stralsund
Greifswald
Kammin
POMERANIA
Stettin
Havelberg
BRANDENBURG
Berlin
Brandenburg
Lebus
LAUSITZ
Bautzen
Meissen
BRESLAU
Glogau
Breslau
Königgratz
Leitomischl
Olmütz
Prague 1348
Cheb (Eger)
Pilsen
BOHEMIA
Brno
MORAVIA
Nitra
Eger

Danzig
Elbing
Marienwerder
TEUTONIC ORDER
Königsberg
Frombork 1243
Kulm
Thorn
DOBRZYN
Włocławek
Płock
Warsaw
Gniezno
Poznan
Kalisz
Lowicz
(GREAT) POLAND
(LITTLE)
Cracow
GALICIA

FRISIA
HOLLAND
Kampen
Haarlem
Amsterdam
Leiden
Delft
Hague
UTRECHT
Deventer
GELDERN
ZEELAND
BRABANT
Antwerp
Mechelen
Brussels
LIÈGE
Namur
HAINAULT
Tournai
Cambrai
Reims
Verdun
LOTHARINGIA
Toul
METZ

BURGUNDY

FRANCHE-COMTÉ

Dijon
Lyon
SAVOY
DAUPHINÉ
Grenoble

Basel 1460
Zürich
Zug
Solothurn
Lucerne
SWISS CONFEDERATION
Lausanne
L Geneva
Geneva
Sion
Chur
St Gottard Pass
Lukmanier Pass
Splügen Pass
Septimer Pass
Great St Bernard Pass
Little St Bernard Pass
Mont Cenis Pass
Constance
TIROL
Brenner Pass
Brixen
The Alps
Trent
SALZBURG
Seckau 1218
STYRIA
Gurk
CARINTHIA
Lavant 1228
KRAIN
Lublana 1462
Aquileia
Trieste
Zagreb
HUNGARY
Veszprém
Bratislava
Esztergom
Győr
Pest
Vác
Kalocsa
Pécs
Dakovo 1229

Strasbourg

MILAN
Milan
Vercelli
Pavia 1361
Turin
Bergamo
Brescia
Cremona
Mantua
Piacenza
Vicenza
Verona
VERONA
Padua
Venice
Treviso
Adriatic Sea
Po
Drava
Sava

© Creative Cartography Ltd © The Hamlyn Group

Tradition and innovation

number, and who and what they should teach. From the thirteenth century thè universities of Europe, led by Paris and Bologna (see Maps 25, 32 and 34) were legally self-governing corporations, effectively independent of both Church and state.

Like the universities, the towns of Europe won their freedom in the high Middle Ages, successfully demanding from the end of the eleventh century charters which granted them exemption from the taxes and jurisdiction of their feudal lords. Northern Italy, its cities more numerous and much more populous than those of any other region, was Europe's, urban region par excellence (compare Maps 28 and 32). To the profits of their far-flung trading colonies (see also Map 26) they were now adding those of the banking and insurance services, which they provided all over Europe, often playing a critical role in political events in consequence. The Bardi and Peruzzi banks had more branches and more capital at the beginning of the fourteenth century than the Medici bank (see Map 35) had a hundred years later, and had far more liquid wealth at their disposal than any monarch. In such a world the skills of literacy and numeracy were necessarily widely distributed. The intense competitiveness and rich opportunities of city life produced on the one hand continuous, often bitter and eventually self-destructive conflict both within and between the cities, and on the other a secular culture of immense vitality, the greatest masterpieces of European building, painting and literature, and a tradition of political and intellectual independence which survived the efforts of German emperors and papal agents alike to subdue it.

The agricultural expansion upon which economic growth and political development rested reached its limit in most places in the late thirteenth century. Falling crop yields and more frequent famine produced the Black Death which between 1347 and 1352 killed up to a third of the population in the worst affected regions (see Map 35). Recurrent epidemics delayed recovery until the end of the century and beyond. Prolonged and savage wars over much of Europe increased the consequent miseries, and swelled the taxes which monarchs extorted from their subjects. The peasant revolts which followed, severely frightening the governors of France and England in particular, were paralleled by the growing bitterness of civil conflict in the towns, and rising signs of popular discontent with the privileges and exactions of the clergy. All these elements were involved in the devastating and fateful wars which originated in criticism of clerical corruption by a distinguished scholar and teacher, John Hus (who died at the stake in 1415) and became a popular rebellion with aristocratic support, against the imperial domination of Bohemia (1419-36; see Map 35). This war foreshadowed the wars of the Reformation era in bloodiness and bitterness as well as in the issues involved.

The growth of government in the twelfth and thirteenth centuries and the miseries of the fourteenth contributed to the creation of a less open and less pluralistic society. The church vindicated its claim to spiritual leadership by persecuting as heretics those who resisted it. They were especially numerous in the Low Countries, Lombardy and the Languedoc, where their presence provided the Capetian kings with an excuse for the brutal conquest of the County of Toulouse (1209-29; see Map 25) and the Pope for the creation of the Inquisition. The Church's demand for Christians to conform

now also encouraged a rising tide of popular hostility towards the Jews, who were ordered to wear distinctive clothing by the Fourth Lateran Council. The withdrawal of royal protection (which was largely responsible for their unpopularity in the first place) as the rise of the Italian banks made their financial services superfluous and the debts owed to them an embarrassment led to their expulsion from England in 1290 and France in 1306; and they were driven from western Germany towards the new lands in the east when a succession of pogroms made them scapegoats for the Black Death. In Spain too, where three cultures had coexisted fruitfully for so long, tolerance broke down, and persecution of the Jews started in earnest in 1391; the Inquisition made up for its late arrival there, in 1480, by pursuing their descendants – particularly those who had converted to Christianity – with special ferocity. Secular monarchs did not hang back. In 1307 the king of France seized the lands of the Knights Templar in his dominion, justifying the action by torturing them until they confessed that they were part of an international satanist conspiracy. A century later the technique was being widely imitated by those who had grudges against their neighbours: accusations of witchcraft were pursued by inquisitors and magistrates with an enthusiasm which would bring scores of thousands to the stake all over early modern Europe.

Nevertheless these reverses did not undo the achievements of the twelfth and thirteenth centuries. Economic failure in some areas was offset by rapid development in others. The Hansa towns of northern Europe formed a political and trading monopoly which dominated their area, and contributed greatly in the thirteenth and fourteenth centuries to the development of the Baltic and the eastern expansion of the Germans (see Maps 34 and 35); the extension of their routes through southern Germany to the Mediterranean and along the Atlantic coast helped to create a larger and more varied European trading community. If the Flemish cloth industry declined, Dutch shipping grew vigorous on the Baltic trade; and the wars in the Iberian peninsula hastened the maritime expansion of Portugal. The tyrannical ambitions of the European rulers were also a sign of the limitations on their power, and of how little they controlled the vital forces of European society; the peasant revolts attacked political weakness as well as financial exaction, and the Inquisition could prevent neither the dissemination of religious disaffection among the people nor the increasing boldness of speculation among the intellectuals both inside and outside the Church. For many Europeans the fifteenth century was not a happy time or, as they saw themselves become the last heirs of antiquity when Constantinople fell to the Ottoman Turks in 1453, a secure one. Nevertheless, theirs was a fortunate inheritance.

35 The economy of the later middle ages
In the 14th century Europe was seized by disease, famine and revolt. Nevertheless new trade routes were established and new centres of production and exchange opened up, especially in central and eastern Europe, to create a larger and more varied economy: compare with Map 28, which this map complements, but does not supersede.

Further reading: M. Elvin, The Pattern of the Chinese Past (Eyre Methuen, 1973); J. J. Saunders, The History of the Mongol Conquest (Routledge & Kegan Paul, 1972); R. W. Southern, The Making of the Middle Ages (Hutchinson, 1953; p.b.); R. W. Southern, Western Society and the Church in the Middle Ages (Penguin, 1970); M. T. Clanchy, From Memory to Written Record (Edward Arnold, 1979); J. K. Hyde, Society and Politics in Medieval Italy (Macmillan, 1973; p.b.); R. I. Moore, The Origins of European Dissent (Allen Lane, 1977).

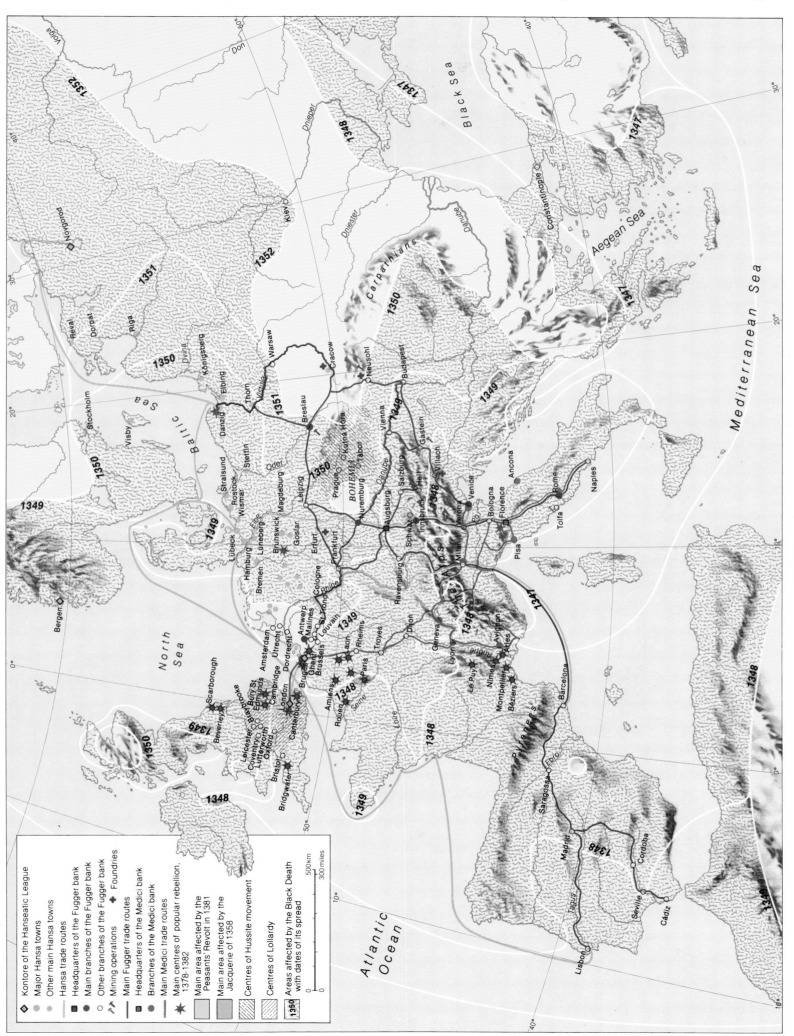

Kontore of the Hanseatic League
Major Hansa towns
Other main Hansa towns
Hansa trade routes
Headquarters of the Fugger bank
Main branches of the Fugger bank
Other branches of the Fugger bank
Mining operations
Foundries
Main Fugger trade routes
Headquarters of the Medici bank
Branches of the Medici bank
Main Medici trade routes
Main centres of popular rebellion, 1378-1382
Main area affected by the Peasants' Revolt in 1381
Main area affected by the Jacquerie of 1358
Centres of Hussite movement
Centres of Lollardy
Areas affected by the Black Death with dates of its spread

© Creative Cartography Ltd © The Hamlyn Group

The age of European supremacy I

Europe and a wider world

AT THE END of the fifteenth century Europe was not evidently the most advanced civilisation. Those of India, the Islamic world and, especially, China were richer and more sophisticated. Yet within 300 years Europe had seized control of the oceans, destroyed the Aztecs, Incas and Mayas of South America (*Map 36*), conquered vast territories throughout the Americas and in India and Siberia, and organised a complex and immensely profitable worldwide commercial system (*see Map 50*).

It seems surprising that China, with its huge land mass, large population and stable political organisation under the Ming dynasty (1368-1644) did not 'discover' Europe. After 1400 sturdy Chinese junks traded extensively in the Pacific and Chinese paper currency circulated widely. In seven expeditions between 1405 and 1433 the Grand Eunuch Cheng Ho sailed to Borneo, the Philippines, Ceylon, Malacca and East Africa. The conservatism of China's governors stifled the initiative. The mandarins disliked Muslims, eunuchs and favourites—Cheng was all three—and regarded trade as exploitation, and the outside world with suspicion. Official records of Cheng's expeditions were destroyed within 30 years, monopolies discouraged commerce, the paper currency collapsed, and external influences were discouraged. The Ottoman Turks, who presented such a desperate threat to Europe (*see Map 42*) had similar inhibitions. The rich bankers of Constantinople in 1500 were foreigners, Greek Christians or (like the 'Fugger of the Orient', Joseph Nasi) Portuguese Jews, and the Ottomans dispatched no ambassadors to the west, translated none of its literature —much of it by now available in print—and relied on slaves in their army to provide new military technology.

The 'age of reconnaissance' was launched from the smallest and least-endowed of European principalities, Portugal. The capture of the North African Moorish city of Ceuta in 1415 was followed by nearly a century of patient exploration of the West African coast, frequently interrupted by war in the Iberian peninsula, and by Portugal's domestic concerns (*see Map 36*). At last Bartholomeu Diaz triumphantly rounded the Cape of Good Hope in 1487, and in 1498 Vasco da Gama reached India. Within a decade and a half the Portuguese, using Asian pilots, bribery, and extensive naval bombardment, established fortresses and trading stations at Goa, which became the spiritual, administrative, and commercial centre of the Portuguese empire, Malacca, the centre of the spice trade in the Orient, and the Moluccas. The port of Mozambique was founded in 1507, and Ormuz, the guardian port of the Persian Gulf, in 1515. In 1557 they made a base on the China coast at Macao. For a few years nearly all the spices for Europe were carried by the Portuguese, but they never established a monopoly of the trade. They were dependent upon a delicate commercial system, always subject to disruption, in which the gold from the Zambeze area bought spices in the Indies, which paid for the expedition on its return.

Discovery begat imitation. The rivalry between Portugal and Castile spread down the West African coast with Castile's capture of the Canary Islands in the 1470s. Portugal (like the crusading powers of the thirteenth and fourteenth centuries) appealed in vain to the Pope to protect the monopoly granted in Papal Bulls of 1454 and 1456. In 1493, five years after Diaz returned from the Cape of Good Hope, Christopher Columbus' ship the *Nina* put into Lisbon, having returned across the Atlantic in a Spanish-sponsored expedition which claimed that it had discovered Cathay (Asia). Columbus, descended from a family of Genoese cartographers, was a careful and accurate navigator. The route of his first voyage to the 'West Indies' became that used by Spanish shipping to and from the New World, and his speed of crossing was rarely beaten in the sixteenth century. Castile claimed, and received, Papal protection for this new route to 'Asia', and an important line of demarcation between Portuguese and Castilian 'Asia' was achieved in the Treaty of Tordesillas (1494), although its precise geographical position was still disputed.

The purpose of Columbus' three subsequent voyages was rather different from that of the Portuguese explorers. He took with him not trading goods, but farmers, artisans, priests, tools, seeds and animals, to establish a new community across the Atlantic. Colonies were established at Española, and Santo Domingo (*see Map 37*). Increasingly, after 1500, as explorers' reports were digested, the suspicion hardened that this was not Asia but a new world. The conviction was strengthened by John Cabot, Amérigo Vespucci and others and confirmed in 1519, when Fernão Magalhães (Magellan) sailed round the tip of southern America. His captain, Del Caso, became the first man to sail round the world (*Map 36*). In less than 30 years the map of the main islands of the Caribbean was established, but that was twice as long as it had taken the Portuguese, with the aid of their Asian pilots, to chart the East Indies.

The early settlements in the Caribbean proved disappointing. They were vulnerable, quarrelsome and economically insecure. European diseases and ill-treatment cut down the native Carib population. Partly to escape the quarrels, various expeditions were sent through the Gulf of Mexico. On the basis of their intelligence a new colony was established in Panama in 1519 and a larger expedition set out for Mexico under the command of the first and greatest of the *conquistadores*, Hernan Cortès (*Map 38*). His letters and four other eyewitness reports of his conquest of Mexico give a uniquely detailed account of their aims and methods. They reveal Cortès trying to prevent unnecessary bloodshed amongst the Aztecs he was conquering, aware of his difficulties in controlling the ill-disciplined forces under him, fascinated by the new culture before his eyes, constantly alive to the classical precedents for the conquest of primitive peoples (such as Julius Caesar's), and persistent in his attempts to maintain the chivalric and knightly values of his native southern Spain. But Cortès could not prevent the destruction of the capital of the Aztecs, Tenochtitlán, (where, subsequently, he founded Mexico City), and to reward the extravagant aspirations of his followers he distributed Aztec villages amongst them in *encomienda*, a system of quasi-manorial tribute.

With the Mexican example before them, other *conquistadores*, with less sympathy and more greed, carved out similar empires for themselves. Guatemala (1523-42), New Granada (1536-9), and central Chile (1540-58) were all conquered, but they never rivalled Mexico and Cuba. *Conquistadores* like Francisco de Pizarro and Nuño de Guzmán bloodily subdued the Incas and Mayas. Wherever there were Indians, the *encomienda* system was established, and the parasitic Spaniards lived off the tribute in the cities which they founded in the New World—Panama, Darien, Santiago, Lima, Santa Fé de Bogotá. The finest fruits of conquest, the first productive silver mines, were discovered at Potosí in central Peru in

36 The European discovery of the world
Late in the 15th century the Europeans began to discover the oceans, and the other advanced peoples, of the world. The Portuguese established a maritime empire in the Far East from the base provided by their earlier exploration of the African coast, while the Spanish conquered a land empire in America from their base in the Caribbean.

1545, which remained the biggest single source of silver in the world for a hundred years (*see Map 37*).

The age of the *conquistadores* was troublesome and brief. They had undertaken great hardships and risked their lives and fortunes, and some had great rewards. Others were overwhelmed by the unexploitable, untapped reserves of space in America. Hernando de Soto, whose expedition reached the Appalachians, and the Mississippi, or Coronado who crossed the Rio Grande and reached the Prairies, could make nothing of the vast expanse of lands, nomadic peoples and roving herds of cattle (*see Map 36*). Francisco de Orellana, who sailed down the Amazon after crossing the Andes, despaired of the dense tropical forests of the Amazon basin. Even those who were successful attracted the suspicions of the Crown, and if they escaped the knives of their rivals were soon replaced by an effective royal administration. Some settled as ranchers and miners. Others, like Cortès, returned to Spain to a bored and litigious retirement.

The motives of the Portuguese seamen and the Castilian *conquistadores* were mixed, powerful and long-established. Memories of crusade were still powerful in the Iberian peninsula. The last province of Castile was captured from the Moors in the same year that Columbus set out for America (*see Map 33*). None of the early explorers would have repudiated the motive which was attributed to Prince Henry the Navigator (master-mind of the Portuguese explorations in the middle of the fifteenth century) by his contemporary biographer: the conversion of the natives to Christianity and the defeat of the Infidel. But Prince Henry was also interested ('as was natural') in profit. The pace of Portuguese discoveries increased once they had reached the gold, slaves, and spices along the Guinea coast. More gold was discovered in the kingdoms of East Africa, and with the spices of the East Indies provided the basic staples of the Portuguese empire. Two powerful legends symbolised the motives of the early explorers: that there was a powerful Christian ruler somewhere to the East (*Prester John*), and a powerful and rich city of gold somewhere in the Orient (*Cathay*).

The first thing which distinguished Europe from other civilisations, and enabled it to discover the world was its ability to imitate, especially in technical developments. The fifteenth century saw, for instance, a fruitful combination of the Arabic type of Mediterranean ship with Atlantic vessels, to produce a craft which could go anywhere and get back again. The combination of lateen and square-rigged sails, developed by Portuguese ship-builders in the caravel, could be worked by a small crew (shortage of water and food was the main hazard of long voyages) and could sail closely to the wind. Other advances in hull design produced ships which could sail their course more accurately. Few expeditions were mounted in first-class ships, but even fewer suffered from defects in their sailing craft. Mounted with guns they proved capable of protecting oceans as well as discovering them. The other tradition alive in the Spanish peninsula was that of mathematics and astronomy, in the hands of Jews. Jewish mathematicians produced traverse tables to indicate approximate journey times and Jewish astronomers produced manuals for the declination of the sun at various latitudes. In Portugal, unlike Spain, Jews were tolerated.

Secondly, Europe did not despise merchants and mercantile wealth. The towns of northern Italy had grown rich upon the trade of the Mediterranean; Italian merchants traded in the bulk-cargoes of grain, salt and fish and, more importantly, with the Arabs in silks, spices and precious metals (*see Maps 28 and 35*). In their manner of conducting their business, sharing their risks, accounting for their profits, and facilitating credit, they were admired and copied in the cities of the southern Netherlands and southern Germany. The Portuguese crown, after initial reluctance, encouraged the participation of merchants in its ventures, and the great fleet which sailed from Lisbon in 1505 was largely financed by foreigners—Genoese, Florentine and German. In later expeditions the Crown undertook the voyages, but sold the entire cargoes, frequently in advance, to merchant syndicates. Once the colonies of the New World were established, it was the merchants of Antwerp who provided the colonists with the goods of the Old World, and the bankers of the Spanish crown in Genoa and Augsburg (like the Fuggers) who distributed the silver from the mines of Potosí across Europe.

Above all, the 'age of reconnaissance' was also the 'age of renaissance'. One of the most brilliant chapters of Jacob Burckhardt's famous book, the *Civilisation of the Renaissance* was entitled 'The Discovery of the World and of Men'. In it he discussed the delicate relationship between two forms of exploration, that of the inner world and the senses, and that of the physical world. He compared the accounts of medieval travellers outside Europe with those of the Renaissance explorers and concluded that the medieval travellers took what they found for granted, neither criticising it nor comparing it with their own experiences. The Renaissance explorer was different. Having gained a sense of historical perspective from the rediscovery of the different culture and civilisation of the ancient world, he was more receptive, intellectually readier to appreciate, without rejecting, the different cultures and civilisations around him. Yet this is difficult to apply to most of the *conquistadores*. And it took two centuries for Europe to absorb the impact of the initial discoveries of the sixteenth century. Only by 1600 were the flora and fauna of the New World adequately described and categorised; it took longer for its carbohydrates (potato, sugar and maize) and vitamins to change the European diet. Only by 1700 was the New World in North America and Brazil beginning to be settled (*Map 38*). Only in the seventeenth century did the Dutch and English develop effective commercial and colonial empires along the lines of the Portuguese or Castilian. When the fruits of discovery had been absorbed, the process could begin again—this time in Siberia, India, Australia and on the margins of America.

Further reading: J. H. Parry, *Europe and a Wider World* (2nd ed. Hutchinson, 1964); *The Age of Reconnaissance* (Weidenfeld and Nicolson, 1963; Cardinal, 1973); C. M. Cipolla, *European Culture and Overseas Expansion* (Collins, 1965, 1967; Penguin, 1970); Bernal Diaz, *The Conquest of New Spain* (Penguin, 1963); J. Burckhardt, *The Civilisation of the Renaissance in Italy* (1860; Phaidon Press, London, 1945).

Bylot-Baffin
1616

Spitzbergen

Arc

Eskimos

North East
Indians

Eskimos

Baffin
Island

Davis
1585/87

Hudson
Straits

Frobisher
1576

Hudson
Bay

Hudson 1610

Button
1612

S. Cabot.
1517

Cabot 1497

Davis 1587

Algonquins

Cartier
1534

John Cabot
1497

Bristol

Drake
1579

Cabrillo
1542

John Cabot
1498

Cabot 1498

Atlantic Ocean

Drake

Californians

American Indians

Varrazano
1523-4

Westerlies

Azores

Eu

Lisbon

John Cabot
1498

Cadiz

Ulloa
1539

Texans

de Soto
1539

Gomez
1524

Ponce de Leon
1515

Diego de Sevilla
1432

Canary
Islanders
1312?/1336

Gonzalo Velho
1416

Nomads of
the Sahara

Becerra
1533

Bahamas Is.

Columbus 1492

Urdaneta 1565

Cortes
1519

Mexico City
(Tenochtitlan)

Caribs
Cuba

Española

N.E. Trades

Nuno de Tristão
1441/43

Diniz Diaz
1443-4

Timbuctoo

East
Sudanese

Aztecs

Cordoba
1517

Mayas

Columbus
1502-4

Columbus
1493-4

Spanish Main

Cape Verde Is.
Cadamostro de Noli.
1456/8

Nuno de Tristão
1445

West
Sudanese

HAUSA

Saavedra 1527

Montejo
1527-8

Columbus
1502-4

A. Fernandez
1446

Niani

MOSSI

Pedro de Evora
1483

N.E. Trades

Dávila
1514

Balboa
1513

Bastidas
1500

Ehinger
1529

Columbus
1498

Vespucci 1499

S. da Costa
1461/70

Guinea coast
peoples

BENIN

Jão de Santarem 1471

Pacific
Ocean

Isthmus of
Panama

Caribs

A. de Hojeda
1498-9

Magellan 1519

Fernando Po
1472

Seguira
1472

Peop
Afric

Pizarro and Almagro
1524/26

Ruiz de Estrada
1526

S.E. Trades

Diego Cão
1485-6

Equator

Mendaña and Quiros 1595-6

Pizarro
1528

Brazilian
Indians

Pinzon
1499-1500

Fernão Noronha
1501/2

João da Nova
1501

Mendaña 1567-69

America
(name first used in 1507)

Terra de
Vera Cruz

KONGO

Incas

Gê-
Botecudos

Drake 1577/80

João da Nova
1502

Saint Helena
Bay

Bantu

Chilean
Indians

Chaco
Indians

Brazilian
Indians

Treaty of Tordesillas 1494

Walfish Bay

Bartholomeu Diaz
1486-88

Hunter-gathering cultures

Nomads and stock-raisers

Primitive cultures

Advanced cultures

Literate civilisations

Routes for voyages of discovery

Drake　Explorers

　Spanish expeditions

　Portuguese

　French

　English

　Dutch

- - -　Political lines of demarcation between Spanish
　and Portuguese exploration

– – –　The world known to Europeans, c. 1450

———　The world known of by Europeans, c. 1450

Mayas　Peoples

←　Approximate prevailing winds (shown for
　the first quarter of the year)

Drake

PORTUGAL
SPAIN

Dias de Solis
1516

Patagonians

Valdivia
1540

Magellan 1519-20

Tristan da Cunha
c. 1510

Vasco da Gama 1497

Westerlies

Cabral 1500

Roaring Forties

Port Saint Jullian
1520

Falkland Is.

Hawkins
1594

Magellan's Straits

Tierra del Fuego

F. de Hocues
1526

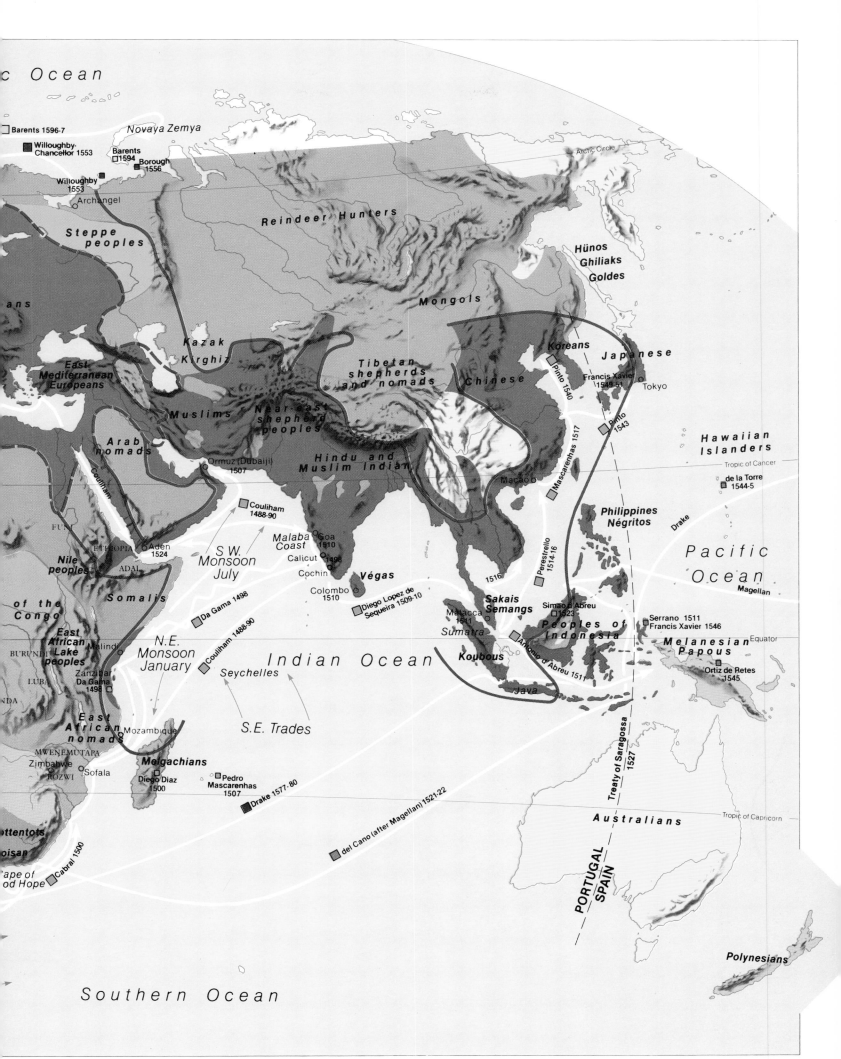

c Ocean

Barents 1596-7

Willoughby-
Chancellor 1553

Novaya Zemya

Barents
1594

Borough
1556

Willoughby
1553

Archangel

Arctic Circle

Reindeer Hunters

Steppe
peoples

Hünos

Ghiliaks

Goldes

ans

Kazak

Kirghiz

Mongols

Koreans

Japanese

East
Mediterranean
Europeans

Pinto 1540

Francis Xavier
1549-51

Tokyo

Muslims

Tibetan
shepherds
and nomads

Chinese

Near-east
shepherd
peoples

Pinto
1543

Arab
nomads

Couliham

Mascarenhas 1517

Hawaiian
Islanders

Hindu and
Muslim India

Ormuz (Dubaiji)
1507

Macao

Tropic of Cancer

de la Torre
1544-5

Nile
peoples

Aden
1524

ETHIOPIA

Couliham
1488-90

Malaba
Coast

Goa
1510

S.W.
Monsoon
July

Calicut
1498

Cochin

Philippines
Négritos

Drake

Pacific
Ocean

ADAL

Somalis

Da Gama 1498

Végas

Colombo
1510

Perestrello
1514-16

Magellan

of the
Congo

Diego Lopez de
Sequeira 1509-10

1516

East
African
Lake
peoples

Malindi

N.E.
Monsoon
January

Couliham 1488-90

Indian Ocean

Sakais
Semangs

Simao d'Abreu
1523

Serrano 1511
Francis Xavier 1546

Melanesian
Papous

Equator

BURUNDI

Matacca
1511

LUBA

Zanzibar
Da Gama
1498

Seychelles

Sumatra

Koubous

Antonio d'Abreu 1511

Ortiz de Retes
1545

NDA

S.E. Trades

Peoples of
Indonesia

East
African
nomads

Mozambique

Java

MWENEMUTAPA

Zimbabwe

Sofala

Meigachians

ROZWI

Diego Diaz
1500

Pedro
Mascarenhas
1507

Drake 1577-80

Treaty of Saragossa
1527

Australians

Tropic of Capricorn

ottentots

oisan

del Cano (after Magellan) 1521-22

PORTUGAL
SPAIN

ape of
od Hope

Cabral 1500

Polynesians

Southern Ocean

© Creative Cartography Ltd © The Hamlyn Group

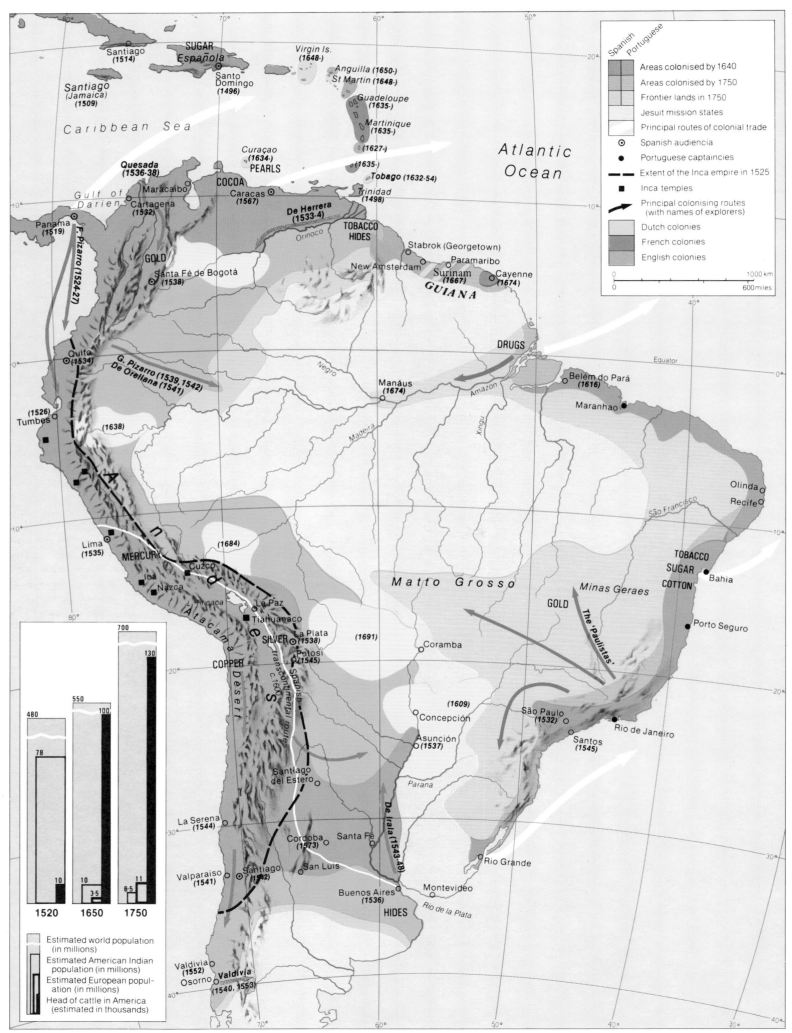

Santiago (1514)

SUGAR Española

Santiago (Jamaica) (1509)

Santo Domingo (1496)

Virgin Is. (1648·)

Anguilla (1650·)
St Martin (1648·)

Guadeloupe (1635·)

Martinique (1635·)

(1627·)

(1635·)

Tobago (1632-54)

Caribbean Sea

Curaçao (1634·)
PEARLS

COCOA

Quesada (1536-38)

Maracaibo

Cartagena (1532)

Caracas (1567)

De Herrera (1533-4)

Trinidad (1498)

Atlantic Ocean

Gulf of Darien

Panama (1519)

F. Pizarro (1524-27)

GOLD

Santa Fé de Bogotá (1538)

TOBACCO
HIDES

Orinoco

Stabrok (Georgetown)

Paramaribo

New Amsterdam
Surinam (1667)
Cayenne (1674)

GUIANA

Quito (1534)

G. Pizarro (1539, 1542)
De Orellana (1541)

(1526)
Tumbes

(1638)

Negro

Manáus (1674)

Amazon

DRUGS

Equator

Belém do Pará (1616)

Maranhao

Olinda

Recife

A
n
d
e
s

Lima (1535)

MERCURY

Ica

Nazca

Cuzco

Titicaca

La Paz

Tiahuanaco

SILVER

La Plata (1538)

Potosí (1545)

Atacama Desert

COPPER

Transcontinental route
c. 1600

Spanish S

(1684)

(1691)

Matto Grosso

Coramba

(1609)

Concepción

Asunción (1537)

Parana

São Francisco

GOLD

Minas Geraes

The 'Paulistas'

São Paulo (1532)

Santos (1545)

Rio de Janeiro

TOBACCO
SUGAR
COTTON

Bahia

Porto Seguro

Santiago del Estero

La Serena (1544)

Cordoba (1573)

Santa Fé

San Luis

De Irala (1543-48)

Valparaiso (1541)

Santiago (1541)

Buenos Aires (1536)

HIDES

Montevideo

Rio de la Plata

Rio Grande

Valdivia (1552)
Osorno

Valdivia (1540, 1553)

Spanish / Portuguese

Areas colonised by 1640
Areas colonised by 1750
Frontier lands in 1750
Jesuit mission states
Principal routes of colonial trade
⊙ Spanish audiencia
• Portuguese captaincies
— — Extent of the Inca empire in 1525
■ Inca temples
→ Principal colonising routes (with names of explorers)
Dutch colonies
French colonies
English colonies

1000 km
600 miles

1520   1650   1750

480 550 700
78   10   130
78   100
10   10   6·5
     3·5 11

Estimated world population (in millions)
Estimated American Indian population (in millions)
Estimated European population (in millions)
Head of cattle in America (estimated in thousands)

© Creative Cartography Ltd. © The Hamlyn Group

Colonies and commerce

37 Colonisation and settlement in South America
The Americas continued to offer apparently limitless land for colonisation until the end of the 19th century, and in the Amazon basin until the present day. This map shows the beginning of the process, under Europe's first colonial powers. The diagram indicating populations refers to the Indian population of North and South America combined.

THE FIRST EUROPEAN colonial empire was that of Spain. By 1600 it was the largest and the most populous and productive. Theoretically, the Spanish crown claimed sovereignty over the Americas west of the line laid down by the treaty of Tordesillas in 1494 (*see Map 36*). In practice, wealth was concentrated in the fertile areas in central and southern America where the ranching of cattle and the cutting of woodland provided the basic necessities for the colonies. Except by the Jesuits, there was little settlement northwards from Mexico or eastwards from Peru. The ranch (or *hacienda*) became the chief productive unit. The other industry was silver, mined by Spaniards and Indians and requiring extensive initial investment. Neither *hacienda* nor mine employed Indians as slaves. A debate amongst theologians at Salamanca in 1550 had decreed that American Indians were not (the term was borrowed from Aristotle's *Politics*) 'slaves', although African natives were.

By 1700, the Spanish empire had suffered infringements. Portuguese smugglers had established themselves at the mouth of the Río de la Plata, a vital trade route through southern America to upper Peru. With Spanish encouragement the Jesuits colonised the wild Indian country in central southern America and reduced Uruguay to an ordered buffer-state. In the Caribbean, Dutch, English and French buccaneers plundered Spanish trade from Curaçao (which itself became Dutch from 1634), Jamaica (English from 1655) and Santo Domingo (French from 1665). But territorial losses were trifling and the Spanish remained the masters of the trade in the Pacific throughout the eighteenth century (*see Map 50*).

The problems of Spain's colonies were not territorial but structural and economic. Spanish trade across the Atlantic became depressed in the decade 1610 to 1620, and remained acutely so for the rest of the century. The interlocking economy of ranches, mines and plantations went into a severe recession, partly as a result of the depletion of the Indian population through plagues and a resulting acute shortage of labour (*Map 37*). The cost of mining and transporting silver outweighed the profit, so that the volume of silver produced reached its peak in the 1580s and dropped to its lowest point for a century in the 1650s. The colonies imported less from the Old World as they became self-sufficient. What trade there was ceased to benefit the merchants of Seville, who found themselves paying heavily for protection against piracy, attacked by the Inquisition for their suspect religious (or racial) background, and required to advance large sums of money to a rapacious Spanish monarchy, to keep its Catholic court solvent and its wars with the heretics active. The profits of the Spanish empire passed to smugglers who paid no duties and who were not obsessed by bullion, being prepared to take their returns in bulk cargoes such as sugar, hides and tallow.

The Portuguese overseas empire suffered the territorial depredations that the Spanish empire largely escaped. From 1580 to 1640, Portugal was politically united with Spain and, under the union, Portugal gained little and lost much (*Map 44*). Her colonies were able to trade only to a limited extent with those of Spain. Portuguese merchants found themselves harassed by the Inquisition, and taxed to pay for the Hapsburg's dynastic ambitions while her colonies, fair game to Spain's enemies, enjoyed no effective protection. Ceylon and Malacca were captured by the Dutch (*Map 39*); Goa declined to insignificance; African Guinea and Angola were conquered and a

profitable strip of northern Brazil was also annexed by the Dutch.

But, unlike those of the Spanish empire, the merchants of Lisbon (in collaboration with the new, independent House of Braganza) adapted, developed and strengthened what was left to them after 1640. They quickly regained Angola and expelled the Dutch from Brazil (*Map 37*). There, in the northern captaincies of Bahía and Pernambuco, João IV, the first Braganza king, established sugarcane. Northern Europe in particular was sugar-starved and in the seventeenth century the plantations of Brazil, equipped with elaborate mechanical gins and refineries, supplied Europe with enough sugar to turn the product from an aristocratic delicacy into something of popular consumption. Sugar became the first trans-oceanic bulk cargo.

To operate the mills and tend and cut the cane required slave-labour. Sugar and slavery were, from the beginning, intimately associated (*Map 51*). In Brazil the natives were nomadic, shy and primitive and their enslavement was forbidden. There were no such problems with African negroes, and the inland slave markets in the Black Monarchies of Angola provided a suitable source (*Map 50*). Boats on an outward voyage from Lisbon shipped slaves at Louanda, sailed to Bahía on the trade winds, and returned to Portugal, again with the wind behind them, filled with refined sugar. It was an ideal navigational and trading pattern.

The Dutch copied the Portuguese with larger mercantile resources, and with speed and success. The Portuguese eastern empire had been gained quickly by piracy and force. It was equally quickly dismembered by the Dutch in the early seventeenth century, using the same methods (*Map 50*). Muslim traders—even Portuguese trading stations—did not hesitate to trade with the new rivals. In some respects, though, the Dutch were different. Their merchants operated as a single trading company. A national charter of privileges guaranteed their monopoly status, organised such administration, jurisdiction and defence as were necessary, and enabled their risks to be shared. As a result, the Dutch operation in the East Indies never suffered from a shortage of capital and it was able to expand the range of goods shipped from the east. Not content with spices, peppers, tea, chinaware and gruff-goods (saltpetre and cottons), the Dutch governor-general introduced coffee-beans into Java and the first small shipment of Javanese coffee reached Amsterdam in 1712. It was a marketing triumph and soon coffee was one of the most profitable items of Dutch trade.

Secondly, the Dutch used the active bullion market in Amsterdam—developed during the days of shipments of Spanish silver to the Netherlands (*Map 44*)—to buy precious metals with which to pay cash for the goods of the East. Because there was no commodity that Europe could readily sell to the Orient the commerce of the East Indies remained, even for the Dutch, vulnerable to changes in the price of bullion in Europe.

Thirdly, the Dutch exploited the 'country' trades, the port-to-port conveyance through the Indian Ocean and towards the China Sea, of pilgrims to Jidda, of piece-goods to the Red Sea and the Persian Gulf from Surat and Bombay; from Madras to the many ports of the Moluccas. Other European nations established rival East India Companies. The English Company prospered during the seventeenth and eighteenth centuries and a French

Colonies and commerce

Compagnie des Indes orientales was founded by Colbert in 1664. But they suffered from government interference, interloping, and the indolence and petty corruption natural to great corporations. None had such a wide basis for the barter of spices and such a well-established mercantile position in the east as the Dutch (*Map 39*).

The Dutch also attempted to establish a commercial presence in the West Indies from the middle of the seventeenth century. But they never secured a firm footing against the English and the French, who were vigorously backed by their respective governments. By 1713 the days of the pirates were over and the pattern of control of the Caribbean islands was clear, governed by a treaty (the Peace of Utrecht in 1713), fully recognised and guarded by naval forces. The West Indies became part of the regular pattern of European diplomacy, and in particular of the rivalry between England and France, both of whom became accustomed to send fleets to the Caribbean at the beginning of any European war. All the colonies of English North America put together were still of less value in 1750 than a dozen sugar islands. The West Indies supplied more English imports and accounted for more English exports both in value and quantity than the American colonies (*Map 50*).

By 1700 the eleven English colonies of the north American mainland occupied a continuous strip of coastal territory (*Map 38*). Two days' travel inland brought one to untouched Indian country. Boston, the largest town, had only 7000-8000 inhabitants. Economic activity was on a small scale. The largest enterprises were those of the tobacco planters of Virginia and Maryland (*Map 51*). If their winters had been warmer they would have grown sugar. As it was they were tied to a product that exhausted the land quickly, required heavy labour, and declined steadily in price throughout the eighteenth century. Only the enormous size of their holdings and their slave labour enabled the Virginian planters to maintain their position. The other colonies were, from a commercial point of view, thoroughly unsatisfactory. Pennsylvania, Delaware, and Philadelphia were modest *émigré*-settled states of self-sufficient farming communities. New York traded with pirates and privateers and was a constant nuisance to the English government. The New England farmers worked small estates and frustrated the English government's attempts to monopolise the area's wood for ships.

The English colonists of the mainland did not only fail to live up to expectations. They also broke laws. In 1651 and again in 1667, the English Navigation Acts had established the basis of a network of rules designed artificially to direct the flow of English colonial commerce. Colonists were to trade only with their mother country. They were encouraged (by bounties) to produce the goods which England lacked and discouraged (by duties) from rivalling home industries. Goods were to be transported, in English ships, direct to the 'mother' country. In practice the legislation was regularly ignored. New England colonists exploited the country trades with both French and English islands of the Caribbean. They sold provisions to the French sugar-islands in time of war and traded directly with continental Europe.

The burden of defending the colonies grew greater in the eighteenth century. French colonisation reflected the absolutism of its founders. From the beginning it was regimented by the state, with the result that the French settled far more of northern America than the British and began to constitute a threat both to the fur trade in the north and to English settlements along the Mississippi. The European war of 1756 to 1763 was also fought in America, between Britain and France. It was natural that the English government should wish to tax its colonists to defray the cost of defence. But by their charters the colonies possessed elected assemblies which, in practice, could neither be dislodged nor ignored. When pressed by the English government, they revolted and won their independence from the Crown in 1776 (*Map 53*).

The success of the rebellion appeared to be a disaster for British colonial expectations. But subsequent developments emphasised what liberal economists like Adam Smith were already preaching—that trade did not depend upon colonial dominion but upon economic power. The Industrial Revolution in Britain, founded in part on the wealth generated by the old colonies, provided the dynamic for a new imperialism. England's reaction to the disaster was to explore new areas for dominion. James Cook explored the remainder of the oceans, discovering Australia in 1775, Mungo Parke set off from the Gambia in search of the Niger twenty years later, and the British East India Company expanded its territorial hold on mainland India.

Another form of liberalism also changed the nature of colonialism at the end of the eighteenth century. During four centuries of the European slave trade, ten million Africans were exported to slavery, of whom some 60% were transported between 1720 and 1820. At this time, the English, French and Portuguese handled 90% of the trade and the English share in most years was equal to the combined total of the others. Public opinion among the educated in Europe had never accepted slavery entirely, but moral unease and rational disquiet had stopped well short of wholesale condemnation. From the late eighteenth century abolitionists in America and England rejected all distinctions. The Quakers in America and the Evangelicals (known as the 'Saints') in England mounted an unprecedented campaign as a result of which slavery was abolished in most of the states of north America north of Pennsylvania (1780) and England abolished the slave trade in its own commerce (1807) [*see Map 51*]. By 1824, slaving was declared piracy on the high seas and the efforts of the British navy to enforce the legislation were a tribute to its preeminence in the oceans. By 1820 Britain, alone of the colonists of Europe, possessed the self-confidence, righteous arrogance and naval force to infuse its commercial dominance with a sense of didactic responsibility which disguised its imperialism as the establishment of a guardianship over the less-developed world.

Further reading: J. H. Parry, *Trade and Dominion* (Weidenfeld and Nicolson, 1971; Cardinal, 1974); C. ver Steeg, *The Making of America: The Formative Years: 1607-1763*; C. R. Boxer, *The Dutch Seaborne Empire* Hutchinson, 1965; Penguin, 1973); C. R. Boxer, *The Portuguese Seaborne Empire* (Hutchinson, 1969; Penguin, 1973); R. Pares, *War and Trade in the West Indies* (Oxford University Press, 1936); P. D. Curtin, *The Atlantic Slave Trade* (Wisconsin University Press, 1967; p.b.).

38 Colonisation and settlement in North America
The colonisation of North America began later than that of the South, and more powers participated in it. The Caribbean became the centre of the most intensive competition between them; England was the main beneficiary and Spain, the original colonising power in central America, the main loser.

Spanish
French
English

Areas colonised by 1640
Areas colonised by 1750
Frontier lands in 1750
Dutch colonies
Jesuit mission states
Principal colonising routes
Aztec empire in 1519
Aztec temples
Forts and fortified trading posts
Fur-trade routes
UTE Indian tribes in frontier regions
Spanish audiencia
Principal routes of colonial trade

0 1000 km
0 600 miles

Hudson Bay

FISH

Rupert's Land
(Hudson Bay Co. Ltd.)

SKINS

Newfoundland

Ft la Tourette
(1684)

Ft St Charles   Ft. St. Pierre

NIPISSING

Tadoussac
(1600)

Île St Jean
Île Royale

OTTOWANS

Québec
(1608)

MAHICANS

FISH

Sault Ste Marie
(1668)

Trois Rivières (1634)
Montréal

St. Lawrence

Nova Scotia

New Hampshire (1629)

HURONS
NEW FRANCE

Fort Orange
(Albany)

Salem (1628)

New Plymouth (1620)

Boston

MOHAWA

Fort Nassau (1614)

New Haven
(1636)

New Amsterdam (New York) (1646)

Rhode Island (1663)

Breuckelen (Brooklyn) (1646)

ROCKY MTS

SERRANO

HUPI

ZUNI

UTE

Santa Fé
(1609)

Missouri

WICHITA

TAWAKONI

KICHA

Philadelphia

GRAIN

NEW NETHERLANDS
(1616; English occ. 1664)

Maryland (1632)

Fort Necessity
(1754)

LOUISIANA

THE THIRTEEN COLONIES

Jamestown (1607)

Virginia (1624)

TOBACCO
RICE
INDIGO

El Paso
(1659)

Coronado
(1540-3)

APACHE

OPATA

De Alarcón
(1540)

Fort Prudhomme
(1682)

APALACHE

San Antonio
(1718)

SKINS

New Orleans
(1718)

Mississippi

Pensacola
(1696)

Ft. Caroline
(1562)

St Augustine
(1565)

Atlantic Ocean

Rio Grande

Monterrey
(1596)

Culiacán
(1531)

Florida
(1513)

The Bahamas
(1646-)

Gulf of Mexico

Havana
(1515)

TOBACCO
SUGAR

Zacatecas

SILVER

Guadalajara
(1531)

Mexico City
(Tenochtitlan)

LEATHER

Cuextatlan

AZTECS

Acapulco

Chichen Itza

MAYAS

Santiago
(1514)

Española (1492)

Santo
Domingo
(1496)

Santiago
(Jamaica)
(1509)

Caribbean Sea

to Manila

Antigua
(1542)

GUATEMALA

Mosquito Coast
(1635)

Léon

Grenada
(1522)

Old Providence I.
(1631-41)

Pacific Ocean

Gulf of Darien

Nombre de Dios

© Creative Cartography Ltd © The Hamlyn Group

RUSSIA

Sakhalin

OUTER
MONGOLIA

Gobi

MANCHURIA

SINKIANG

INNER MONGOLIA

Willow Palisade

Mukden

Sea of
Japan

Peking

Pao-ting

Great Wall

T'ai-yuan

Pyongyang

KOREA

Lan-chou

Huang ho

Chi-nan

Seoul

TIBET

Hsi-an

Kai-feng

Taegu

Pusan

East
China
Sea

Fukuoka

Hirado

Nagasaki

Osaka

JAPAN

CHINA

Ch'eng-tu

Nanking

Wu-ch'ang

An-ch'ing

Yangtze

Su-chou

Hang-chou

Kagoshima

Kuei-yang

Nan-ch'ang

Ch'ang-sha

Fu-chou

T'an-sui

T'ai-wan

Ryukyu Is.

Yün-nan-fu

Kuei-lin

Hsi-chiang

Ch'uan-chou

Anpeijo

Takao

BURMA

Canton

Pescadores Is.

Macao

Hanoi

Haiphong

Pegu

Rangoon

Vinh

Kagayan

SIAM

Hué

Suran

Kachan

Faifo

GREAT
VIETNAM

Manila

San Miguel

PHILIPPINES

Paknam

Bangkok

CAMBODIA

Phnom Penh

Saigon

South
China
Sea

Ringoru

Singora

Pattani

Kotabaru

MALAYA

Brunei

Pacific Ocean

Malacca

Johore

SUMATRA

BORNEO

Ternate

Halmahera

Chidor

Jambi

Kotawarinki

CELEBES

Moluccas

Bacan

Seram

Ambon

Banda

NEW GUINEA

Bantam

Batavia

Makassar

JAVA

Surabaya

(Port.)

TIMOR

Arafura Sea

Indian
Ocean

	Manchu homeland
→	Route of Manchu entry into China
	Territories under Manchu control by 1640
	Territories under Manchu control by 1645
	Territories under Manchu control by 1650
	Territories under Manchu control by 1660
	Territories under Manchu control by 1685
	Territories under Manchu control 1690-1730
◉	Imperial capital
○	Seats of governors of Manchu Empire
⊕	Seats of Governors-General of Manchu Empire
◆	Manchu Banner garrisons
	Japanese trading routes until 1633
	Japanese official 'red seal ships' trading routes
	Harbours used by Japanese trading vessels
⊙	Places with Japanese townships
○	Places where Japanese resided
	Main routes of Japanese armies. 1592-6
	Main routes of Japanese armies. 1597-8
	Netherlands territory
	Spanish territory

1000 km
600 miles

The age of European supremacy III

The Eurasian land empires

BOTH CHINA and Japan looked back to the philosophy of Confucius and developed it in different ways into a powerful ideology serving the practical needs of empire. In China, Confucianism stood for benevolent and patriarchal bureaucracy with a mildly conservative, conformist and inward-looking stamp. In Japan, by contrast, it was a newer ideology, only officially adopted by the Tokugawa dynasty in the early seventeenth century, expressly imported upon a Chinese model to uphold a warrior aristocracy (turned bureaucracy) and an autocratic emperor (*see Maps 39 and 40*).

Ming China was an impersonal empire. An ambitious forceful emperor could act decisively but the weight of tradition guarded by the mandarins of the largest and most impressive bureaucracy of the early modern world limited his power. Central government was located in the planned capital of Peking after 1421, and its six ministries supervised major areas of imperial life through a carefully organised provincial administration which extended to the borders of old Han China. Mandarins were recruited nationally through rigorous examinations. Incompetence and corruption were checked by the Office of Censors, to which young bureaucrats were seconded to censure their elders and advance themselves through their zeal and integrity.

The military power of the empire (by contrast) was separate and subordinate. Positions in the army were hereditary, and the quality of the armed forces gradually deteriorated. Troops were stationed defensively along the (partially) reconstructed Great Wall. Although the Tartars advanced to the gates of Peking in 1556, the Ming dynasty was largely spared heavy pressure on its landward frontiers.

The prosperity of the Chinese empire in the sixteenth century reflected its political stability. It was first disrupted by the Japanese invasion of Korea in 1592 and 1597 (*Map 39*). The Japanese were repulsed, but the economic stagnation of many regions in the next century increased the relative cost of the administration, and peasant rebellions enfeebled the central government. The emperor, surrounded by up to 10,000 eunuchs, withdrew to the seclusion of his court, and left power entirely in the hands of a divided bureaucracy. These weaknesses were exploited by the Manchu, militarily formidable neighbours on the north-east border who, partly under Mongol influence, rejected Chinese overlordship about 1609. They took Peking in 1644 and in another four decades had firm control over the whole of China and Taiwan. Whereas the Mongol Yüan dynasty had ruled China through foreigners, the Manchu relied on the established machinery of imperial government to control the former empire, while their vast new territories were ruled by a newly-created Court of Colonial Affairs that worked through local rulers and chiefs (*see Map 40*).

Sixteenth-century Japan was an island kingdom, with no real central government, political stability or civilian rule. In theory sovereignty resided in the emperor, in the court at Kyoto, but in practice power had passed through civil war from the hands of his hereditary military commander (the *shogun*) to local overlords (*daimyōs*) who commanded a hereditary caste of warriors (the *samurai*). Under the *daimyōs* Japan suffered a century of fierce warfare and shifting allegiances. Powerful Buddhist monasteries and merchant guilds added to the forces of fragmentation, while self-governing leagues of farmers and landowners were formed to resist the *daimyōs*.

From this confusion a series of military leaders emerged to attempt, often with great cruelty, to impose their authority upon Japan. Odo Nobunaga took Kyoto in 1568 and destroyed the Buddhist temples, massacring 20,000 monks. His lieutenant and successor Hideyoshi eliminated the remaining opposition, appointed himself chief minister and legalised the position of the *samurai* as an exclusive nobility of the sword. Hideyoshi's ambitious and unsuccessful invasions of Korea failed to consolidate his rule and it was left to his former councillor, Tokugawa Ieyasu (appointed *shogun* in 1603) to complete the work of his predecessors by imitating rather than irritating the Chinese empire. He founded a bureaucracy, imported Confuciansim, established a new imperial capital at Edo (Tokyo) and provided the basis for the *Pax Tokugawa* that lasted for two hundred years.

The *Pax Tokugawa* was, like the Manchu dynasty in China, an oriental *ancien régime*. The rigid caste system exploited the peasantry and allowed no social mobility. 'The offspring of a toad is a toad; the offspring of a merchant is a merchant' was the saying in Japan. Japanese towns and merchants benefitted particularly from peace. By 1691 Edo, with its population of over half a million, became one of the largest cities in the world. Here, as in other Japanese cities, the wealth of merchant townsmen supported a refined patrician culture, similar to that in the towns of China.

In both China and Japan, the Confucian *ancien régime* excluded Europeans. Portuguese overtures at Canton were rebuffed and only allowed to return to China at Macao in 1557 (*see Maps 36 and 50*). The Dutch operated from Taiwan from 1626 until they were expelled in 1662. Only the Spanish maintained a regular presence for trade at four open coastal ports, and only the Jesuits were allowed into Peking, where they accepted Chinese customs and dressed their Christianity in Confucian disguise until they too were expelled, in the eighteenth century. But their missionary efforts (like Europe's trading ventures) remained superficial. In Japan, the Europeans were initially more successful. From 1540 the Portuguese (exploiting political uncertainty and the dislike of Buddhist monks) established a lucrative trade monopoly based on Nagasaki, and fostered Christian churches and seminaries. Under Tokugawa rule official tolerance quickly diminished; persecution began in 1629. By 1650 some 2,000 Christians (including 70 European priests) had been killed. From 1639 trade with outsiders was forbidden except that Chinese and Dutch traders were allowed to call at Nagasaki once a year. China and Japan remained almost closed to the wider world until the nineteenth century, when the impetus of western imperialism destroyed their isolation (*see Map 64*).

The great Islamic powers in the sixteenth and seventeenth centuries were Ottoman Turkey, Safavid Persia and Mughal India (*see Maps 41 and 42*). They had much in common. Each was centred about a great capital city: Istanbul, Isfahan and Delhi. For each, Islam was not only a religion but a social and political code, essentially urban, worn lightly by some of its adherents and subject to some internal dissension, but still a common bond. Each city throughout the Islamic world had its mosque, built on an axis oriented on the heavenly city, Mecca, to which all Muslims turn in prayer. Arabic was a *lingua franca* for religion, government and law.

For all three empires, the sixteenth century was one of

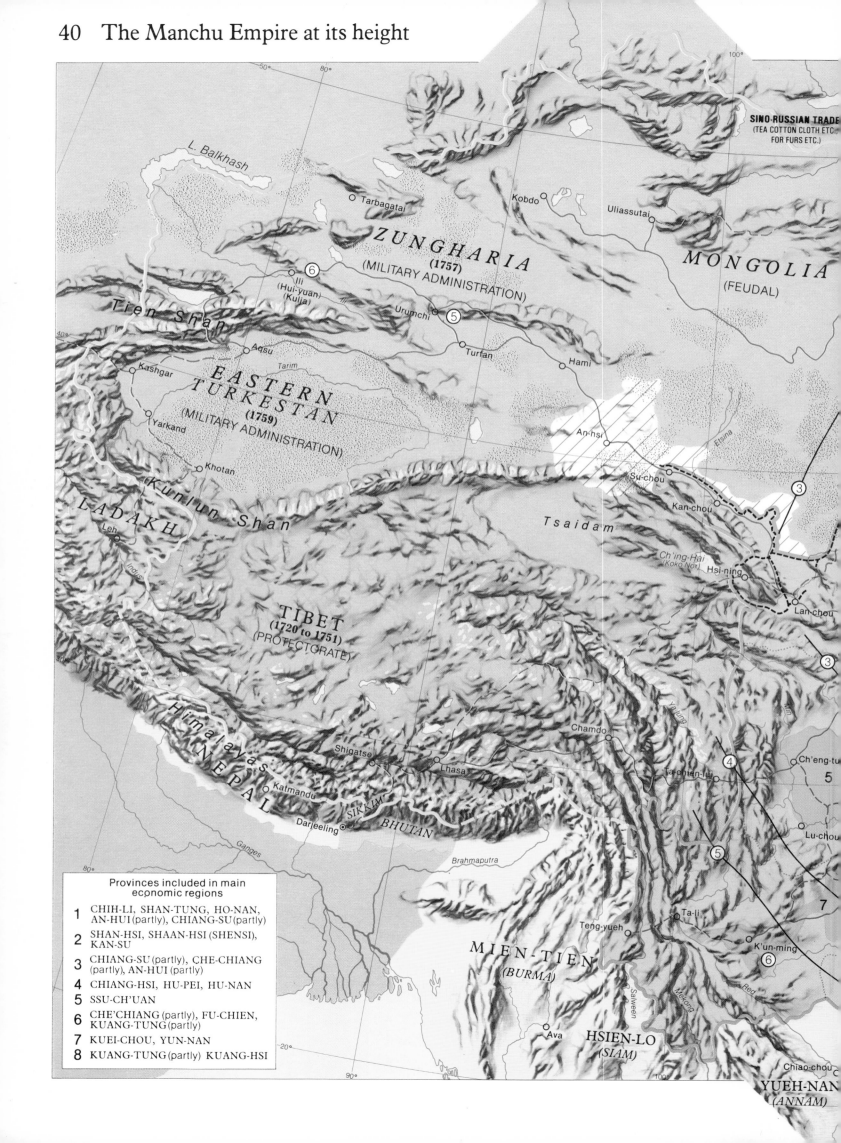

SINO-RUSSIAN TRADE
(TEA COTTON CLOTH ETC.
FOR FURS ETC.)

L. Balkhash

Tarbagatai

Kobdo

Uliassutai

MONGOLIA
(FEUDAL)

ZUNGHARIA
(1757)
(MILITARY ADMINISTRATION)

6
Ili
(Hui-yuan)
(Kulja)

Tien Shan

Urumchi

5

Aqsu

Tarim

Turfan

Hami

Kashgar

EASTERN
TURKESTAN
(1759)
(MILITARY ADMINISTRATION)

Yarkand

An-hsi

Su-chou

Kunlun Shan

Khotan

Tsaidam

Kan-chou

3

LADAKH

Leh

Ch'ing-Hai
(Koko Nor)

Hsi-ning

Indus

Lan-chou

TIBET
(1720 to 1751)
(PROTECTORATE)

3

Yalung

Chamdo

4

Himalayas

NEPAL

Shigatse

Ta-chien-lu

Ch'eng-tu

5

Katmandu

Lhasa

Darjeeling

SIKKIM

BHUTAN

Brahmaputra

5

Ganges

Ta-li

7

Teng-yueh

Lu-chou

MIEN-TIEN
(BURMA)

K'un-ming

6

Salween

Mekong

Red

Ava

HSIEN-LO
(SIAM)

Chiao-chou

YUEH-NAN
(ANNAM)

Provinces included in main economic regions

1 CHIH-LI, SHAN-TUNG, HO-NAN, AN-HUI (partly), CHIANG-SU (partly)

2 SHAN-HSI, SHAAN-HSI (SHENSI), KAN-SU

3 CHIANG-SU (partly), CHE-CHIANG (partly), AN-HUI (partly)

4 CHIANG-HSI, HU-PEI, HU-NAN

5 SSU-CH'UAN

6 CHE'CHIANG (partly), FU-CHIEN, KUANG-TUNG (partly)

7 KUEI-CHOU, YUN-NAN

8 KUANG-TUNG (partly) KUANG-HSI

Nerchinsk

Kiakhta

Mai-mai-ch'eng

Urga

Aigun

Tsitsihar

MANCHURIA

G o b i

Ördös

Amur

Sungari

Liao

Chi-lin

Ning-hsia

Sui-yuan
Kuei-hua
Kalgan
Je-ho
Mukden
(Sheng-ching)
Nui-chuang

Yalu

CHAO-HSIEN
(KOREA)

T'ai-yuan
PEKING
T'ien-chin
Pao-ting
Cheng-ting
Te-chou
Lin-ch'ing
Chi-nan

Mouth of Huang-ho
after 1853

Teng-chou

P'ing-jang

Ching-ch'eng

JAPAN

Wei
Hsi-an

Huang-ho

1

2

K'ai-feng
Hsu-chou

Huai-an

Mouth of Huang-ho
before 1853

YANGTZE-MANCHURIA
TRADE
(COTTON CLOTH AND TEA
FOR SOYA BEANS ETC.)

Nagasaki

Han

Hsiang-yang

Yang-chou

Nanking
Ho-fei
Chen-chiang
Su-chou SC
T'ai
Hu-chou C Sung-chiang
S
Hang-chou

Shang-hai

3

SINO-JAPANESE TRADE
(SILKS, SUGAR, DRUGS ETC.,
FOR COPPER ETC.,)

Wan-hsien
Yangtze
Han-k'ou
An-ch'ing
Chiang-ling
Han-yang Wu-ch'ang
Chiu-chiang
Shao-hsing W
Ning-po

Chung-ch'ing

4

Yo-chou
L. Po-yang
Ching-te-chen P

L. Tung-ting
Ch'ang-te
Ch'ang-sha
Nan-ch'ang
Wen-chou

Hsiang-t'an

Kuei-yang

Heng-yang

Fu-chou

3

L'IU-CH'IU ISLANDS

Kan-chou
Ting-chou
Ch'üan-chou
6

T'AI-WAN – MAINLAND
COAL EXPORT TRADE

Kuei-lin
Hsi-chiang
Chang-chou
Amoy
Ch'ao-chou

T'an-sui
T'AI-WAN
(1683)
(Civil administration)

4

5
Nan-ning
Wu-chou
8
Fo-shan I
Macao
(Portuguese)
Canton
Hui-chou
Swatow

SINO-S.E. ASIAN TRADE
(FABRICS, METAL GOODS, PORCELAIN ETC.,
FOR WOODS, RICE, RAW COTTON ETC.)

SINO-WESTERN TRADE
(SILVER OPIUM (ILLEGALLY) ETC.,
FOR TEAS, SILKS, PORCELAIN)

Chiung-chou

HAI-NAN

The Ming Empire c.1600
Regions of the Manchu Empire administered
by the Court of Colonial Affairs
Regions acquired by the Manchu,
administered by imperial bureaucracy
(1683) Date of establishment of Manchu rule
Tributary states of Manchu Empire
Tributary states of Lhasa
Wall rebuilt late 14th century
Wall rebuilt 15th-16th centuries
Wall rebuilt 16th century
Major imperial courier routes
② Maximum time in weeks permitted for
mounted courier from Peking
Other courier and trading routes
Willow Palisades (northern limit of legal
migration by Han Chinese)
Economic regions: core areas
Economic regions: peripheral areas
⊙ Major trading centre
◉ Port open to western trade after 1757
Grand Canal
Desert

0   500 km
0   300 miles

I   Ironware exporting centre
W   Wine exporting centre
P   Porcelain exporting centre
S   Silk exporting centre
C   Cotton exporting centre
SC Silk and cotton exporting centre

© Creative Cartography Ltd © The Hamlyn Group

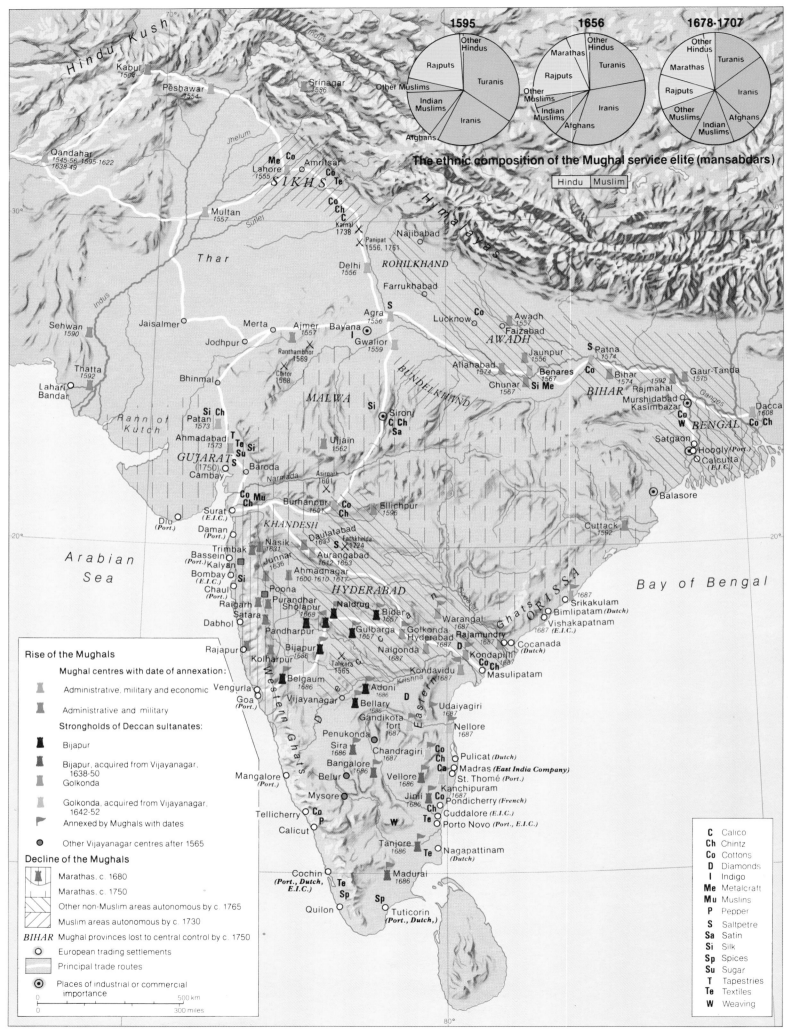

The ethnic composition of the Mughal service elite (mansabdars)

1595 | 1656 | 1678-1707

Hindu | Muslim

Rise of the Mughals

Mughal centres with date of annexation:

- Administrative, military and economic
- Administrative and military

Strongholds of Deccan sultanates:

- Bijapur
- Bijapur, acquired from Vijayanagar, 1638-50
- Golkonda
- Golkonda, acquired from Vijayanagar, 1642-52
- Annexed by Mughals with dates
- Other Vijayanagar centres after 1565

Decline of the Mughals

- Marathas, c. 1680
- Marathas, c. 1750
- Other non-Muslim areas autonomous by c. 1765
- Muslim areas autonomous by c. 1730
- *BIHAR* Mughal provinces lost to central control by c. 1750
- European trading settlements
- Principal trade routes
- Places of industrial or commercial importance

0 ____ 500 km
0 ____ 300 miles

C	Calico
Ch	Chintz
Co	Cottons
D	Diamonds
I	Indigo
Me	Metalcraft
Mu	Muslins
P	Pepper
S	Saltpetre
Sa	Satin
Si	Silk
Sp	Spices
Su	Sugar
T	Tapestries
Te	Textiles
W	Weaving

© Creative Cartography Ltd © The Hamlyn Group

41 The India of the Mughals
Between 1526 and 1636 the Mughals, from a base in Afghanistan, acquired control over most of the Indian subcontinent by seizing military and administrative centres along the main trade routes. Until the reign of Aurungzib (r.1668-1707) a balance between its various peoples was maintained in their administration; thereafter growing disunity and disaffection among the ruling elites undermined Mughal control, to the benefit of the intruding European powers.

42 The Ottoman Turks
The Ottoman challenge to Christendom began in the early 14th century. The capture of Constantinople in 1453 was followed by increasingly rapid expansion until the empire reached its strategic limits under Süleyman the Magnificent (r.1520-66).

43 The rise of Muscovy
Moscow's position at the intersection of the great trade routes and the ruthless determination of its Grand Dukes to subordinate every resource and institution to their power, suppress their fellow princes and shake off the rule of the Mongols (to whom Ivan III stopped paying tribute in 1480) made Moscow the unchallenged centre of the emergent Russian empire.

creation, growth and consolidation. The Mughal dynasty was founded by Babur (d.1530), a military adventurer who saw himself as the heir to the Mongol empire of Chingiz Khan. In 1522, he seized Qandahar, the key to northern India, and took Lahore. Mughal authority was established throughout northern India within four years (see Map 41), and reached its height under Akbar (r.1556-1605). Similarly, the Ottoman Turks had established themselves in Anatolia, captured Constantinople in 1453 and continued to expand their empire, until it reached its height under Süleyman the Magnificent (r.1520-66) (see Map 42). He alarmed Christian Europe by capturing Belgrade in 1521 and the island of Rhodes in 1522, arriving at the gates of Vienna in 1529 and 1532. Persia, too, had its Akbar or Süleyman, in Shah Abbas I, known as the Great (r.1587-1629), whose reign dominated the memory of Persia through the seventeenth century.

In each case, the easy talent for the absorption of different cultures and racial and ethnic groups characterised these regimes in their early period of expansion (Map 41). Akbar I declared himself, in 1572, sole arbiter of religious matters in his realms and repealed all discriminatory taxes on racial and religious minorities within the empire. Avowing a policy of toleration, he embarked upon discussions with various religions, including the Portuguese Jesuits, and finally devised a new universal faith. Ottoman Turkey gave the Catholic peasantry of Hungary and the orthodox inhabitants of Greece a welcome release from the seigneurial burdens and intolerance of Reformation Europe. Christians, Muslims and Jews served in the famous slave-based Janissary corps of the Ottomans.

Their achievements brought the Muslim powers wealth and sophistication, but also created a burden of empire which could not be indefinitely sustained. Each, in turn, ended its expansion in the seventeenth century with enormous internal problems. Feeding and fuelling their inflated capitals became a major problem in itself when the decline in economic activity in the seventeenth century affected the Islamic empires, as it had done, to a lesser extent, the Oriental ones. Frontiers and the long lines of communication with them were an enduring problem. The Mughal Jahangir sent his armies into the Deccan, which all Mughal emperors aspired to conquer, and which became the obsession of his successor in the decade 1670-80 (see Map 41). The Mughals also struggled with military potentates in irrepressible Bengal and worried over the frontier city of Qandahar. In Persia Shah Abbas was forced into offensive war in Khorasan. Even Süleyman the Magnificent admitted defeat outside Vienna and for the most part in the western Mediterranean. His Ottoman successors were forced to loosen their grip on Algiers and Tunis, suffered rebuffs from the Muscovites on the Steppes, saw Cossack oarsmen in the Bosforos and were troubled by insubordinate tributary princes in Transylvania.

In the face of these problems, each empire in its turn looked to autocracy, centralisation and militarism as the immediate solution. But structural change did not come easily. In the Ottoman empire, the Janissaries rebelled frequently (the outbursts were customarily announced by the overturning of the barrack-room soup-cauldron). In Persia, Shah Abbas' standing army of Christians from Georgia and the Caucasus also rebelled. Centralisation caused provincial rebellions, such as those in Wallachia, Moldavia and Turkestan in the Ottoman empire and

Bengal in the Mughal empire. These revolts were serious because provincial governors exploited them to influence the imperial succession. Across the Islamic world, court intrigue surrounding the succession of the shah, sultan or emperor was a constant danger. There was no formal law of succession in any of the empires. Emperors existed by right of conquest and survived by their ability to eliminate rivals. The harems of the rulers ensured a regular supply of pretenders, and brutal practices were adopted to limit them. The Ottomans had a law which allowed successful emperors to put their rivals to death by strangulation with a silken bow-string. The Mughals tried to ensure a clear succession by nomination, but their efforts were ruined by ambition or bad blood. In Persia the practice of blinding royal princes who were potential contenders grew up from the end of the sixteenth century, and later both Persia and Turkey adopted the formal imprisonment of every heir to the throne. Enforced seclusion and incarceration led to an observable decline in the quality of their rulers.

The Islamic empires began to quarrel amongst themselves. War between Persia and the Ottomans, intermittent from 1502 onwards, became more violent in the seventeenth century. In the process the Islamic states adopted more exclusive ideologies; the Sunnite faith was preferred by the Ottomans and Shi'ite orthodoxy by the Persians. Both became less inclined to tolerate Christian and Jewish minorities. A rebellion among the Christians of Greece brought the European fleet (against orders) to Lepanto, where it won the sixteenth century's greatest offensive victory against the Ottomans. European merchants could not be excluded from the Islamic capitals, whose lavish tastes demanded fine cloth and precious metals. In their wake, later in the seventeenth century, came the rising military and naval power of Europe, whose colonial expansion the Islamic powers would find difficult to resist.

Despite the absorption of many Slavs into the Ottoman and Hapsburg empires, and the subjection of others to the Tartars, two separate Slav empires existed in the early modern world. On the borders of Europe Poland stretched from the Baltic to the Black Sea, while under Ivan III (r.1462-1505) the Grand Duchy of Muscovy threw off the Tartar yoke and made Moscow the centre of a Russian empire (see Maps 43 and 48). Both states expanded during the sixteenth century. In 1569 the kingdom of Poland, endowed with strong representative institutions, a vigorous aristocracy and (until 1572) a hereditary monarchy of the European kind, joined in a condominium with the Grand Duchy of Lithuania, to which it had been driven closer by the common threat from Muscovy. The expansion of Muscovy was far more remarkable. The whole area around the independent city of Novgorod was subjugated in 1478, the Kazan Khanate in 1552, and Astrakhan in 1556. From the accession of Ivan IV in 1553 the realm of Muscovy expanded in each year by an area equal to the size of Holland until, by 1600, it was as large as the whole of Europe.

Prosperity encouraged expansion. Russia gained the route across the Urals to Siberia and control of the Volga and the routes to the Caspian Sea, and would have liked a port on the Baltic. Russian fur-trappers moved easily across Siberia and by the middle of the seventeenth century, reached the Pacific Coast and the borders of China (see Map 70). New towns were established on the Volga and Belaya as visible signs of the wealth of the silk,

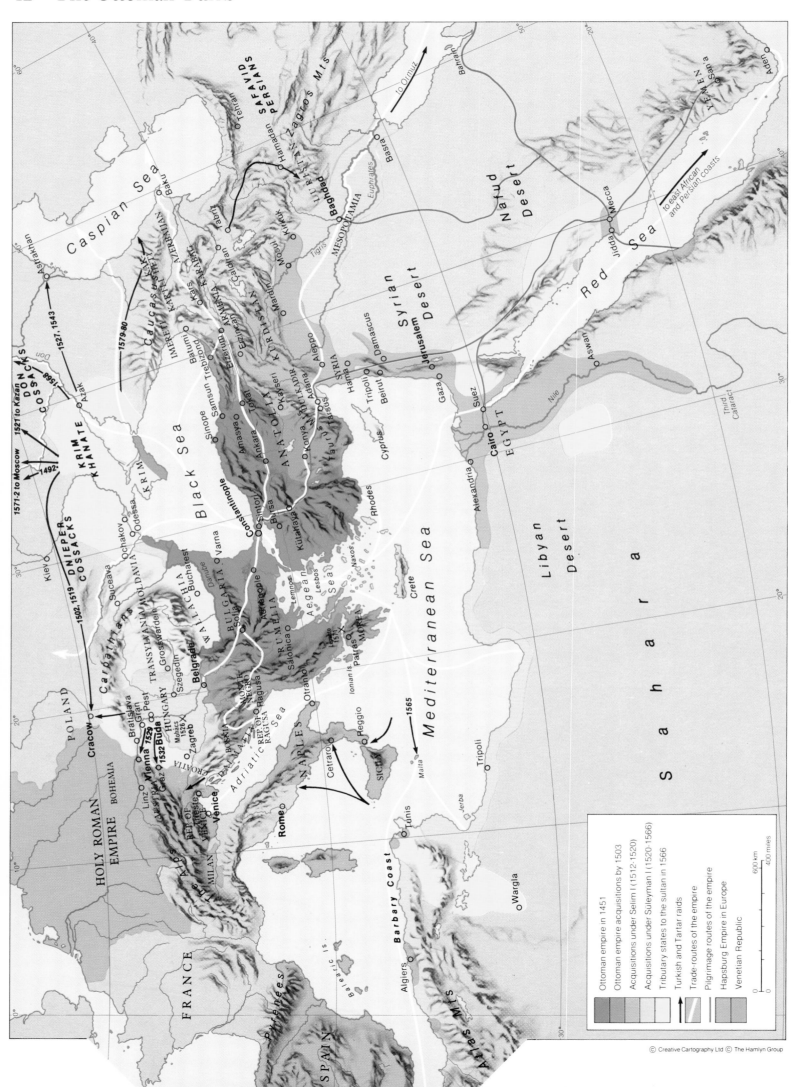

Caspian Sea

SAFAVID PERSIANS

Zagros Mts

LURISTAN

Baghdad

MESOPOTAMIA

Euphrates

Basra

to Ormuz

Bahrain

Nafud Desert

Red Sea

Mecca

Jidda

to east African and Persian coasts

YEMEN San'a

Aden

Astrakhan

1527, 1543

1556

1521 to Kazan

1571-2 to Moscow

1492

1579-80

DON COSSACKS

Don

Azak

KRIM KHANATE

KRIM

Kiev

1502, 1519

DNIEPER COSSACKS

Caucasus Mts

IMERETI KARTLI AZERBAIJAN

KAKETI

Batumi

Baku

Tehran

Hamadan

Tabriz

KARABH

Kars

Calfran

ARMENIA

Erzerum

Erzincan

Mosul

Kirkuk

Tigris

Mardin

KURDISTAN

SYRIA

Aleppo

Hama

Tripoli

Damascus

Beirut

Syrian Desert

Jerusalem

Gaza

Suez

Cairo

EGYPT

Alexandria

Aswan

Nile

Third Cataract

Libyan Desert

Trebizond

Erzurum

Okavseri

DULKADIR

Adana

Tarsus

Taurus Mts

Cyprus

Black Sea

Sinope

Samsun

Amasya

Ankara

Tokat

ANATOLIA

Konya

Bursa

Constantinople

Sinope

Kütahaya

Rhodes

Mediterranean Sea

Ochakov

Odessa

Suceava

MOLDAVIA

WALLACHIA

Bucharest

Danube

BULGARIA

Sofia

Varna

Adrianople

RUMELIA

Salonica

Aegean Sea

Lemnos

Lesbos

Naxos

Crete

Carpathians

TRANSYLVANIA

Grosswarden

Szegedin

Belgrade

MONT ENEGRO

Ragusa

REP. OF RAGUSA

Adriatic Sea

Otranto

Ionian Is.

Lepanto 1571

Patras

MOREA

Cracow

POLAND

Bratislava

Gran

Pest

1529

1532 Buda

HUNGARY

Mohacs 1526

Zagreb

CROATIA

BOSNIA

BALKANS

Linz

Vienna

Güz

AUSTRIA

Trieste

Venice

REP. OF VENICE

Alps

MILAN

HOLY ROMAN EMPIRE

BOHEMIA

Reggio

1565

Cetraro

SICILY

Malta

Tripoli

Jerba

NAPLES

Rome

FRANCE

SPAIN

Pyrenees

Balearic Is.

Tunis

Algiers

Barbary Coast

Atlas Mts

Sahara

Wargla

Ottoman empire in 1451

Ottoman empire acquisitions by 1503

Acquisitions under Selim I (1512-1520)

Acquisitions under Süleyman I (1520-1566)

Tributary states to the sultan in 1566

Turkish and Tartar raids

Trade-routes of the empire

Pilgrimage routes of the empire

Hapsburg Empire in Europe

Venetian Republic

600 km

400 miles

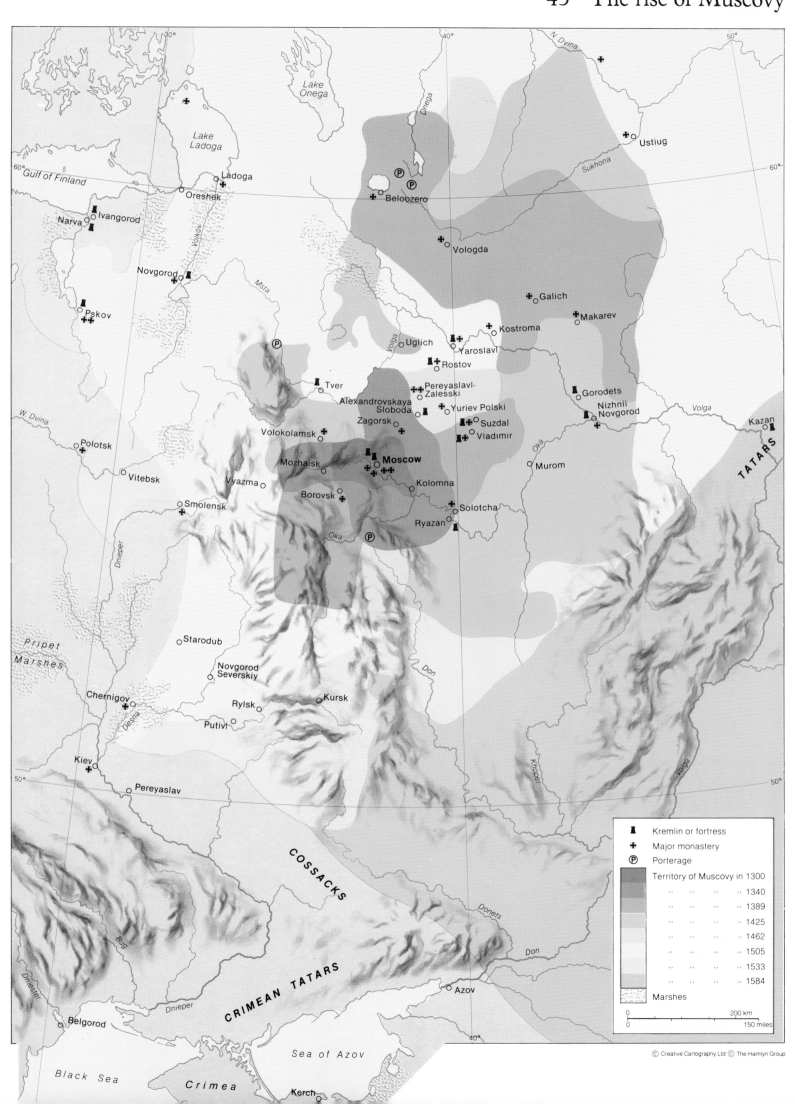

Lake Onega

N Dvina

Ustiug

Lake Ladoga

Onega

Sukhona

Gulf of Finland

Ladoga

Oreshek

Ivangorod

Narva

Novgorod

Pskov

Volkov

Msta

W Dvina

Beloozero

Vologda

Galich

Makarev

Kostroma

Uglich

Yaroslavl

Rostov

Volga

Tver

Pereyaslavl-Zalesski

Alexandrovskaya Sloboda

Yuriev Polski

Gorodets

Nizhnii Novgorod

Volga

Kazan

TATARS

Zagorsk

Suzdal

Vladimir

Volokolamsk

Mozhaisk

Moscow

Murom

Oka

Polotsk

Vitebsk

Vyazma

Kolomna

Borovsk

Solotcha

Smolensk

Ryazan

Oka

Dnieper

Starodub

Don

Pripet Marshes

Novgorod Severskiy

Desna

Chernigov

Rylsk

Putivl

Kursk

Khoper

Volga

Kiev

Pereyaslav

Don

Bug

Donets

Dnieper

COSSACKS

Don

Belgorod

CRIMEAN TATARS

Azov

Dniester

Kerch

Black Sea

Crimea

Sea of Azov

	Kremlin or fortress
✚	Major monastery
Ⓟ	Porterage
	Territory of Muscovy in 1300
	" " " " 1340
	" " " " 1389
	" " " " 1425
	" " " " 1462
	" " " " 1505
	" " " " 1533
	" " " " 1584
	Marshes

0   200 km
0   150 miles

© Creative Cartography Ltd © The Hamlyn Group

The Eurasian land empires

rug and precious metals trade with Persia. Meanwhile Poland extended its authority over the old Hanseatic ports of the Baltic, Danzig and Riga, (*Map 48*) and the resulting prosperity was demonstrated in newly-founded universities, churches and printing presses.

The foundations of Russia were entirely different from those of Poland. The essence of the Russian state lay in its patrimonialism. The tsars (as the grand dukes styled themselves officially from 1547, to emphasise their legendary descent from a brother of the Emperor Augustus) stressed that, on their hereditary lands, they were *gosudar*, supreme lord, ruler, autocrat. The land stewards of the patrimony (the *votchina*) provided the basis for the expanded and from the 1550s reorganised state official-dom (the *prikazi*). Trade in the Duchy had always been the private possession of the grand dukes and the tsars extended this monopoly over wholesale commerce and the manufacturing and mining industries of Russia at large.

Outside the domain of the grand dukes of Muscovy were the lands of the *boyars* (the aristocracy) and the Church. Since feudalism had never been established in Russia there was no vassalage or conditional land tenure to provide a law common to the aristocracy and the tsar. As Moscow extended its influence the *boyars* were gradually subjected to the will of the tsar, beginning in the 1470s when Ivan III denied their freedom to serve another prince. In the sixteenth century the tsars created new nobles and rewarded loyal service. In 1564 Ivan IV (the 'Terrible') divided the country clearly between his domain (*oprichnina*) and the rest (*zenichina*) so that in the former he could enforce his authority more vigorously. *Oprichniki*, a group of tsar's bailiffs, were permitted to abuse or kill the *boyars* in the domain with impunity, and to loot their properties. Although the *oprichniki* were withdrawn in 1572 the power of the *boyars* was destroyed and private land in secular hands no longer played a significant role in Muscovite Russia. The church retained its wealth, and the monasteries and kremlins (some of which were designed by German military engineers) of the duchy of Moscow provided a solid base for the government and internal security of the tsars. The Russian Orthodox church, with its own patriarchal structure, fitted well with the tsars' pretensions, and each reinforced the authority of the other.

Conquered territories were treated as the tsar's patrimony. Independent cities such as Novgorod lost their privileges, and mass deportations, which became common in the expansion of Russia, emphasised that, as a German traveller remarked in the middle of the sixteenth century, 'All the people consider themselves *kholops*, that is slaves of their Prince'. Serfdom also spread outwards from the patrimony of the tsar, where no peasant considered himself the owner of land or property. As peasants seized the opportunities which expansion offered to abandon the domain and colonise the new territories of the Kazan and Astrakhan the tsars abandoned the custom which had given peasants freedom to leave their masters on one day in each year, began to keep a close watch on their debts and dues, made systematic enquiries of their own rights and finally, in 1592, introduced serfdom. Most Russian peasants had become serfs by 1650.

By prodigious efforts and at great cost the tsars transformed Russia into a gigantic royal domain. The costs were highest in the seventeenth century. Dynastic uncertainties, peasant rebellions, revolts of the Cossacks to the south and of Lithuanians to the west, produced civil disturbance beside which that of Europe at the same time pales into insignificance. In the long run the autocratic system of the tsars emerged victorious, and under Peter 'the Great' (*r.1682-1725*) the Russian *ancien régime* began.

Not so in Poland. The Lithuanian-Polish condominium collapsed three years after it was established. With the extinction of the Jagiellonian dynasty, Poland adopted an elective kingship (in form rather like that of the neighbouring Holy Roman Empire) but without a strong, well-endowed dynasty like the Hapsburgs to give it direction and muscle (*compare Map 44*). In the elections of the following centuries members of the European ruling dynasties were chosen as kings and pursued their own dynastic interests to the detriment of Polish peace and security. Poland's magnates (unlike the *boyars*) successfully defended their individual patrimonies and held the great offices of state. In a state racially, culturally, religiously, ethnically and politically divided, the monarch's authority rapidly gave way to the creeping political paralysis (disguised by the weaknesses common to all states in the seventeenth century and by a certain conservative tolerance born of potential anarchy) which became evident in the eighteenth century and would make Poland the despair of the *philosophes* and the prey of the autocrats.

Further reading: R. Dawson, *Imperial China* (Hutchinson, 1972; Penguin, 1976); P. Spear, *A History of India*, Vol. 2 (Penguin, 1965); A. R. Lewis, *Knights and Samurai* (Temple Smith, 1974); H. Inalcik, *The Ottoman Empire* (Weidenfeld & Nicolson, 1973); R. E. Pipes, *Russia under the Old Regime* (Weidenfeld & Nicolson, 1974; Penguin, 1979); F. Braudel, *The Mediterranean and the Mediterranean World in the Age of Philip II* (Collins, 1972-3; Fontana, 1975).

Europe divided

THE DECISIVE event of the early sixteenth century was the Protestant Reformation. It split Europe into two camps. Like all powerful ideologies, Protestantism had a distinct message which divided families, cities and states. At first it was fostered in the fast-expanding universities. Later, Protestants would establish their own academies in Strasbourg, Geneva and elsewhere to teach their vigorous analysis, refine their own theology, and attack that of their opponents. The cities of Europe were also growing rapidly (*Map 46*), and in them, the new ideology found an interested literate laity. Persuasive Protestant preachers and theologians—Martin Luther in Wittenberg, Ulrich Zwingli in Zurich, Jean Calvin in Geneva, Jacob Sturm in Strasbourg—aided by the enormous diffusive power of the new printing press, could compel attention, create controversy and capture converts.

Ideologies are seldom fully developed in their first generation. Lutheranism spread from Wittenberg in Germany from 1517. During its first decade it had a liberating effect in much of western Europe, but it became the official religion only in German-influenced areas, spreading with the support of princes and their courts (*Map 45*). It offered no new view of society; when groups of Anabaptists, who did so, emerged in Lutheran areas preaching indifference towards constituted authority, and even sometimes a sharing of worldly possessions, they were always as firmly repressed as they were by the Catholic Charles V at Münster in 1535.

The second generation reform—Calvinism—spread from Geneva from 1536. It was ideologically more compelling. It offered a new model for society without the inherent anarchy of Anabaptism. Calvin created a new model Church with committees of pastors and elders to enforce its hard, clear, effective moral discipline. Refugees from Catholic persecution throughout Europe came to Geneva. They were sent out again as an élite—the Saints—to conquer, destroy and replace the 'great worldly Babylon'.

The seed of the Calvinist Church was found in the blood of martyrs. Initially, official persecution created refugees. Later, in the second half of the sixteenth century, sectarian conflict dominated the politics of Europe. Calvinists held up to ridicule, menace and abuse the Catholic images, crosses, shrines, feast-day processions, burials and marriage services. The Dutch religious wars started in this way with the 'iconoclastic' riots of 1566. Catholics retaliated against the defiling of their sacred things by taking the blood of Protestants. The massacre of St Bartholomew in France in 1572 began as a government-inspired attempt to eliminate Protestants but became, under popular Catholic enthusiasm, a season of pogroms in major French cities, and a climax to the forty years of religious wars.

At first, Calvin had tried to convert peacefully; but under the pressure of persecution, his successor in Geneva, Beza, openly advocated the deposition of the persecutors. And faced with persecution, Calvinism was forced back on to a narrow social base. It became the religion of urban republics, sometimes reaching out for support from other social groups—lesser princes, turbulent magnates, backwoods gentry or the urban poor—but always retaining its urban and semi-republican ethos.

By the 1560s, the Roman Church seemed everywhere on the defensive. All Europe north of the Alps and the Pyrenees was lost or endangered; the princes were uncertain, the nobility heavily Protestant, the clergy converting.

But Roman Catholicism developed a powerful authoritarian counter-ideology. The formal statement of this came in the decrees of the Council of Trent, which concluded its sessions in 1563. When it had first met, summoned by the Emperor in 1545, its purpose had been to reunite and purify the Church and to reverse the 'Monarchical' tendencies of the Papacy. Its effect was otherwise; instead of restoring authority to the bishops, it confirmed their subjection to the Papacy, and presented in hardened form the doctrine of the absolute obedience of both laity and clergy to the Papal See.

Thenceforth Rome became like one of the courts of the great European princes. The Hapsburgs—whose own swelling courts were the envy of the rest of Europe—fought their wars, centralised their government, increased their taxes, sold offices, sent out permanent ambassadors to Europe and elsewhere and planned their capitals (*Map 44*). The popes did likewise, and with Spanish-Hapsburg strength behind them, Catholicism triumphed in Europe and America (*Map 37*). Spanish power even protected Italy against the Turks (*Map 52*).

The Catholicism of the Counter-Reformation became the religion of princely courts and bureaucratic and hierarchical societies. Its spiritual force came with the Jesuits. Their powerful casuistry was disseminated through a network of educational institutions in Europe and in the New World. Their political influence grew, and gradually they became linked to the Spanish court. Thanks to the Portuguese Jesuits, Philip II gained the crown in Portugal in 1580. The Jesuits promised him the crowns of England and France too. Spanish interests lurked behind the Jesuits who penetrated Lutheran Sweden and Orthodox Russia. It was as Spanish agents that they were expelled from Japan in 1640.

The Catholic Counter-Reformation reached its climax in 1630. Bavaria, Poland, Austria, France and the southern half of the Netherlands had been recovered by preaching and by force. In 1621 Rome had celebrated the destruction of Protestantism in Bohemia. In 1629, La Rochelle, the last Huguenot citadel of France, had been reduced (*Map 49*). In the same year, the Jesuits were advancing northwards to the Baltic. The victories were not all at the expense of Protestantism. To the east they attached a portion of the Greek Orthodox church to their cause, and Catholic missionaries counted the Red Indian of Canada, the war-like daimyos of Japan and even—they liked to think—the Confucian Mandarins of China among the souls they had saved.

But in one major respect, Catholic victories were pyrrhic ones. In the decades of persecution the Catholic princes of Europe expelled the Calvinists and with them their financial reserves and mercantile and manufacturing skills. The industrial heart of Europe was displaced. After the iconoclastic riots the Protestants persecuted in the Spanish Netherlands moved north and east across the Rhine. The massacre of Saint Bartholomew sent French silk workers from Lyons across the Jura. In the seventeenth century, the Catholic reconquests scattered Calvinists from Bohemia, the Palatinate and the Baltic to Protestant regions. As a result, the towns of Holland and Zealand—Amsterdam, Haarlem, Delft—inherited the prosperity of Catholic Antwerp, and the cloth industry of Hondschoote (*Map 46*). The North Sea cities—Bremen, Hamburg and Emden—were enriched from the shattered urban life of the Catholic southern Netherlands. The cities of the Rhineland—the Palatinate and Alsace—

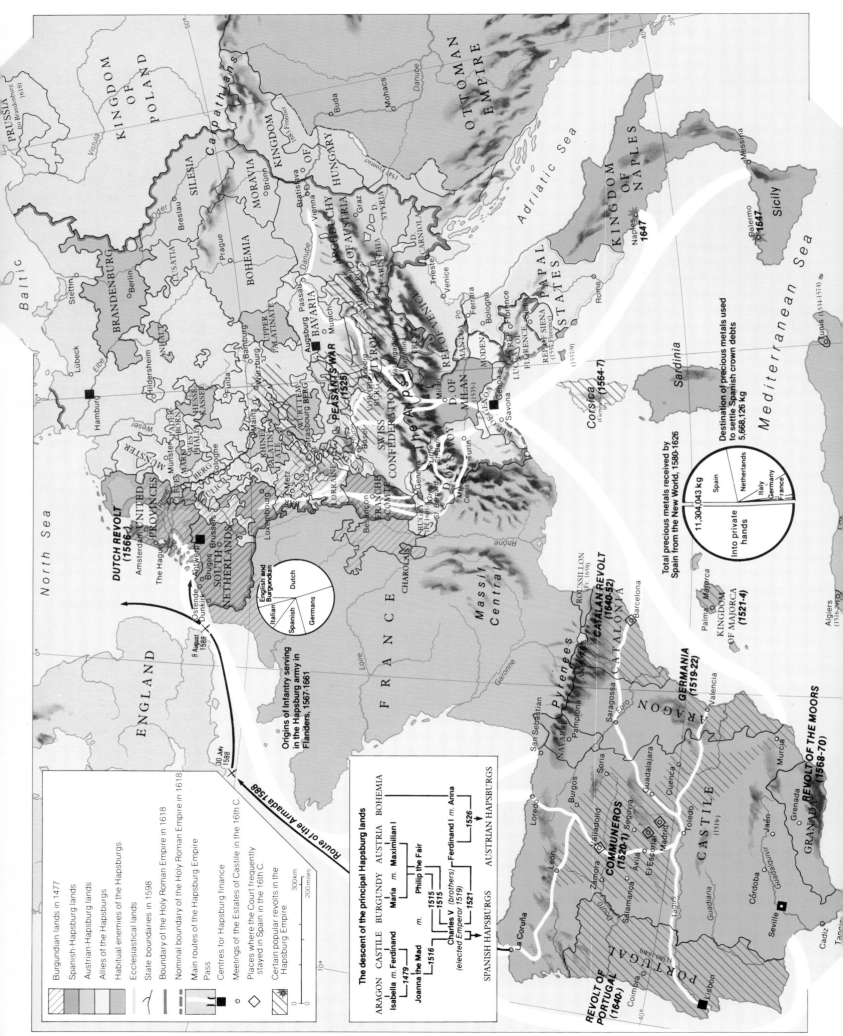

44 The Hapsburg empire
The devolution of the succession to four royal houses on Charles of Hapsburg between 1515 and 1519 and his election as Holy Roman Emperor in 1519 created a unique empire. Its territorial extent, claim to absolute rulership and championship of Catholicism threatened almost every interest and made it the focus of European politics for the next two hundred years.

45 Reformation and Counter-Reformation in Europe
The spread of Protestantism and the development of a variety of sects within it provided Europe with a range of ideologies to match the profusion of its courts and the increasing complexity of its social structure. The Catholic Reformation assisted the traditional powers to counter it with new vigour.

46 The rise of the Atlantic economies
In 1500 the Mediterranean was still the commercial, industrial and financial heart of Europe. In the years of economic crisis which began about 1610 the 'Atlantic economies' of England and Holland advanced at the expense of Spain and Italy through technical innovation, colonial expansion and the exploitation of the resources of the Baltic.

47 The Thirty Years War
The 'Thirty Years War' was in reality a series of conflicts between a succession of contenders for supremacy in post-Reformation Europe, among which France emerged victorious. The scale, duration and bitterness of warfare led to a degree of depopulation which crippled the empire for generations, although its extent cannot be measured with precision.

benefitted from the Calvinists expelled from France and from the prince-bishoprics of the Empire. Switzerland was a reservoir into which France, Germany and Italy drained its refugees. On the Atlantic coast, tolerant, Anglican England was a refuge for Huguenot weavers.

The economic consequences would have been less serious if Europe's economy had continued to expand. In the sixteenth century – particularly in the first 50 years – the population of Europe was growing, its cities were more wealthy, its economic activity increasing. The merchants of Antwerp, Venice and Seville traded further and deeper across the Baltic, through Germany, into the Levant, into Brazil and across to America (*Maps 35 and 46*). But this pace and confidence could not be sustained at an even rate. Shortly after 1600 it halted or slowed down. First here, then there, the economy of the European states trembled mysteriously. What was the cause of this 'decay of trade'? Was it purely economic? There certainly were weaknesses in the economic system of Europe: it was vulnerable to plagues and disease; its transport remained cripplingly limited; technological change was slow; markets for manufactured goods were relatively small. Was it purely financial? Certainly the decline in the amount of silver imported from the New World (and still the main material for coinage) went hand in hand with the general contraction. Was it the climate? Europe was indeed colder and wetter in this century than in the sixteenth and some historians have spoken of a 'mini ice-age'. Or was it the result of the growing burden of administrative centralisation, particularly in Catholic states? We do not know precisely. What is clear is that the effects of stagnation were felt unevenly in Europe.

Spain, despite its overseas wealth and its military power felt the European-wide shortage of resources most keenly. It had ceased to be able to feed itself. Disastrous plagues in the 1590s decimated its inland population; its coins depreciated to become shadows of their former sovereign glory (*Map 46*). Italy and the Mediterranean felt the same process less severely. Further north, Holland escaped these ravages. Financial constriction was avoided and capital introduced by *emigrés* was put to good use in modest technological endeavours. The Dutch became drainage engineers across the whole of northern Europe, thus releasing new land for cultivation. Their famous fly-boats brought a revolution in bulk-carrying cargoes at sea. Their industries produced products which were saleable across a broad European market – cheap, durable cloth, mass-produced Delft tiles, sugar-enriched wines, salted fish. In the wake of the Dutch Wars, which reached a truce in 1609, Amsterdam became the successor of Antwerp as Europe's mercantile centre. Its Protestant neighbours also found their currencies and their economies more stable, their cities growing. This new strength enabled the Dutch to break into the oceans of the world and establish themselves at the centre of an East Asiatic empire which lasted until the twentieth century (*Maps 50 and 67*).

Economic crisis and European war came together. From 1618, the energies of Europe were turned inwards to be consumed in the long, destructive contest of the Thirty Years War (*Map 47*). This was a complex of wars, a pattern of rival imperialism amongst the European land-empires. Spanish ambitions in the Netherlands and the Baltic, Saxon ambitions in Germany, Swedish ambitions in the Baltic, all encouraged the fears and hopes of their various satellite powers. At the beginning, it was also a

war of ideologies, of the Counter-Reformation against Calvinism. As such it flowed across boundaries and was never a purely German affair. The war began in Bohemia with the mobilisation by the Elector Palatine of his Protestant allies in England, Holland, and other minorities elsewhere to support his election as King of Bohemia. It could have started earlier, perhaps when the conversion to Protestantism of the elector of Cologne had caused the Cologne war in 1583, or when the death of the duke of Cleves in 1609 could have plunged Europe into war but for the timely assassination of King Henry IV of France. Ranged against the Elector Palatine was the Hapsburg Empire. For the Hapsburgs it was a parasitic war. Economically bankrupt (as they admitted) after expelling their productive subjects, war seemed the only way of nourishing their court and the privileged society which regularly consumed more than it generated. It enabled them to suck from the heretics the sustenance they could not create themselves. The Austrian Hapsburgs devoured Bohemia, Bavaria, the Upper Palatinate, just as the Lutheran princes – Denmark, Sweden and Saxony – absorbed Lusatia and the German coastal littoral as the reward of supporting their fellow Protestants.

But the Thirty Years War marked the end of religious ideology. In their imperialism, the European monarchs took up strange alliances across the ideological divide. Protestant Sweden intervened in Germany in 1631, funded by Catholic France. Catholic Bavaria joined the Protestant princes in Europe against the Hapsburgs. Albrecht von Wallenstein, of doubtful personal religious conviction, fought the Emperor's wars for him as a mercenary and used Protestant bankers. The material destruction which caused the depopulation of swathes of Germany (especially the Elbe and lower Rhine regions) and the devastation of its cities, discredited the ideologies that had permitted such savagery. The peace of Westphalia, which ended the wars in 1648, was not attended by a representative of the Papacy or ratified by the Pope.

When all was over, who had gained and who lost? Politically, it is clear. The Spanish empire in Europe was broken, the Hapsburg Empire was shaken. Saxony and Bavaria had demonstrated their independence; Brandenburg followed where they led (*Map 52*). Above all France had a firm government, clearly defined boundaries, and boundless influence in Germany (*Map 49*). But the Thirty Years War destroyed far more than Spanish hegemony. It destroyed a whole system. In the cataclysm, the hierarchical courts of the Counter-Reformation, with their patronage, their swollen officialdom, and parasitic economies, were broken. Even some Protestant countries with courts – such as England – suffered the same fate. The international churches were broken too; the Roman Catholic church destroyed the international effectiveness of the Calvinists only to weaken itself fatally in facing the challenge of scepticism in the next century. The new forms of government – sober republics and mercantilist-minded absolutist states based on rationalised privileges – which had recently germinated, began to show themselves after 1660. The European *ancien régime* was beginning.

Further reading: R. H. Tawney, *Religion and the Rise of Capitalism* (J. Murray, 1926; Penguin, 1938); A. G. Dickens, *Reformation and Society in Sixteenth-Century Europe* (Thames & Hudson, 1966; p.b.); *The Counter Reformation* (Thames & Hudson, 1969; p.b.); J. H. Elliott, *Europe Divied* (Fontana, 1968); C. V. Wedgwood, *The Thirty Years War* (Cape, 1938).

FINLAND (1528)

ESTONIA (1542)

LIVONIA (1542)

COURLAND (1561)

Riga

TEUTONIC ORDER PRUSSIA (1530) (under Polish Suzerainty from 1466)

Königsberg

KINGDOM OF POLAND

Warsaw (1572)

Consensus Poloniae, 1570/1595

Confessio Pentapolitana, 1545

MORAVIA Confessio Hungarica, 1562

Danube

Uppsala

Danzig

Vistula

(Northern Mission) (1673/78/88)

Stettin

Oder

BOHEMIA

Prague (1576-1612)

Confessio Bohemica, 1575

Breslau

SILESIA

Vienna (1524)

Graz (1581-1621)

Baltic Sea

SWEDEN (1527)

Confessio Augustana, 1593

Lund

Lübeck

POMERANIA

MECKLENBURG (1548-9)

BRANDENBURG (1539)

Berlin

SAXONY (ELECTORATE) (1539)

Wittenberg (1524)

Dresden

Leipzig

Zwickau

Salzburg

Regensburg (1538)

BAVARIA

Munich (1573/83)

Innsbruck

NORWAY (1539)

Confessio Augustana, 1536/1607

Skagerrak

DENMARK

Confessio Hafnica, 1530

SCHLESWIG (1542)

HOLSTEIN (1542)

Elbe

Hamburg

Magdeburg (1525)

(DUCHY) (1526)

Mühlhausen

HESSE-KASSEL

FULDA

Augsburg (1573/83)

Ulm

WÜRTTEM-BERG (1534)

DonauWörth

North Sea

Bremen

EMDEN (1526) (1542)

BREMEN

Bc. MÜNSTER

Dortmund

Cologne

Rhine

Maastricht

NASSAU (1528)

Frankfurt (1539)

WÜRZBURG

B. BAMBERG

ANSBACH (1528)

Halle

Worms (1546)

Speyer (1559)

RHINE PALATINATE

UPPER PALATINATE

Nuremberg

Strasbourg

Basel (1529)

Münster

Zurich

Luzern

Groningen

Utrecht

Münster

Amsterdam

Leiden

Breda

Ghent

Antwerp

Middleburg

Tournai

Lille

Confessio Belgica, 1559/61 (1594/97)

Meaux

Troyes

Paris (1500)

Rouen

SCOTLAND

Scottish Mission (1653/94)

Saint Andrews

Confessio Scotica, 1560

Glasgow

ENGLAND

English Mission (1623/88)

York

Norwich

Canterbury

Act of Supremacy, 1534
Act of Uniformity, 1549
Act of Uniformity, 1552
Recatholicisation, 1554
Act of Uniformity, 1559

English Channel

IRELAND (1536)

Dublin

FRANCE

Confessio Gallicana, 1559

Alençon

Angers

Loire

Saumur

Marmoutiers

(French Congregation,

Bourges

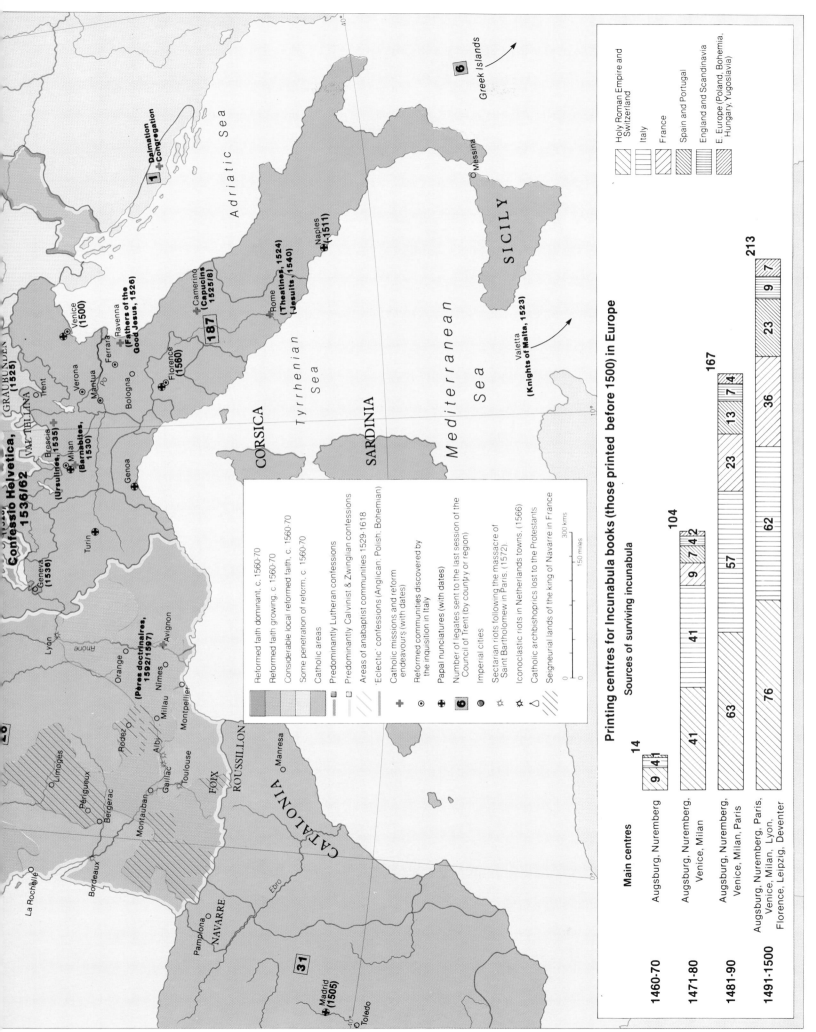

Printing centres for Incunabula books (those printed before 1500) in Europe

Atlantic
Ocean

FISH

FISH

SWEDEN

• Stockholm

North
Sea

Baltic Sea

POLAND

FISH

DENMARK

Copenhagen

• Edinburgh

Danzig
(Guilders)

Whitby

Oder

Lübeck

Hamburg

Berlin

Breslau

Vistula

York

FISH

Magdeburg

Malvern Close

Hatfield Chase
Holland Fen

Norwich

UNITED
PROVINCES

Haarlem

Amsterdam

HOLY ROMAN
EMPIRE

Prague

Cracow

Great
Yarmouth

Leiden

(Guilders)

Weser

London
(Pound Sterling)

Canvey Is.

Bristol

Bromley
Marsh

Bruges

Antwerp

Cologne

Rhine

Nuremberg

Tatra
Mts.

Southampton

Ghent
Dunkirk

Louvain

Plymouth

Dieppe

Amiens

Rouen

(Florins)

Strasbourg

Augsburg

Vienna

Danube

Seine

Paris

FRANCE

(Ecus)

Graz

Drava

Loire

Tours

The Alps

Udine

Bay of
Biscay

Geneva

Milan

Brescia
Verona

Trieste

Lyon

Turin

Cremona

Padua

Venice

OTTOMAN
EMPIRE

Bordeaux

Garonne

Po

Bologna

Genoa

(Ducats)

Florence

Ancona

Adriatic Sea

Toulouse

Rhône

Nîmes

Avignon

Leghorn

Pyrenees

Marseilles

Rome

Valladolid

SPAIN

Barcelona

Naples

Madrid

Lisbon
(Cruzados)

Toledo

Valencia

GRAIN

Cordoba

Alicante

Palermo

Messina

Seville

Granada

Mediterranean Sea

Syracuse

Cadiz

Algiers

Tunis

To and from
the New World

POPULATION OF
SELECTED TOWNS 1600

⊙ over 250,000
⊙ 80-120,000
⊙ 50-70,000
○ 30-40,000
• other towns

POPULATION DENSITIES c.1620
(per sq. km.)

rising population
static population
declining population

Over 40 inhabitants
20-40   "
5-20   "
Under 5   "

Areas of cloth production
Areas of metal production
Areas drained by Dutch engineers
in the seventeenth century
Trade routes
Movement of exchange rates of major European
currencies against the Dutch guilders on the
Amsterdam market across the century. 1609-1700/9.
For France and Portugal, the base year is 1619.
● devaluation   ◐ evaluation

0   400 km
0   200 miles

© Creative Cartography Ltd © The Hamlyn Group

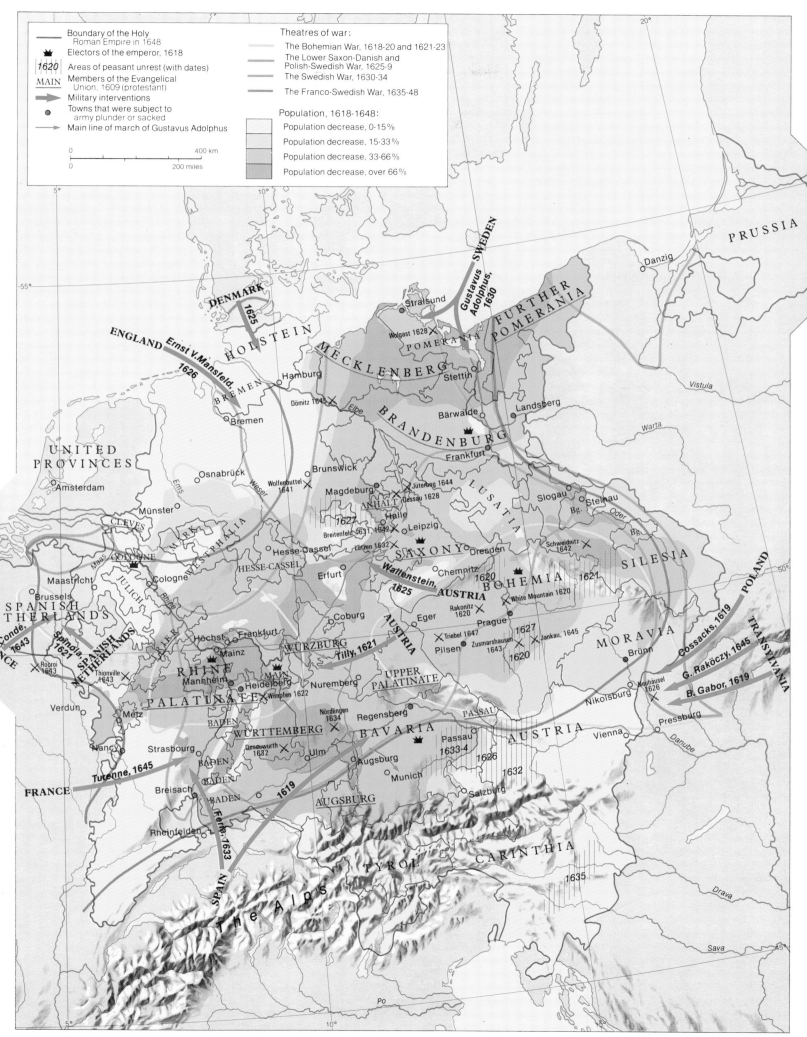

Boundary of the Holy
Roman Empire in 1648
Electors of the emperor, 1618
1620 **Areas of peasant unrest (with dates)**
MAIN
Members of the Evangelical
Union, 1609 (protestant)
Military interventions
Towns that were subject to
army plunder or sacked
Main line of march of Gustavus Adolphus

Theatres of war:
The Bohemian War, 1618-20 and 1621-23
The Lower Saxon-Danish and
Polish-Swedish War, 1625-9
The Swedish War, 1630-34
The Franco-Swedish War, 1635-48

Population, 1618-1648:
Population decrease, 0-15%
Population decrease, 15-33%
Population decrease, 33-66%
Population decrease, over 66%

0　　　　　　400 km
0　　　　　200 miles

PRUSSIA
Danzig
SWEDEN
Gustavus Adolphus, 1630
FURTHER POMERANIA
Stralsund
Vistula
DENMARK
1625
Wolgast 1628 ✕
POMERANIA
HOLSTEIN
ENGLAND
Ernst v.Mansfeld, 1626
MECKLENBERG
Stettin
Landsberg
BREMEN
Hamburg
Dömitz 1645 ✕
Elbe
Bärwalde
BRANDENBURG
Warta
Bremen
Frankfurt
UNITED PROVINCES
Osnabrück
Wolfenbüttel 1641 ✕
Brunswick
Magdeburg ✕
Jüterbog 1644 ✕
LUSATIA
Amsterdam
Slogau
Steinau
Ems
ANHALT
Dessau 1628 ✕
Oder
Bg.
Münster
Weser
1627
Halle
Bg.
CLEVES
Breitenfeld 1631 ✕ 1642 ✕
Leipzig
Schweidnitz 1642 ✕
MARK
Hesse-Cassel
Lützen 1632 ✕
SAXONY
Dresden
SILESIA
COLOGNE
WESTPHALIA
HESSE-CASSEL
Erfurt
Chemnitz
1620
Maastricht
Cologne
Wallenstein, 1625
AUSTRIA
BOHEMIA
1621
JULICH
Rhine
White Mountain 1620 ✕
POLAND
SPANISH NETHERLANDS
Brussels
Coburg
Eger
Rakonitz 1620 ✕
Prague
Cossacks, 1619
Condé, 1643
Spinola, 1621
Höchst
Frankfurt
WÜRZBURG
Triebel 1647 ✕
1627
Jankau, 1645 ✕
MORAVIA
TRANSYLVANIA
FRANCE
SPANISH NETHERLANDS
Mainz
Tilly, 1621
Pilsen
Zusmarshausen 1643 ✕
1620
Brünn
G. Raköczy, 1645
Rocroi 1643 ✕
Thionville 1643
RHINE
MAIN
AUSTRIA
Neuhäusel 1626 ✕
B. Gabor, 1619
Verdun
Mannheim
Heidelberg
Wimpfen 1622 ✕
Nuremberg
UPPER PALATINATE
Nikolsburg
PALATINATE ✕
Nördlingen 1634 ✕
Regensberg
PASSAU
Vienna
Pressburg
Metz
BADEN
WÜRTTEMBERG ✕
BAVARIA
Danube
Nancy
Donauwürth 1632 ✕
Ulm
Passau 1633-4
AUSTRIA
Strasbourg
BADEN
Augsburg
1626
Turenne, 1645
BADEN
Munich
1632
FRANCE
Breisach
BADEN
1619
Salzburg
AUGSBURG
Rheinfelden
Feria, 1633
1635
SPAIN
TYROL
CARINTHIA
THE ALPS
Drava
Sava
Po

© Creative Cartography Ltd © The Hamlyn Group

Norwegian Sea

Arctic Circle

White Sea

LAPLAND

Archangel

Bergen

TRONDHEIM
1658-60 to Sweden
JÄMTLAND
(1645)
HÄRJEDALEN

Västerbotten

Gulf of Bothnia

Österbotten

CARELIA
(1617)

L. Onega

KINGDOM OF DENMARK AND NORWAY

KINGDOM OF SWEDEN

COPPER
IRON
Falun

Vasa

FINLAND

Lake Ladoga

Christiania

Åland Island

Uppsala
Västeras

Helsingfors

Gulf of Finland

Vyborg

RUSSIAN EMPIRE

Reval
Narva

INGRIA
(1583-95, 1617-)

Novgorod

Stockholm

HEMP

ESTONIA
(1561)

(1658)

L. Vänern

L. Vättern

Linköping

Dagö
(1582)

Ösel
(1645)

(1582)

Gulf of Riga

LIVONIA
(1621/29-1721)

Skagerrak

HALLAND

Jönköping

GRAIN FLAX HIDES

GOTLAND
(1645)

Riga
(1621/29)

DUCHY OF COURLAND

Düna

Smolensk

Jutland

Calmar

TIMBER COPPER IRON

Baltic Sea

Memel

Frederiksodde

Helsingborg
Brömsebro

Copenhagen
SKANE
(1658)

Zeeland
The Sound

Funen

Bornholm
(1658 to Sweden)

(Swedish occupation 1629-35)

Königsberg

PRUSSIA
under Polish
suzerainty to 1657

GRAIN

Minsk

Schleswig

Danzig

Lübeck

POMERANIA
(1648)

Elbing

GRAIN

LITHUANIA

Hamburg
(1648-1715)

Wismar

MECKLEN BERG

FURTHER POMERANIA

Bremen

Stettin

Pripet

BRANDENBURG

Elbe

Berlin

RUSSIANS

Vistula

Warsaw

KINGDOM OF POLAND

Kiev

Breslau

SILESIA

Prague

Cracow

PODOLIA
(1672-99)

COSSACKS

Carpathians

Dnieper

Dniester

Vienna

Danube

TURKISH EMPIRE

Legend

- Sweden in 1560
- (1561) Acquisitions by Sweden 1560-1660
- Swedish colonisation in Finland
- Denmark and Norway
- Poland in 1569 (maximum extent)
- Poland in 1700
- Northern limit of oak-trees (for Norway and Sweden)
- Seas and lakes frozen in winter

0   400 km
0   200 miles

The age of European supremacy V

The ancien régime

IN 1660, EUROPE emerged from a half-century of violent convulsions. The whole continent was at peace for the first time in over a generation. The last 'great rebellion' ended with the restoration of Charles II in England. Descartes' logical philosophical method enthroned human reason and seemed capable of resolving every intellectual problem. Demographic stagnation and areas of economic depression would persist into the eighteenth century, but this in its way was a facet of the social and political stability which was not radically disturbed for more than a century.

The basis of this stability was the pre-eminence of rich, hereditary landed oligarchies, most of which enjoyed nobility. Every state in Europe (except certain Swiss cantons) recognised the existence of a nobility. The French revolutionaries identified the principle of noble privilege as the essential component of the 'ancien régime' to whose destruction they were committed.

The doomed nobility of France was the prime example of European nobility. France was held to comprise three orders or estates–clergy, nobility and the third estate. This originated in the medieval division of society into those who prayed, those who fought, and those who worked. The noble order had a complex hierarchy of titles and enjoyed substantial precedence and privileges, notably personal exemption from taxation. By 1660, it not only fought but prayed (the overwhelming proportion of Louis XIV's bishops were old nobles) and worked for the state (his ministers were also old nobles). It enjoyed a certain lifestyle in which manual work, which included the retail trades, was forbidden and which, in practice, required the possession and cultivation of land. Perhaps a third of France was owned by the nobility, and this proportion was about average for Europe. In Denmark, by comparison, 85% of the land was owned by the nobility. In England, 400 noble families owned a quarter of the soil.

The attributes of the nobleman were universally agreed upon. 'Persons of Quality' (like the Englishman, Dr Burney) roamed across Europe, armed with a sheaf of letters of recommendation which opened up the polite society of metropolis and court along their route (see Map 52). The allurements of town and court life were irresistible and European nobles were divided between those who could afford them and the 'mere' squires who could not. In France, where residence in the royal palace of Versailles was the ultimate privilege, establishments had to be maintained in Paris, at court and in the country. Most ostentatious of all were the magnates of the Hapsburg empire, who not only resided at court in their Viennese palaces, but also built impressive country seats, of which the Esterhaz ('the Hungarian Versailles') was the most famous. With the European nobility went a European language (French), a cosmopolitan entertainment (music) and a common cultural attitude subsequently called 'Enlightenment'.

The central political problem for the nobility was to obtain a stable, firm government to maintain their privileges without at the same time encouraging despotism, or breeding democracy. In his *Leviathan* (1651), Thomas Hobbes, defending all forms of strong government, had argued that a sovereign power was the only source of authority, law and morality. 'The sovereign power . . . is as great as men can be imagined to make it. And although of so unlimited a power, men may fancy many evil consequences, yet the consequences of the want of it, which is perpetual war of every man against his neighbour, are much worse'. Tyranny, said Hobbes, was only a pejorative term for monarchy.

Hobbes' justification for the absolute power of the prince was used in France by Louis XIV's apologist, Bishop Bossuet, to construct a coherent theory of absolutism. The activity of Louis XIV enthralled Europe for fifty years and the memory of it haunted the eighteenth century (see Map 49). In many respects Louis XIV built upon the achievements of the Cardinal ministers Richelieu and Mazarin, who had introduced the bureaucratic mechanism of provincial government in the *intendants*, initiated an expansionist foreign policy, chastened the rebellious nobles in the *Frondes* (1648-53) and increased taxation. In other ways, Louis XIV's baroque taste for glory and sense of theatre led contemporaries to overestimate his absolutism. Nonetheless, he did dramatically expand the borders of France at the expense of the Hapsburgs, expel the Huguenots from his realm in 1685, and maintain a huge standing army and a developed navy. As a result, there was a reaction after his death since he had seriously undermined the privileges of the nobility, encountered peasant uprisings and resistance within the Catholic establishment, and built up a colossal debt which was stabilised only by multiple bankruptcies in the succeeding reign.

Nevertheless, others in eighteenth-century Europe followed Louis XIV's taste for glory. Prussia became a kingdom when the Elector Frederick III of Brandenburg was given a royal dignity in 1701 and crowned 'King in Prussia'. His military reforms created a standing army which his son used to make Prussia one of the leading powers in Europe (see Map 52). In Austria, Maria Theresa (r.1740-80) compensated for the loss of Silesia by imitating Louis XIV in her hereditary lands of Austria, Bohemia and Hungary. Even countries with a strong tradition of representative institutions established painfully in the wars of the seventeenth century, such as Sweden and the Netherlands, faced autocratic monarchs like Gustavus III (r.1772-92) and Wilhelm V (r.1766-1806). They constructed their pastiche Versailles, where royal, imperial, or ducal courts could enjoy the delicate interplay between ruler, minister, courtier, mistress and financier. Imitations stretched from Naples to Madrid, from Vienna to St Petersburg. But, significantly, the only miniature Versailles on English soil–Blenheim Palace–was constructed not for a monarch but for a general in retirement from the last of Louis XIV's wars.

As armies grew, the profession of arms took on a new meaning. Higher standards of discipline were exacted from officers. For the rank and file, developments included impressment, parade-ground drill and execution by firing squad. Other continental autocrats undertook expansionist wars with the same thread-bare justifications as Louis XIV's mixture of strategic, commercial and dynastic motives, but they added a pseudo-scientific jargon of the 'balance of power' to justify the Peace of Utrecht in 1713 or the first partition of Poland in 1773. Some have spoken of a century of limited warfare, but when reason of state demanded it there was brutality and extensive war. Louis XIV's armies devastated the Palatinate. Frederick II's laid waste Silesia. To pay for the wars, the autocrats established bureaucracies and increased indirect taxation on goods, windows, documents and stamps.

Like Louis XIV the eighteenth-century autocrats

The ancien régime

encountered opposition from philosophers, provincial nobles, peasants and the bourgeoisie. The philosophic Enlightenment is not easy to dissect. Philosophers, moralists, historians and political thinkers in eighteenth-century France, England and Germany gradually developed an optimistic faith in the power of human reason to reach a composite truth encompassing man and nature. They saw themselves engaged in a common battle against tyranny in politics, dogma in religion, superstition in science, prejudice in morals and hypocrisy in manners. The movement spread from England, where opposition to Louis XIV's absolutism was articulated in the works of John Locke, who set out to prove that absolutism was inconvenient, dangerous, unnatural and a threat to property. But Voltaire was, through his long life and prodigious output, the most formidable *philosophe*. His greatest works were composed during the last years of his life at his Swiss retreat, les Délices. His wit made the *ancien régime* ridiculous; his moral fervour made it hateful throughout the courts and salons of Europe. The philosophers created a climate of opinion in which change was seen as necessary and good. In their stress upon Truth, Equality and Liberty, they laid the foundations for the ideology of the revolutions.

The most divisive issues were the position of established religion and tolerance for minorities. Everywhere the established church was closely interlocked with the state and the aristocracy. Initially autocrats supported the church and repressed religious extremists, whether Huguenots, Jansenists or Quakers. But increasingly the 'enlightened' despots sought approval from their *philosophe*-inspired aristocrats and began to tolerate minorities. The expulsion of the Jesuits, (who had once been the confessors and advisors of the princes) proved universally popular. Their wealth and power had rendered them a source of much envy, particularly for their trading companies to the New World. They were expelled from Portugal in 1759 and the order was dissolved twenty-five years later. Austria tolerated Jews from 1781; the Huguenots were officially tolerated in France from 1787. Everywhere the exclusive religion of free-masonry appealed to aristocrats for whom an embattled and obscurantist church held no attractions. Under the influence of the *philosophes* the monarchs and aristocrats of Europe rendered the established churches vulnerable in the coming revolutions.

The opposition of provincial nobilities to the autocrats was patchy and sporadic. In Prussia the nobility was so involved with the army and administration that it obediently followed where the kings led. In Russia, Catherine the Great (r.1762-46) took care not to offend the nobility. But elsewhere in Europe, the provincial nobilities – in Ireland, America, Belgium or Hungary – felt that the powers of government had increased, were increasing and should be reduced (*see Maps 53 and 54*).

Peasant revolts were, likewise, sporadic. There were serious ones in Hungary in 1678-81, 1703-11, 1735, 1751, 1755, 1763-4, 1765-6 and 1784. They were provoked by increases in seigneurial dues but extended to complaints about taxes and tithes. Twenty thousand peasants were involved in the revolt of 1755, and in the Transylvanian rising of 1784 30,000 rebels butchered hundreds of nobles and their families. Similar revolts occurred in Russia. Further west, there was no serious peasant uprising after those at the end of Louis XIV's reign until the *Grande Peur* (Great Fear) of July 1789 (*Map 54*). The

reasons lie in agricultural prosperity and the diminishing frequency of crisis years in which famine, plague, war and heavier taxation struck simultaneously and left the peasant with nothing to lose but his life.

The cornerstones of this economic growth, particularly towards the middle of the eighteenth century, were the towns, and a non-noble élite – the *bourgeoisie* – dominated the towns as the nobles dominated the countryside. Many continental towns had a legally defined group of burghers (*bourgeois*), enjoying privileges and qualifying for the status through heredity, favouritism and great wealth. They were not a new group in the eighteenth century, but they grew both in numbers and wealth. By 1800, they easily outnumbered the titled nobility in western Europe, being about ten per cent of the population, though no more than three per cent in Hungary or Russia. Their wealth rapidly increased through trade, the professions, government investment and contracts, and prudent industrial ventures. Merchants in Marseilles, Bristol, Nantes, Cadiz, Cork, Hamburg; manufacturers in Manchester, Lyons and Barcelona; lawyers in the capital cities and judicial centres of Europe – all contributed to the expanding *bourgeoisie*.

It would be premature to speak of a bourgeois 'class-consciousness' anywhere before 1815 in sufficient strength to threaten the nobility or the autocrats. Only in particular circumstances did the bourgeois make use of their increased preponderance. When the forces of order failed to repress sedition, riots were sparked off by strikes, fears of bread shortage, taxation and religion. Riots in Geneva in 1781, in the towns of Holland in 1787, and in Paris in 1789 heightened the political awareness of the *bourgeoisie*. Religious dissent also separated some *bourgeois* from the common assumptions of their age sufficiently to articulate alternative ones. Baptist, Congregationalist, and Quaker merchants in England, Presbyterian manufacturers in Cork, Protestant financiers in Nîmes, Montpellier and Montauban, Jewish bankers in Berlin, Frankfurt or Hamburg were all apart from or opposed to the values of the *ancien régime* despite its palsied attempts at toleration towards the end of the eighteenth century. It is not a coincidence that the most outspoken leaders in England, America and France in the age of revolutions came from religious minorities.

In the hands of far-sighted autocrats structural change in the *ancien régime* would not have been impossible. But here lay the congenital weakness of absolutism. The painters of the eighteenth century leave nothing to the imagination. From their canvases rulers and their consorts stare out, pop-eyed and pompous, their bewigged, vacuous expressions revealing the emptiness of their minds. By the end of the eighteenth century western Europe lay in the hands of mad old George III in England, booby Wilhelm V in the Netherlands, erratic Joseph II in Austria and inadequate Louis XVI in France. Dominated by their diseases, their wives and their families, they present a picture not of individual misfortune, but of the generic and ineradicable disease of the *ancien régime*.

Further reading: A. Goodwin (ed.) *The European Nobility in the Eighteenth Century* (A. & C. Black, 1953); N. Hampson, *The Enlightenment* (Penguin, 1968); R. Mousnier, *Peasant Uprisings in Seventeenth-Century France, Russia and China* (Allen & Unwin, 1970); W. Doyle, *The Old European Order, 1660-1800* (Oxford University Press, 1978; p.b.); Voltaire, *Candide* (Penguin, 1970); *The Autobiography of Edward Gibbon* (Oxford University Press, World's Classics, 1907).

49 The ancien régime in France
The gradual absorption of the great fiefs by the French crown and the decay of regional institutions permitted the creation of a centralised bureaucratic government which, despite widespread and often prolonged local resistance, laid the foundations of absolute monarchy and territorial expansion.

50 Trade and dominion
The major European powers had established their colonial spheres of influence by 1750, and the colonies were returning substantial profits. Sugar, slaves and spices were among the most lucrative commodities, and North America, the Caribbean and India the principal theatres of wars to control them.

51 Slave economies of the Western Hemisphere
Reliance on imported slave labour was reflected in the changing patterns of crops and industries in the New World – each shown here at its period of greatest activity – as well as in regional variation. The early closure of the trade to the United States deprived its slave population of the unsubdued reinforcements from Africa who contributed significantly to the revolts endemic elsewhere.

52 The Enlightenment in Europe
The Europe of the *ancien régime* was an agglomerate of vested interests – churches, guilds, corporations, aristocrats – whose members shared a cosmopolitan culture, increasing luxury and the excitement of the philosophical Enlightenment in their courts and salons. Some monarchs imitated the absolutism of Louis XIV, their ambitions demonstrated in their new palaces.

Royal domain in 1477

Fiefs which fell to the Crown in 1477-1527

Patrimony of Charles, Duke of Bourbon, escheating to the crown in 1527

Other fiefs still outstanding in 1550

Ven Region with estates (provincial assemblies) in the sixteenth century

Art Region with estates surviving to 1661

⊙ *Siège* of a *parlement*

1643 Intendency centres in c. 1716 (with dates of first permanent *intendants*)

Généralités in c 1716

Certain peasant revolts and town revolts

SPANISH

C. of NETHERLANDS

Flanders

FLEMISH

WALLOON

HOLY

ROMAN

EMPIRE

Dunkirk
Calais
Ardres
Gravelines
St Omer
LUSTUCRU 1662
Aire
Lille
Tournai
Bonn
Artois
Arras **1659**
Bouchain
Charleroi
Arenburg
Cambrai
Maubeurge
Aresnes **1659**
Landrecies
Rocroi **1678**
Mont Royal
Oberstein
Lantrecke
Amiens **1633**
1628, 1638, 1642
Picardy **1477**
St. Quentin
Guise
C. of Sedan **1678**
Mézières
Longwy
Luxemburg
Arenburg
Sarrelouis
Sundgau
Landau
Wissembourg

C. of Eu

Cherbourg

Le Havre **1630**
Rouen **1631, 1634, 1636, 1639**
Normandy
La Fère
Soissons **1634**
Rethel
Montmédy
Verdun
D. of Bar **1634**
Metz
Thionville
Phillippsburg **1681/4**
Haguenau
Strasbourg **1643**
Kehl

Brest
St Malo
Caen **1630**
1631, 1639
NU-PIEDS 1639
Alençon **1525**
Perche **1474-83**
Alençon **1638**
Ile de France
D. of Valois **1515**
Reims
Marne
Champagne
Vertus **1636**
Troyes **1630, 1641, 1642**
Toul
Lorraine
Münster
Schlettstadt
Colmar
Freiburg **1643**
Breisach

Rennes **1634**
1636, 1639
TORRÉBEN 1675
C. of Maine
Le Mans **1489**
D. of Brittany 1491

Belle Isle

Nantes
Loire
Angers **1656**
Anjou **1525**
Tours **1630**
Touraine
D. of Vendôme **1525**
Orléanais **1498**
Orléans **1638**
Nemours
D. of Nemours
Auxerre
Nivernais
Paris **1634**
1631, 1648-9, 1653
Belfort
1648
FRENCH
GERMAN
Franche-Comté **1674**
Dijon **1635**
1630
Besançon
Dôle **1678/9**
D. of Burgundy **1477/82**
SWISS CONFEDERATION

Poitou
Ile de Ré
La Rochelle
Aunis
Poitiers **1633**
1631-2, 1639, 1641
La Marche
Bourges **1641**
1639
Nevers **1639**
Bourbonnais
Moulin **1634**
1633, 1636, 1640
C. of Charolais **1684**
Châlons
1684

TARD-AVISÉS, CROQUANTS 1593-4, 1636, 1637
Saintonge
Angoulême
Angoumois
Limoges **1632**
Limousin
Auvergne
Riom **1623**
Clermont Ferrand **1636-7, 1640, 1641-3**
Forez
Lyonnais **1597**
Bresse
Lyon **1632, 1641-2**
DUCHY OF SAVOY
The Alps

TARDANIZATS 1655-6
Blaye
Périgueux **1637**
C. of Périgord
CROQUANTS 1593-4, 1637
Bordeaux **1630**
1631, 1635, 1649, 1651-3, 1675
Guyenne
Garonne
Dordogne
Massif Central
C. of Rouergue
C. of Rouergue
ROURE 1670
Dauphiné
Grenoble **1638**

Albret
TARD-AVISÉS 1707
CROQUANTS 1643
Montauban **1643**
CAMISARDS 1702-7
Orange **1713**
C. of Venaissin
Avignon
C. of Provence **1481**

Bayonne
Armagnac
CROQUANTS 1642
Auch **1613**
Nîmes
AUDIJOS 1663
Navarre
Pau
Tarbes
V. C. of Béarn 1620
Toulouse **1635**
CROQUANTS 1594
Languedoc
Montpellier **1613**
1639, 1644-5
Marseille **1631, 1649, 1650, 1658**
Aix **1629**
1630, 1649, 1659
Toulon

Comminges
C. of Foix **1569**
The Pyrenees
Narbonne **1635**
1642
1642

◆ Fortresses constructed or strengthened by Vauban

Linguistic eastern frontier of France

French border in 1715

0 — 200 km

0 — 100 miles

Acquisitions in 1552, confirmed in 1648 (Metz, Toul and Verdun)

Acquisitions 1643-1661

Acquisitions 1662-1715

Areas "reunited" with the French Crown by Louis XIV 1684-1697

Duchy of Lorraine (occupied by France 1634-59 and 1670-1697)

Ten Imperial cities in Alsace over which France acquired jurisdiction in 1648 and which were annexed in 1672

© Creative Cartography Ltd © The Hamlyn Group

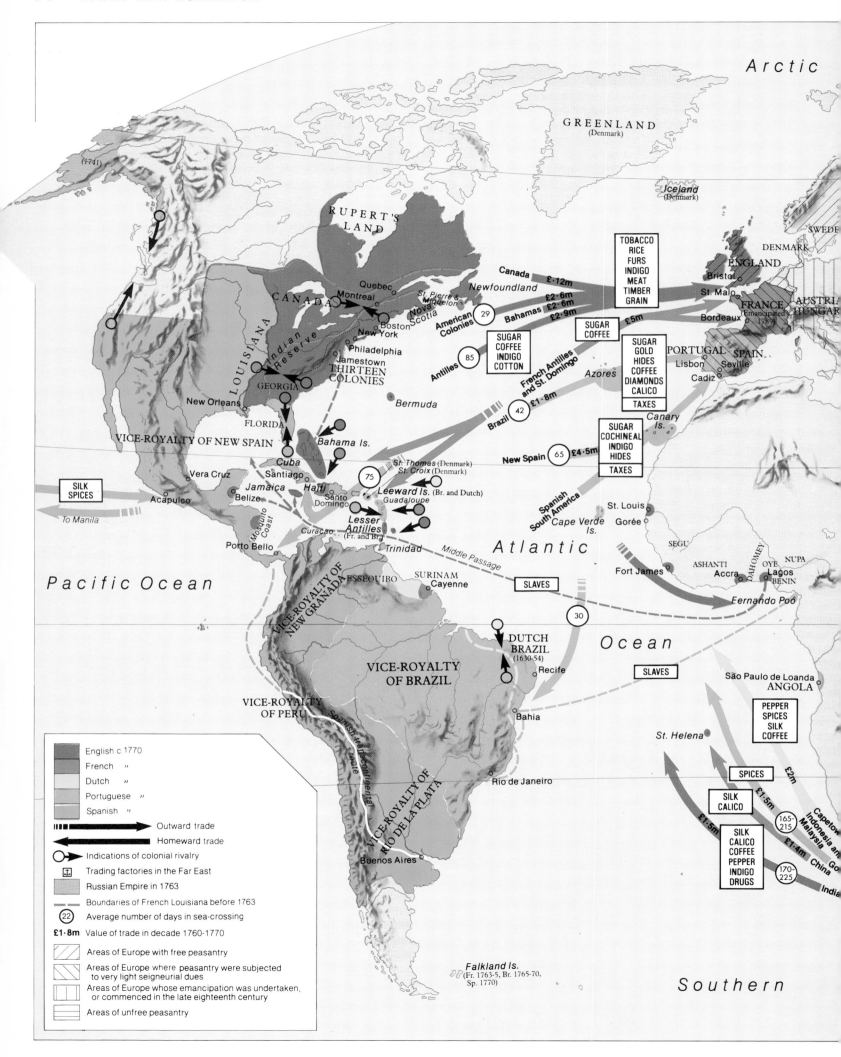

Arctic

GREENLAND
(Denmark)

Iceland
(Denmark)

RUPERT'S
LAND

SWEDE

DENMARK

ENGLAND
Bristol

CANADA

TOBACCO
RICE
FURS
INDIGO
MEAT
TIMBER
GRAIN

Canada £·12m

Quebec
Montreal
St. Pierre &
Miquelon
Nova
Scotia
Boston
New York
Philadelphia
Jamestown
THIRTEEN
COLONIES

Newfoundland

Bahamas £2·6m
£2·6m
£2·9m

29

SUGAR
COFFEE
INDIGO
COTTON

85

American
Colonies

Antilles

St. Malo
FRANCE
(Emancipated
1789)
Bordeaux

AUSTRI
HUNGAR

£5m

SUGAR
COFFEE

French Antilles
and St. Domingo

PORTUGAL SPAIN
Lisbon
Cadiz
Seville

SUGAR
GOLD
HIDES
COFFEE
DIAMONDS
CALICO

TAXES

LOUISIANA
Indian
Reserve

GEORGIA

New Orleans

Azores

£1·8m

Brazil

42

Canary
Is.

SUGAR
COCHINEAL
INDIGO
HIDES

TAXES

FLORIDA

VICE-ROYALTY OF NEW SPAIN

Bermuda

Bahama Is.

New Spain

65

£4·5m

SILK
SPICES

Vera Cruz

Acapulco

To Manila

Cuba
Santiago

Jamaica
Belize

Porto Bello

Mosquito
Coast

Santo
Domingo

Haiti
Curaçao

St. Thomas (Denmark)
St. Croix (Denmark)

75

Leeward Is. (Br. and Dutch)
Guadaloupe

Lesser Antilles
(Fr. and Br.)

Trinidad

Middle Passage

Spanish
South America
Cape Verde
Is.

St. Louis
Gorée

SEGU

ASHANTI
Accra

NUPA

DAHOMEY
OYE
Lagos
BENIN

Atlantic

Pacific Ocean

ESSEQUIBO

SURINAM
Cayenne

VICE-ROYALTY OF
NEW GRANADA

SLAVES

Fort James

30

Ocean

Fernando Poó

DUTCH
BRAZIL
(1630-54)
Recife

SLAVES

São Paulo de Loanda
ANGOLA

VICE-ROYALTY
OF BRAZIL

VICE-ROYALTY
OF PERU

St. Helena

PEPPER
SPICES
SILK
COFFEE

Bahia

Rio de Janeiro

*Spanish first transcontinental
route*

VICE-ROYALTY
OF RIO DE LA PLATA

Buenos Aires

SPICES

£2m

£1·5m

SILK
CALICO

£1·4m

Capetown
Indonesia an
Malaysia
China

165-
215

SILK
CALICO
COFFEE
PEPPER
INDIGO
DRUGS

£1·5m

170-
225

India

Falkland Is.
(Fr. 1763-5, Br. 1765-70,
Sp. 1770)

Southern

English c. 1770
French "
Dutch "
Portuguese "
Spanish "

Outward trade
Homeward trade
Indications of colonial rivalry
Trading factories in the Far East
Russian Empire in 1763
Boundaries of French Louisiana before 1763
Average number of days in sea-crossing

22

£1·8m   Value of trade in decade 1760-1770

Areas of Europe with free peasantry
Areas of Europe where peasantry were subjected
to very light seigneurial dues
Areas of Europe whose emancipation was undertaken,
or commenced in the late eighteenth century
Areas of unfree peasantry

(1741)

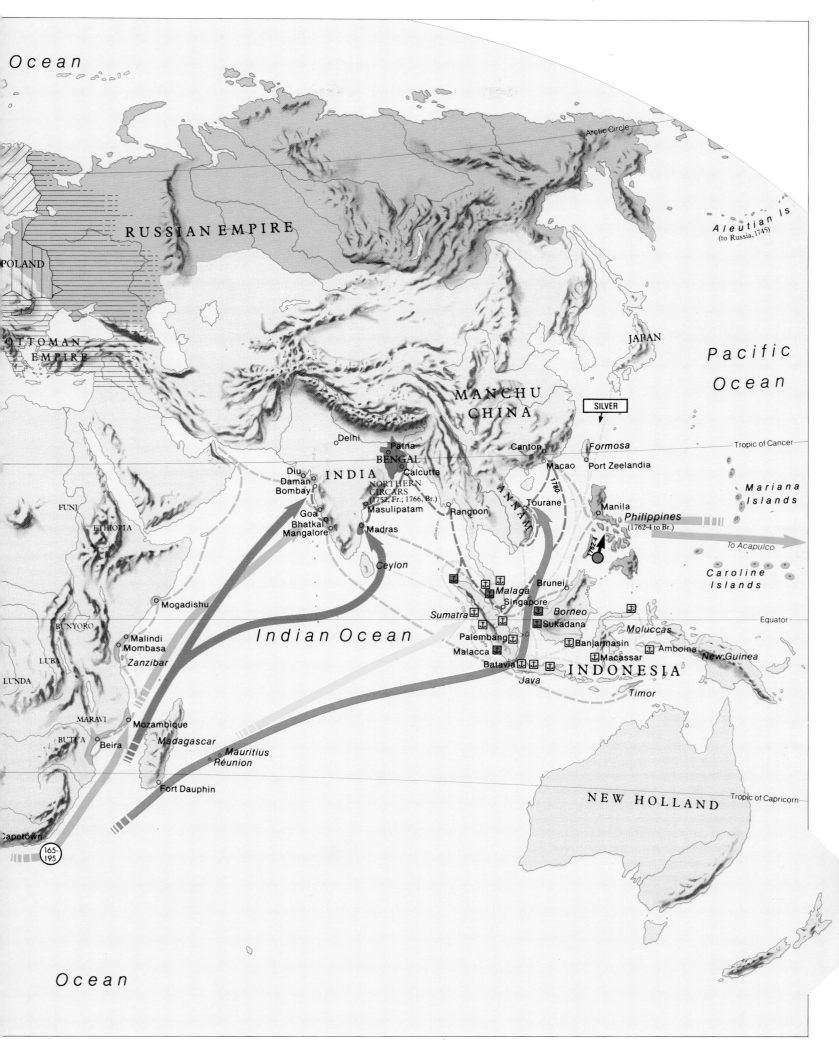

Ocean

RUSSIAN EMPIRE

POLAND

OTTOMAN
EMPIRE

Arctic Circle

Aleutian Is
(to Russia, 1745)

JAPAN

Pacific

Ocean

MANCHU
CHINA

SILVER

Delhi

Patna
BENGAL

Canton

Formosa

Tropic of Cancer

Diu
Daman
Bombay

INDIA

Calcutta
NORTHERN
CIRCARS
(1752, Fr.; 1766, Br.)
Masulipatam

Macao

Port Zeelandia

1780

*Mariana
Islands*

FUNJ

ETHIOPIA

Goa
Bhatkal
Mangalore

Madras

Rangoon

ANNAM

Tourane

Manila

1762-4

Philippines
(1762-4 to Br.)

To Acapulco

Ceylon

*Caroline
Islands*

Mogadishu

Brunei

Malaga
Singapore

Sumatra

Borneo

Sukadana

Moluccas

Equator

BUNYORO

Malindi
Mombasa

Zanzibar

Indian Ocean

LU'BA

LUNDA

Palembang

Malacca

Java

Batavia

Banjarmasin

Macassar

Amboina

New Guinea

INDONESIA

Timor

MARAVI

BUTCA   Beira

Mozambique

Madagascar

*Mauritius
Réunion*

Fort Dauphin

NEW HOLLAND

Tropic of Capricorn

Capetown

165-
195

Ocean

© Creative Cartography Ltd © The Hamlyn Group

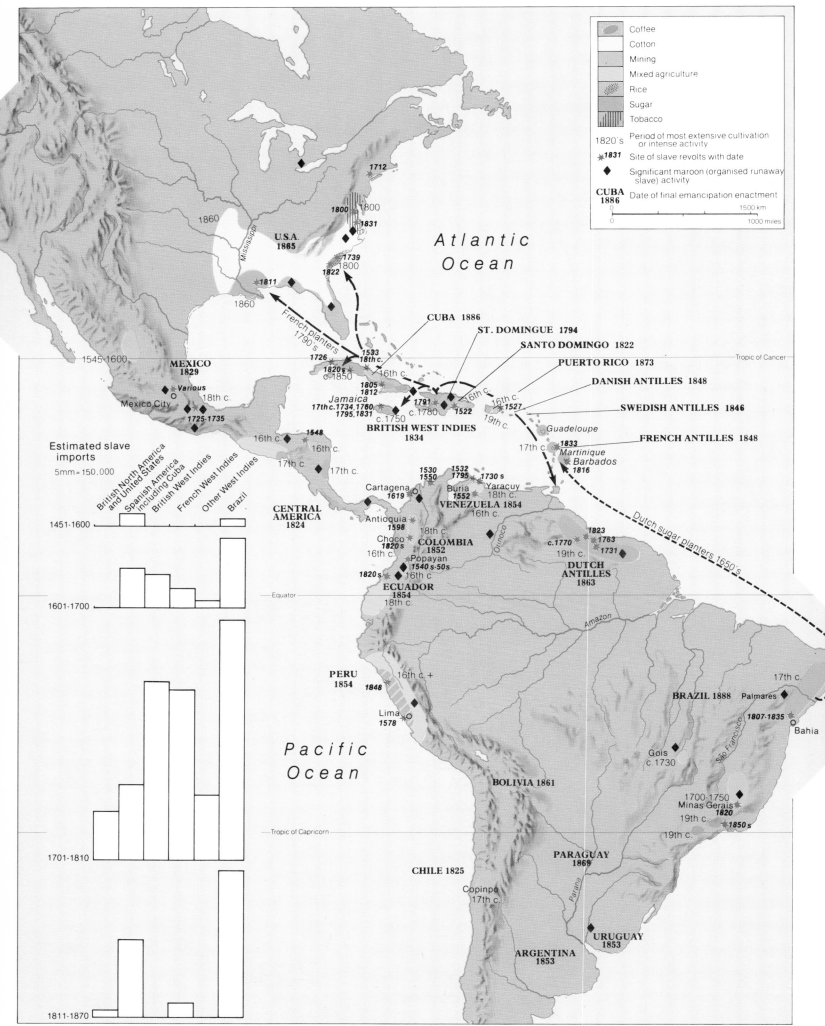

Legend:
- Coffee
- Cotton
- Mining
- Mixed agriculture
- Rice
- Sugar
- Tobacco

1820's — Period of most extensive cultivation or intense activity

*1831 — Site of slave revolts with date

◆ — Significant maroon (organised runaway slave) activity

CUBA 1886 — Date of final emancipation enactment

1500 km
1000 miles

Atlantic Ocean

Pacific Ocean

1712

U.S.A. 1865
1800
1831
1860
1739 1800
1822
1811
1860

French planters 1790's

1545-1600
MEXICO 1829
Various
Mexico City
18th c.
1725-1735

CUBA 1886
ST. DOMINGUE 1794
SANTO DOMINGO 1822
PUERTO RICO 1873
DANISH ANTILLES 1848
SWEDISH ANTILLES 1846
FRENCH ANTILLES 1848

1533 18th c.
1726
1820's c.1850
16th c.
1805 1812
Jamaica 17th c. 1734,1760, 1795,1831
c.1750
1791 c.1780
1522
BRITISH WEST INDIES 1834
16th c.
16th c.
1527
19th c.

Guadeloupe
1833
Martinique
Barbados *1816*
17th c.

16th c.
16th c.
1548
17th c.
CENTRAL AMERICA 1824
Cartagena *1619*
Antioquia *1598*
Choco *1820's*
16th c.
Popayan *1540's-50s*
1820's 16th c.
ECUADOR 1854
18th c.

1530 1550
1532 1795
1730's
Buria
1552
Yaracuy 18th c.
VENEZUELA 1854
16th c.

Orinoco
c.1770 19th c.
1823 1763 1731
DUTCH ANTILLES 1863

Dutch sugar planters 1650's

Amazon

PERU 1854
16th c. +
1848
Lima 1578

Equator

BRAZIL 1888   Palmares   17th c.
1807-1835
Bahia
Gois c.1730

BOLIVIA 1861

1700-1750
Minas Gerais
1820
19th c.
1850's
19th c.

Tropic of Capricorn

PARAGUAY 1869

CHILE 1825
Copinpo 17th c.

URUGUAY 1853

ARGENTINA 1853

Estimated slave imports
5mm = 150,000

Categories:
- British North America and United States
- Spanish America including Cuba
- British West Indies
- French West Indies
- Other West Indies
- Brazil

1451-1600

1601-1700

1701-1810

1811-1870

Tropic of Cancer

© Creative Cartography Ltd © The Hamlyn Group

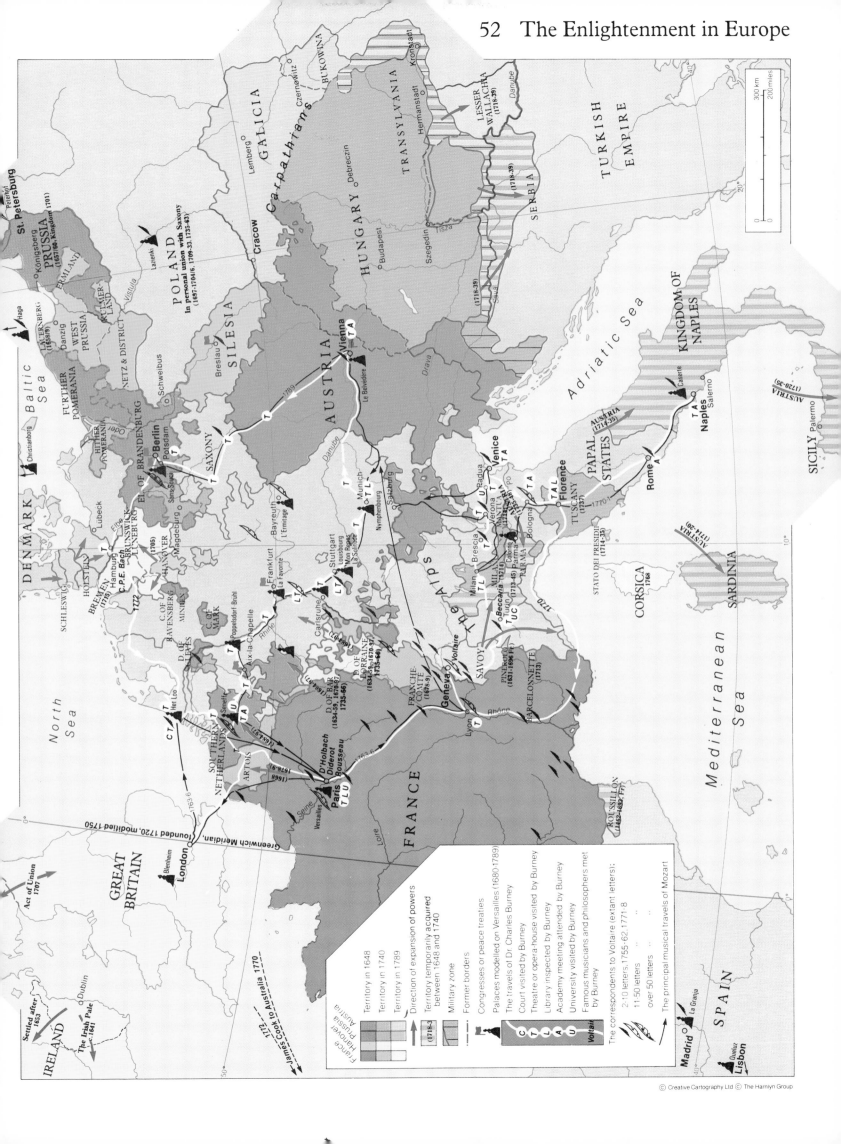

IRELAND
Settled after 1653
○ Dublin
The Irish Pale 1641

GREAT BRITAIN
Act of Union 1707
Blenheim
● London

James Cook to Australia 1770
1772

Greenwich Meridian founded 1720, modified 1750

SPAIN
Madrid ●
La Granja
Queluz
Lisbon ●

North Sea

Baltic Sea

Peterhof
St. Petersburg

DENMARK
Christiansborg
Haga
SCHLESWIG
HOLSTEIN
BREMEN (1715) Hamburg
Lübeck
Elbe

PRUSSIA
(1657/60 Kingdom 1701)
Königsberg
ERMLAND
LAUENBERG (1656/9)
FURTHER POMERANIA
Danzig
WEST PRUSSIA
KULMER-LAND
HITHER POMERANIA
NETZ & DISTRICT
Schweibus
Oder

POLAND
In personal union with Saxony
(1697-1704/6, 1709-33, 1735-43)
Lazienki
Vistula
Cracow

GALICIA
Lemberg
BUKOWINA
Czernowitz

Carpathians

TRANSYLVANIA
Kronstadt
Hermanstadt
(1718-39)

LESSER WALLACHIA (1718-39)
Danube

TURKISH EMPIRE
SERBIA (1718-39)
Sava
Tisza

HUNGARY
Debreczin
Budapest
Szegedin

EL. OF BRANDENBURG
● Berlin
Potsdam
Sans-Souci
BRUNSWICK-LÜNEBURG
C.P.E. Bach
(1705)
HANOVER
Magdeburg
1772

SILESIA
Breslau
Schweidnitz

SAXONY
Bayreuth
L'Ermitage
Frankfurt
La Favorite
Carlsruhe
(1691-97)

AUSTRIA
Vienna
Le Belvédère
1789

D. OF BAR (1634-59, 1670-97, 1735-66)
LORRAINE (1634-59, 1670-97, 1735-66)
Stuttgart
Louisburg
Mon Repos
La Solitude

Munich
Nymphenburg
Salzburg

The Alps

Munich

D'Holbach
Diderot
Rousseau
Paris
Versailles
Seine
Loire

FRANCE
FRANCHE-COMTÉ (1678-9)
Geneva
Voltaire
Lyon
Rhône

SAVOY
PINEROLO (1631-1696 Fr.)
Turin

Milan
MIL.A (1714)
Brescia
Verona
Padua
Venice
Beccaria
Parma
PARMA (1713-45)
Bologna
MODENA
Colorno

BARCELONNETTE (1713)
ROUSSILLON (1462-1652 Fr.)

PAPAL STATES
Florence
TUSCANY
AUSTRIA (1714-35)
Rome
1770

Adriatic Sea

KINGDOM OF NAPLES
Caserte
Naples
Salerno
AUSTRIA (1720-35)

SICILY
Palermo

CORSICA 1768
SARDINIA
AUSTRIA (1714-20)
STATO DEI PRESIDII (1714-35)

Mediterranean Sea

The Enlightenment in Europe legend

		Territory in 1648
France	Prussia	Territory in 1740
Hanover	Austria	Territory in 1789

Direction of expansion of powers
(1718-39) Territory temporarily acquired between 1648 and 1740
Military zone
Former borders
Congresses or peace treaties
Palaces modelled on Versailles (1680-1789)

The travels of Dr. Charles Burney:
C Court visited by Burney
T Theatre or opera-house visited by Burney
L Library inspected by Burney
A Academy meeting attended by Burney
U University visited by Burney

Voltaire — Famous musicians and philosophers met by Burney

The correspondents to Voltaire (extant letters):
2-10 letters, 1755-62, 1771-8
11-50 letters
over 50 letters

The principal musical travels of Mozart

© Creative Cartography Ltd © The Hamlyn Group

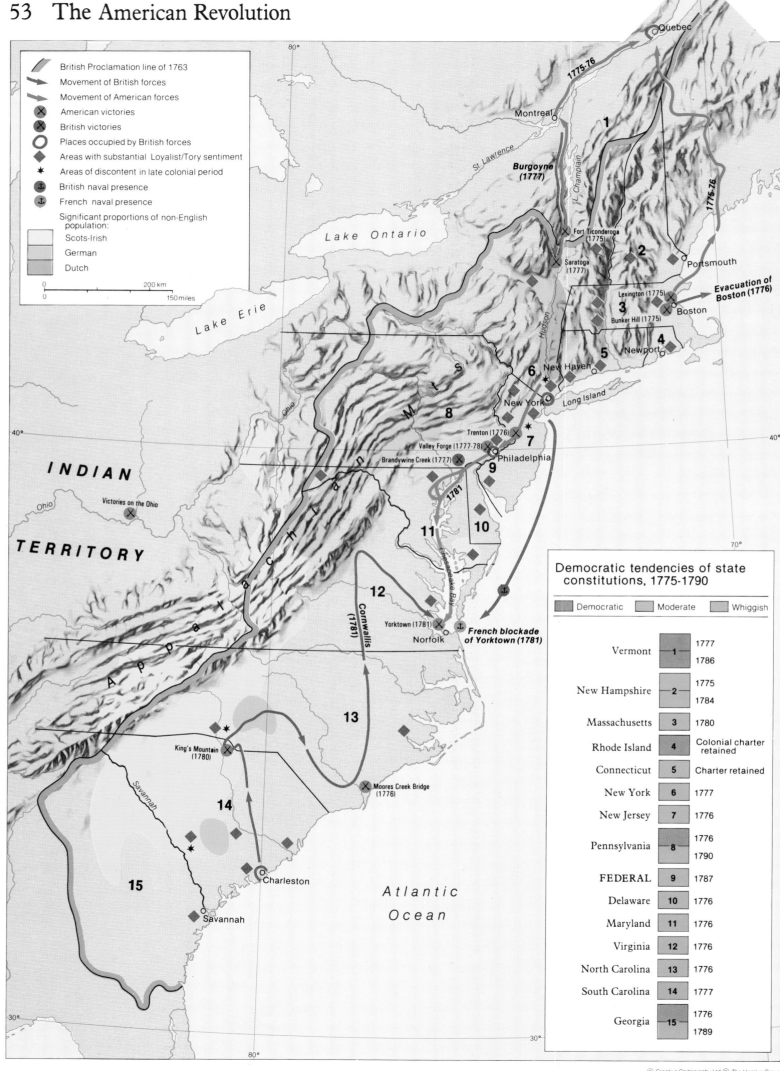

Legend

- British Proclamation line of 1763
- Movement of British forces
- Movement of American forces
- ⊗ American victories
- ⊗ British victories
- ○ Places occupied by British forces
- ◆ Areas with substantial Loyalist/Tory sentiment
- ✳ Areas of discontent in late colonial period
- ⚓ British naval presence
- ⚓ French naval presence

Significant proportions of non-English population:
- Scots-Irish
- German
- Dutch

0   200 km
0   150 miles

Quebec
1775-76
Montreal
St. Lawrence
1775-76
Burgoyne (1777)
Lake Ontario
L. Champlain
Fort Ticonderoga (1775)
1   Portsmouth
2
Saratoga (1777)
Lexington (1775)   Evacuation of Boston (1776)
3   Boston
Bunker Hill (1775)
4   Newport
5   New Haven
Lake Erie
6
Hudson   New York   Long Island
8   7
Trenton (1776)
Valley Forge (1777-78)   Philadelphia
Brandywine Creek (1777)   9
INDIAN   1781
Ohio   10
Victories on the Ohio   11
TERRITORY   Chesapeake Bay
12
Cornwallis (1781)   Yorktown (1781)   French blockade of Yorktown (1781)
Norfolk
13
King's Mountain (1780)
Moores Creek Bridge (1776)
Savannah
14
Charleston
15   Atlantic Ocean
Savannah

Democratic tendencies of state constitutions, 1775-1790

- Democratic
- Moderate
- Whiggish

State		Date(s)
Vermont	1	1777 / 1786
New Hampshire	2	1775 / 1784
Massachusetts	3	1780
Rhode Island	4	Colonial charter retained
Connecticut	5	Charter retained
New York	6	1777
New Jersey	7	1776
Pennsylvania	8	1776 / 1790
FEDERAL	9	1787
Delaware	10	1776
Maryland	11	1776
Virginia	12	1776
North Carolina	13	1776
South Carolina	14	1777
Georgia	15	1776 / 1789

53 The American Revolution
Much of the Thirteen Colonies remained largely unaffected by the war, but the concentration of British power along the coast hampered attempts to suppress the revolution. As it gained ground the predominantly bourgeois leadership showed preference for 'Whiggish' rather than 'democratic' principles–for example, for appointive rather than elective office, and a narrow, property-based franchise–in the forms of government which were adopted.

54 The French Revolution
Under the pressure of internal opposition and external attack (which by autumn 1793 threatened to extinguish the revolution) the National Assembly, which had dismantled the *ancien régime* in France, gave way to the growing chaos of the Terror and the Directorate. But its main achievement was permanent. As Goethe said, 'Here begins a new age in the history of the world.'

55 The Europe of Napoleon
The conquests of the French revolutionary armies were accompanied everywhere by the collapse of the *ancien régime*, to be replaced by the prefectoral system of government and the legal code which Napoleon had devised for France; despite the victory of 'legitimacy' in 1815 the *Code civil* continued to provide a basis for liberal regimes in Europe throughout the 19th century.

WHEN ALEXIS DE TOCQUEVILLE published his work, *The Ancien Régime and the Revolution* in 1856, he showed how much of the French Revolution was foreshadowed in the *ancien régime* (*see Map 49*). Its revolutionary principles were born of the *philosophes*; centralisation of power in the state had already been achieved by the Bourbons; the peasantry was already emancipated; the process of reducing society to an aggregate of individuals, each purged of the bonds of blood, guild or corporation, had already begun. Above all, the French Revolution had been anticipated elsewhere, once with success (in the American War of Independence, 1775-83) and elsewhere in Europe with failure (notably in Geneva, 1780-82; the Netherlands, 1787-9; and Belgium, 1789).

These revolutions have been called 'democratic'. Some turned out that way, but they were not begun by democrats, and were not the result of a revolutionary movement. The collapse of the *ancien régime* came from conflicts between the ruling nobilities and autocrats. Leadership came, initially, not from the street, but from the provincial nobility–the outraged, but sober and conservative gentry. Among their leaders were George Washington, a successful soldier, a landowner, and a conscientious representative of the House of Burgesses in his state, Jan van der Capellen, the radical noble who urged the Dutch to resist their prince and govern the state themselves, and a clutch of noble radicals in the French estates general, such as the vicomte de Noailles or the affable marquis de Condorcet.

The nobility allowed the revolts to happen, but the bourgeoisie rapidly became the standard-bearers. Outraged lawyers and notables organised themselves across the east coast of America, following the example of Boston, into Sons of Liberty from 1763 (*see Map 53*). In Holland, the Patriot party grew up among the regent patricians (who ruled the towns) and their supporters so that, by 1784, they numbered 28,000 volunteers and held their first national convention. In Belgium, urban oligarchs who opposed the absolutism of Joseph II joined the clergy in a revolutionary society 'for altar and hearth' in June 1789. In France the resistance of the law-courts (the issue, as in America, was a stamp duty) encouraged the calling of an estates general in May 1789. Amongst the delegates, two-thirds were from the 'third estate', which was dominated by royal officials and lawyers from the professional bourgeoisie. Their self-confidence and their involvement in the machinery of state encouraged them to undertake a structural reform unparalleled in any other European state.

The successful revolutions reveal their ideology clearly. In the ringing terms of the American *Declaration of Independence* (1776) or the French *Declaration of the Rights of Man and Citizens* (1789) lie the manifestoes against privilege and for liberty and nationhood, blueprints for every nineteenth-century liberation movement. Liberty was a marvellous battle-cry, corrosive of all frontiers, classes, governments, boundless in its application. In the glorious dawn of 1789, when trees of liberty were being planted in France, some even dreamt of 'the possibility of a single Nation and the facility with which the Universal Assembly sitting in Paris will conduct the whole human race'. Subsequently, the National Assembly in France would grant citizenship to the great champions of liberty, Washington, Wilberforce, Schiller and Pestalozzi.

Nationalism was as corrosive as liberty but more exclusive in its impact. In August 1789, the Estates General in France transformed themselves into the National Assembly. They destroyed privilege because it damaged national integrity. A new mythology of patriotism was hastily fostered, to encourage a sense of invincible unity. Stones from the demolished Bastille were carried as souvenirs to all corners of France. In July 1793, the new nation's apparatus of flags, anthems, and identity cards was completed by an order to erect an altar of the fatherland, on which would be engraved the Declaration of Rights with the inscription 'The citizen is born, lives and dies for the Fatherland'.

When the Estates General referred to 'the people' in, for instance, the French *Declaration*, they meant 'the nation'. They therefore sounded more democratic than, in practice, they intended to be. This impression was reinforced because their first sessions were accompanied by the enormous popular unrest in Paris which led to the fall of the Bastille on the 4th July 1789 and the *Grande Peur* (Great Fear) of the peasantry which destroyed seigneurial charters and documents and lent a mobbish atmosphere to their opening deliberations.

Since their independence could only be achieved through armed rebellion the American revolutionaries had no opportunity to put their ideology into practice in normal conditions. In France, on the contrary, the National (or 'Constituent') Assembly had three years to reconstruct every aspect of French life until, exploited by revolutionary exiles from England, Holland and Belgium, enthusiasm for attacking the *ancien régime* in all its manifestations caused France to declare war on Austria in 1792. The principles of this reconstruction were legal equality, representative government (with wide, but not universal, suffrage), the complete sovereignty of the state and a centralised administration. They were expressed by the reorganisation of local government into 83 departments established on rational lines; a national system of weights and measures (in metric units) and a national system of education. Torture was abolished; privileged guilds were dismantled; the Jews were emancipated; customs dues abandoned; seigneurial obligations suppressed. No exclusive corporation was spared. The property of the French church was nationalised and assigned to repay government debts. In a proposed constitution for the clergy, all clerics were to be chosen on democratic principles, the religious orders dissolved and the papacy excluded from influence in the French national church. By the outbreak of war, old France had been destroyed and the most lasting institutional achievements of the age of revolutions established.

Changes on this scale bred reaction, and this changed the nature of the revolution. Louis XVI, encouraged by *emigré* royalists and the indignation of crowned heads across Europe, took flight to the frontier, only to be stopped at La Varenne. His trial and execution excited republican fervour in the National Assembly, Paris and elsewhere, and confirmed counter-revolutionary fears. Clerical opposition to the civil constitution of the clergy also divided France bitterly. Militant revolutionaries in the cities (which were already anti-clerical) became open enemies of the church and religion, and made the priests the scapegoats for the revolution's own shortcomings. Rural France remained stubbornly Catholic and rural insurrection after 1790 in the Vendée and the south of France was uniformly against the revolution. The old

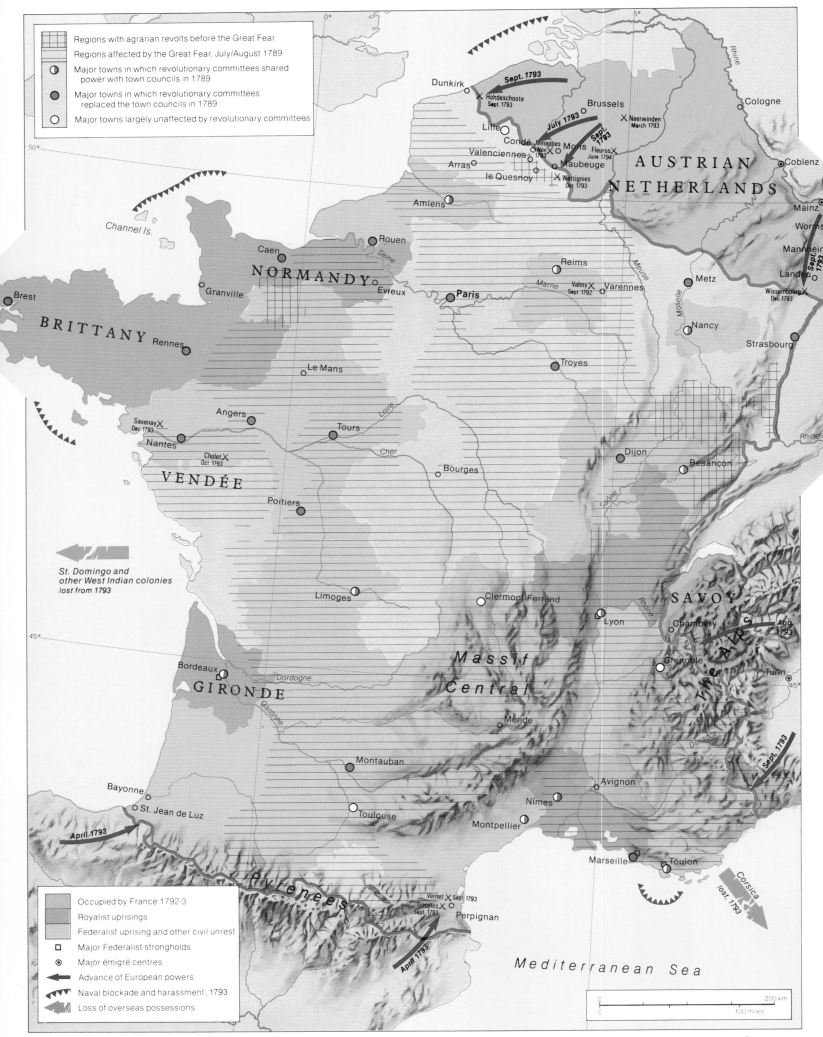

Legend (upper left):

- Regions with agrarian revolts before the Great Fear
- Regions affected by the Great Fear, July/August 1789
- Major towns in which revolutionary committees shared power with town councils in 1789
- Major towns in which revolutionary committees replaced the town councils in 1789
- Major towns largely unaffected by revolutionary committees

Legend (lower left):

- Occupied by France 1792-3
- Royalist uprisings
- Federalist uprising and other civil unrest
- Major Federalist strongholds
- Major émigré centres
- Advance of European powers
- Naval blockade and harassment, 1793
- Loss of overseas possessions

Map labels:

AUSTRIAN NETHERLANDS

Dunkirk · Hondschoote Sept. 1793 · Sept. 1793 · Brussels · Cologne
Lille · Condé · Jemappes Nov. 1793 · Mons · Neerwinden March 1793
Valenciennes · Fleurus June 1794 · Sept. 1793
Arras · le Quesnoy · Maubeuge · Wattignies Oct. 1793
July 1793

Amiens · Coblenz · Mainz · Worms · Mannheim · Landau Sept. 1793 · Wissembourg Dec. 1793

Channel Is.

Caen · Rouen · Reims · Metz · Nancy · Strasbourg
NORMANDY · Evreux · Seine · Marne · Valmy Sept. 1792 · Varennes · Moselle
Granville · Paris · Meuse · Rhine

Brest

BRITTANY Rennes · Le Mans · Troyes

Savenay Dec. 1793 · Angers · Tours · Loire · Cher · Dijon · Besançon
Nantes · Cholet Oct. 1793 · Bourges · Saône
VENDÉE · Poitiers

St. Domingo and other West Indian colonies lost from 1793

Limoges · Clermont-Ferrand · SAVOY
Lyon · Chambéry · Aug. 1793
Massif Central · Grenoble · Turin
Bordeaux · Dordogne · Rhône · Durance · Sept. 1793
GIRONDE · Garonne
Mende · Avignon
Montauban · Nîmes
Bayonne · St. Jean de Luz · Toulouse · Montpellier
April 1793 · Pyrenees
Marseille · Toulon · Corsica lost, 1793
Vernet Sept. 1793 · Trouilles Sept. 1793 · Perpignan
April 1793

Mediterranean Sea

200 km
100 miles

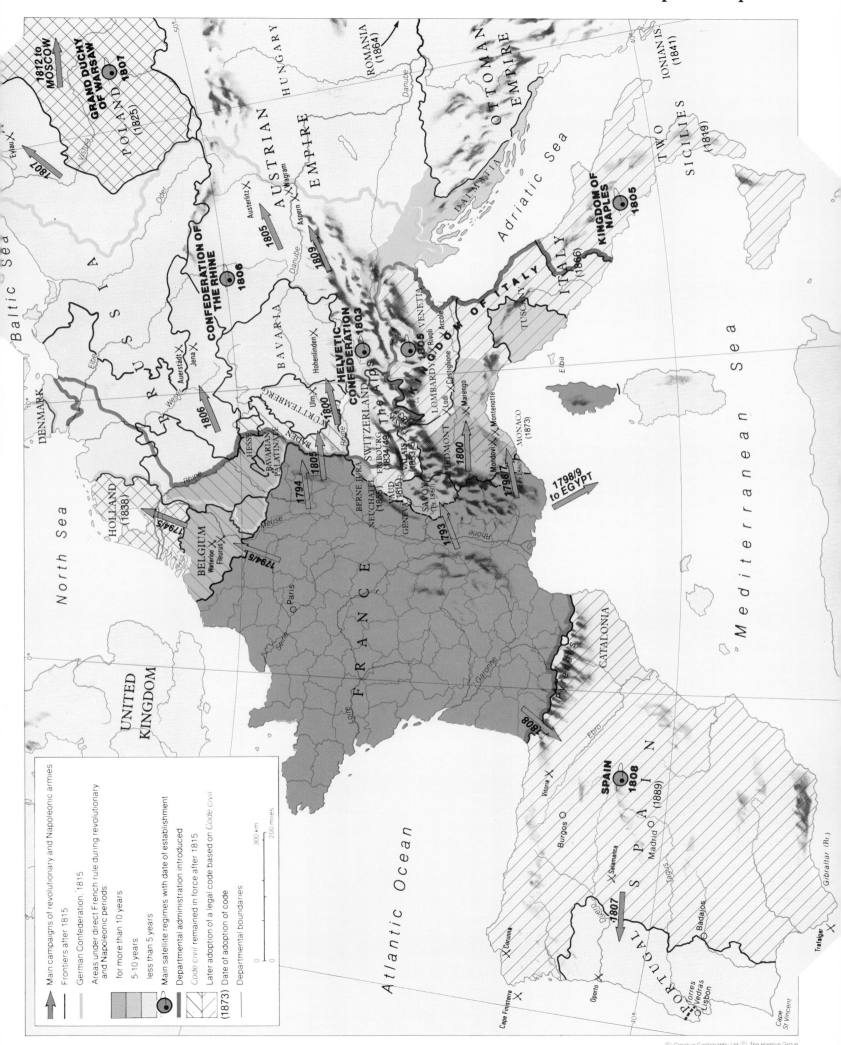

Baltic Sea

North Sea

DENMARK

UNITED KINGDOM

Atlantic Ocean

P R U S S I A

POLAND (1825)

GRAND DUCHY OF WARSAW 1807

1812 to MOSCOW

1807

Eylau X

Oder

Vistula

Elbe

Wesel

AUSTRIAN EMPIRE

HUNGARY

ROMANIA (1864)

OTTOMAN EMPIRE

Danube

Austerlitz X

1805

Aspern X

Wagram X

1809

Jena X

Auerstädt X

1806

Hohenlinden X

1800

Ulm X

WÜRTTEMBERG

BADEN

Rhine

CONFEDERATION OF THE RHINE 1806

BAVARIA

HESSE

BAVARIAN PALATINATE

1805

HELVETIC CONFEDERATION 1803

SWITZERLAND

The Alps

FRIBOURG 1834/48

NEUCHÂTEL (1865)

BERNE JURA

GENEVA (1815)

VALAIS 1833/5

SAVOY (Fr. 1860)

PIEDMONT

1800

1793

1794

Rhône

MONACO (1873)

Mondovi X Montenotte X

1796/7

Pinerolo X

KINGDOM OF ITALY 1805

LOMBARDY

Lodi X Castiglione X

VENETIA

Rivoli X

Arcole X

Marengo X

DALMATIA

Adriatic Sea

TUSCANY (1866)

I T A L Y

Elba

KINGDOM OF NAPLES 1805

TWO SICILIES (1819)

IONIANS (1841)

Mediterranean Sea

1798/9 to EGYPT

HOLLAND (1838)

1794/5

BELGIUM

Waterloo X

Fleurus X

1794/5

Meuse

F R A N C E

Paris O

Seine

Loire

Garonne

1808

PYRENEES

CATALONIA

Ebro

S P A I N

Vitoria X

SPAIN 1808

Burgos O

Madrid O (1889)

Salamanca X

Tagus

1807

Duero

Coruña X

Badajoz O

PORTUGAL

Oporto O

Torres Vedras X

Lisbon

Cape Finisterre X

Cape St Vincent

Gibraltar (Br.)

Trafalgar X

Legend:
- Main campaigns of revolutionary and Napoleonic armies
- Frontiers after 1815
- German Confederation, 1815
- Areas under direct French rule during revolutionary and Napoleonic periods:
  - for more than 10 years
  - 5-10 years
  - less than 5 years
- Main satellite regimes with date of establishment
- Departmental administration introduced
- *Code civil* remained in force after 1815
- Later adoption of a legal code based on *Code civil*
- (1873) Date of adoption of code
- Departmental boundaries

300 km

200 miles

© Creative Cartography Ltd © The Hamlyn Group

The age of revolutions

army and navy did not remain loyal to the new régime; its senior officers provided the bulk of the *emigrés*. From the barracks in the cities, the new National Guard, with its distinctive *sans-culottes* trousers spread the openly democratic force of Jacobinism throughout France.

Republicanism, atheism and Jacobinism inspired the language and euphoria of the revolution after 1792. They also excited streetfighters, spies, police and the dictatorial zealots of the committees of Public Safety. At the heart of 'the Terror' (as contemporaries referred to it) lay Paris itself. The way to securing the loyalty of Paris lay in the provision of its food supplies and in winning the confidence of the street-revolutionaries. The Directory (the effective successor of the National Assembly) which ruled France after 1795, failed in both tasks. Food supplies were consistently scarce and the Paris revolutionaries (like the Jacobins in the army) were bitterly divided between factions supporting various politicians of the Terror–Robespierristes, Dantonistes, etc. Nationally, the Directory became increasingly troubled both by those who feared reaction and by those who feared fresh popular violence. It depended increasingly upon force. Generals began to loom larger in its affairs and one of them, Napoleon Bonaparte, accepted the role offered him by some of the disenchanted. A *coup d'état* in November 1799 (Brumaire, year VIII, in the new calendar) installed him in power as First Consul of the Republic. Five years later, he inaugurated a hereditary empire, completing the transformation from revolution to dictatorship.

Napoleon was, in many ways, the incarnation of an eighteenth-century enlightened despot (*see Map 55*). Like his hero, Frederick the Great, he codified, rationalised, centralised, and militarised, without an *ancien régime* to cramp his style either at home or abroad. Napoleon's achievement was to define how much of the revolution should survive. In France, his *Code Napoléon* distilled the decisions of the Constituent Assembly into a readily understood and easily imposed constitutional settlement administered through departmental prefects. But he anaesthetized France against the republicanism, atheism and democratic Jacobinism of the Terror. His police harried one-time liberals and Jacobins in cities and in the army. The empire proclaimed the death of republicanism. His concordat with the Papacy in 1801 added to the widespread reaction against the excesses of the previous decade. Napoleon was so successful in reconciling the former nobles and oligarchs to his empire that there was little obstacle to the revival of traditional titles and the re-integration of the old French ruling-class and its monarchy in 1815. If the French Revolution had been a 'democratic' revolution, then Napoleon ensured its failure.

Napoleon's greatest achievement was outside France in the wider empire (*Map 55*). Here, too, he built upon revolutionary antecedents. The ideology of the French Revolution had crossed national frontiers in the 1790s, particularly affecting the areas where revolts had previously failed. Groups of social and political dissenters–'Jacobins'–appeared in clubs and taverns in every city in Europe. They prepared the way for the French revolutionary armies which established themselves in the 1790s in Holland, Belgium, Switzerland and most of Italy.

Initially, France respected the self-determination of these 'allies' in revolution. Subsequently the Directory was less tolerant. In Belgium (which, as the Republic of the United Belgian Provinces, had seceded from the Hapsburg Empire in 1790) a rigged plebiscite was held; property belonging to the 'accomplices' of tyranny was confiscated and an enfeebled French currency introduced. By 1795 Belgium had become once more a mere geographical expression, having been divided into nine French departments ruled from Paris. The Rhineland and north-western Italy were similarly treated, without the tiresome pretence of a plebiscite. The Dutch Provinces, Switzerland, Lombardy and Dalmatia were permitted the semblance of separate identity as the Batavian, Helvetian, Cisalpine and Illyrian republics. The inner collapse of the Directory and the European reaction against domination dressed as liberation left only Belgium secure in French hands by 1799.

Napoleon could rebuild the French continental empire because the memory of the revolutionary wars was still green in Europe. This time, the armies exported the code, the prefects, police, and conscription (over half the army at Moscow in 1812 was non-French) and imported the treasures of Florence, Venice and the Near East. Even countries like Prussia, which remained independent, could not avoid the influence of Bonapartism. Prussian reformers began to look to the destruction of serfdom, to open the army (cautiously) to non-nobles, and to preach a distinctive nationalism.

There was remarkably little popular resistance within the Napoleonic empire to this extension of French power. Where popular risings did occur, they were the product of traditional rivalries (the Tyrolese in 1808 against the Bavarians) or religious affiliations (in Spain in 1808 and Russia in 1812). In Italy, apart from the extreme Francophobe *Carbonari*, who pledged themselves to counter-revolution after 1809 (*see Map 60*), the French constructed national institutions which would form the basis of Italian movements for unification in the nineteenth century. In Germany too, Napoleon's rationalisation of frontiers, emancipation of serfs and Jews, and abolition of restrictions on commerce, earned him support from men as varied in outlook as Metternich, Hegel, Goethe and Beethoven.

Only in the great land empires of Ottoman Turkey and tsarist Russia, and the maritime empire of England did Napoleon fail to leave any lasting monument. When these powers were finally victorious after the battle of Waterloo (1815) against Bonaparte it was believed that the subsequent Congress of Vienna would recreate the *ancien régime*. In fact in France as throughout most of continental Europe this proved impossible. Boundaries, administrations, armies, laws and patterns of thought had all been irreversibly changed by the revolutionary experience. And one of the guarantors of the Congress of Vienna was England which, following its own distinctive path, undertook by peaceful means the changes that the men of 1789 had accomplished by force and emerged as the champion in nineteenth-century Europe of their liberal and nationalist principles.

Further reading: E. J. Hobsbawm, *The Age of Revolution* (Weidenfeld & Nicolson, 1962; Abacus, 1977); J. R. Pole, *The Foundations of American Independence*, 1763-1815, (Bobbs-Merrill, 1972); J. M. Roberts, *The French Revolution* (Oxford University Press, 1978; p.b.); R. Cobb, *The Police and the People* (Oxford University Press, 1970; p.b.); A. de Tocqueville, *The Ancien Régime and the French Revolution*, trans. S. Gilbert (Fontana, 1966).

The age of European supremacy VII

The Industrial Revolution

As FRANCE was the progenitor of political revolution in the nineteenth century, England was the home of the industrial revolution. Industrial innovation was not new in itself, but the series of self-perpetuating and apparently unstoppable developments which were set in motion by the advances made in eighteenth-century Britain transformed the life of man and the nature of human society more profoundly – and more rapidly – than anything that had happened since the appearance of agriculture (*see Map 2*).

The industrial revolution originated in new methods for the exploitation of coal, iron and steam-power, which complemented and stimulated one another to create a massive increase in production, wealth and population. 'Carboniferous capitalism' (as it has been christened) had advanced far enough in Britain by 1815 to enable her to take a decisive lead in post-Napoleonic Europe (*Map 56*). Belgium followed the same course (under British influence) after its independence in 1830, and parts of Germany and France had experienced the same changes by 1870 (*see Map 57*).

Coal, already mined on an unprecedented scale in England in the seventeenth century, was transported from the coalfields of Northumberland and Durham by sea to provide the capital with domestic fuel. In the eighteenth century, it provided a source of energy which ended the domination of wind and water. By 1800, Britain was using 11 million tons of coal a year; by 1870, 100 million tons. The mines of the Newcastle area attracted civil and mechanical engineers as well as surveyors and managers of a higher calibre than anywhere else in Europe.

By the end of the seventeenth century iron too was worked on a large scale in England. But the vital process of producing pig iron by using coal (reduced to the form of smelting coke) – established by Abraham Darby at Coalbrookdale in 1709 – increased the supply and reduced the cost. Iron freed the engineer from dependence upon wood and expensive soft metals. Its uses seemed endless. Pig iron output in Britain rose from about 20,000 tons in 1720 to 250,000 tons in 1806. By 1830 Britain produced more iron than continental Europe and America combined.

The steam engine used the new source of energy and the new material. Atmospheric engines were already used in England in the early eighteenth century to drain water from mines. In the 1760s, James Watt (1736-1819) produced a genuine steam engine. In the 1770s, he went into partnership with a metal manufacturer from Birmingham, Matthew Boulton, and their manufactory marketed a stationary steam engine which could force draught to blast furnaces, drain mines and power factories. As Boulton wrote in 1781, 'The people in London, Manchester and Birmingham are steam-mill mad'.

The application of steam-power to transport followed. Eighteenth-century turnpike trusts had improved English roads but the canal boom of the 1780s, which completed the improvement of river navigation undertaken since the seventeenth century, was vital for the transporting of bulk cargo such as iron ore and coal in the early industrial revolution (*Map 56*). While there were some steam-powered barges in the early nineteenth century, railways united the forces of iron, coal and steam-power. The first regular working railway – from Stockton to Darlington – was completed in 1825. By 1840, there were 1500 miles of trunk route in operation and many more under construction. By 1870 the English network was complete with over 15,000 miles of 'iron road'.

Britain also developed the first sizeable factory industry in cotton products, which were soon being exported throughout the world. The cloth industry in England flourished in the eighteenth century, producing woollens and worsteds, linens and, on a smaller scale, cottons. Everywhere in Europe the fabrication of these cloths was farmed out to rural spinners and weavers and finishing undertaken in the towns by the merchant entrepreneurs. Capacity was low and price was high because up to eight spinners were required to keep one weaver at work. The famous spinning jenny which was invented in 1770 by James Hargreaves replaced the old spinning wheel in the hands of rural workers. Cheaper cloth and the delays and expense of transport made industrial concentration an attractive prospect. Samuel Crompton (1753-1817) produced a hybrid jenny which could easily be steam-powered and arranged in factories. Cartwright's powered loom, introduced after 1800, offered the same advantages. By the turn of the century, the cotton mills were marching across the Lancashire Plain. Less than two million pounds weight was imported through Liverpool in 1700; over 50 million pounds by 1800.

The industrial revolution wrought enormous changes. The construction of the railways, for instance, brought work to armies of navvies, transformed the value of land and stimulated unprecedented financial speculation. Their operation changed the meaning of time and distance. London, a capital city which (like every capital in Europe) had grown prodigiously in the eighteenth century, was the focus for many of these changes. But it was the new industrial towns of the Black Country and Lancashire Plain, mushrooming out to meet each other in conurbations, which experienced most keenly the first industrial revolution. Manchester, its population rising from 75,000 in 1800 to 400,000 in 1850, was surrounded by industrial towns expanding around their factories, workshops, blast furnaces and coke ovens. In them, change was untrammelled by institutions. Plans and regulations came too late. Streets of terrace houses were thrown up cheaply, often without sewerage and water. Poverty and insanitary conditions had been dispersed in the countryside, but in towns they were concentrated and reached horrifying proportions. Typhoid and cholera epidemics broke out throughout Europe in 1832 and again in 1848 and 1849 (*Map 58*). Because of the inadequate sewers, the water-borne germ was spread by polluted rivers. Many other diseases – notably scarlet fever and small-pox – were endemic and dangerous killers. The problem was an intensely serious one in England because by 1851 more than half the population was living in cities.

Migration to, and mobility within, these new industrial cities emphasised the chasm between rich and poor. Housing, income, living standards, life-expectancy, education, geography, all reinforced the distinction. Every nineteenth-century industrial city had its West End and its East End, later its inner-city slum and its outer-city suburb. Amongst some contemporaries, it aroused guilty feelings which spilled over into early socialism. Others turned sour and escapist, reacting (like Wordsworth) to 'Industry's command' by retreating to a romantic nature and idealised past. Friedrich Engels was inspired to radical politics after seeing the industrial

Percentage area of each county enclosed by Act of Parliament, 1700-1845

over 30% enclosed

10% – 30% enclosed

under 10% enclosed

Major trunk canals

Navigable rivers, 1850

Principal railways completed by 1850

• Main railway junctions and depots

Shire boundaries

Major economic activities by 1870

W   Woollen manufacturing

C   Cotton textile manufacturing

H   Hosiery manufacturing

S   Silkworking

J   Jute manufacturing

Cu   Copper mining and smelting

T   Tin mining and smelting

L   Lead mining and smelting

I   Iron mining and smelting

M   Metalware and cutlery

SB   Shipbuilding

B   Brewing

FP   Food processing and refining

CG   Salt, soap, chemicals and glass

Sh   Shoes and leather

P   Pottery

SL   Slate quarrying

Coal working

Selected urban populations in 1801 and 1851
vertical scale : 2mm=15,000 persons

0   150 km

0   100 miles

Outer Hebrides

Inner Hebrides

North West Highlands

Grampian Mts.

Inverness

Aberdeen

Caledonian Canal

Fort William

J Dundee

Perth

Stirling

Dunfermline

Forth-Clyde Canal

Edinburgh

Greenock SB SB

Glasgow SB

Paisley M M

C C M

M

Southern Uplands

Newcastle-on-Tyne

Carlisle

SB SB
I Sunderland
SB
Durham

Workington

L L
L L
L L
Cu L
L
Darlington CG I Middles-brough
L
I

Pennines

Barrow in Furness
SB
Lancaster

Irish Sea

Blackpool

Preston C C
Blackburn C C C Bradford W Leeds
C Halifax W W Aire-Calder Nav.
Bolton C W Wakefield
Wigan C C Oldham Barnsley
Liverpool CG Salford M
FP Manchester Sheffield
Birkenhead CG Warrington Doncaster
SB CG
Chester L
CG Crewe

York

Ouse

Derwent

FP Hull

North Sea

Grimsby

Lincoln

Chesterfield Canal

Holyhead Cu

Bangor

Cambrian Mts.

SL
L

Stoke-on-Trent

Trent and Mersey Canal

S
L
M

S Nottingham

Derby H

B
Burton on Trent
Ironbridge I
Newtown L M Leicester
Wolverhampton L H
M
Birmingham M
Coventry Rugby
Northampton
Sh
Worcester Peterborough

Trent Nav.

Nene Nav.

Great Ouse

Norwich W

W W
W W W
W
W W

Cambridge W
Bedford W Ipswich

Grand June. Canal

Oxford Canal

Hereford

Brecon

Merthyr I
L
Swansea I

Wye

Severn

I
Gloucester W
Thames and Severn Canal
Oxford
Didcot

W W W
Colchester

Newport FP
Cardiff
Bristol FP W
Bath
Kennet and Avon Canal

Swindon
Reading

Thames

FP London
B M SB Chatham

SB

Dover
Folkestone

Royal Military Canal

L
W
Salisbury

W W
Dorchester
W W W
Exeter W
Southampton
Portsmouth
Brighton
Bournemouth

Cu T
Redruth Plymouth
Camborne Cu T Torbay
Cu T
Penzance

English Channel

Bolton Salford Oldham Manchester

© Creative Cartography Ltd © The Hamlyn Group

56 The Industrial Revolution in Great Britain
The complementary exploitation of coal, iron and steam power produced the rapid diversification of economic activity and huge increases in production which made Britain the first industrial society, rapidly becoming wealthier, more populous and more urban, in the first half of the 19th century.

57 The Industrial Revolution in Europe
Except in Belgium, industrialisation did not gather pace in continental Europe until the second half of the 19th century. Its 'second phase', dominated by steel, chemicals and electricity, was led by Germany. In the most backward regions industrialisation was far too late to absorb an explosion of rural population which created acute social tensions and rising emigration.

58 Cholera 1817–1952
The growth of world-wide communications with colonialism and of concentrated urban populations with industrialisation made western man terrifyingly vulnerable to infectious diseases until they could be checked by the advances in medical knowledge, sanitation and public health.

unrest around Manchester; his friend, Karl Marx, an exile from the European Revolutions of 1848, used the industrial cities of England as his model for a class struggle in which, by the law of history, the industrial proletariat would shortly triumph.

Marx was proved wrong in Europe in the generation after 1848, partly because prosperity increased and was not confined to a narrow oligarchy. Real income per head rose substantially in Britain after 1850, for this was a century of falling prices in food as well as clothing and housing. Agricultural changes enabled England to meet the increased demand for food for its rapidly expanding population until the 1870s. These changes had already made the English countryside physically, economically and socially different from the rest of Europe by 1800. Open fields, where the absence of hedges between neighbouring plots preserved customary agricultural techniques, stretched across all the plains of Europe with the exception of the Po Valley, Flanders and England. There in the course of the seventeenth and eighteenth centuries, enclosed fields, farmed with all the intensity of a cottage garden, dramatically broke with traditional communal practices and made innovation possible in crops and methods. Economically, the English country-side was less isolated from its markets than that of the rest of Europe. Socially, no other country had such a large class of tenant farmers, capable of investing so much in agricultural expansion, new machinery, stock and seed. As a result, Britain avoided the iron law of population asserted by T. R. Malthus, that in history population always expanded beyond the means to sustain it.

Marx was also proved wrong because state legislation and new technology alleviated the problems of the industrial city. The state intervened in factory safety, public health and education in Britain in the later nineteenth century. The technology of conveying fresh water in iron pipes and sewerage in glazed pottery pipes reduced the dangers of water-borne infection; western Europe was clear of cholera by 1911. Cleaner gas heating, electric lighting, electric trams and underground railways all improved urban life dramatically by 1900. Co-operative shops and chain stores improved marketing and distribution in towns. As a result, it was the philosophy of infinite material progress rather than Marxism which appeared to be confirmed at every turn to urban man in the late nineteenth century.

The benefits and wealth generated by the industrial revolution were not confined to Britain. In 1850, Britain was the manufacturer, clothier, banker, shipper, insurer and transporter to the world, a pre-eminence demonstrated at the Great Exhibition of 1851. London invited the whole world to its shop-window, confident that its wares would outstrip all-comers. But the pre-eminence did not last for long. Flanders began its industrial revolution in the 1830s; the Rhur in the 1850s and 1860s imitated British technology, frequently used British capital and engineers and sometimes avoided British mistakes. By the

1870s, the second phase of the industrial revolution (as it is now commonly called) had begun in Germany and the United States (see Maps 57 and 69). In this second phase, a new trinity of steel, electricity and petro-chemicals dominated the industrial world. By 1900, Germany and the United States produced more steel than Britain. The United States developed – with its natural resources and tycoons – the technology of the internal combustion engine. Germany, with the help of state intervention and adventurous bankers, exploited electrical technology for power, transport and communications. After the turn of the century, the exploitation of hydro-electric power in the Alps helped France and Italy at last to increase the pace of their progress towards industrialisation. English manufacturers, secure in their belief in progress, the continued primacy of coal and their imperial self-sufficiency, fitted snugly into a liberal society where tradition and innovation had been reconciled, and met competition with complacency. They were inevitably less conspicuous in the Great Exhibitions in Paris in 1867, Chicago in 1880 and Melbourne in 1891 than they had been in 1851. In Europe, as in Britain, food prices fell, spreading the benefits of industrial change amongst the citizens of the new industrial towns and compelling change amongst the peasantry of Europe which felt the demands from the new markets.

In another important respect, the industrial revolution was a 'Prometheus Unbound'. In 1846 the abolition of tariffs on corn imported into England was, in retrospect, a recognition that the days of British self-sufficiency were numbered. The opening-up of the prairies in the 1870s and 1880s in America (Map 68), the application of mechanised farming methods there, and the impact of railways and steamships on transport, resulted in the large-scale importation of American wheat to Europe. A similar pattern was established with the imports of butter, cheese and Canterbury lamb from New Zealand (using refrigerated shipping) in the 1880s. The canned meat trade also developed from South America to Europe. The export of European capital across the world and the migration of Europeans which followed it, emphasised European predominance in the nineteenth century (see Map 67). But it also, with the development of world communications by telegraph and telephone, and the new patterns of trade established in the wake of the industrial revolutions, created the basis for a world community in the twentieth century.

Further reading: D. S. Landes, *The Unbound Prometheus* (Cambridge University Press, 1969); A. P. Milward and S. B. Saul, *The Economic Development of Continental Europe (1780-1870)* (Allen & Unwin, 1973; p.b.); A. Briggs, *Victorian Cities* (Odhams, 1964; Penguin, 1968); E. P. Thompson, *The Making of the English Working Class* (Gollancz, 1963; Penguin, 1970); C. Morazé, *The Triumph of the Middle Class* (Weidenfeld & Nicolson, 1966); K. Marx, *Capital*, Volume 1 (1867; trans. F. B. M. Fowkes, Penguin, 1968).

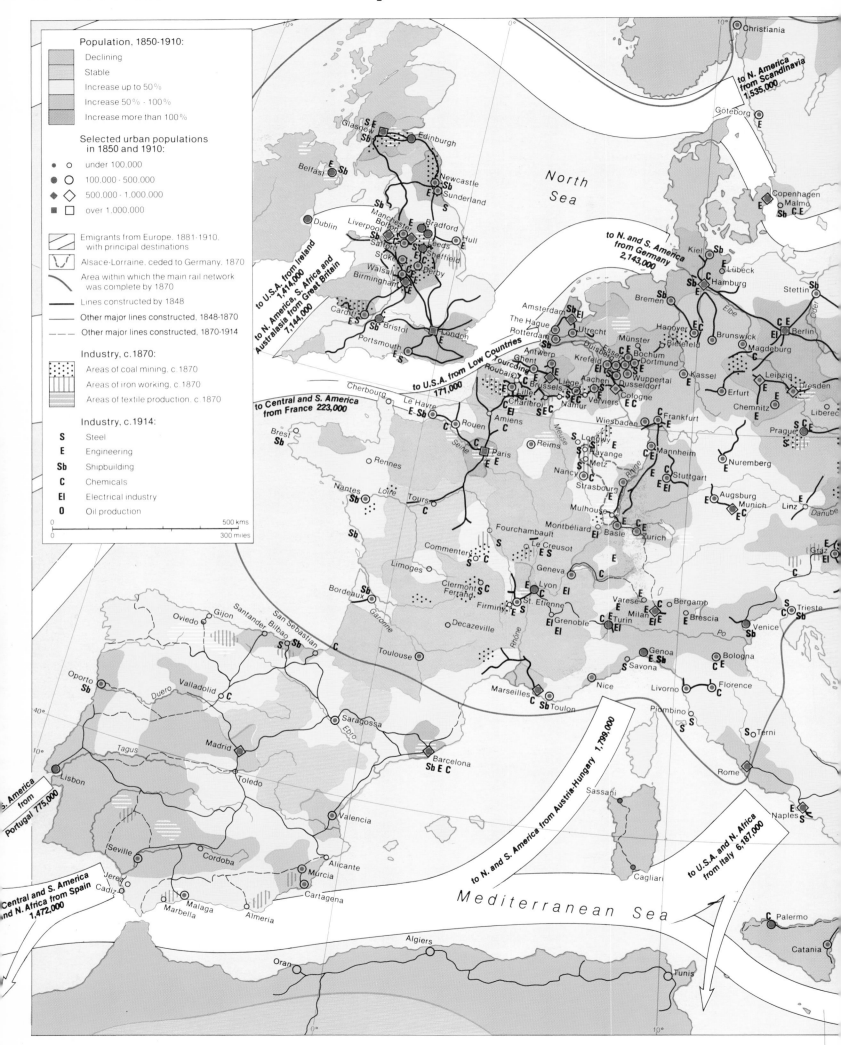

Population, 1850-1910:
- Declining
- Stable
- Increase up to 50%
- Increase 50% - 100%
- Increase more than 100%

Selected urban populations in 1850 and 1910:
- under 100,000
- 100,000 - 500,000
- 500,000 - 1,000,000
- over 1,000,000

Emigrants from Europe, 1881-1910, with principal destinations

Alsace-Lorraine, ceded to Germany, 1870

Area within which the main rail network was complete by 1870

Lines constructed by 1848

Other major lines constructed, 1848-1870

Other major lines constructed, 1870-1914

Industry, c.1870:
- Areas of coal mining, c.1870
- Areas of iron working, c.1870
- Areas of textile production, c.1870

Industry, c.1914:
- S Steel
- E Engineering
- Sb Shipbuilding
- C Chemicals
- El Electrical industry
- O Oil production

500 kms
300 miles

North Sea

Mediterranean Sea

to N. America from Scandinavia 1,535,000

to N. and S. America from Germany 2,143,000

to U.S.A. from Ireland 1,414,000
to N. America, S. Africa and Australasia from Great Britain 7,144,000

to U.S.A. from Low Countries 171,000

to Central and S. America from France 223,000

to N. and S. America from Austria-Hungary 1,799,000

to U.S.A. and N. Africa from Italy 6,187,000

to S. America from Portugal 775,000

to Central and S. America and N. Africa from Spain 1,472,000

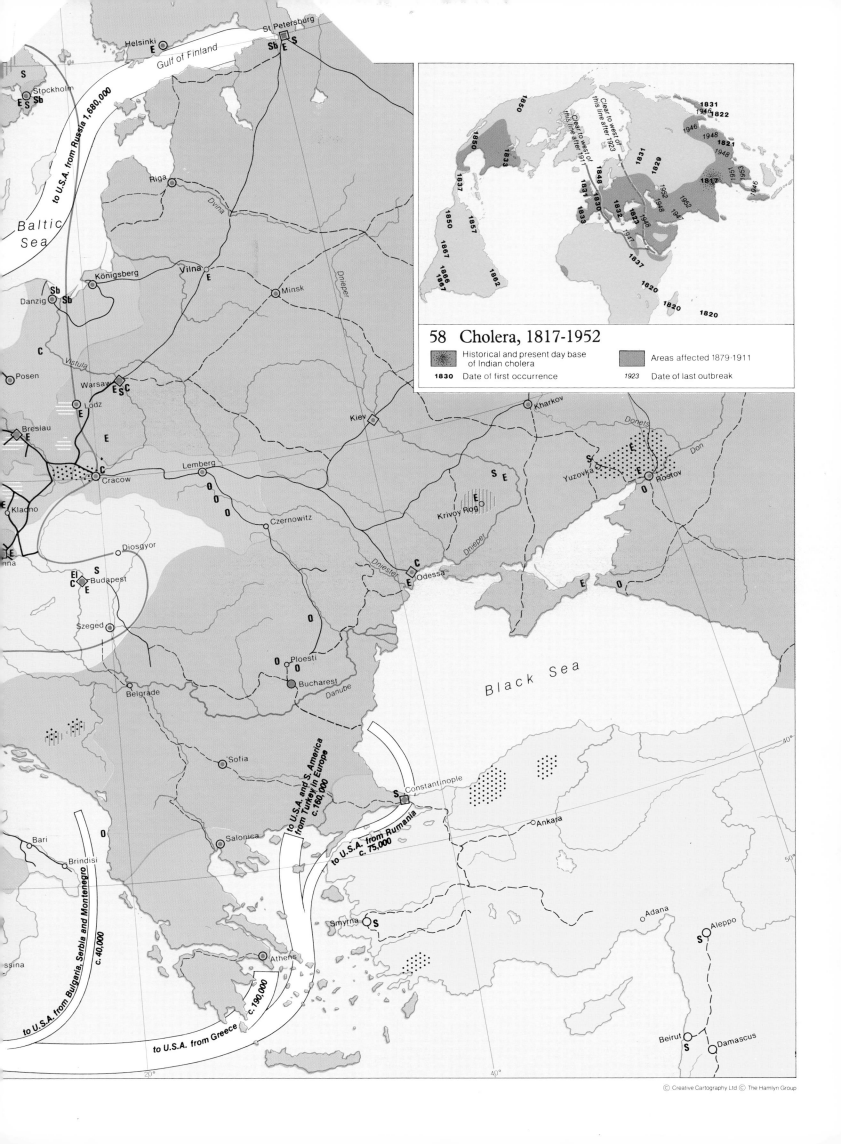

Helsinki E

Gulf of Finland

St Petersburg Sb E

Sb E

S

Stockholm

E S Sb

Baltic Sea

to U.S.A. from Russia 1,680,000

Riga

Dvina

Königsberg

Vilna E

Minsk

Dnieper

Danzig Sb Sb

Posen

C

Vistula

Warsaw E S C

Lodz E

Breslau E

Kladno

Cracow C

Lemberg O O O

Kiev

Kharkov

Donets

S E E

Yuzovka E E

Rostov

Don

nna Y E

Diosgyor

El C S

Budapest E

Czernowitz

Krivoy Rog E

Dnieper

Dniester C

E Odessa

E O

Szeged

O

Ploesti O

Bucharest

Danube

Black Sea

Belgrade

Sofia

to U.S.A. and S. America from Turkey in Europe c. 160,000

to U.S.A. from Rumania c. 75,000

Constantinople S

40°

Ankara

Bari

O

Brindisi

Salonica

Smyrna S

Adana

50°

to U.S.A. from Bulgaria, Serbia and Montenegro c. 40,000

ssina

to U.S.A. from Greece

c. 190,000

Athens

Aleppo S

Beirut S

Damascus

58 Cholera, 1817-1952

Historical and present day base of Indian cholera

Areas affected 1879-1911

1830 Date of first occurrence

1923 Date of last outbreak

1850

1850

1833

1837

Clear to west of this line after 1923

Clear to west of this line after 1911

1831

1829

1831 **1946** **1822**

1946

1821

1948

1948

1817

1965 1956

1946

1831

1848

1851 1830

1833

1832 1823 1948

1830 1832

1833

1952

1952

1947

1941

1850

1857

1948

1837

1947

1867

1866 1867

1862

1820

1820

1820

20°

40°

© Creative Cartography Ltd © The Hamlyn Group

80°

Curaçao

Cartagena
Maracaibo
Coffee
Margarita
Trinidad

Panama
Mompós
Cattle
Caracas
× Carabobo 1821
San Carlos

Canal Zone (U.S. occ. 1903)

PANAMA 1903

COLOMBIA 1819

VENEZUELA 1830

Sheep
Orinoco
Coffee
Angostura
Sugar

Georgetown
Paramaribo
Cayenne

BRITISH GUIANA

DUTCH GUIANA

FRENCH GUIANA

Atlantic Ocean

× Boyacá 1819

Bogotá

Cattle

GREATER COLOMBIA 1819-30

8

7

9

× Bombona 1822

Equator 0°

ECUADOR 1830

× Pichincha 1822
Bananas Quito

Guayaquil

Cattle

5

3

1

2

RUBBER

Negro

TIMBER

Gurupá

Belém

To Brazil: 3m. 1835-1913 from Portugal, Spain, Italy

Equator 0°

4

6

FEDERATION OF PERU AND BOLIVIA 1836-39

Sugar

Trujillo

COPPER

SILVER

PERU 1821

Lima
Callao
× Junin 1824
× Ayacucho 1824
× Pisco

Cuzco

RUBBER

TIMBER

RIO NEGRO

Manaus

Amazon

RUBBER

ACRE

10

11

13

14

RUBBER

MATO GROSSO

15

B R A Z I L 1822

Xingu

PARÁ

Tocantins

Cotton

MARANHÃO

Maranhão

Coffee

Ceará

CEARÁ

Cocoa

RIO GRANDE DO NORTE

Sugar

PARAIBA

Pernambuco

PERNAMBUCO

Coffee

ALAGÔAS

Tobacco

S. Francisco

BAHIA

Bahia

GOIÁS

Minas Novas

Coffee

Pacific Ocean

NITRATES

La Paz

SILVER TIN COPPER

Chuquisaca

BOLIVIA 1825

Tacna

Arica
GUANO
Iquique

18

Potosí

CHACO

16

17

19

Corumbá

PARAGUAY 1811

20

MINAS GERAIS

Diamantina

SÃO PAULO

Coffee

ESPIRITO SANTO

To Uruguay from Italy, Spain

20°

Antofagasta

Copiapó

23

Jujuy

Salta

× 1812

Tucumán

× 1812

COPPER MANGANESE TIN SILVER

ARGENTINA 1810

24

TIMBER

Asunción

21

22

Sao Paulo

Santos

Rio de Janeiro

SANTA CATARINA

Cattle

RIO GRANDE DO SUL

Cattle

Porto Alegre

To Argentine: 4.5m. 1857-1913 from Italy, Spain

La Serena

Valparaiso

Santiago

Chacabuco 1817
× Maipú 1818

CHILE 1818

Concepción

Valdivia

Mendoza

Córdoba

San Luis

Cattle

Cereals

Sheep

Cattle

Santa Fé

Rosario

Buenos Aires

URUGUAY 1828

Montevideo

River Plate

Sheep

Patagonia

25

26

Falkland Islands (Br. 1833)

Tierra del Fuego

27

1	to Brazil 1905	
2	to Brazil 1904	
3	to Ecuador 1880-1922	
4	to Ecuador 1880-1942	
5		
6	to Peru 1942	
7	to Brazil 1904-5	
8	to Brit. Guiana 1899	
9	to Brazil 1900	
10	to Bolivia 1867-1903	
11		
12	to Bolivia 1867	
13	to Bolivia 1867-1909	
14	to Bolivia 1867-1902	
15	to Brazil 1927	
16	to Paraguay 1935	
17	to Bolivia 1880-1935	
18	to Chile 1883	
19	to Brazil 1870	
20		
21	to Argentina 1874	
22	to Brazil 1895	
23	to Chile 1884	
24	to Argentina 1874	
25	to Argentina 1881	
26	to Chile 1902	
27	to Argentina 1881	

Mountain

Desert and semi-desert

Temperate forest and scrub

Tropical forest and scrub

Grasslands

Population:
c.1880 c.1910

● ○ 100,000 and over

● ○ 200,000 and over

□ 1,000,000 and over

○ Other towns under 100,000

── Main railways c.1910

──▶ Bolivar's route 1817-24

─ ─ San Martin's route 1817-22

── Borders c.1830

─ ─ Subsequent border changes

━━ Border of Greater Colombia, 1819-30 and border of Federation of Bolivia and Peru, 1835-39

⟹ European immigration (showing country of origin)

0   1000 km
0   600 miles

© Creative Cartography Ltd © The Hamlyn Group

59 Independent Latin America
Protected from hostile European intervention by Britain and America (the Monroe doctrine was proclaimed in 1823), the liberation movements ended the Spanish American empire, but failed to create a united republic—Bolívar's Gran Colombia—in its place. Disputes over land, minerals and access to the coast continued to weaken and divide the new states.

60 Reaction and revolution in Europe
The revolutions of 1848, though directly responsible for a change of regime only in France, marked a decisive stage in the progress of liberal ideas and the aspirations of national minorities. These had presented a growing and increasingly successful challenge to the *status quo* imposed by the Congress of Vienna of 1815.

ALTHOUGH REACTION appeared triumphant in the aftermath of 1815, as conservative rule was restored to most of Europe (*Map 60*), the twin forces of liberalism and nationalism which had been unleashed by the French revolution continued their volcanic rumblings beneath the surface of international politics. Liberalism stressed freedom of internal and international trade, the removal of traditional constraints on the free operation of the market (including the abolition of institutions such as slavery and serfdom, the stripping of monopolistic corporate privileges, and the emancipation of religious minorities), minimal governmental interference in the economy or society, liberty of the individual, and responsible representative government through parliaments as against arbitrary, hereditary rule. Drawing on the thought of the Scottish economist Adam Smith, the English political theorists Locke, Jeremy Bentham, and James Mill, and the French *philosophes*, liberalism was the ideological expression of the interests of the rising middle classes in industrial societies. It was natural, therefore, that it should find its political home in this period in the world's foremost industrial society, Britain. Measures such as the emancipation of Catholics (1828), the first parliamentary reform act (1832), and the abolition of slavery in the British empire (1833) were typical liberal achievements. With the abolition of the Corn Laws (the tariff on imported corn) in 1846, Britain moved into the era of free trade from which, because of her industrial and commercial dominance in the world's markets, she continued to prosper for several decades. Although it was not until about 1858 that a Liberal Party coalesced in Parliament, liberal principles dominated English politics at home and abroad for much of the earlier period, and it was to England that liberals elsewhere tended to look for inspiration and support.

A striking example was the liberation of Latin America from Spanish and Portuguese colonial rule (*Map 59*). The leaders of the liberation movement, Francisco de Miranda, Simón Bolívar, and José de San Martín, were much influenced by the ideas of English liberalism, and by the American and French revolutions. After the collapse of the short-lived first Venezuelan republic, proclaimed in 1811, Miranda was imprisoned in Spain (dying in gaol in 1816), while Bolívar fled to neighbouring New Granada, and thence after 1814 to Jamaica and Haiti. During the next three years he organised his army anew, and in 1817 he returned to Venezuela, landing at Angostura. From there he led his troops (among whom were several thousand European, particularly British, volunteers) in a series of epic campaigns through difficult country, capturing Bogotá in 1819, and Quito in 1822. Meanwhile in the south of the continent San Martín had formed his 'Army of the Andes' in Argentina. In one of the most remarkable campaigns in military history, San Martín led his forces across the Andes and into Chile, fewer than half surviving the journey. After inflicting defeat on the Spaniards at the battle of Chacabuco, he was able to proclaim the independence of Chile in 1818. By 1821 he had made a triumphal entry into Lima after a thousand-mile sea voyage with his men in a fleet commanded by the British admiral, Lord Cochrane. The two liberators met at Guayaquil in 1822, but they fell out, and Bolívar wrested leadership of the movement from his rival. After 1825, with the liberation of the sub-continent virtually complete, Bolívar devoted his energies to preserving the unity of 'Gran Colombia'—but in vain. By

the time of his death in 1830 the former Spanish Empire had fragmented into small units. By contrast the former Portuguese territory of Brazil remained united after its bloodless separation from Portugal in 1822 under the Emperor Pedro I. The liberation process had received strong support from the USA, whose President, James Monroe, in 1823 enunciated his celebrated 'doctrine' prohibiting European intervention against the nascent republics, and from Britain, whose Foreign Secretary, Canning, in 1826 declared that he had 'called the New World into being to redress the balance of the Old'.

In the Old World, however, liberals faced more formidable opposition as conservative governments concerted their defensive measures in the 'congress system'. This was the term applied to the four-power alliance of Britain, Russia, Prussia, and Austria, in November 1815, whereby the signatories agreed to meet periodically in congress to discuss common measures to preserve the *status quo* as enshrined in the Treaty of Vienna (*Map 60*). However, as the system, masterminded by the Austrian statesman Metternich, was rapidly revealed to be a 'Holy Alliance' of conservative forces determined to crush liberal tendencies throughout Europe, Britain gradually dissociated herself from the arrangement. Britain objected to the French military intervention in Spain in 1822, conducted with the blessing of the Holy Alliance, which repressed a liberal revolt there. Austrian intervention in Italy to crush liberal rebellions, particularly those of the secret nationalist society, the *Carbonari*, further aroused British indignation. The marriage of liberalism and nationalism found its ultimate consummation in the Greek War of Liberation between 1821 and 1829 (*Map 63*). Romantic revolutionaries from all over Europe, among them Lord Byron, flocked to the Greek cause and sang its praises. Russia, perceiving an opportunity of stealing a further march on the Turks, supported the Greeks. In the naval battle of Navarino (1827) British, French, and Russian forces defeated the Turks.

With conservatism now in some disarray, the liberals took an important stride forward in 1830, when the last of the French Bourbons, the arch-reactionary Charles X, was overthrown in the 'July Revolution' and replaced by the Orleanist dynasty of Louis Philippe. Shortly afterwards a liberal revolution in Belgium dissolved the union with Holland, and the new state received guarantees of its independence and neutrality by the Treaty of London (1839). The success of the July Revolution gave rise to further revolts, but these were crushed by conservative governments. A Polish attempt to regain independence was extinguished by the Russians. Under the July Monarchy, France pursued a guardedly liberal course in home politics, a rapprochement with Britain abroad, a policy of imperial expansion in Algeria (where a vicious colonial war was waged to subdue local resistance which endured until 1847), and an economic policy which, while it enriched sections of the bourgeoisie, left France lagging further behind Britain in industrial development (*compare Maps 56 and 57*). The Orleanist régime was increasingly criticised for its corruption, and a severe economic crisis in 1846-7 sounded its death-knell.

The year 1848, the year of revolutions throughout Europe, was the supreme crisis of conservatism (*Map 60*). Beginning in Sicily in January, a wave of revolutions swept through the continent, throwing nearly all conservative governments off balance, and giving a fresh

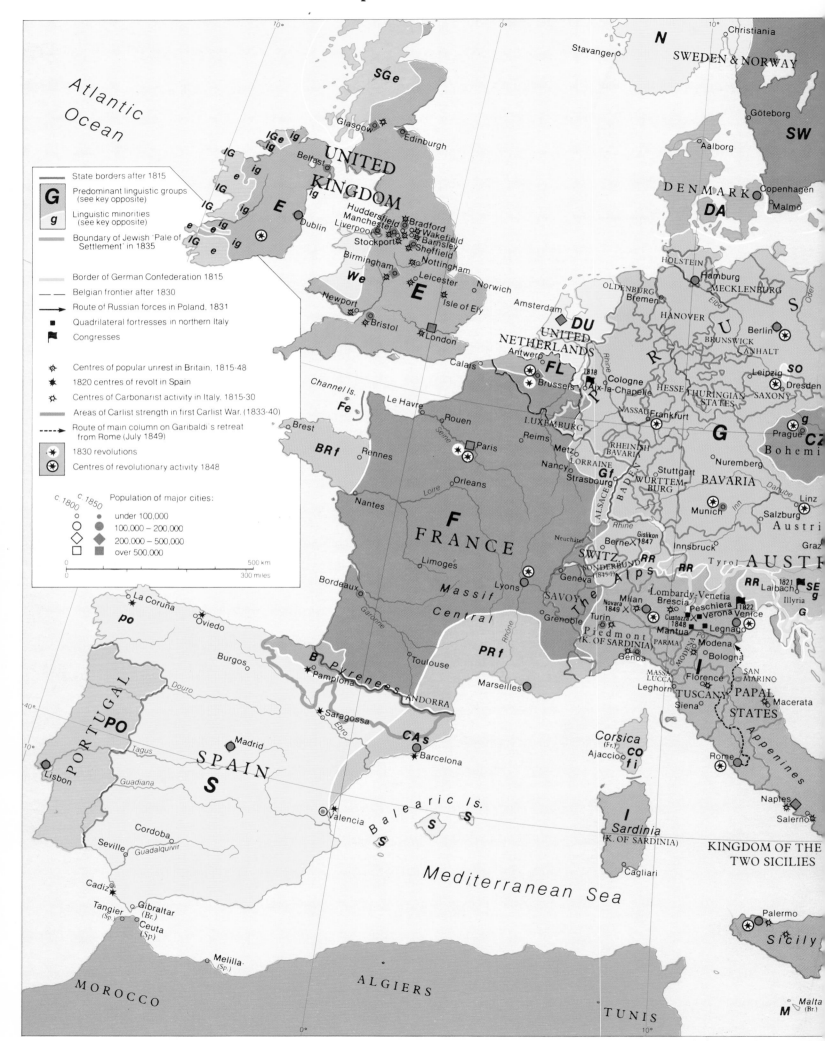

Atlantic Ocean

State borders after 1815

G Predominant linguistic groups (see key opposite)

g Linguistic minorities (see key opposite)

Boundary of Jewish 'Pale of Settlement' in 1835

Border of German Confederation 1815

Belgian frontier after 1830

→ Route of Russian forces in Poland, 1831

■ Quadrilateral fortresses in northern Italy

⚑ Congresses

✷ Centres of popular unrest in Britain, 1815-48

✳ 1820 centres of revolt in Spain

✩ Centres of Carbonarist activity in Italy, 1815-30

Areas of Carlist strength in first Carlist War, (1833-40)

Route of main column on Garibaldi's retreat from Rome (July 1849)

1830 revolutions

Centres of revolutionary activity 1848

Population of major cities:
- c. 1800 / c. 1850
- ○ ● under 100,000
- ○ ● 100,000 – 200,000
- ◇ ◆ 200,000 – 500,000
- □ ■ over 500,000

0 — 500 km
0 — 300 miles

SWEDEN & NORWAY
Christiania
Stavanger
Göteborg
SW
Aalborg
DENMARK
Copenhagen
DA
Malmö
HOLSTEIN
Hamburg
MECKLENBURG
OLDENBURG
Bremen
HANOVER
S
U
BRUNSWICK
Berlin
ANHALT
P
R
Leipzig
SO
Dresden
SAXONY
THURINGIAN STATES
HESSE
Cologne
Aix-la-Chapelle
Frankfurt
NASSAU
Prague
g
CZ
RHEINISH BAVARIA
Bohemia
G
Nuremberg
Stuttgart
BADEN
WÜRTTEM-BURG
Munich
Salzburg
Austri
Linz

SGe
Glasgow
Edinburgh
IGe ig
IG ig
e
UNITED
KINGDOM
Belfast
ig
IG ig
e
IG ig
E
Dublin
e
IG e
ig
Huddersfield
Manchester Bradford
Liverpool Wakefield
Stockport Barnsley
Sheffield
Birmingham Nottingham
We Leicester
Newport E Norwich
E Isle of Ely
Bristol London

Amsterdam
UNITED
NETHERLANDS
DU
Antwerp
FL
1818
Brussels
LUXEMBURG
Calais
Channel Is.
Fe
BR f
Le Havre
Rouen
Reims
Seine
Metz
Paris
Nancy LORRAINE
Rennes
Orleans
Loire
Strasbourg
ALSACE
Gf
Nantes
F
FRANCE
Limoges
Rhine
Neuchâtel
Berne X
Gislikon
1847
SWITZ.
SONDERBUND
1845-7
Geneva
The Alps
Bordeaux
Garonne
Massif
Central
Lyons
Grenoble
SAVOY
Turin
Novara
1849 X
Piedmont
(K. OF SARDINIA)
PR f
Rhône
Toulouse
ANDORRA
Marseilles
Pyrenees

N
Rhine
Elbe
Oder
Danube
Inn
Graz
Tyrol
AUSTR
RR
RR
RR
Innsbruck
RR
Milan
Lombardy-Venetia
Brescia Peschiera
Custozza X Verona Venice
1848 Mantua Legnago
PARMA Modena
MODENA Bologna
MASSA
LUCCA Florence
Leghorn TUSCANY
Siena
1821
Laibach SE
Illyria
G
1822
SAN
MARINO
PAPAL
STATES
Macerata
Appenines

La Coruña
po
Oviedo
Burgos
Douro
PORTUGAL
PO
Lisbon
Tagus
Guadiana
SPAIN
Madrid
S
B
Pamplona
Saragossa
Ebro
CAs
Barcelona
Valencia
S
S
S
S
Balearic Is.
Cordoba
Seville
Guadalquivir
Cadiz
Tangier
(Sp.)
Gibraltar
(Br.)
Ceuta
(Sp.)
Melilla
(Sp.)
MOROCCO

Corsica
(Fr.)
CO
Ajaccio f i
Rome
Sardinia
(K. OF SARDINIA)
Cagliari
KINGDOM OF THE
TWO SICILIES
Naples
Salerno
Mediterranean Sea
ALGIERS
TUNIS
M Malta
(Br.)
Sicily
Palermo

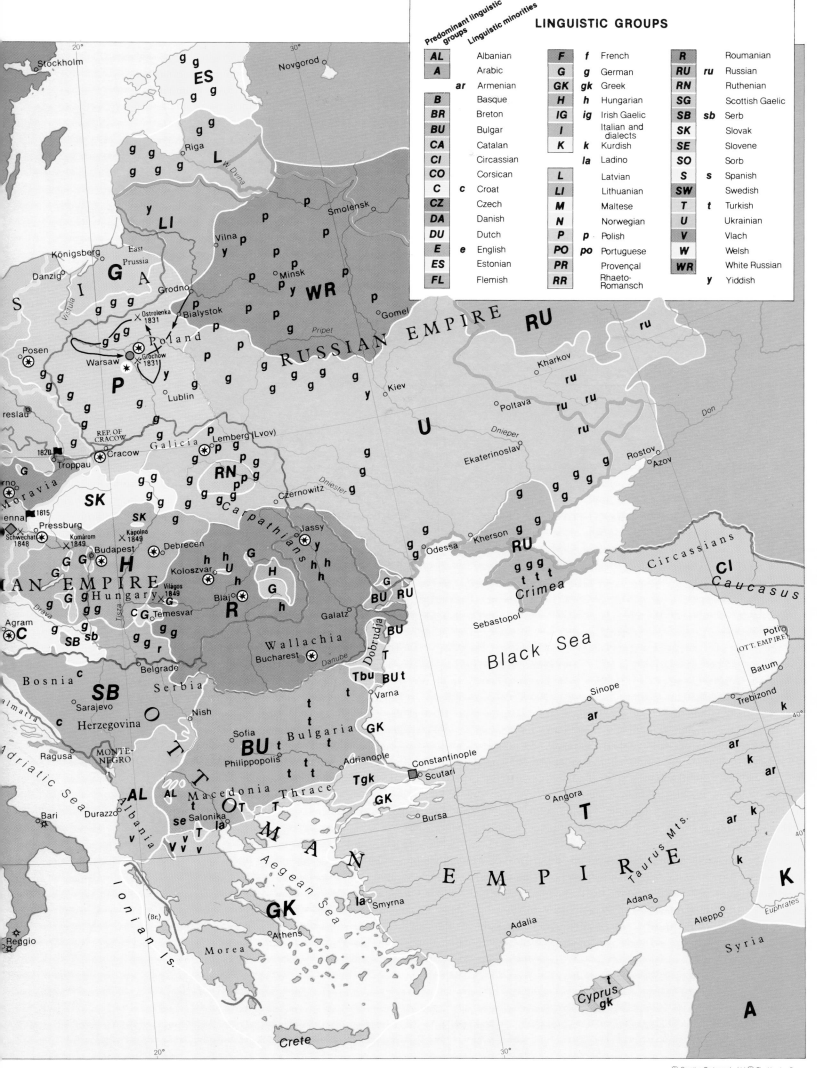

LINGUISTIC GROUPS

Liberalism and nationalism

impetus to democratic and nationalist ideals. In France the July Monarchy was replaced by the short-lived Second Republic, which, after the suppression of radical left-wing elements in June 1848, elected Louis Napoleon (nephew of the first Emperor) as President. By 1852 he had transformed the régime into the Second Empire, styling himself Napoleon III, and maintaining a firm grip on power, by a mixture of populism, authoritarianism, and opportunism, until 1870. In Prussia popular disturbances led King Frederick William IV to agree to 'merge Prussia into Germany' and to reign as a constitutional monarch. Similar movements were sparked off in the smaller German states, and a Constituent National Assembly met at Frankfurt from May 1848 to April 1849. Meanwhile the revolutionary surge had reached the Austrian Empire where an uprising in Vienna in March 1848 led to the fall of Metternich. A Constituent Assembly in Vienna emancipated the peasantry from surviving feudal burdens. In June 1848 a Slav Congress in Prague demanded national rights for the subject peoples of the empire. However, resolute military action by the Austrian general Windischgraetz crushed the revolution in Prague and later in Vienna. Under the leadership of Schwarzenberg, Hapsburg power was restored. In Hungary a nationalist revolution led by Kossuth was repressed by 1849 after the Hungarians had been defeated by Austrian, Croat, and Russian forces. Revolution against Austrian rule in Italy, supported by King Charles Albert of Piedmont, was defeated, though the Venetian republic held out until August 1849. By then the revolutionary surge had subsided, and conservative governments nearly everywhere had reasserted control. But 1848 had demonstrated the vulnerability of reactionary régimes, and the year of revolutions marked a decisive stage on the road to nationhood of several peoples, most notably those of Italy and Germany.

The *Risorgimento*, the movement for Italian unification, was a diversified and at times incoherent movement, whose supporters often differed over both means and ends, even over the practicability and desirability of the complete unification of the peninsula. The liberal constitutionalists, among whom the Piedmontese statesman Cavour was outstanding, proved to be the dominant group, but they were challenged by the republicans, whose leaders Mazzini and Garibaldi inspired revolutionaries everywhere, the former by his speeches and writings, the latter by his romantic heroism. A third group, the 'neo-Guelphs', believed that the Papacy was the natural head of a united Italy, and this notion was given some stimulus by the early actions of Pope Pius IX, elected in 1846. However, in the revolution of 1848 Pius fled from Rome, and he returned only after Garibaldi's Roman Republic had been destroyed by French troops. The political unification of Italy took place in several stages (*Map 62*). The first, and most important, took place in 1859-60 when France, in alliance with Piedmont, defeated Austria in war, and secured the liberation of Lombardy and its union with Piedmont. In return Napoleon exacted his '*pourboire*' ('tip') in the form of the cession of Savoy and Nice to France by Piedmont. The independent northern duchies decided to join the union. Cavour was inclined to call a halt at this stage, but his hand was forced by Garibaldi who sailed for Sicily with his 'thousand', and, in a brilliant campaign, conquered Sicily and moved up through Naples towards Rome. In order to forestall an attack by Garibaldi on Rome (which,

it was feared, would bring about outside intervention), the Piedmontese king Victor Emmanuel II moved south to block the way against Garibaldi. Rome and Venetia remained outside the kingdom of Italy proclaimed in 1861. Further attempts by Garibaldi in 1862 and 1867 to seize Rome were thwarted. In 1866 Venetia fell into Italian hands as a result of the defeat of Austria by Prussia, but it was not until 1870, after the French defeat by Prussia, that Rome was at last captured and the *Risorgimento* appeared complete.

The *Risorgimento* was the foremost example of the union of liberalism and nationalism. By contrast the process of German unification (*Map 61*) was marked by the gradual divorce of the two movements, particularly after 1848, as nationalism came to be increasingly aligned with conservative elements. Italian unification, it was sometimes said, was merely a mask for Piedmontese expansion. There was some truth in this (as was shown by the failure of the new Italy to prevent the ever-widening divergence between the developed north and the primitive south); but in the case of Germany there could be no doubt that the country was united primarily in the form of conquest by Prussia. The dominant genius of German unification was Bismarck (Prussian minister-president 1862-7 and federal chancellor 1867-90) who towered over international politics in the later part of the century even more effectively than had Metternich earlier. Bismarck proceeded, like Cavour, by a deft mixture of diplomacy and war. Unlike Cavour he had, in the Prussian army, a military machine which could win decisive victories without heavy reliance on allies. Prussian victories in three wars within seven years secured German unification. The war with Denmark in 1864 secured Austro-Prussian occupation of the duchies of Schleswig and Holstein. The war with Austria in 1866 saw the decisive defeat of Austria at Sadowa-Königgrätz, the formation of the North German Confederation of German states under Prussian leadership, and the eclipse of Hapsburg aspirations to German leadership. Henceforth it was certain that Prussia would dominate Germany and that Austria would be excluded from the new national state. The final stage came in 1870-1 with the victory over France at Sedan which brought the collapse of the Second French Empire, and the birth of the new German Empire which incorporated not only the south German states but also the annexed French provinces of Alsace and Lorraine, with their substantial German-speaking populations. In January 1871 the Prussian king William I was proclaimed German Emperor in a ceremony held at Versailles. The dream of the romantic German nationalists of the early part of the century seemed fulfilled. But the methods by which German unification had been brought about, and the type of state which was now established, socially conservative and politically authoritarian, hardly fulfilled the hopes of the German liberals. Henceforth nationalism was increasingly to be the handmaiden not of liberalism but of reactionary forces, notably imperialism.

Further reading: H. Kohn, *Nationalism: its Meaning and History* (Anvil Books, 1965); J. H. Lynch, *The Spanish American Revolutions* (Weidenfeld & Nicolson, 1973); P. N. Stearns, *The Revolutions of 1848* (Weidenfeld & Nicolson, 1974); D. Mack Smith, *The Making of Italy, 1796-1870* (Michigan University Press, 1959); W. N. Medlicott, *Bismarck and Modern Germany* (English Universities Press, 1965).

61 The unification of Germany
Under the leadership and, after the defeat of Austria in 1866, the domination of Prussia, Germany was unified to form a highly centralised and authoritarian state, and the leading military and industrial power of continental Europe.

62 The unification of Italy
Despite the brilliance and international fame of the republican heroes Mazzini and Garibaldi, the traditional leadership of Piedmont retained effective control of the Italian *risorgimento*. After 1870 the benefits of political unity were limited by deep and persistent economic and social divisions.

63 The Balkans in the nineteenth century
As the Ottoman empire retreated, the rise of nationality in the Balkans led through provincial autonomy and war to independence. The political and strategic interests of the great powers ensured their constant, often dangerous, and eventually fatal intervention.

Border of German Confederation 1815
Border of North German Confederation 1867
Border of German Empire 1871
Prussia 1815
Prussian gains by 1867
German States still independent 1867-71
X   Battle

0   150 km
0   100 miles

SWEDEN

Baltic Sea

North Sea

DENMARK

Copenhagen

SCHLESWIG
Flensburg
Schleswig
Kiel
HOLSTEIN

Heligoland
(Br. to 1890)
Cuxhaven
Wilhelmshaven

Frisian Is.

Lübeck
LÜBECK
Hamburg
HAMBURG
Rostock
MECKLENBURG-
SCHWERIN
MS
MECKLENBURG-
STRELITZ
Stettin

Memel
Tilsit
Königsberg

East Prussia
A

Danzig
P R U S S I A
Pomerania
West Prussia
Posen
Posen
Vistula
Warsaw

RUSSIAN EMPIRE
Poland

Oldenburg
OLDENBURG
BREMEN
Bremen
Weser

Wittenberg
Brandenburg
Berlin
Brandenburg

Oder

Amsterdam
NETHERLANDS
The Hague

HANOVER
Osnabrück
SCHAUMBURG-
LIPPE
LIPPE-
DETMOLD
Detmold
Münster

Hanover
Brunswick
BRUNSWICK
B
Magdeburg
Dessau
ANHALT
Halle
Göttingen
TS
TS
Saxony
Leipzig

Dresden
Breslau
Silesia

REP. OF
CRACOW
(to Austria 1846)
Cracow

Galicia

Westphalia
Dortmund
Essen
Düsseldorf
WALDECK
Kassel
H
EL.te. OF
HESSE
THURINGIAN
STATES
P
Erfurt
SAXONY

Antwerp
Brussels
BELGIUM

Cologne
P
Marburg
RHENISH
PRUSSIA
Coblenz
NASSAU
P
GR. D.
OF
HESSE
Fulda

Karlsbad
Prague
Pilsen
Bohemia

Sadowa Königgrätz
1866

Olmütz
Brünn
Moravia

LUXEMBURG
(to Belgium
1839)
Sedan
1870
Luxemburg
Trier
O LICHTEN-
BERG
Ludwigshafen
RHEINISH
BAVARIA
Mainz
FRANKFURT
AM MAIN
Frankfurt
Main
GR.D.OF
HESSE
Würzburg
Mosel

Elbe

Metz
Saarbrücken
Lorraine
Meuse
Nancy

Mannheim
Heidelberg
Fürth
Nuremberg
Regensburg
Danube

AUSTRIAN
Lower
Austria
Pressburg
Slovakia

Strasbourg
(From Fr.1871)
Alsace
BADEN
Karlsruhe
Stuttgart
WÜRTTEMBERG
Ulm
HOHEN-
ZOLLERN

BAVARIA
Augsburg
Munich
Inn

Linz
Vienna

EMPIRE
Budapest
Hungary
Danube
Drava

FRANCE

Mulhouse
Belfort
Basel

Freiburg
Lake of
Constance
Constance
Zurich

LIECHTENSTEIN

Neuchâtel
(Pr. 1815-57)
Bern
SWITZERLAND
Lausanne
L. Geneva

Salzburg
Upper
Austria
Innsbruck
Tyrol
The Alps

Graz
Styria
Carinthia

Laibach
Carniola
Trieste
Fiume

Croatia
Adriatic Sea

Lyon
Grenoble
Turin
Milan
Venice
Po

5° 10° 15° 20°
45° 50° 55°

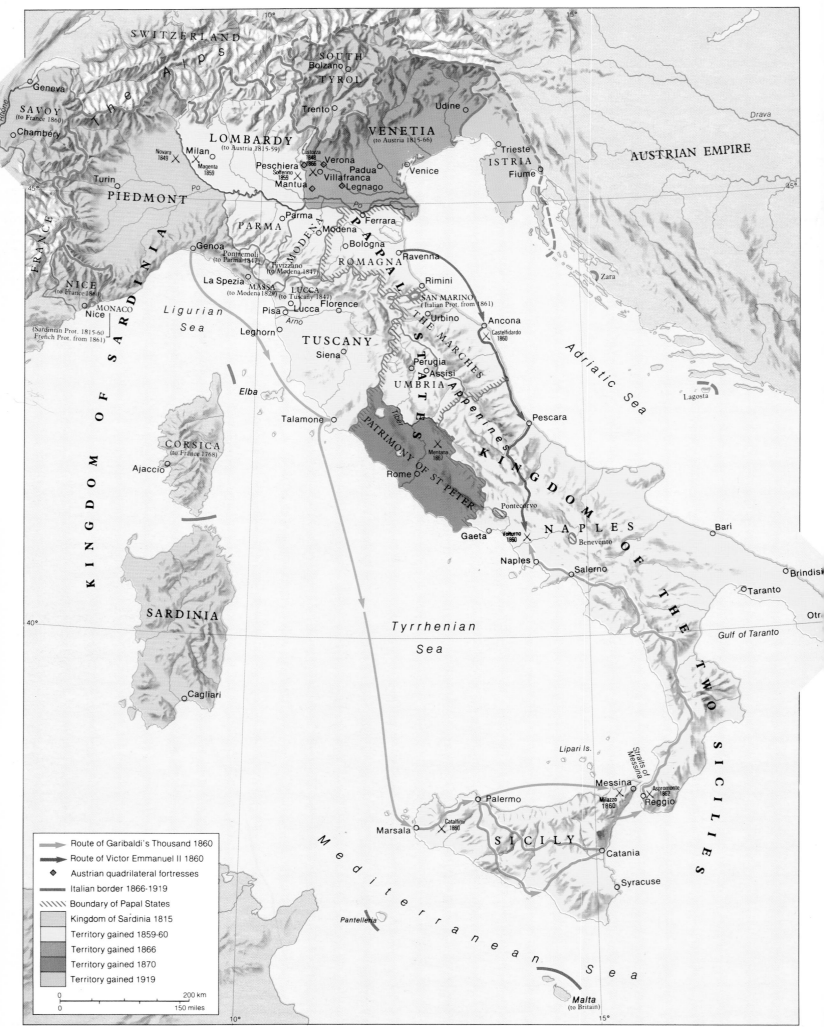

SWITZERLAND

Geneva

SAVOY
(to France 1860)

Chambéry

The Alps

SOUTH
Bolzano
TYROL

Trento

Udine

Trieste
ISTRIA
Fiume

AUSTRIAN EMPIRE

Drava

PIEDMONT

Turin

LOMBARDY
(to Austria 1815-59)

Novara
1849

Milan

Magenta
1859

Peschiera

Mantua

Custozza
1848
1866

Verona

Padua

Villafranca

Legnago

VENETIA
(to Austria 1815-66)

Solferino
1859

Venice

FRANCE

NICE
(to France 1860)

MONACO

Nice

(Sardinian Prot. 1815-60
French Prot. from 1861)

Genoa

Pontremoli
(to Parma 1847)

Fivizzano
(to Modena 1847)

La Spezia

MASSA
(to Modena 1829)

PARMA

Parma

MODENA

Modena

Bologna

ROMAGNA

Ferrara

PAPAL

Ravenna

Rimini

Zara

LUCCA
(to Tuscany 1847)

Pisa

Lucca

Florence

Arno

SAN MARINO
(Italian Prot. from 1861)

Urbino

Ancona

THE MARCHES

Castelfidardo
1860

Adriatic Sea

Lagosta

Ligurian
Sea

Leghorn

TUSCANY

Siena

Perugia

Assisi

STATES

UMBRIA

Apennines

Pescara

KINGDOM OF SARDINIA

Elba

Talamone

PATRIMONY OF ST PETER

Tiber

Mentana
1867

Rome

Pontecorvo

Gaeta

Volturno
1860

Benevento

NAPLES

Bari

CORSICA
(to France 1768)

Ajaccio

SARDINIA

Tyrrhenian
Sea

Naples

Salerno

Brindisi

Taranto

Otr

Gulf of Taranto

KINGDOM OF THE TWO

Cagliari

Lipari Is.

Straits of
Messina

Messina

Aspromonte
1862

Reggio

SICILIES

Palermo

Milazzo
1860

Marsala

Catalfimi
1860

SICILY

Catania

Syracuse

Mediterranean
Sea

Pantelleria

Malta
(to Britain)

Legend:
→ Route of Garibaldi's Thousand 1860
→ Route of Victor Emmanuel II 1860
◆ Austrian quadrilateral fortresses
— Italian border 1866-1919
/// Boundary of Papal States
Kingdom of Sardinia 1815
Territory gained 1859-60
Territory gained 1866
Territory gained 1870
Territory gained 1919

0   200 km
0   150 miles

© Creative Cartography Ltd © The Hamlyn Group

Budapest

AUSTRIA-HUNGARY

Agram
(Zagreb)

Croatia-Slavonia

Temesvar

Banat

Drava

Danube

Klausenburg
(Cluj)

Transylvania

Moldavia

Carpathians

RUSSIA

Odessa

Bessarabia

(Moldavian, 1856–1878)

Galatz

Transylvanian Alps

ROUMANIA
(Autonomous 1829, independent 1878)

Wallachia

Sereth

45°

BOSNIA
(Austrian Prot. 1878,
annexed 1908)

HERZEGOVINA

Dalmatia

Sava

Bosna

Belgrade

Krajova

Bucharest

Dobrudja

Constanta

(a. 1878)

Danube

(a. 1913)

Sarajevo

Drina

Kragujevac

(a. 1913)

Ragusa

Cattaro

MONTENEGRO

Sanjak of Novibazar

Novibazar

(a.
1913)

(a. 1913)

SERBIA
(Autonomous 1817,
independent 1878)

Morava

Aleksinac
× 1876

Nishi

(a. 1878)

Sofia

BULGARIA
(Autonomous 1878, independent 1908)

Iskcr

Balkan Mts.

Plevna
1877

Stara Zagora

Varna

Black
Sea

Burgas

Scutari

Adriatic Sea

Durazzo

Üsküb (Skopje)

× Kumanovo
1912

Vardar

(a. 1913)

Eastern Roumelia
(Autonomous 1878,
to Bulgaria 1885)

Philippopolis
(Plovdiv)

(a.1913)

Struma

Maritza

(a. 1913)

Kirk Kilisse
× 1912

Adrianople

× Luleburgaz
1912

(a. 1913)

Constantinople
San Stefano

Scutari

Bosphorus

Monastir
(Bitola)

Macedonia

Salonika

Kavalla

Thrace

Sea of Marmara

Marmara

ALBANIA
(Independent 1913)

(a.1913)

Thasos

Gallipoli

Samothrace

Imbros

40°

Pindus Mts.

Corfu

Janina

Epirus

Larissa

Aegean

Lemnos

Dardanelles

OTTOMAN

EMPIRE

Ionian
Sea

Santa
Maura

Thessaly
(a. 1881)

Sea

(a.1913)

Northern
Sporades

Skiros

Mitilini
(Lesbos)

Cephalonia

Ionian
(a.1863)
Is.

Missolonghi
1826 ×

Livadia
(Independent 1830)

Euboea

Chios

Smyrna

Zakynthos
(Zante)

Patras

Gulf of Corinth

GREECE

Corinth

Piraeus

Athens

Andros

Nikaria

Samos

Tripolis
(Morea)

Peloponnese

Cyclades

Naxos

Cos

Dodecanese Is.
(Italian occupation 1912)

Rhodes

Navarino
× 1827

Milos

Cerigo
(Kythira)

Sea of Crete

Karpathos

35°

CRETE
(Autonomous 1898)
(to Greece 1908)

(to Egypt 1824–40)

Mediterranean Sea

25°

········ Borders proposed by Treaty of San Stefano,
          March 1878

– – –   Borders established by Congress of Berlin,
          June–July 1878

———   Borders, 1914   a. Acquired

0   200 km

0   150 miles

© Creative Cartography Ltd © The Hamlyn Group

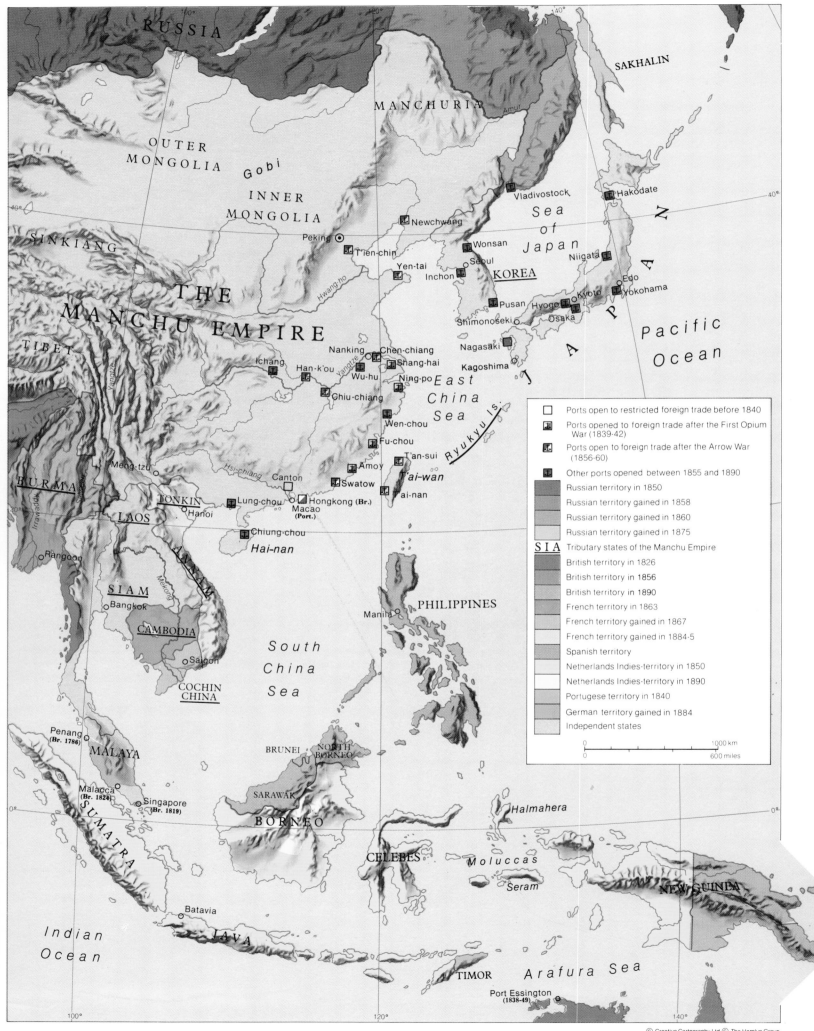

RUSSIA

MANCHURIA

Amur

SAKHALIN

OUTER
MONGOLIA

Gobi

INNER
MONGOLIA

SINKIANG

Vladivostock ☐

Hakodate ☐

Sea
of
Japan

Newchwang ☐

Peking ⊙

T'ien-chin ☐

Wonsan ☐

Niigata ☐

Yen-tai ☐

Seoul
Inchon ☐

KOREA

Hwang-ho

THE

MANCHU EMPIRE

TIBET

Yangtze

Pusan ☐

Hyogo ☐ ○ Kyoto
Osaka

Shimonoseki ○

Edo ○
Yokohama ☐

J
A
P
A
N

Pacific
Ocean

Ichang ☐

Han-k'ou ☐

Nanking ○ Chen-chiang ☐
Shang-hai ☐
Wu-hu ☐
Ning-po ☐

Nagasaki ☐

Kagoshima ○

Chiu-chiang ☐

East
China
Sea

Wen-chou ☐

Ryukyu Is.

Meng-tzu ○

Hsi-chiang

Fu-chou ☐

T'an-sui ☐

BURMA

Irrawaddy

Canton ☐

TONKIN

Lung-chou ☐

Amoy ☐
Swatow ☐

T'ai-wan

Hongkong (Br.)
Macao
(Port.)

T'ai-nan ☐

LAOS

Hanoi ○

Chiung-chou ☐

Rangoon ○

Hai-nan

SIA

Mekong

SIAM

Bangkok ○

A
N
N
A
M

CAMBODIA

Saigon ○

COCHIN
CHINA

South
China
Sea

Manila ○

PHILIPPINES

Penang
(Br. 1786)

MALAYA

Malacca
(Br. 1824)

Singapore
(Br. 1819)

SUMATRA

BRUNEI

NORTH
BORNEO

SARAWAK

BORNEO

CELEBES

Halmahera

Moluccas

Seram

NEW GUINEA

Batavia ○

JAVA

Indian
Ocean

TIMOR

Arafura Sea

Port Essington
(1838-49)

☐ Ports open to restricted foreign trade before 1840

☐ Ports opened to foreign trade after the First Opium War (1839-42)

☐ Ports open to foreign trade after the Arrow War (1856-60)

☐ Other ports opened between 1855 and 1890

Russian territory in 1850

Russian territory gained in 1858

Russian territory gained in 1860

Russian territory gained in 1875

Tributary states of the Manchu Empire

British territory in 1826

British territory in 1856

British territory in 1890

French territory in 1863

French territory gained in 1867

French territory gained in 1884-5

Spanish territory

Netherlands Indies-territory in 1850

Netherlands Indies-territory in 1890

Portugese territory in 1840

German territory gained in 1884

Independent states

0   1000 km
0   600 miles

© Creative Cartography Ltd © The Hamlyn Group

The age of imperialism

64 The European
penetration of the Far East
The 'Opium War' of 1839-42
demonstrated the inability of
the Manchu (Ch'ing) empire
to withstand the expansion
of the European powers.
Their domination of the Far
East was established as much
by exacting commercial
privileges as by territorial
occupation.

THE LATE NINETEENTH and early twentieth centuries witnessed an unprecedented extension of European power over non-Europeans. Hence the frequent characterisation of the period as an 'age of imperialism'. This was, however, as much a time of imperial decline as of imperial expansion. Indeed, the debilitation of the older imperial systems—most notably those of Austria, Ottoman Turkey, and China—and the ensuing diplomatic rivalries, were two of the primary causes of the imperial expansion of countries such as Britain and France.

The vulnerability of the old empires became steadily more apparent in the course of the nineteenth century. Austria, bludgeoned into submission by Prussia, not only lost most of its lands in Italy and its position as the leading German power (*Maps 61 and 62*) but was compelled by resurgent Hungarian nationalism to acquiesce in 1867 to the *Ausgleich* ('compromise') whereby the empire was transformed into a 'Dual Monarchy' based on the joint domination of Germans and Hungarians over Slavs. Although unity under Austro-Hungarian rule made considerable economic sense (as was proved when the area broke up into several states after 1918 – *Map 77*) Austro-Hungarian output and industrialisation lagged far behind that of Germany. While the Hapsburg régime continued to command impressive reserves of institutional and ideological strength, the nationalist Revolutions of 1848-9 and 1866-7 had demonstrated its essential frailty. The spread of the ideas of romantic nationalism and the rise of Pan-Slav feeling championed by Russia rendered the Austro-Hungarian system increasingly unstable.

Slav opposition to the Hapsburgs was heightened by the success of Slav and other subject nationalities in south-east Europe in gaining independence from the Turks (*see Map 63*). The long territorial retreat of the Ottoman Empire, which had begun in 1699, greatly accelerated in the nineteenth century. The Empire made repeated attempts to recover its strength by internal reforms and modernisation, and it enjoyed strong support from other powers (especially Britain, which sought to maintain Ottoman integrity for fear of Russian encroachment on Constantinople and the Dardenelles). Nevertheless one after another of the European subject nationalities wrested autonomy and eventually independence from the Turks. In 1830, after a bitter struggle, Greece won its independence, and by 1878 Serbia and Roumania were independent and Bulgaria virtually so.

Meanwhile Ottoman power on the southern shore of the Mediterranean was also disappearing. France conquered Algeria between 1830 and 1848, annexed Tunis in 1881, and harboured ambitions in Morocco (which, however, preserved a precarious independence until 1912) (*see Maps 66 and 74*). Egypt had asserted its autonomy under Muhammad Ali in the early nineteenth century, but his successors drove the country into bankruptcy and financial submission to Britain and France. With the construction of the Suez Canal (opened in 1869) the British began to fear that control of the area by a hostile power might endanger the security of their communications with India. The outbreak of an Egyptian nationalist revolution in 1881 was the occasion for the occupation of the country by British forces the following year. Although successive British governments affirmed their intention to withdraw, a 'veiled protectorate', in which Egypt became in all but name a British possession, endured for nearly three-quarters of a century.

It was, as Gallagher and Robinson point out, 'more than any other cause, the danger of a general Ottoman collapse [which] set off the partition of Africa and brought on the rise of new European empires in north and tropical Africa'. The 'scramble for Africa' (*see Map 74*) in the 1880s and 1890s saw nearly the whole continent subjected to European rule. Britain secured the lion's share of the territorial spoils as she expanded up the Nile valley into east Africa and inland from the west African coast. In southern Africa the discovery of gold and diamonds led to a vast influx of European capital and labour and laid the foundations of the greatest economic power on the continent. An elaborate railway system was constructed, and British rule was extended northwards beyond the Zambeze to the shores of Lakes Nyasa and Tanganyika. The French too moved into the hinterland from their north and west African coastal footholds and established their suzerainty over most of the Sahara and as far south as the Congo basin. Other European powers nibbled at more modest morsels. Bismarck, although sceptical of the value of imperial possessions, gained the German annexation of Tanganyika, Togoland, Kamerun, and South-West Africa. Portugal, deprived of her former vast dominion in Brazil (*Map 59*), consoled her national pride by consolidating her position in Portuguese West Africa (Angola) and Mozambique, rebuffing the rapacious advances of acquisitive European rivals. Italy too, disillusioned with the failure of the post-*risorgimento* régime to recreate Italian greatness, tried her hand at empire-building, only to encounter humiliating disaster when her army was defeated at Adowa by the army of Abyssinia, the one indigenous imperial system in Africa to survive into the twentieth century.

In east Asia (*see Map 64*) it was the decline of the Ch'ing (Manchu) empire in China that afforded the opportunity for rapid European expansion into the area as the decline of the Mughal Empire had already done in India (*see Map 65*). In 1839 an attempt by the Chinese Government to enforce a prohibition on the importation of opium led to war with Britain. By the Treaty of Nanking in 1842 China was obliged to cede Hong Kong to Britain and to make a series of commercial concessions, including the opening of several ports to British traders. The T'ai P'ing Rebellion (1850-64), a popular upheaval which convulsed sixteen of China's eighteen provinces, provided the pretext for further European intervention. Anglo-French victories between 1856 and 1860 led to further 'unequal treaties' which extended European commercial and cultural penetration of China. The decrepitude of the Ch'ing Empire made possible the expansion of French sovereignty from its base at Saigon to the whole of Indo-China. Defeated by Japan in 1894-5, China was compelled to yield up her suzerainty over the tributary state of Korea. The Sino-Japanese war was the signal for a 'scramble for China' in the late 1890s, in which the imperial powers vied for railway and other concessions and occupied Chinese ports (*see Map 73*). Chinese resentment of European encroachments found expression in the so-called 'Boxer Rebellion'. This eruption of anti-foreign feeling, spearheaded by a secret society of 'Righteous and Harmonious Fists', enjoyed the support of a faction of the imperial government. In 1900 a multinational military expedition relieved a siege of the foreign legations in Peking. The vindictive terms subsequently imposed by the imperial powers appeared to spell the doom of the Ch'ing dynasty.

The age of imperialism

Although formal European rule had not been extended to the greater part of the country, and in spite of American attempts to preserve Chinese integrity by the enunciation of the 'open door' principle in 1899, the Chinese government had by the end of the century effectively been deprived of mastery in its own house. China was thus an outstanding example of 'informal imperialism', the process whereby imperial powers secured commercial, legal, or diplomatic privileges which gave them influence, in some cases a predominant voice, in the internal affairs of nominally independent states. Another such case was Persia where Britain and Russia carved out spheres of influence in the declining Qajar empire.

The weakening of the old empires, and the consequent power vacuums in much of Asia and Africa, cannot alone explain the phenomenal growth of European imperialism in the late nineteenth century. A number of further explanations have been advanced. Imperialism, it is suggested, was the result of a search for outlets for 'surplus capital'. Was it rather a necessary consequence of heightened trade rivalries and moves towards protectionism in Europe? Or did it derive from the need of manufacturing economies for assured sources of supply of cheap raw materials? Or from the need of rapidly expanding populations to find outlets for emigration and settlement? Some historians tend to discount economic motives and stress rather the more purely political origins of the imperial urge. It is thus portrayed as a stepchild of frustrated nationalisms, as a plaything of diplomatic rivalries, or as an attempt by ruling élites to siphon off internal social unrest by the stimulation of 'jingoist' imperial enthusiasms. Although there are grains of truth in several of these suggested causes the search for a 'general theory' of imperialism has been unsuccessful — perhaps not surprisingly in the case of such a far-flung and variegated phenomenon.

Just as there is no historical consensus as to the causes of imperialism, so views diverge as to its nature and effects. Some emphasise its negative aspects: the use of force and repression to establish and maintain imperial rule; the barbarities perpetrated in some colonies by imperialist agents and officials (as in the Congo, governed for a time as the private estate of the King of the Belgians); the distortion of colonial economies to meet the needs of metropolitan countries; the subordination of the interests of indigenous peoples to those of European settlers; the racialism of most imperial powers; the extinction of some non-European cultures; the alienation and psychological dislocation arising from the sudden imposition of westernisation. Against all this it is argued that imperialism did not rely only on brute force but in many cases constructed sophisticated governmental systems incorporating indigenous institutions and co-opting local élites. Moreover, it was the imperial powers, led by Britain, that sought (with considerable success) to eliminate the African slave trade in the course of the nineteenth century (*compare Map 51*). To the positive side of the balance-sheet are also often added the development of modern economic infrastructures, the spread of education and literacy, the application of modern medical techniques to the battle against disease (*compare Map 66*), the unification of large areas containing diverse religions, tribes, and ethnic groups into single units, and the establishment of the rule of law.

Resistance to imperialism reflected its ambivalent impact, for opposition to colonial incursions tended to be more effective the more it borrowed from the ideas and techniques of imperial societies themselves. The British victories over the Indian mutiny (1857-9), the Ashanti of the Gold Coast (1874), the Zulus of South Africa (1879), and the Mahdist forces in the Sudan (1885) showed that technologically inferior anti-imperialist forces might win occasional battles but could not expect enduring success against imperial armies in straightforward military confrontations. By contrast, the Indian National Congress (founded in 1885), based on a marriage of western with Indian techniques of political mobilisation, and profoundly influenced by British liberalism, succeeded in compelling the Government of India (which had replaced the East India Company after the mutiny as the agency of British rule) to concede a growing share of political power to Indians (*Map 65*). In this respect the Indian experience served as a model for some other anti-imperial movements and for some other (particularly British) colonial administrations. A similarly ambiguous response to European penetration may be detected in the declining old empires: the constitutional revolution in Persia in 1905, the Young Turk revolution in the Ottoman Empire in 1908, and the republican revolution in China led by Sun Yat-Sen in 1911, were at once against western imperial domination and in themselves evidence of the impact of western political and social ideas.

Among all the imperial powers, one held for a while almost undisputed predominance. Britain indeed attained in the third quarter of the nineteenth century a position more nearly approaching world mastery than perhaps has ever been achieved by any other power in history. It was not merely that Britain had amassed what was territorially the largest empire ever known (*see Map 67*). Britain maintained its long lead over competitors in industrial innovation and production almost until the end of the century. Until the 1870s she produced more coal than all other countries put together. She was similarly dominant in the production of iron. Britain produced one-third of the world's industrial output in 1870. Britain's foreign trade (in which Lancashire cotton was the largest single element) was greater than that of any two other countries until the 1890s. The pound sterling remained the basis of the international payments system until well into the twentieth century. Britain was the world's largest foreign investor until the First World War (most of the exported capital flowing to the Americas, India, and South Africa, rather than to the new empire). Britain dominated the world's system of transport and communications: herself possessed of the world's best network of roads and railways, she supplied the capital and the technology for the construction of railways in five continents; she owned the majority of the world's submarine cables. Above all, she dominated world shipping: until almost the eve of the First World War the British merchant fleet comprised a larger tonnage than that of all other countries put together. Shielding this massive aggregation of economic might was the Royal Navy, the world's most powerful seaborne force. The age of imperialism was, in truth, the British era.

Nevertheless, by the turn of the century Britain's overwhelming predominance was beginning to be eroded. By 1890 the USA had overtaken Britain in the production of iron, and by 1900 in the production of coal and steel (*Map 69*). Germany too had outstripped Britain

65 South Asia around 1900 India became a British Crown Colony after the suppression of the mutiny of 1857-59. Territorial consolidation, the importation of British administrative and educational institutions and economic development (which, however, destroyed the self-sufficiency of the village economies and opened the way to chronic rural over-population) had created by 1900 Britain's greatest imperial possession and a growing independence movement.

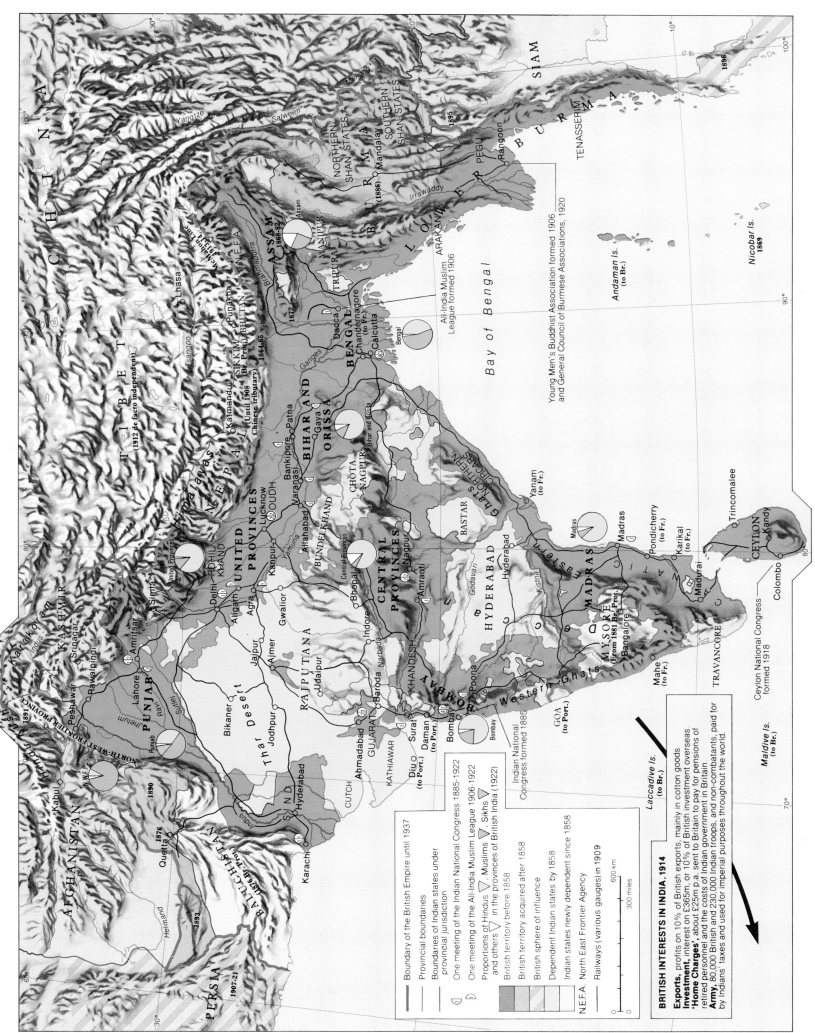

CHINA

SIAM

AFGHANISTAN

PERSIA

BALUCHISTAN

TIBET
(1912 de facto independent)

Himalayas

McMahon Line (1914)

NEPAL

BHUTAN
(Until 1908 Chinese tributary)

SIKKIM
(Br. Prot.)

ASSAM
1868-82

N.E.F.A.

NORTHERN
SHAN STATES

SOUTHERN
SHAN STATES

MANIPUR

TRIPURA

ARAKAN

LOWER   BURMA

PEGU

TENASSERIM

BURMA

Bay of Bengal

Andaman Is.
(to Br.)
1869

Nicobar Is.
1869

BENGAL

BIHAR AND
ORISSA

UNITED
PROVINCES

OUDH

BUNDELKHAND

CHOTA
NAGPUR

Central Provinces

CENTRAL
PROVINCES

BASTAR

NORTHERN
CIRCARS

Eastern Ghats

MADRAS

HYDERABAD

MYSORE
(From 1881 Br. Prot.)

BOMBAY

RAJPUTANA

GUJARAT

KATHIAWAR

CUTCH

SIND

PUNJAB

KASHMIR

NORTH-WEST FRONTIER PROVINCE

HINDU KUSH

Karakoram

Thar Desert

KHANDESH

Western Ghats

GOA
(to Port.)

CEYLON

TRAVANCORE

KANDY

Colombo

Trincomalee

Madurai

Karikal
(to Fr.)

Pondicherry
(to Fr.)

Madras

Mahe
(to Fr.)

Bangalore

Poona

Hyderabad

Yanam
(to Fr.)

Amraoti

Nagpur

Bhopal

Indore

Baroda

Ahmadabad

Surat

Daman
(to Port.)

Diu
(to Port.)

Bombay

Karachi

Hyderabad

Jodhpur

Bikaner

Ajmer

Jaipur

Udaipur

Gwalior

Agra

Delhi

Aligarh

Kanpur

Lucknow

Allahabad

Varanasi

Yamuna

Patna

Bankipore

Gaya

Bihar and Orissa

Dacca

Calcutta

Chandernagore
(to Fr.)

Bengal

Assam

Manipur

Ganges

Brahmaputra

Simla

Amritsar

Lahore

Punjab

Jhelum

Ravi

Sutlej

Indus

Rawalpindi

Peshawar

Srinagar

Kabul

Quetta

Helmand

Katmandu

Lhasa

Tsangpo

Salween

Mekong

Irrawaddy

Mandalay

Rangoon

Yangtze

Godavari

Kistna

Narbada

Maldive Is.
(to Br.)

Laccadive Is.
(to Br.)

All-India Muslim League formed 1906

Young Men's Buddhist Association formed 1906
and General Council of Burmese Associations, 1920

Indian National Congress formed 1885

Ceylon National Congress formed 1918

1895

1896

1886

1872

1891

1890

1876

1893

1907-21

1864-65

1868-82

BRITISH INTERESTS IN INDIA, 1914

Exports, profits on 10% of British exports, mainly in cotton goods.
Investment, interest on £365m, or 10% of British investment overseas.
'Home Charges', about £25m p.a. sent to Britain to pay for pensions of
retired personnel and the costs of Indian government in Britain.
Army, 80,000 British and 230,000 Indian troops, and non-combatants, paid for
by Indians' taxes and used for imperial purposes throughout the world.

Boundary of the British Empire until 1937
Provincial boundaries
Boundaries of Indian states under
provincial jurisdiction
One meeting of the Indian National Congress 1885-1922
One meeting of the All-India Muslim League 1906-1922
Proportions of Hindus ▽, Muslims △, Sikhs ▷
and others ▽ in the provinces of British India (1922)
British territory before 1858
British territory acquired after 1858
British sphere of influence
Dependent Indian states by 1858
Indian states newly dependent since 1858
N.E.F.A. North East Frontier Agency
Railways (various gauges) in 1909

600 km

300 miles

© Creative Cartography Ltd © The Hamlyn Group

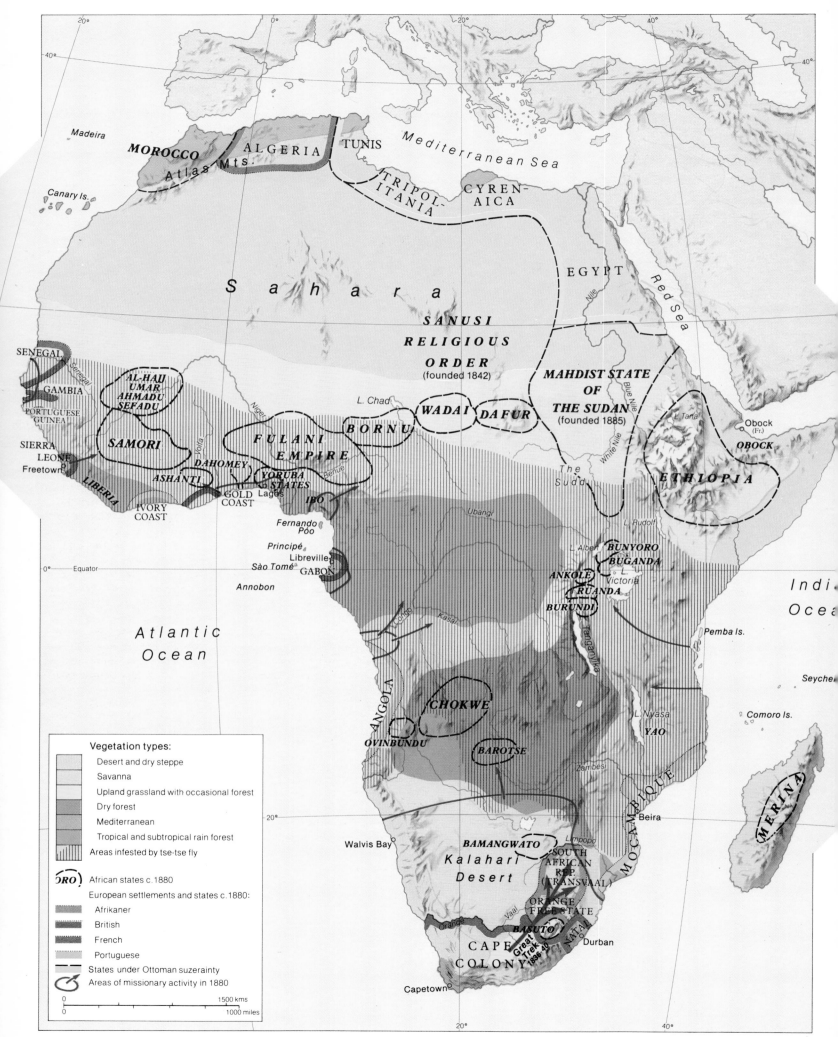

Madeira

Canary Is.

MOROCCO ALGERIA TUNIS
Atlas Mts.
TRIPOL-
ITANIA CYREN-
AICA

Mediterranean Sea

EGYPT

Red Sea

S a h a r a

SANUSI
RELIGIOUS
ORDER
(founded 1842)

MAHDIST STATE
OF
THE SUDAN
(founded 1885)

SENEGAL

GAMBIA

PORTUGUESE
GUINEA

SIERRA
LEONE
Freetown

LIBERIA

IVORY
COAST

AL-HAJJ
UMAR
AHMADU
SEFADU

SAMORI

DAHOMEY

ASHANTI

GOLD
COAST

Lagos

FULANI
EMPIRE

YORUBA
STATES

IBO

L. Chad

WADAI **DAFUR**

BORNU

Senegal

Niger

Volta

Benue

White Nile

Blue Nile

L. Tana

Obock
(Fr.)

OBOCK

ETHIOPIA

The
Sudd

Fernando
Póo

Principé
Libreville
Sào Tomé GABON

Annobon

Ubangi

L. Rudolf

L. Albert **BUNYORO**
BUGANDA

L.
Victoria

ANKOLE
RUANDA

BURUNDI

Congo

Kasai

Tanganyika

Pemba Is.

India
Ocea

Equator

Atlantic
Ocean

ANGOLA

CHOKWE

OVINBUNDU

BAROTSE

L. Nyasa

YAO

Zambesi

Seyche

Comoro Is.

MOÇAMBIQUE

Beira

MERINA

Walvis Bay

BAMANGWATO

Kalahari
Desert

Limpopo

SOUTH
AFRICAN
REP.
(TRANSVAAL)

ORANGE
FREE STATE

Vaal

Orange

BASUTO

CAPE
COLONY

Great
Trek
1836-40

NATAL

Durban

Capetown

Vegetation types:

Desert and dry steppe

Savanna

Upland grassland with occasional forest

Dry forest

Mediterranean

Tropical and subtropical rain forest

Areas infested by tse-tse fly

ƆRO) African states c.1880
European settlements and states c.1880:

Afrikaner

British

French

Portuguese

States under Ottoman suzerainty

Areas of missionary activity in 1880

0   1500 kms
0   1000 miles

© Creative Cartography Ltd © The Hamlyn Group

66 Africa on the eve of the scramble

Before 1880 most of the African continent was unknown to Europeans, and very little of it ruled by them. They were confined to the coast by disease (also the greatest obstacle to African development), the hostility generated by the slave trade, and the fact that comparable profits from other sources seemed unlikely.

67 Foundations of a world economy

European colonial expansion created a world economy united not only by the establishment of regular communications (telegraph cables joined most parts of the civilised world by 1900) and the exchange of goods and people, but by financial ties through capital investment even more widespread than territorial dominion.

in industrial production by the turn of the century (*Map 57*). By 1913 the USA was producing more than one-third of the world's manufactured goods, whereas Britain's share of world output had slipped below one-tenth. By 1900 Britain was the only major nation which still adhered to free trade, and although Britain still dominated world trade some voices began to be raised in favour of protectionism. Nor was it only economically that Britain now began to appear vulnerable. Britain, alone among the European powers, had no system of conscription and no large standing army. Between 1899 and 1902 she suffered a shattering blow to her prestige in the Boer War: although she was ultimately victorious Britain's difficulties in crushing the Dutch colonists in South Africa cruelly exposed her military weakness and her diplomatic isolation. British policy-makers now began to wonder whether the vast territorial acquisitions of the late nineteenth century had not extended the empire beyond Britain's capacity to sustain or defend it. In 1905 the head of the British Foreign Office suggested that the British Empire might give the appearance 'of some huge giant sprawling over the globe, with gouty fingers and toes stretched in every direction, which cannot be approached without eliciting a scream.'

British paramountcy was further challenged by the development of European alliance systems. In 1879 Bismarck had formed a 'Dual Alliance' between Germany and Austria-Hungary. In 1882 this was expanded to a 'Triple Alliance' by the addition of Italy. Meanwhile Bismarck sought to contain Russia by drawing her into a *Dreikaiserbund* (League of Three Emperors) in company with Austria-Hungary. The heightening of Balkan rivalries between Russia and Austria-Hungary made this impossible to preserve intact, and in 1887 Bismarck replaced it with the so-called 'Re-insurance Treaty', a bipartite arrangement between Germany and Russia. However, in 1890 Bismarck was dismissed by the new German Emperor, William II. The delicate balance of Bismarck's alliance system collapsed with him: Germany now jettisoned Russia and threw in her lot wholeheartedly with Austria-Hungary. This led between 1891 and 1894 to what Bismarck had always feared most and what his entire diplomacy had been concerned to prevent—the crystallisation of a Russo-French alliance which presented Germany with the danger of a war on two fronts.

Although the phrase 'splendid isolation', as sometimes applied to British foreign policy in the late nineteenth century, is misleading if taken literally, it is true that Britain in the 1890s held aloof from either camp. The traditions of her foreign policy earlier in the century had been anti-Russian rather than anti-German. It was against Russia that Britain had combined with France, Turkey, and Sardinia to fight in the Crimean War (1854-6). At the

Congress of Berlin in 1878 the British prime minister, Disraeli, had helped to deprive Russia of the fruits of her victory in the Russo-Turkish war, and had secured a reversal of the Treaty of San Stefano which Russia had sought to impose on Turkey (*see Map 63*). Throughout the period Britain had been concerned by the apparent threat to her Indian empire posed by Russian advances in central Asia (*Map 70*) – which stimulated Britain too to advance her frontiers in northern India (*see Map 65*). Britain was further inhibited from identifying herself with the Russo-French alliance by colonial disputes with France, particularly over North Africa. In 1898 a minor Anglo-French confrontation at Fashoda (*see Map 74*) blew up into a serious crisis which seemed to bring Britain and France to the brink of war.

Nevertheless, by the end of the century it was the German Empire, with its dynamic economy, its thrusting foreign policy, its assertive demand for a 'place in the sun', and its expanding naval programme, which seemed to represent the chief threat to Britain's international hegemony. Although Anglo-German discussions about a possible alliance continued until 1901, it became apparent that the fundamental interests and sympathies of the two powers were diverging. It is the Anglo-Japanese alliance, concluded in 1902, which is traditionally held to mark the end of Britain's 'isolation', but this did not commit Britain to either of the main European power blocs. Even the 'ententes' signed with France in 1904 and with Russia in 1907 were ostensibly concerned merely with the settlement of outstanding colonial disputes. But they were followed by naval and military conversations which, although short of an alliance, insensibly drew Britain closer to France and Russia. In the diplomatic crises of 1905 and 1911 over Morocco and of 1908 and 1912-13 over the Balkans the lines hardened between the 'Triple Entente' and the 'central powers'. In the years before 1914 all the European powers greatly increased their expenditure on armaments. Meanwhile, as the struggle for mastery in Europe intensified, the rise of new powers on the periphery of the international system foreshadowed the sudden collapse, at the moment of its greatest imperial extension, of Europe's mastery of the world.

Further reading: A. J. P. Taylor, *The Struggle for Mastery in Europe* (Oxford University Press, 1954; p.b.); E. J. Hobsbawm, *The Age of Capital* (Weidenfeld & Nicolson, 1975; Abacus, 1977); John Gallagher and Ronald Robinson, *Africa and the Victorians* (Macmillan, 1961; p.b.); D. K. Fieldhouse, *The Theory of Capitalist Imperialism* (Longman, 1967); John K. Fairbank, Edwin O. Reischauer, and Albert M. Craig, *East Asia: The Modern Transformation* (George Allen & Unwin, 1965); J. Berque, *Egypt: Imperialism and Revolution* (Faber, 1972).

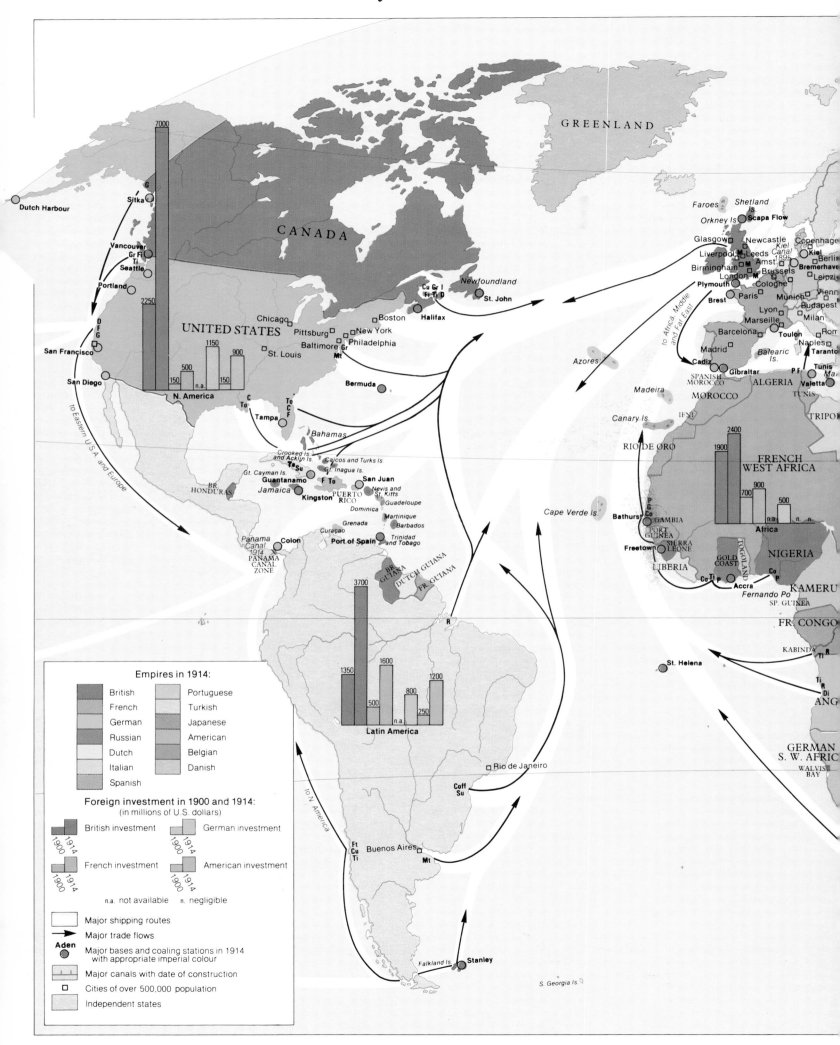

GREENLAND

CANADA

Dutch Harbour

7000

G
Sitka

Vancouver
Gr Fi
Seattle

Portland

2250

D F G

San Francisco

San Diego

UNITED STATES

Chicago
Pittsburg
Baltimore
St. Louis
Philadelphia
New York
Boston
Halifax
St. John
Newfoundland

Cu Gr I
Fi Ti D

Gr
Mt

C
To
To C F
Tampa

Bermuda

Bahamas

Crooked Is.
and Acklin Is.
Caicos and Turks Is.
Gt. Inagua Is.
Gt. Cayman Is.
Guantanamo
Jamaica
Kingston
F To
San Juan
PUERTO RICO
Nevis and
St. Kitts
Dominica
Guadeloupe
Martinique
Barbados
Grenada
Curaçao
Port of Spain
Trinidad
and Tobago

BR. HONDURAS

Panama
Canal
1914
PANAMA
CANAL
ZONE
Colon

1150
500   900
150   150
n.a.
N. America

Azores

Madeira

Canary Is.

Cape Verde Is.

St. Helena

Falkland Is.   Stanley

S. Georgia Is.

BR. GUIANA
DUTCH GUIANA
FR. GUIANA

3700

1350   1600
500   800   1200
n.a.   250
Latin America

R

Coff
Su

Rio de Janeiro

Ft
Cu
Ti
Buenos Aires
Mt

Faroes   Shetland Is.
Orkney Is.   Scapa Flow

Glasgow   Newcastle   Copenhage
Liverpool   Leeds   Kiel   Kiel
Birmingham   Canal   Berlin
M   1895   M   Bremerhave
London   Amst.   Leipzi
Plymouth   Cologne
Brussels
Paris   Munich   Vienn
Brest   Lyon   Budapest
Marseille   Milan
Barcelona   Rom
Madrid   Balearic
Is.   Toulon   Naples   Taranto
Cadiz   Gibraltar   P F   Tunis
SPANISH   Valetta   Ma
MOROCCO   ALGERIA
TUNIS
MOROCCO   TRIPOL

to Africa, Middle
and Far East

RIO DE ORO

2400
1900
700   900
500
n.a.   n.   n.
Africa

FRENCH
WEST AFRICA

IFNI

Bathurst   GAMBIA
P G Co
PORT.
GUINEA
Freetown   SIERRA
LEONE
LIBERIA   GOLD
COAST
TOGOLAND
NIGERIA
Co Ti P
Accra
Co P
Fernando Po
SP. GUINEA
KAMERU

FR. CONGO

KABINDA
Ti
Ti
Di
ANG

GERMAN
S. W. AFRIC
WALVIS
BAY

to Eastern U.S.A. and Europe

to N. America

Empires in 1914:

British	Portuguese
French	Turkish
German	Japanese
Russian	American
Dutch	Belgian
Italian	Danish
Spanish	

Foreign investment in 1900 and 1914:
(in millions of U.S. dollars)

British investment   German investment
1914   1914
1900   1900

French investment   American investment
1914   1914
1900   1900

n.a. not available   n. negligible

☐ Major shipping routes

→ Major trade flows

Aden ● Major bases and coaling stations in 1914
with appropriate imperial colour

▮ Major canals with date of construction

☐ Cities of over 500,000 population

Independent states

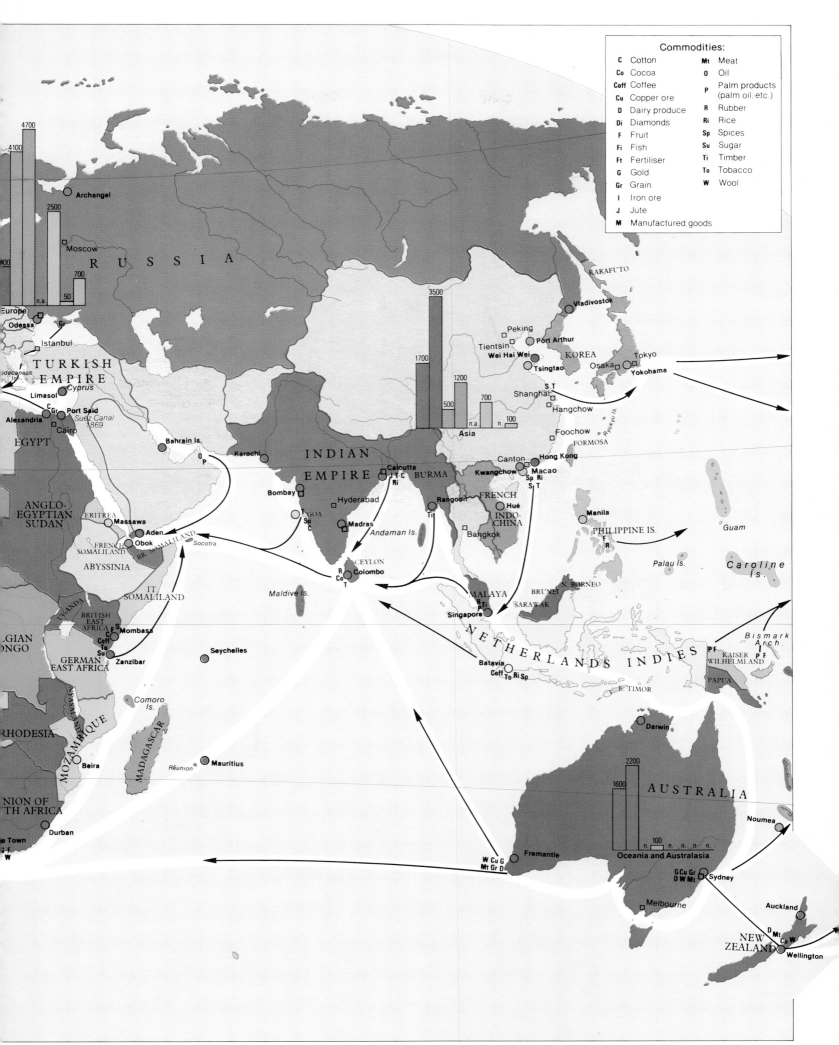

The emergence of the modern world I

Rivals to European supremacy

THE SUDDEN eclipse of European world power in the mid-twentieth century was foreshadowed by the emergence as potential 'super-powers' of the USA, Russia, and Japan. Although each of them followed a very different path of development, they shared certain general characteristics. All three underwent vast expansion in population, territory and production. They industrialised on a massive scale, transforming themselves in the process from overwhelmingly rural to predominantly urban societies. In each the rapid pace of economic and social change led to acute strains between traditional and modernising institutions and ideologies. And all three alternated between periods of expansionist involvement in international politics and periods of self-absorption and isolationism.

No nation in modern history can match the phenomenal growth of the USA within a few generations from the small agrarian community of the thirteen colonies *(Map 53)* to a continental civilisation commanding the world's greatest concentration of economic and military power. The territorial expansion of the USA westwards to the Pacific *(see Map 68)* proceeded in three broad stages. By 1819 all of the region between the old seaboard states and the Mississippi had been admitted to the Union except Michigan (admitted in 1837) and Wisconsin (admitted in 1848). By 1858 five states had been carved out of the vast hinterland of the Louisiana Purchase obtained by Jefferson from France in 1803 for approximately $15,000,000 and admitted to the Union. In addition, Florida, purchased from Spain in 1819, attained statehood in 1845. The third stage was the settlement of the south-western lands detached from Mexico. Texas, revolted against Mexico in 1836 and constituted an independent state until it was admitted to the Union in 1845; American victory in war against Mexico (1846-8) added the present states of Arizona, Nevada, California, and Utah, plus other areas; and the Gadsden Purchase of 1853 acquired a further small strip (now the southern parts of Arizona and New Mexico). Meanwhile a dispute with Britain over the Oregon Territory was settled in 1846 by the concession to the USA of the mainland as far north as the 49th Parallel. Finally, in 1867 Alaska was purchased from Russia for $7,200,000.

Territorial expansion depended on settlement, which proceeded against formidable physical and human obstacles. The fast-flowing, navigable rivers eastwards from the Mississippi Valley were vital in locating ports and creating subject economic hinterlands. In the more arid and gently sloping high plains of the trans-Mississippi west, trails rather than rivers marked the lines of movement and settlement. *Map 68* shows how aridity delayed agricultural settlement on the high plains; the wave of migrants leapt across to the west (often encouraged by gold and silver strikes), leaving the interstices to be filled in from the 1870s onwards. Settlement was encouraged by the sale of federal land for as little as $1.25 an acre. After the Homestead Act of 1862 lots of up to 160 acres could be acquired for nothing after 5 years of continuous residence. The human obstacle of the indigenous Amerindian population was overcome by ruthless expropriation and mass murder. By 1838 most of the remaining Indians from the east had been moved to the Indian territory of Oklahoma. In a series of wars (1861-68 and 1875-90) the western tribes were subjugated and confined to reservations.

The growth of the USA's population was no less spectacular. The population was 3,929,000 in 1790; by 1830 it was 12,866,000; by 1880 it was 50,155,000; and 105,710,000 by 1920. Immigration rose to an annual average of over a million by the peak decade before 1914 *(see Map 57)*. After 1881 the massive flow of 'new immigration' came from southern and eastern Europe. Within the country there was huge internal migration from east to west and from south to north. The overwhelming majority of the migrants settled in towns, so that the urban population of the USA, which was only 3·3% of the total in 1790, increased to 16% by 1860 and to 33% by 1900. By 1920 the majority of Americans lived in towns.

The transition from an agrarian to an urban vision of society was perhaps the most revolutionary change in the American consciousness. The Civil War of 1861-65, in which eleven southern states attempted to secede from the Union and form a separate 'Confederacy', was in essence a conflict between a traditional agrarian society and a dynamic industrial community. Slavery was not really the issue: emancipation was more a consequence than a cause of the war. At first President Abraham Lincoln, the leader of the northern states, stressed that he did not seek to abolish slavery in the south. But he insisted that he was under solemn oath to 'preserve, protect, and defend' the Union. Only in January 1863 did he issue the Proclamation of Emancipation. The defeat of the Confederacy in April 1865 came five days before the assassination of Lincoln. The Civil War was the costliest in American history, leaving over 600,000 dead, but it welded the nation together indissolubly and helped to determine the direction of American social and economic development. The abolition of slavery, confirmed by the northern victory, brought new forms of economic exploitation and misery to the freed slaves from which their descendants began to escape only after the 1930s when large-scale negro migration to the north began. But the war destroyed the power of 'King Cotton'. As Arthur M. Schlesinger Sr. wrote: 'The collapse of plantation capitalism signalized the rise of industrial capitalism.'

The industrialisation of the USA *(see Map 69)* was based on a perpetually replenished pool of immigrant labour, on the discovery and exploitation of the continent's tremendous concentration of natural resources, on the development of a sophisticated system of communications, and on the rapid application to industry of technological innovations by dynamic and ruthless entrepreneurs. Between 1860 and 1890 coal production increased more than tenfold and iron production nearly elevenfold. By 1910 US production of iron and steel exceeded that of Britain, France, Germany, and Austria-Hungary put together and by the 1920s the USA produced (and consumed) about three-quarters of the world's oil. New industries rose in the early twentieth century, most notably automobile manufacture. The mass production of motor cars, pioneered by Henry Ford, transformed American (and eventually world) society as well as the economy: the 'assembly line' became the characteristic form of factory organisation. The stream of immigrant labour for long hampered the growth of effective labour unions in the USA. Resentment of the activities of the 'robber barons' (magnates of railroads, oil, steel, meatpacking and high finance) and fear of the trend towards economic concentration in 'trusts' and combines led to sporadic industrial unrest, sometimes violent. But labour union membership and power

68 The westward growth of the U.S.A.
Systematic extension of its territory by diplomacy, purchase and conquest both within and beyond its frontiers transformed the United States from a small agrarian community into a major continental civilisation. The arid high plains beyond the Mississippi constituted the principal barrier to the settlement of the newly acquired lands.

69 The industrial growth of the U.S.A.
Abundant mineral resources, a limitless supply of labour from the surplus populations of the Old World and great agricultural wealth, brought together by a transcontinental railway system completed in its essentials in the 1890s, made the United States the greatest industrial power in the world by the early 20th century.

In the 19th century the long expansion of Russia into Asia, in quickening pursuit of land, minerals and icefree ports, brought her into conflict with the Middle Eastern and Asian interests of the European powers, and eventually with Japan. Behind the moving frontier colonisation by migrants from European Russia steadily encroached upon the nomadic peoples.

71 The emergence of modern Russia
After the checks imposed by war and revolution the industrialisation of Russia, which had progressed very rapidly from the 1890s to 1914, was resumed with the first five-year plan in 1929. At the same time the beginning of forced collectivisation – reversing the movement towards individual peasant proprietorship in the decades immediately before and after the revolution – further depressed the low levels of agricultural productivity which dogged both the old and the new regime.

remained much weaker than in many other industrial countries. Nevertheless, an inchoate but widespread desire to tame 'big business' and to humanise untrammelled capitalism helped give rise to the Progressive movement which dominated American politics in the early twentieth century. As the USA emerged as the world's greatest economic power she took a more outward-looking and expansive role in world affairs. As a result of victory in the Spanish-American War (1898), she acquired Cuba, Hawaii, and the Philippines (*see Map 85*). Having thus joined the ranks of imperial powers the USA became, particularly under Presidents Theodore Roosevelt (1901-9) and Woodrow Wilson (1913-21), a major actor in international diplomacy.

Although Russia, unlike the USA, was already a major power in the early nineteenth century, her development lagged far behind that of America. Indeed, a sense of 'backwardness' and of social and cultural inferiority haunted many Russian thinkers and politicians in the nineteenth century, and contrasted markedly with the thrusting self-confidence of maturing American capitalism. From the 1840s onwards Russian social thought was dominated by the debate between the 'Slavophiles', who believed that Russia's salvation lay in a return to her Orthodox religious traditions, and 'Westernisers', such as Belinsky and Herzen, who attacked religion and adopted many of the liberal and radical ideas of western Europe. The absence in Russia of a substantial mercantile and industrial bourgeoisie, however, prevented liberalism from becoming a major force in Russian politics. The autocracy, until its demise in 1917, consequently played a much more central and directing role in social and economic development than did governments in most other major countries (*see Map 71*).

More than anything else it was the overwhelming agrarian problem which dominated economic and political discussion in Russia. In 1861 the 'Tsar-Liberator', Alexander II, promulgated the emancipation of the serfs. But Alexander's emancipation decree, as much a symbolic watershed as Lincoln's, proved as much a disappointment. The peasants remained burdened by the large redemption payments which they were compelled to make for their lands. The communal system of tenure tied the peasant to the land and perpetuated primitive techniques of cultivation. By the end of the century the rapid rise in the rural population of European Russia from 50 million in the early 1860s to 82 million by 1897 had produced a crisis of rural over-population (*see Map 57*). The establishment of a Peasant Land Bank in 1882 and the encouragement of emigration to the virgin lands of Siberia (to which some three million peasants had moved by 1914) hardly touched the surface of the problem (*Map 70*). The legislation inspired by P. A. Stolypin between 1906 and 1911 represented the most serious effort by the tsarist régime to come to grips with the agrarian problem. Stolypin announced that he proposed to back 'the sound and the strong'. His legislation was designed to encourage a shift from communal to private tenure, the consolidation of land into compact units, the movement of surplus population from the country to the towns, the promotion of more advanced techniques of cultivation, and the creation of a surplus of agrarian income, beyond bare subsistence, to create a market in the country for the manufactured products of the towns. Significant progress had been achieved by 1914 but war, revolution, and civil war led to a collapse

of the rural economy (*see Map 76*). The Bolshevik Revolution of 1917 made the peasants proprietors of their land, but only in the late 1920s did agricultural production again reach pre-war levels. Stalin's programme of forced collectivisation after 1929, accompanied by mass murder of recalcitrants, plunged Russian agriculture once again into chaos. Russian agricultural productivity remained far behind that of western Europe and north America, and Russia, an exporter of grain before the revolution, was compelled in the 1970s to import large quantities of grain from her capitalist rivals, the USA and Canada.

Russian industrial development was far more impressive and was indeed the foundation of her emergence as a 'super-power'. Throughout the nineteenth century Russian industry remained primitive and expansion slow. Only towards the end of the century was there really significant development and growth. Russian industrialisation was characterised by a very high reliance on foreign (particularly French) capital, by a stress on mining and metallurgy, by concentration in large units of production, and by heavy state involvement in industrial development. All of these characteristics except the first endured into the post-revolutionary period (*Map 71*). The foremost exponent of industrialisation under the old régime was S. Y. Witte who presided over economic policy for most of the period between 1892 and 1906. These were years of very swift economic expansion, with an average annual growth rate in the 1890s of eight per cent. A renewed surge of growth took place between 1906 and 1913. The dislocations of war between 1914 and 1921 were catastrophic for Russian industry. 'War communism' between 1918 and 1921 brought overnight nationalisation, attempts to introduce workers' control, and near-total economic collapse. The 'New Economic Policy' (NEP) after 1921 permitted a limited return to capitalism, and by 1929 industrial production had surpassed the pre-war level. The 'five-year plan' instituted by Stalin in 1929 marked the beginning of the most intensive period of industrial expansion – particularly striking because it took place against a background of economic depression in the capitalist world (*Map 78*). Although official Soviet figures are dubious there is no question that during this period Russia was ruthlessly propelled into the front ranks of industrial producers. The progress continued after the Second World War, and between 1950 and 1980 the Soviet economy grew from about one-third to more than two-thirds the size of that of the USA. However, much of Soviet industry remained relatively primitive, and it was notable that in the 1960s Russia once again began to rely on large-scale imports of foreign capital and advanced western technology.

The eastward territorial expansion of Russia in the nineteenth century (*see Map 70*) was no less impressive than that of the USA to the west. But Russian imperialism encountered serious internal and external difficulties. The empire contained vast numbers of non-Russian subject nationalities, many (in the east) educationally and socially backward, others (in the west) relatively advanced, most resentful of Russification and highly nationalistic. The Jews, confined to the so-called 'Pale of Settlement' (*see Map 60*), were particularly prominent in the revolutionary socialist movement which grew rapidly after the 1890s. Defeat by Japan in 1904-5 (*Map 73*) was the catalyst for revolution in 1905, which came close to

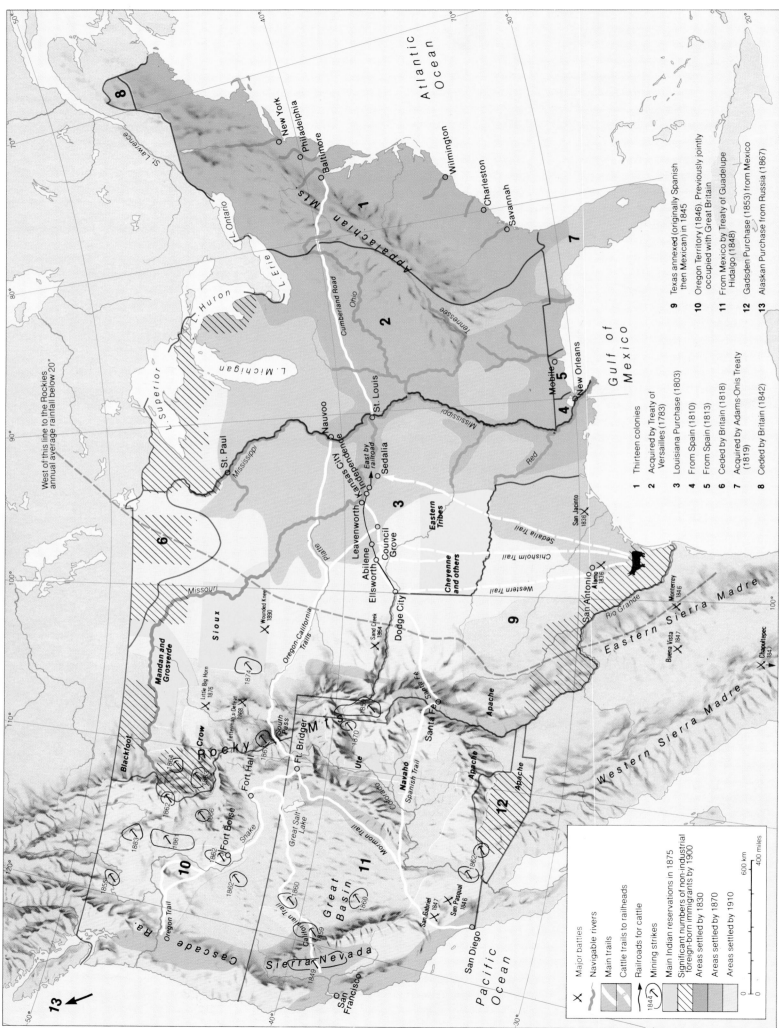

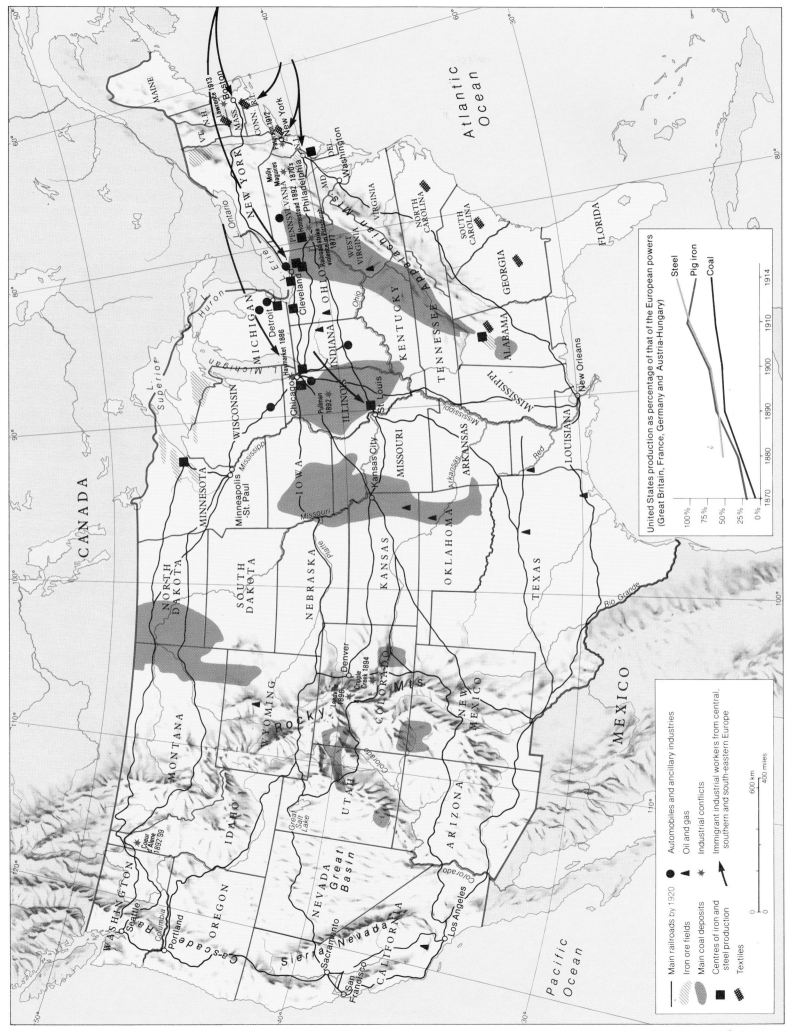

Atlantic Ocean

MAINE

VT. N.H.

MASS. Boston
Lawrence 1913

CONN. R.I.

NEW YORK

New York

Paterson 1912

L. Ontario

L. Erie

PENNSYLVANIA
Molly Maguires 1870's

Philadelphia

DEL.

MD.

Washington

Homestead 1892
Railroad strike
violence at Pittsburgh
1877

WEST VIRGINIA

VIRGINIA

NORTH CAROLINA

SOUTH CAROLINA

FLORIDA

Cleveland

OHIO

Ohio

KENTUCKY

TENNESSEE

GEORGIA

ALABAMA

MISSISSIPPI

New Orleans

Detroit
Haymarket 1886

MICHIGAN

L. Huron

L. Superior

L. Michigan

INDIANA

Chicago

Pullman 1892

ILLINOIS

St. Louis

MISSOURI

Kansas City

ARKANSAS

Arkansas

Red

LOUISIANA

Mississippi

WISCONSIN

Minneapolis
-St. Paul

Mississippi

MINNESOTA

IOWA

Missouri

OKLAHOMA

TEXAS

Rio Grande

MEXICO

CANADA

NORTH DAKOTA

SOUTH DAKOTA

NEBRASKA

Platte

KANSAS

Denver

Cripple Creek 1894

Leadville 1896

COLORADO

Rocky Mts.

NEW MEXICO

WYOMING

MONTANA

IDAHO

Great Salt Lake

UTAH

Colorado

ARIZONA

Colorado

Coeur d'Alene 1892-99

WASHINGTON

Seattle

Columbia

Portland

OREGON

Cascades

NEVADA

Great Basin

Sierra Nevada

Sacramento

San Francisco

Los Angeles

CALIFORNIA

Pacific Ocean

United States production as percentage of that of the European powers
(Great Britain, France, Germany and Austria-Hungary)

Steel

Pig iron

Coal

100%
75%
50%
25%
0%

1870 1880 1890 1900 1910 1914

600 km
400 miles

Main railroads by 1920

Iron ore fields

Main coal deposits

Centres of iron and
steel production

Textiles

Automobiles and ancillary industries

Oil and gas

Industrial conflicts

Immigrant industrial workers from central,
southern and south-eastern Europe

© Creative Cartography Ltd © The Hamlyn Group

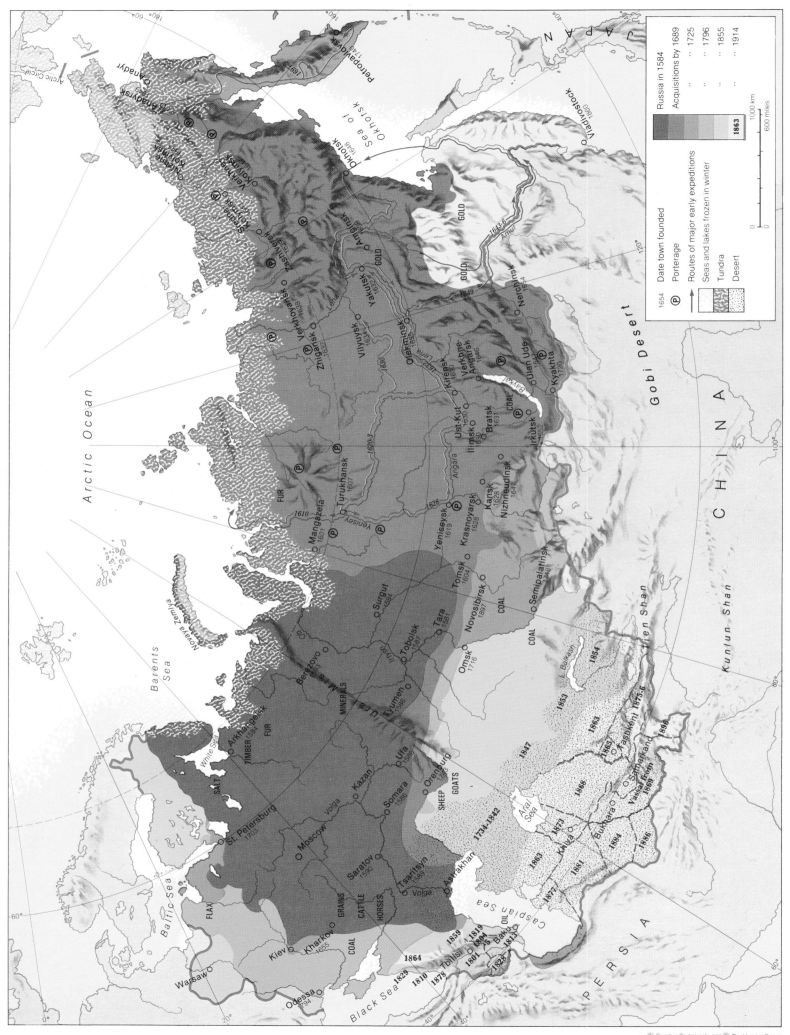

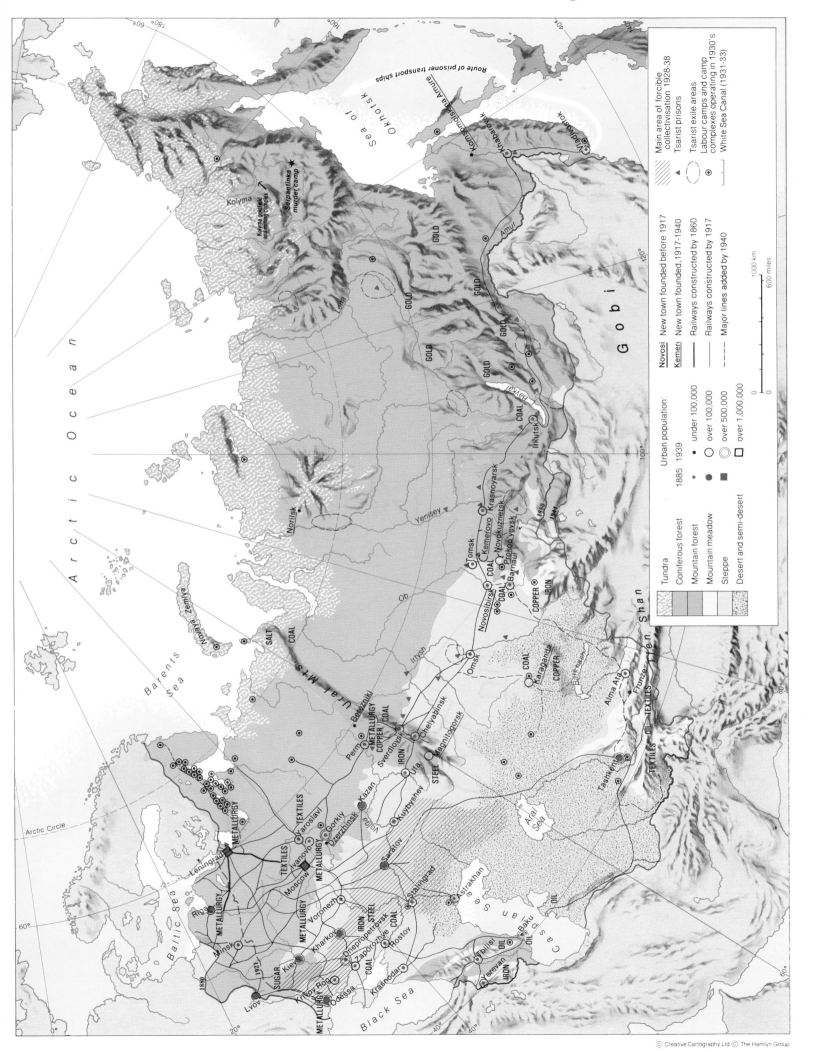

Main area of forcible
collectivisation 1928-38
Tsarist prisons

Tsarist exile areas
Labour camps and camp
complexes operating in 1930's
White Sea Canal (1931-33)

Novosi New town founded before 1917
Kemer New town founded.1917-1940
Railways constructed by 1860
Railways constructed by 1917
Major lines added by 1940

Urban population:
1885 1939
under 100,000
over 100,000
over 500,000
over 1,000,000

1000 km
600 miles

Tundra
Coniferous forest
Mountain meadow
Mountain meadow
Steppe
Desert and semi-desert

Arctic Ocean

Sea of
Okhotsk

Route of prisoner transport ships

Kom-somolsk-na-Amur

Khabarovsk

Vladivostok

Kolyma

Serpantinka
murder camp

Kolyma gold-field
and mining complex

Amur

GOLD
GOLD
GOLD
GOLD
GOLD
GOLD

Gobi

Lena

Baykal

COAL
Irkutsk

Tien   Shan

Yenisey

Krasnoyarsk
Kemerovo
Tomsk   COAL   Novokuznetsk
COAL   Prokop'yevsk
COAL   Barnaul
Novosibirsk   IRON
COPPER

Norilsk

Ob

Irtysh

Omsk

COAL
Karaganda
COPPER

Balkhash

Alma Ata
Frunze
TEXTILES
OIL

Tashkent
TEXTILES

Aral
Sea

Ural Mts.

SALT   COAL

Bereznki

METALLURGY   COAL
Perm   COPPER
Sverdlovsk
IRON
Ural
Chelyabinsk
Magnitogorsk
STEEL

Barents
Sea

Novaya
Zemlya

Arctic Circle

Baltic Sea

Leningrad   METALLURGY

Riga   METALLURGY

Minsk

Lvov
METALLURGY

Odessa
METALLURGY

Krivoy Rog
SUGAR   Kiev

1880
1921

Yaroslavl
TEXTILES
Ivanovo   TEXTILES
Moscow   METALLURGY
METALLURGY
Voronezh
Kharkov   IRON
Dnepropetrovsk   STEEL
Zaporozhye   COAL
Rostov
Krasnodar

Gorkiy
Dzerzhinsk
Kazan
Volga
Kuybyshev

Saratov

Stalingrad

Astrakhan

OIL

Caspian   Sea

Tbilisi   OIL
Baku
Yerevan   IRON
OIL

Black Sea

© Creative Cartography Ltd   © The Hamlyn Group

toppling the régime. The concession of a Duma (Parliament) in 1905 was soon whittled away by the autocracy which retreated into hidebound conservatism. The liberal-democratic interlude of the February Revolution in 1917 gave way by October to a 'proletarian dictatorship' which by the late 1920s had degenerated into an autocracy far more brutal than that of the tsars.

The modernisation of Japan, like that of Russia, was closely bound up with her relationship with the rest of the world. Until the mid-nineteenth century Japan had kept herself almost hermetically sealed from contact with other powers. But in 1853 an American naval squadron under Commodore Perry visited Japan. This marked the start of the opening of Japan to foreign trade and foreign influences (see Map 64). In 1858 Russia, Britain, the USA, and France imposed 'unequal treaties' on Japan which, although much resented by the Japanese, confirmed foreign privileges in the country.

The modern history of Japan is generally seen as dating from 1868 when the Tokugawa shogunate ended and authority reverted to the young Meiji Emperor. The 'Meiji Restoration' began with an explicit statement of receptiveness to foreign ideas pronounced in the Emperor's 'Charter Oath': 'Knowledge', he declared, 'shall be sought from all over the world and thus shall be strengthened the foundations of the imperial polity.' There followed soon afterwards the abolition of feudalism. Revolts by conservative elements, particularly in 1877, were suppressed, and the government continued a wide-ranging programme of modernising reforms. In 1885 a cabinet system of government was established, and in 1889 a westward-looking constitution was adopted; this led to the convening of a legislative assembly in 1890. The legal codes were revised, occidental fashions in ideas, clothes, and food spread, and the foundations of a mass education system were laid. By 1905 over 90% of children attended primary schools. Secondary and higher education (particularly technical colleges) developed rapidly after the turn of the century. A modern army and navy were established.

The basis for these reforms was the transformation of the economy of Japan. Industrialisation, in which the government played a major role, was concentrated particularly in strategic industries such as munitions and ship-building and in textiles (see Map 72). There was a twentyfold expansion in the export of finished goods between 1868 and 1897. The late 1890s and the years after 1895 were boom periods; the outbreak of the First World War led to greatly increased demand for Japanese goods, and the period 1915-20 saw a huge spurt forward. Between 1900 and the late 1930s output of manufactured goods increased more than twelvefold. By 1936 Japan had overtaken Britain as the world's leading exporter of cotton piece goods. By the late 1930s Japan had developed what was in many ways a mature and diversified industrial economy. Industrialisation naturally led to

rapid urbanisation: whereas in 1895 only 12% of the population lived in towns, by the mid-1930s the urban population had increased to 45% of the total. But the Japanese economy had certain weaknesses. On the one hand there were large numbers of small, relatively primitive units of production; on the other, there developed the zaibatsu, massive industrial conglomerates, of which the most important in the 1920s and 1930s were Mitsui and Mitsubishi, which were probably the two largest private economic empires in the world. The zaibatsu, by means of corruption and other forms of covert control, exercised a generally baneful influence over Japanese politics and society. But the most serious weakness of the Japanese economy was her increasing dependence on imported raw materials: by 1930 she was a net importer of coal, and depended on imports for 85% of her iron and steel, 79% of her oil, and a large part of her food. The desire to break out of this apparent stranglehold helped to strengthen imperialist elements in Japan.

Japanese imperialism was in large measure a response to the imperialism of western powers. It began in the 1870s with the incorporation of the Ryuku Islands into Japan and the imposition of an 'unequal treaty' on Korea (see Map 73). Rivalry with China in Korea was largely responsible for the outbreak of the Sino-Japanese War in 1895 in which Japan won a stunning victory. But pressure from Russia, France, and Germany compelled Japan to yield up her claim to have won Port Arthur and the Liaotung Peninsula. The seizure of the peninsula by Russia only three years later aroused strong Japanese animosity, and the conclusion of the alliance with Britain in 1902 placed Japan in a position to confront Russia without fear of intervention. In 1904 she attacked Russia, won another startling victory, and regained the leasehold of the Liaotung Peninsula, and control of south Sakhalin and the Russian-built railways in southern Manchuria. Russia further recognised Japanese paramountcy in Korea, and by 1910 Japan felt strong enough to annex Korea outright.

The emergence of the USA, Russia, and Japan as powers of the first rank was, therefore, already far advanced by 1914 when there began the series of cataclysmic shocks which, within little more than a generation, was to shatter the old European-dominated world order.

Further reading: S. E. Morrison, H. S. Commager, and W. E. Leuchtenberg, A Concise History of the American Republic (Oxford University Press, 1977); Richard Hofstader, The Age of Reform (Random House, 1955; Cape, 1962; p.b.); Hugh Seton-Watson, The Russian Empire 1801-1917 (Oxford University Press, 1967); Lionel Kochan, The Making of Modern Russia (Cape, 1962; Penguin, 1970); Richard Storry, A History of Modern Japan (Cassell, 1962; Penguin, 1968); William W. Lockwood, The Economic Development of Japan (Oxford University Press, 1955).

72 The modernisation of Japan
The Meiji restoration of 1868 ended the traditional seclusion of Japan and returned power to the imperial government. A deliberate programme of westernisation in government and society was accompanied by a state-directed transformation of the economy to make Japan a modern industrial power.

73 The Far East around 1900
After defeating China in the war of 1894-5 Japan competed with the western powers and Russia in a 'scramble for China' which the imperial government, paralysed by corruption and internal dissension, was powerless to resist. Japan confirmed its new status as a world power by overwhelming Russia in the war of 1904-5.

74 European imperialism in Africa
The partition of Africa in the 'scramble' of 1880-1914 was less a development of earlier activity there than an extension of the rivalries of the Great Powers in Europe. The new political geography had little correspondence with African reality; nevertheless it largely survived the decolonisation of the 1950s, 60s and 70s.

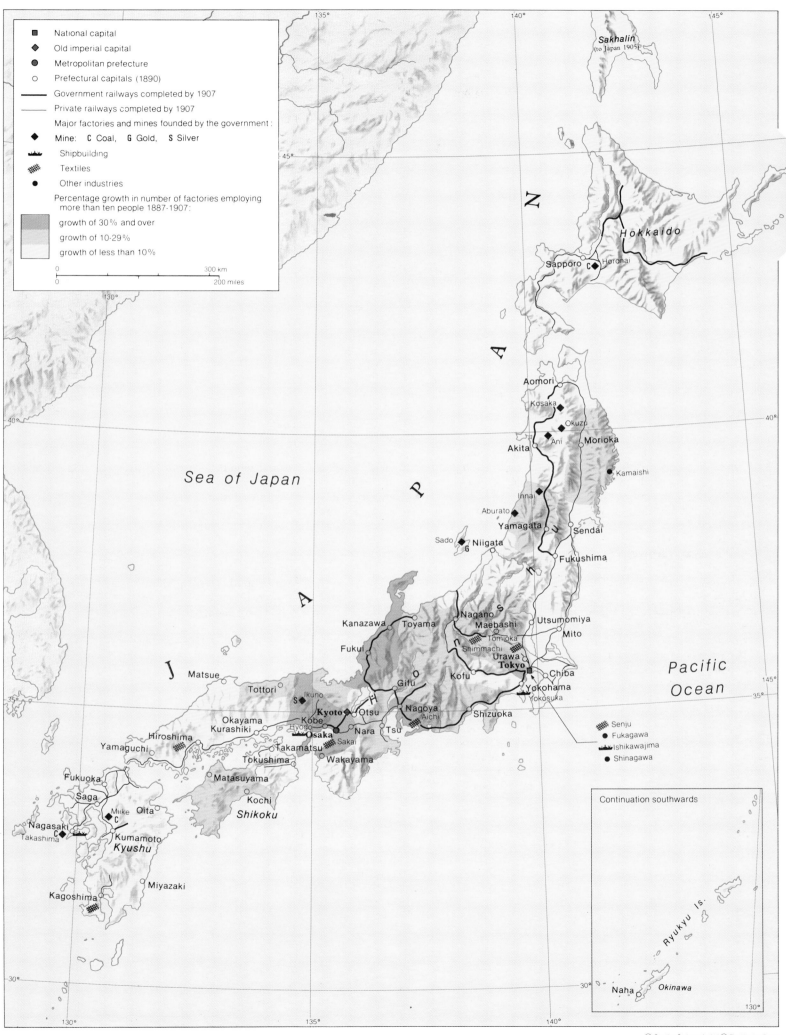

National capital
Old imperial capital
Metropolitan prefecture
Prefectural capitals (1890)
Government railways completed by 1907
Private railways completed by 1907
Major factories and mines founded by the government:
Mine: C Coal, G Gold, S Silver
Shipbuilding
Textiles
Other industries
Percentage growth in number of factories employing
more than ten people 1887-1907:
growth of 30% and over
growth of 10-29%
growth of less than 10%

300 km
200 miles

Sakhalin
(to Japan 1905?)

Hokkaido

Sapporo Horonai C

N

A

P

Aomori
Kosaka
Okuzu
Akita Ani Morioka
Kamaishi
Innai
Aburato Yamagata
Sado Niigata Sendai
G Fukushima

Sea of Japan

Nagano
Kanazawa Toyama Maebashi Utsumomiya
Tomioka Mito
Fukui Shimmachi
Urawa
Tokyo Chiba
Kofu Yokohama
Matsue Gifu Yokosuka
J Tottori Nagoya Shizuoka
Ikuno Otsu Aichi
S Kyoto
Okayama Kobe Nara Tsu
Kurashiki Hyogo Osaka Sakai
Hiroshima Takamatsu
Yamaguchi Tokushima Wakayama
Matasuyama

Senju
Fukagawa
Ishikawajima
Shinagawa

Pacific
Ocean

Kochi
Shikoku

Fukuoka
Saga
Miike
Nagasaki Oita C
Takashima C Kumamoto
Kagoshima Kyushu

Miyazaki

Continuation southwards

Ryukyu Is.

Naha Okinawa

© Creative Cartography Ltd © The Hamlyn Group

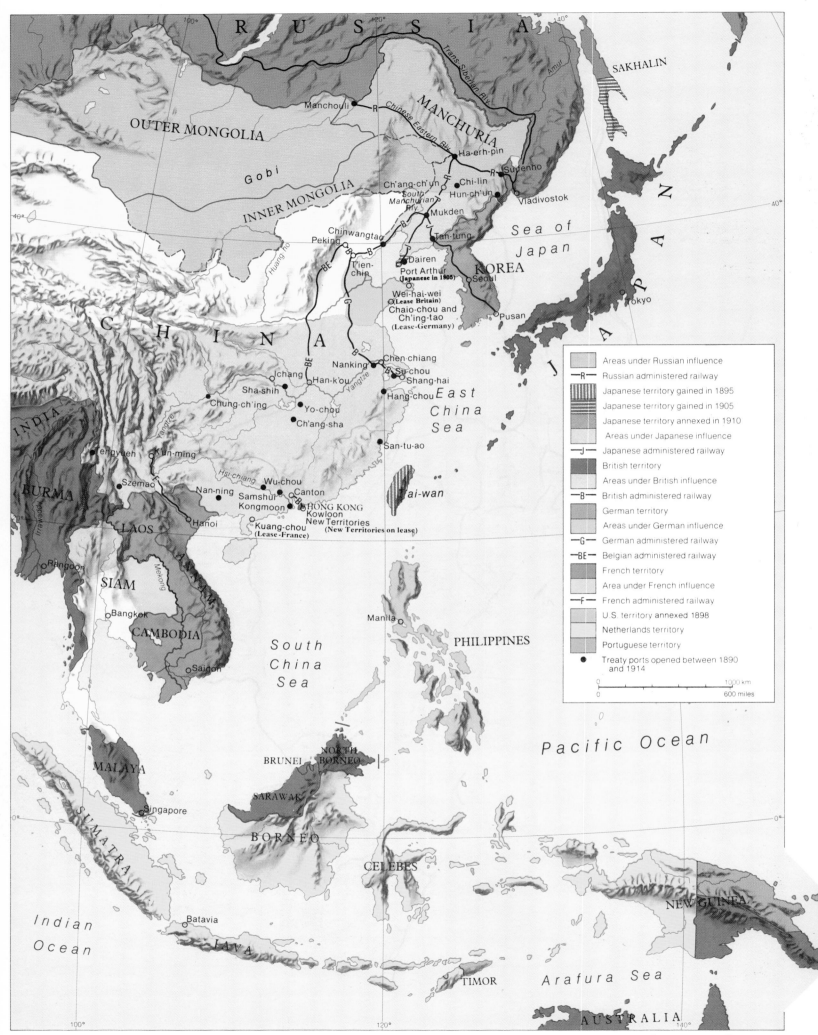

Legend:

- Areas under Russian influence
- —R— Russian administered railway
- Japanese territory gained in 1895
- Japanese territory gained in 1905
- Japanese territory annexed in 1910
- Areas under Japanese influence
- —J— Japanese administered railway
- British territory
- Areas under British influence
- —B— British administered railway
- German territory
- Areas under German influence
- —G— German administered railway
- —BE— Belgian administered railway
- French territory
- Area under French influence
- —F— French administered railway
- U.S. territory annexed 1898
- Netherlands territory
- Portuguese territory
- ● Treaty ports opened between 1890 and 1914

1000 km
600 miles

© Creative Cartography Ltd © The Hamlyn Group

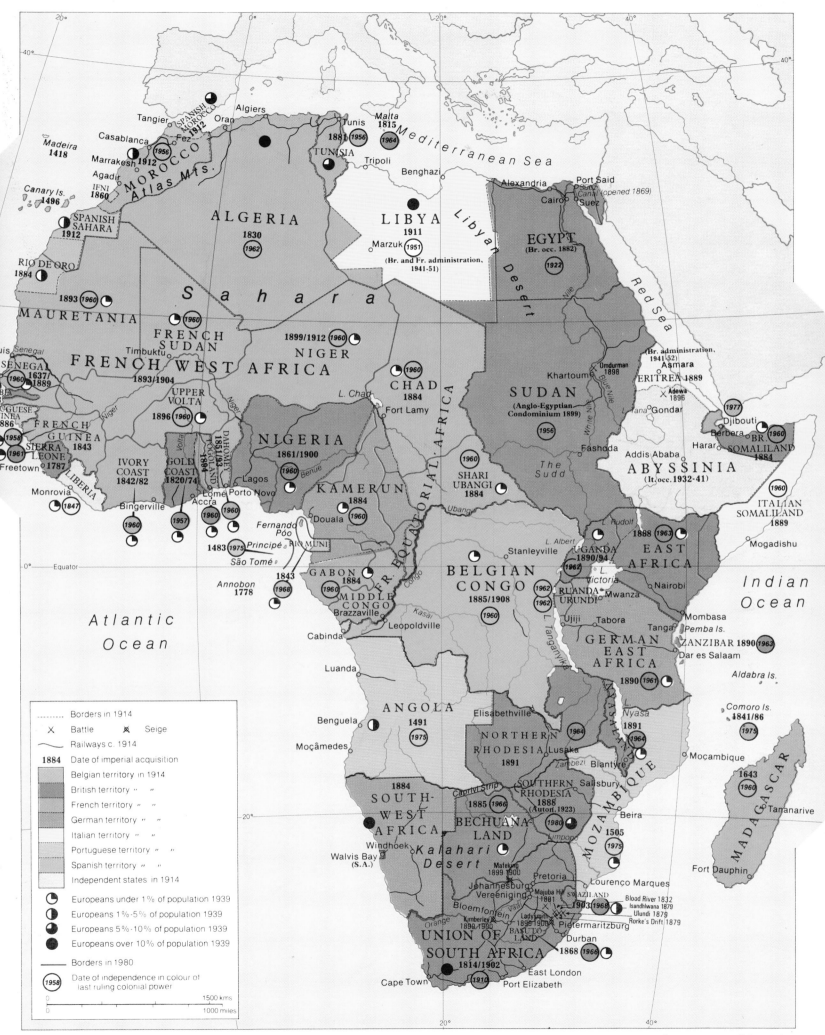

Madeira 1418
Canary Is. 1496
Tangier
Algiers
Oran
Tunis 1881 (1956)
Malta 1815
TUNISIA (1964)
Tripoli
Benghazi
Casablanca
Fez
Marrakesh 1912 (1956)
MOROCCO
Atlas Mts.
Agadir
IFNI 1860
SPANISH SAHARA 1912
RIO DE ORO 1884
MAURETANIA 1893 (1960)
Luis Senegal
SENEGAL 1637/1889 (1960)
GUINEA 1886 (1958)
SIERRA LEONE 1787 (1961)
Freetown
Monrovia
LIBERIA (1847)
Bingerville (1960)
IVORY COAST 1842/82
GOLD COAST 1820/74 (1957)
UPPER VOLTA 1896 (1960)
Timbuktu
FRENCH SUDAN
FRENCH WEST AFRICA 1893/1904
NIGER 1899/1912 (1960)
DAHOMEY 1851/93 (1960)
TOGOLAND 1884
Lomé Porto Novo (1960)
Accra
Lagos
NIGERIA 1861/1900 (1960)
KAMERUN 1884 (1960)
Douala
Fernando Póo
Principé 1483 (1975)
São Tomé
RIO MUNI
Annobon 1778
1843 (1968)
GABON 1884 (1960)
MIDDLE CONGO
Brazzaville
Leopoldville
Cabinda
Luanda
ANGOLA 1491 (1975)
Benguela
Moçâmedes

SPANISH MOROCCO 1912

ALGERIA 1830 (1962)

Sahara

LIBYA 1911 (1951)
Marzuk
(Br. and Fr. administration, 1941-51)

Mediterranean Sea
Libyan Desert

Alexandria
Cairo
Port Said
Suez Canal (opened 1869)
Suez
EGYPT (Br. occ. 1882) (1922)

L. Chad
CHAD 1884 (1960)
Fort Lamy

FR. EQUATORIAL AFRICA

SHARI UBANGI 1884 (1960)

Khartoum
Omdurman 1898
SUDAN (Anglo-Egyptian Condominium 1899) (1956)
Blue Nile
Fashoda
The Sudd
White Nile
Adowa 1896
Addis Ababa
ABYSSINIA (It. occ. 1932-41)
Gondar
L. Tana
Asmara
ERITREA 1889
(Br. administration, 1941-52)
Djibouti (1977)
Berbera
Harar
BR. SOMALILAND 1884 (1960)
Mogadishu
ITALIAN SOMALILAND 1889 (1960)

Red Sea

Nile

Ubangi
Congo
Kasai
L. Albert
Stanleyville
BELGIAN CONGO 1885/1908 (1960)
RUANDA-URUNDI (1962)
L. Rudolf
UGANDA 1890/94 (1962)
L. Victoria
Mwanza
Ujiji
Tabora
EAST AFRICA 1888 (1963)
Nairobi
Mombasa
Pemba Is.
ZANZIBAR 1890 (1963)
Dar es Salaam
Tanga
GERMAN EAST AFRICA 1890 (1961)
L. Tanganyika
Aldabra Is.

Indian Ocean

Atlantic Ocean
Equator

NORTHERN RHODESIA 1891
Elisabethville
Lusaka
1964
NYASALAND 1891 (1964)
Blantyre
L. Nyasa
Comoro Is. 1841/86 (1975)
Mocambique
Beira
MOZAMBIQUE 1505 (1975)

SOUTH-WEST AFRICA 1884
Windhoek
Walvis Bay (S.A.)
Kalahari Desert
BECHUANALAND 1885 (1966)
Caprivi Strip
SOUTHERN RHODESIA 1888 (Auton. 1923) (1966)
Salisbury
Zambezi
Limpopo
1980
Mafeking 1899/1900
Pretoria
Johannesburg
Vereeniging
Majuba Hill 1881
SWAZILAND 1903 (1968)
Blood River 1832
Isandhlwana 1879
Ulundi 1879
Rorke's Drift 1879
Bloemfontein
BASUTOLAND 1868 (1966)
Kimberley 1899/1900
Ladysmith 1899/1900
Pietermaritzburg
Durban
UNION OF SOUTH AFRICA 1814/1902 (1910)
Cape Town
East London
Port Elizabeth
Lourenço Marques

MADAGASCAR 1643 (1960)
Tananarive
Fort Dauphin

Legend:
- - - - Borders in 1914
X Battle
⚔ Seige
～ Railways c. 1914
1884 Date of imperial acquisition
Belgian territory in 1914
British territory " "
French territory " "
German territory " "
Italian territory " "
Portuguese territory " "
Spanish territory " "
Independent states in 1914
◗ Europeans under 1% of population 1939
◖ Europeans 1%-5% of population 1939
◕ Europeans 5%-10% of population 1939
● Europeans over 10% of population 1939
— Borders in 1980
(1958) Date of independence in colour of last ruling colonial power

1500 kms
1000 miles

© Creative Cartography Ltd © The Hamlyn Group

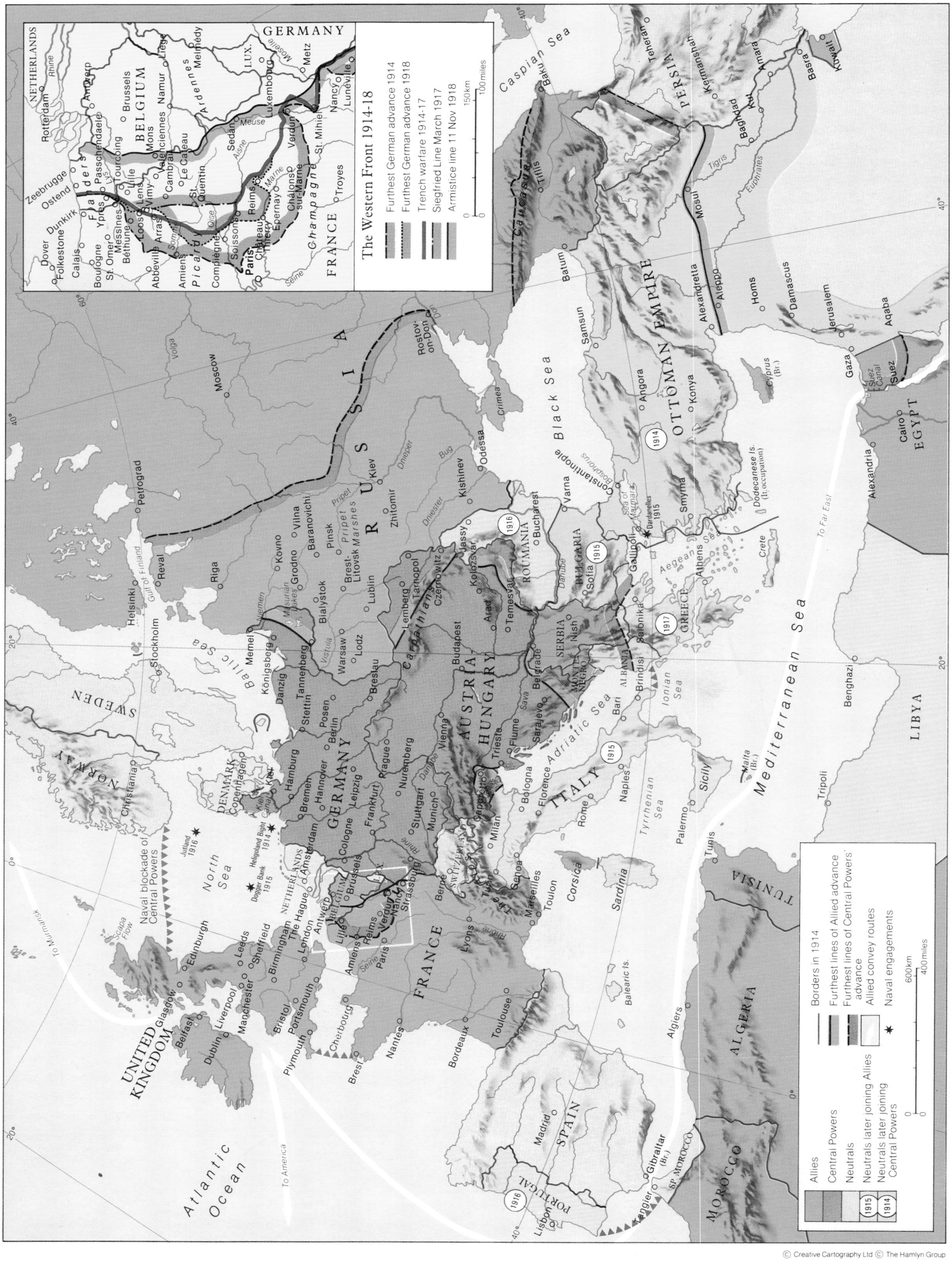
The Western Front 1914-18
Furthest German advance 1914
Furthest German advance 1918
Trench warfare 1914-17
Siegfried Line March 1917
Armistice line 11 Nov 1918
150km
100miles
GERMANY
NETHERLANDS
BELGIUM
LUX.
FRANCE
Flanders
Picardy
Champagne
Ardennes
Allies
Central Powers
Neutrals
Neutrals later joining Allies
Neutrals later joining Central Powers
Borders in 1914
Furthest lines of Allied advance
Furthest lines of Central Powers' advance
Allied convey routes
Naval engagements
600km
400miles
Naval blockade of Central Powers
Jutland 1916
Heligoland Bight 1914
Dogger Bank 1915
Dardanelles 1915
To Murmansk
To America
To Far East
UNITED KINGDOM
FRANCE
GERMANY
AUSTRIA-HUNGARY
RUSSIA
SWEDEN
NORWAY
DENMARK
SPAIN
PORTUGAL
ITALY
SWITZERLAND
SERBIA
MONTENEGRO
ALBANIA
ROUMANIA
BULGARIA
GREECE
OTTOMAN EMPIRE
PERSIA
EGYPT
LIBYA
TUNISIA
ALGERIA
MOROCCO
SP. MOROCCO
Atlantic Ocean
North Sea
Baltic Sea
Black Sea
Caspian Sea
Mediterranean Sea
Adriatic Sea
Aegean Sea
Ionian Sea
Tyrrhenian Sea
Caucasus
Carpathians
Pripet Marshes
Masurian Lakes

The emergence of the modern world II

The First World War and its aftermath

75 The First World War
The supremacy of defensive over offensive techniques made the Great War one of relatively little movement, especially on the Western Front, and enormous casualties, engaging armies many times larger than ever before. The resources of the belligerent powers were deployed and their civilian populations involved to a quite unprecedented degree, making this the first 'total' war.

THE OUTBREAK of the First World War in August 1914 may be explained as, first and foremost, the product of a German bid for world power. The immense growth of German industrial and military might since 1871 (*see Map 57*) had nourished the development of dynamic political ambitions for a German-dominated 'Mitteleuropa', a colonial empire including a German 'Mittelafrika' (*see Map 74*), and the permanent subjugation of all Germany's potential European rivals. Underlying all this was hatred of the Slavs, fear of 'encirclement' by the Triple Entente, and resentment of Britain's empire, of her navy, and of her dominance of world trade and of the international capital market (*Map 67*). The German government intended, by means of a war, to establish the Reich as a super-power on a par with Britain. By 1914 the Germans, conscious that they would have to fight in both the east and west, and aware of Russia's programme of military modernisation, felt it was 'now or never'. The opportunity came in June with the assassination by Serbs of the Austrian Archduke Franz Ferdinand in Sarajevo. Austria, encouraged by Germany, sent Serbia an ultimatum designed to be so harsh as to ensure rejection. The Serbs, although they were fired by a burning Slav nationalism, and were confident of Russian support, accepted nearly all Austria's demands. But the Austrians, under German influence, nevertheless declared war on Serbia. Russia's immediate decision to mobilise dispelled any prospect of localisation of the conflict, and Germany quickly declared war on Russia and France. German violation of Belgian neutrality led Britain to join Russia and France. The Ottoman Empire, fearing partition by the Entente powers, allied itself with Germany. The Entente powers were joined by Japan in August 1914, and by Italy in May 1915, and, after German U-boat (submarine) attacks on merchant shipping, by the USA in April 1917.

The First World War was more catastrophic in its impact on nearly every sphere of human activity than any previous war. Although some fighting occurred in Asia and Africa and at sea, the conflict was at its most intense in Europe (*Map 75*). Relying on the pre-war Schlieffen plan, the Germans launched a sweeping thrust through Belgium into France, hoping to knock her out in six weeks, thus enabling Germany to turn her full strength against Russia. However the German army was halted at the River Marne, and the war in the west settled down to static trench warfare for four years, leaving millions of German, French, and British dead. In the east the conflict was more mobile but no less bloody. With the issue unresolved on the two central fronts both sides sought alternative strategies. But neither the British landing at Gallipoli in 1915-16 nor the German attempt to starve Britain into surrender by blockade was successful in breaking the impasse.

In its military character (although not its scale) the war was in general fought by traditional means, the key elements being infantry, cavalry, and artillery. But the war boosted technological innovation, and the appearance of tanks and warplanes, although in limited numbers, was a portent of the revolution in warfare of the mid-twentieth century. In most belligerent countries, particularly in Europe, the war had a shattering impact on society, economy, and government. Conscription, food shortages, attacks on civilian populations, war propaganda and hysteria were nothing new in human warfare. But what rendered this perhaps the first 'total war' in history was the vast expansion in the role of

government in directing social and economic organisation: *laissez-faire* was dead.

By late 1917 Germany had won the war in the east and in March 1918 imposed the draconian Treaty of Brest-Litovsk on Russia (*Map 76*). But although Germany was now free to concentrate on the western front, the entry of the USA to the war, with its huge reservoir of manpower and resources, ensured an eventual Allied victory. By late 1918 a final German push in the west had failed, her allies Austria-Hungary and Turkey had collapsed, and revolution had broken out in Germany. Although no enemy armies were yet on German soil, an armistice took effect on 11 November 1918.

The war had convulsive effects on the old empires. In Russia the Tsar abdicated after a liberal revolution in March 1917 (the 'February Revolution' after the Old Style calendar then still used in Russia). The new Provisional Government determined to keep Russia in the war, but it was discredited and demoralised by continuing defeat, desertion, and dislocation, and by a rising demand for peace. The ascent to power of Lenin's Bolsheviks (the extreme left wing of the Russian Social Democratic Party) in November 1917 (the 'October Revolution') was founded on his promise of 'peace, bread, and land'. Although defeated in elections in December 1917, and forced to surrender large areas in the west to the Germans at Brest-Litovsk, the Bolsheviks clung to power and by 1921 had defeated both their internal enemies and interventionist armies of capitalist powers. In the last days of the war the German and Austrian Emperors were swept off their thrones by revolution. Short-lived socialist republics in eastern and central Europe soon collapsed, however, leaving Russia for the next quarter-century as the sole exemplar of a communist state. Perhaps the most momentous of the anti-imperial revolutions was that of Mustafa Kemal (later known as Ataturk). From 1919 onwards he drove Greek forces out of Asia Minor, to be followed by the enforced exodus of the ancient Greek communities of the Black Sea and Aegean littorals (*Map 5*). He expelled all occupying forces, reversed the imposed peace treaty, deposed the Sultan, and pronounced the end of the Islamic Caliphate (symbol of Islamic political unity since the death of the Prophet). Ataturk consolidated Turkey as a national state, and propelled her on a path of modernisation which was to inspire a later generation of post-colonial politicians in Asia and Africa.

Allied war aims, as enunciated in the American President Wilson's 'Fourteen Points', had presaged a relatively generous peace. In the event the treaties imposed on the defeated powers after a peace conference at Paris in 1919 humiliated the vanquished without in the long run benefiting the victors. Germany, convicted in the Treaty of Versailles of 'war guilt', was forced to cede territory in the east and the west, to pay massive reparations, and to constrict her armed strength within narrowly defined limits (*Map 77*). East Prussia was divided from the rest of Germany by a narrow strip of land gained by the new Polish state – the 'Polish corridor'. Austria, reduced to a German-speaking rump around Vienna, was barred from uniting with Germany. Hungary too was diminished to a small national state, losing two-thirds of her pre-war territory and population. The old empires were replaced by a patchwork of small 'successor states', formed in ostensible accordance with the principle of 'national self-determination'. But far from resolving

The First World War and its aftermath

national problems the new political structure in Europe aggravated them. All the new states contained substantial national minorities; the defeated powers resented the 'dictated peace' and itched to regain lost territories; the successor states lived in terror of the 'revisionist' ambitions of their former masters. Outside Europe too the peace treaties helped to stimulate local nationalisms. The Anglo-French carve-up of the ex-Ottoman Fertile Crescent provoked Arab unrest. The Chinese, who had hoped that the 'Fourteen Points' would lead the western powers to treat them on a basis of equality, resented the transfer to Japan of former German territories in China. Wilson, disillusioned by the selfish aggrandisement of his allies, acceded to their demands in order to gain their acquiescence to the Covenant of the League of Nations, the world organisation which he hoped would guarantee peace. However the League's prospects were gravely damaged by the US Senate's repudiation of the Charter. The USA remained outside the League and embarked on an 'isolationist' course for the next two decades.

The international economic order, shattered by the war, never fully recovered. Britain's former pre-eminence as a producing, trading, and investing centre was in tatters. In company with others Britain was humiliatingly obliged to 'renegotiate' her war debts to the USA. The victorious powers had hoped to finance their debt payments out of German reparations, but these were not forthcoming, and even the French occupation of the Ruhr in 1923 failed to secure payment on the desired massive scale. Germany, together with most of central and eastern Europe after the war, was gripped by hyperinflation which had profoundly unsettling social effects. During the middle and late 1920s a partial recovery of the international economy occurred. But the crash on the New York Stock Exchange in 1929 was the signal for descent into the most severe economic crisis of the century, by which only Soviet Russia and some undeveloped countries remained unafflicted (*Map 78*). Banks failed, stock markets collapsed, businesses were bankrupted, international trade slumped, demand for all types of goods plummeted, and further millions were thrown out of work. Everywhere confidence in liberal capitalism was shaken, and the general reaction was to resort to protectionist, beggar-my-neighbour policies with competitive devaluations and high tariff walls. The British, American, and French currencies were forced off the gold standard. Even Britain abandoned free trade in 1932. Some measure of recovery was achieved in the later 1930s, but a functioning international economic system was not resurrected. Meanwhile the insecurities induced by the Great Depression had helped to engender political deformations which wrecked the flimsy constructions of the peace treaties.

Economic recession and aggressive nationalism, heightened by frustration with the consequences of the peace treaties, led to the rise of violent authoritarian movements and their seizure of the reins of government. Demagogic militarist dictatorships became the order of the day. Mussolini's fascist movement in Italy, which took power in 1922, formed the prototype for such régimes, with its accent on brute force, national prestige, and imperial expansion, and its contempt for intellectuals and for parliamentary democracy. The insecure Weimar constitution in Germany was by 1933 reeling under the impact of economic collapse (with six million unemployed) and fierce rivalry between communists and socialists. In 1933, after emerging in free elections as the largest party in Germany, Hitler's National Socialists (Nazis) took power with the support of conservatives. A ruthless totalitarian state apparatus replaced the rickety Weimar structure: Jews, socialists, trade unionists and liberal intellectuals were attacked and placed in concentration camps, the *Reichstag* (Parliament) was burned down, books were thrown on bonfires, and a pagan, racialist, anti-democractic ideology was inculcated by state propaganda. The economy was regenerated by massive expansion of the armaments industries. The bourgeois decencies of imperial and Weimar Germany gave way to the cult of 'blood and soil' and to hysterical mob adulation of the leader. Authoritarian régimes, often with a similar tinge, sprang up in much of Europe, notably in Spain after the bloody civil war of 1936-9 (*see Map 80*). In Soviet Russia too a savage despotism developed, with the usual apparatus of secret police, censorship, torture, prison camps, repression of all opposition, rule through a single party, and stress on economic self-sufficiency (*Map 71*). Stalin, who by the late 1920s had eliminated all potential rivals for power in the USSR, launched the country on a hectic course of heavy industrialisation, collectivisation of agriculture, and military reinforcement, accompanied by mass murder of *kulaks* (peasant proprietors), 'purges' of dissidents, and show trials. Japan, severely affected by the Depression, descended into the 'dark valley' of militarism. The efforts of the *Kuomintang* government of China to counter fragmentation into regional warlordism by unifying the country economically and politically evoked fears of a threat to Japanese economic interests and helped to stimulate Japanese expansionism into Manchuria and China (*Map 79*). On the other side of the Pacific also, democracy failed to withstand the impact of economic crisis, with dictators assuming power in Brazil and Argentina after military coups in 1930. Only in the states around the North Atlantic seaboard did liberal democracy survive in the late 1930s as the characteristic form of government, and even here economic enfeeblement, social malaise, and fear of war seemed to portend collapse in the face of totalitarian attack.

Further reading: H. W. Koch, *The Origins of the First World War* (Macmillan, 1972); B. H. Liddell Hart, *The First World War* (2nd ed. Cassell, 1970; Pan, 1972); E. H. Carr, *The Russian Revolution from Lenin to Stalin* (Macmillan, 1979); J. K. Galbraith, *The Great Crash* (Hamish Hamilton, 1955; Penguin, 1969); A. J. Nicholls, *Weimar and the Rise of Hitler* (Macmillan, 1968).

76 Revolution in Europe
In the civil war which followed the Russian revolution of October 1917 the 'White' (anti-Bolshevik) forces were supported by the western powers, and especially by Poland which, its independence confirmed by the Congress of Versailles, sought territorial expansion. Elsewhere in Europe revolutionary outbreaks were widespread from the last months of the Great War, but were ultimately abortive.

77 Central Europe between the Wars
The peace treaties divided the old dynastic empires into what purported to be nation-states but in fact contained large national minorities. In consequence they engaged in continuous border disputes while living in perpetual dread that the defeated powers, Germany, Hungary and Bulgaria, would seek to overturn what they regarded as a 'dictated' peace.

78 The Depression
The crash of the New York Stock Exchange in October 1929 was followed by the collapse of businesses and of financial confidence all over the developed world. While new industries developed in many regions the high unemployment and acute depression which followed, especially in areas dependent on traditional industries, imposed additional strains on democratic regimes, many of which failed to survive.

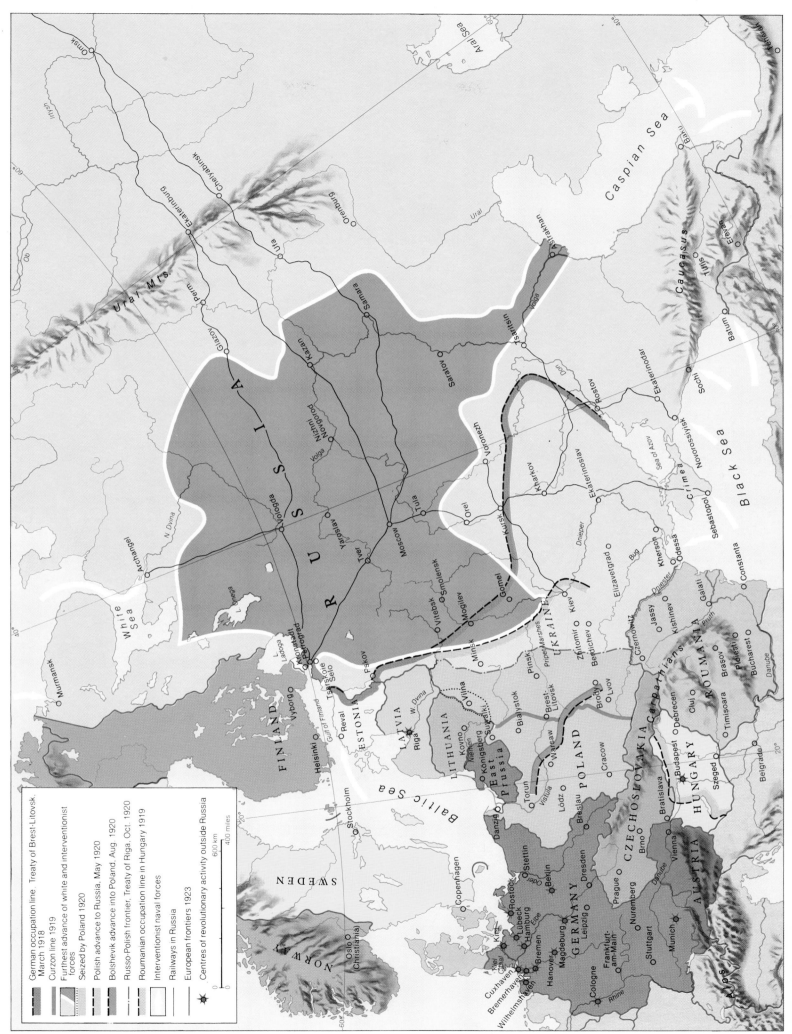

Omsk

Irtysh
Ob

Ishim

Chelyabinsk

Ekaterinburg

Ural Mts.

Perm
Tobol
Ufa

Orenburg
Ural

Caspian Sea

Baku
Elevan

Caucasus

Tiflis

Batum

Sochi

Astrakhan

Volga

Don

Ekaterinodar

Novorossiysk

Black Sea

Constanta

Sebastopol

Crimea

Sea of Azov

Tsaritsin

Rostov

Odessa

Kherson

Elizavetgrad

Ekaterinoslav

Kharkov

Voronezh

Saratov

Samara

R U S S I A

Kazan

Nizhni
Novgorod

Volga

Vologda

N Dvina

Archangel

White Sea

Murmansk

L. Onega

L. Ladoga

Yaroslav

Tver

Moscow

Tula

Orel

Kursk

Gomel

Smolensk

Mogilev

Vitebsk

Minsk

Pripet Marshes

Pinsk

Zhitomir

Berdichev

UKRAINE

Kiev

Lvov

Brody

Brest-
Litovsk

Bialystok

Dnieper

Bug

Czernowitz

Jassy

Kishinev

Prut

Galati

ROUMANIA

Brasov

Ploiesti

Bucharest

Danube

Cluj

Debrecen

Oradea

Szeged

Belgrade

HUNGARY

Budapest

Bratislava

Vienna

AUSTRIA

Alps

CZECHOSLOVAKIA

Carpathians

Brno

Prague

Cracow

POLAND

Lodz

Warsaw

Torun

Breslau

Oder

Dresden

Leipzig

Berlin

GERMANY

Magdeburg

Hanover

Frankfurt-
am-Main

Nuremberg

Stuttgart

Munich

Elbe

Rhine

Cologne

Bremen

Hamburg

Lübeck

Rostock

Stettin

Danzig

East
Prussia

Königsberg

Memel

Kovno

LITHUANIA

Suwalki

Vilna

Riga

LATVIA

W. Dvina

ESTONIA

Reval

Pskov

Tsarskoe
Selo

Petrograd

Kronstadt

Vyborg

Helsinki

Gulf of Finland

FINLAND

Stockholm

SWEDEN

Copenhagen

Kiel Canal

Cuxhaven

Bremerhaven

Wilhelmshaven

Baltic Sea

Oslo
(Christiania)

NORWAY

Nuremberg

Ural

Aral Sea

Volga

Syr Darya

Ural Mts.

© Creative Cartography Ltd © The Hamlyn Group

German occupation line. Treaty of Brest-Litovsk.
March 1918

Curzon line 1919

Furthest advance of white and interventionist
forces

Seized by Poland 1920

Polish advance to Russia, May 1920

Bolshevik advance into Poland, Aug. 1920

Russo-Polish frontier, Treaty of Riga. Oct. 1920

Roumanian occupation line in Hungary 1919

Interventionist naval forces

Railways in Russia

European frontiers 1923

Centres of revolutionary activity outside Russia

600 km

400 miles

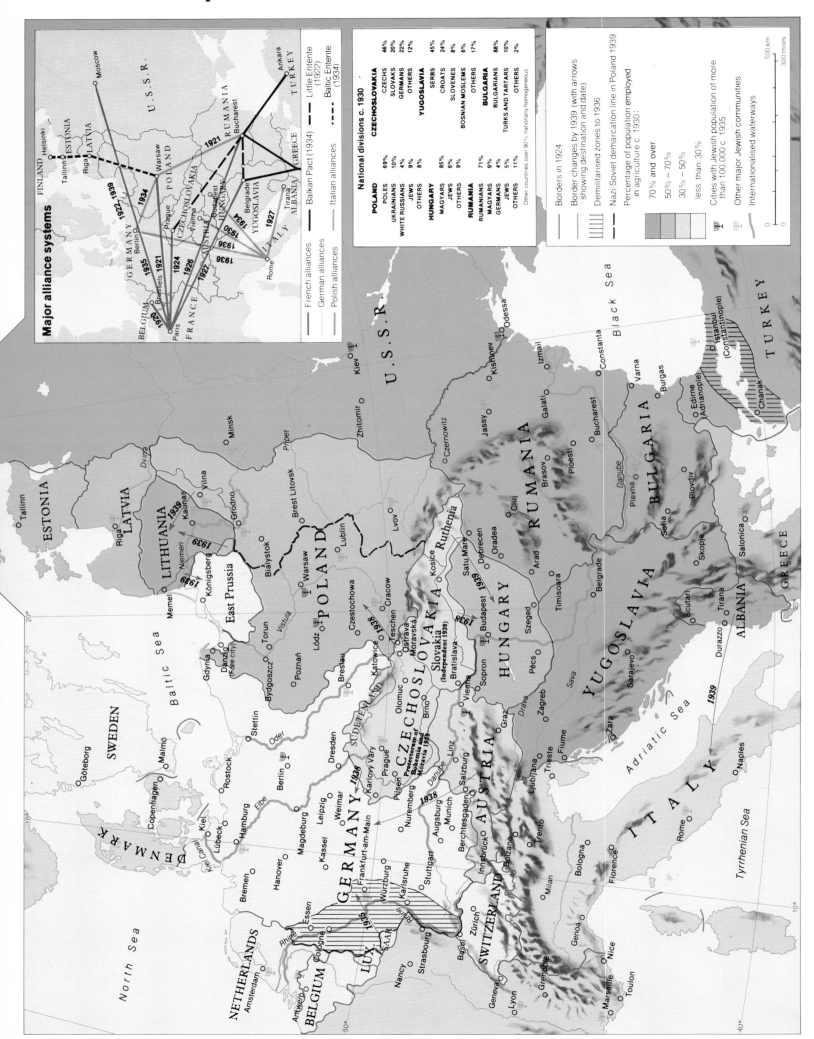

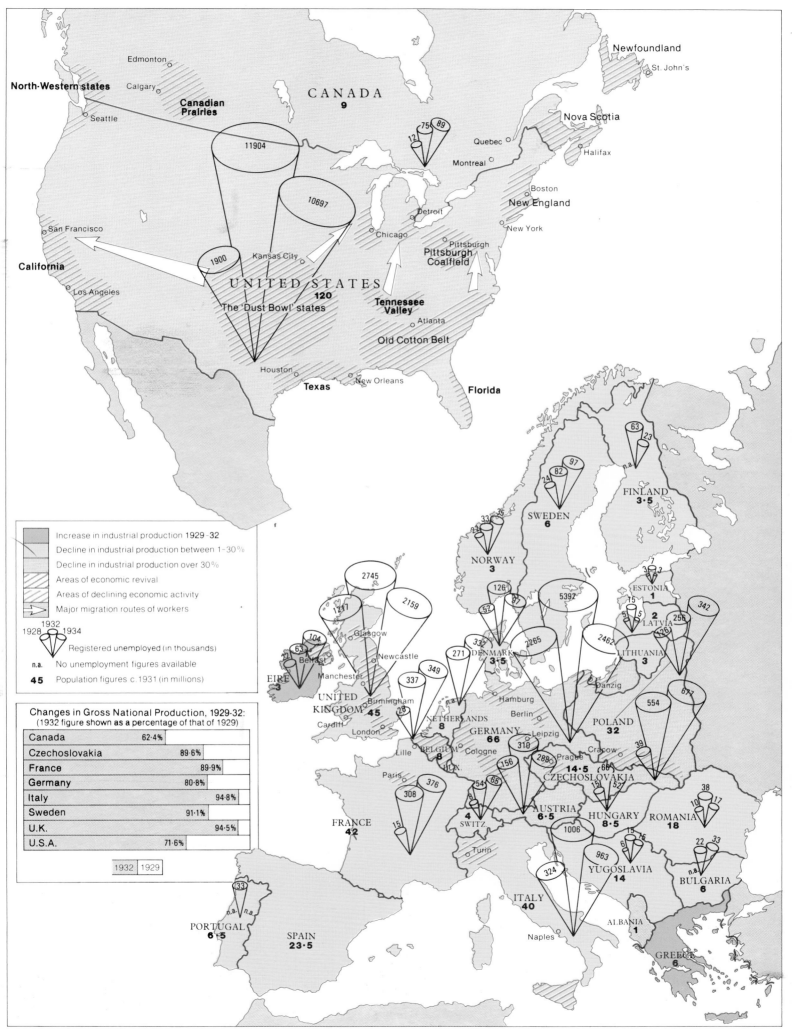

North-Western states

Edmonton
Calgary
Seattle

Canadian Prairies

CANADA
9

11904

Newfoundland
St. John's

Nova Scotia

75 89

12

Quebec

Halifax

Montreal

10697

Detroit

Boston

New England

San Francisco

Chicago

New York

Pittsburgh

Pittsburgh Coalfield

1900

Kansas City

California

Los Angeles

UNITED STATES
120
The 'Dust Bowl' states

Tennessee Valley

Atlanta

Old Cotton Belt

Houston

New Orleans

Texas

Florida

Legend:
- Increase in industrial production 1929-32
- Decline in industrial production between 1-30%
- Decline in industrial production over 30%
- Areas of economic revival
- Areas of declining economic activity
- Major migration routes of workers

1928 1932 1934
Registered unemployed (in thousands)

n.a. No unemployment figures available

45 Population figures c.1931 (in millions)

Changes in Gross National Production, 1929-32:
(1932 figure shown as a percentage of that of 1929)

Canada	62·4%
Czechoslovakia	89·6%
France	89·9%
Germany	80·8%
Italy	94·8%
Sweden	91·1%
U.K.	94·5%
U.S.A.	71·6%

1932 1929

63 23
n.a.

FINLAND
3·5

82 97
24

SWEDEN
6

33 36
23

NORWAY
3

3 3
7

ESTONIA
1

15
5
2

342
256
126

LATVIA
2

LITHUANIA
3

2745

1217

2159

126
52 97

5392

2462

2265

2265

Glasgow
Newcastle

104
63
21

Belfast
Manchester

EIRE
3

Birmingham

UNITED KINGDOM
45

Cardiff
London

337 349
23

271

332

DENMARK
3·5

Hamburg
Berlin

Danzig

554

677

POLAND
32

39

NETHERLANDS
8

GERMANY
66

Leipzig

310

288

Prague

Cracow

66

CZECHOSLOVAKIA
14·5

15 52

Lille

BELGIUM
3

LUX.

Cologne

156

54 65

8

38
10 17

ROMANIA
18

Paris

376

308

FRANCE
42

15

SWITZ.
4

AUSTRIA
6·5

HUNGARY
8·5

15 16
8

22 33
n.a.

BULGARIA
6

1006

963

YUGOSLAVIA
14

324

Turin

ITALY
40

ALBANIA
1

Naples

33
n.a. n.a.

PORTUGAL
6+5

SPAIN
23·5

GREECE
6

© Creative Cartography Ltd © The Hamlyn Group

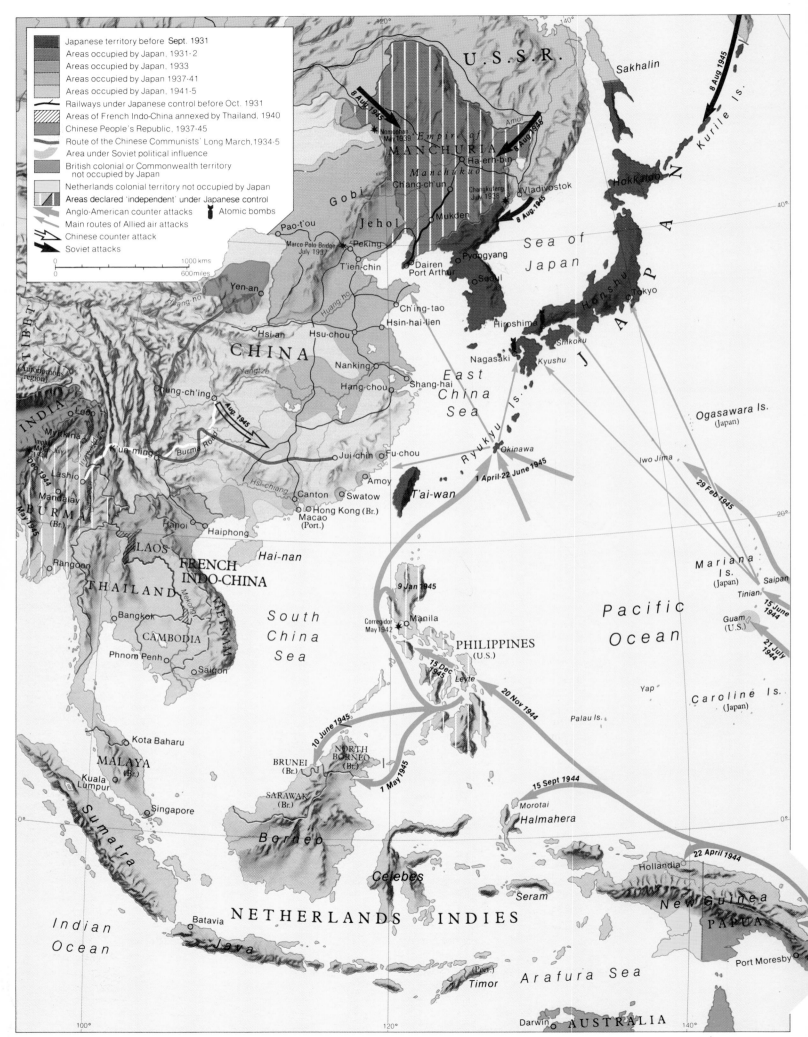

Legend:
- Japanese territory before Sept. 1931
- Areas occupied by Japan, 1931-2
- Areas occupied by Japan, 1933
- Areas occupied by Japan 1937-41
- Areas occupied by Japan, 1941-5
- Railways under Japanese control before Oct. 1931
- Areas of French Indo-China annexed by Thailand, 1940
- Chinese People's Republic, 1937-45
- Route of the Chinese Communists' Long March, 1934-5
- Area under Soviet political influence
- British colonial or Commonwealth territory not occupied by Japan
- Netherlands colonial territory not occupied by Japan
- Areas declared 'independent' under Japanese control
- Anglo-American counter attacks   Atomic bombs
- Main routes of Allied air attacks
- Chinese counter attack
- Soviet attacks

1000 kms
600 miles

U.S.S.R.

Sakhalin

Kurile Is.

8 Aug 1945

MANCHURIA

Nomonhan May 1939

Empire of

Manchukuo

Ha-erh-bin

Chang-ch'un

Changkufeng July 1938

Vladivostok

Hokkaido

Gobi

Jehol

Mukden

8 Aug 1945

Pao-t'ou

Peking

Marco Polo Bridge July 1937

T'ien-chin

Dairen
Port Arthur

Pyongyang

Seoul

Sea of Japan

Huang-ho

Yen-an

Ch'ing-tao

Hsin-hai-lien

Hiroshima

Honshu

Tokyo

Hsi-an

Hsu-chou

CHINA

Nanking

Hang-chou

Shang-hai

Nagasaki

Kyushu

Shikoku

East China Sea

Yangtze

Chung-ch'ing

Aug. 1945

J A P A N

INDIA

Ledo

Myitkyina

Imphal Mar-July 1944

K'un-ming

Burma Road

Jui-chin

Fu-chou

Ryukyu Is.

Okinawa

1 April-22 June 1945

Ogasawara Is. (Japan)

TIBET
(Autonomous region)

Lashio

Mandalay

BURMA (Br.)

May 1945

Hsi-chiang

Canton

Amoy

Swatow

T'ai-wan

Iwo Jima

29 Feb 1945

Rangoon

Hanoi

LAOS

Haiphong

Hai-nan

Macao (Port.)

Hong Kong (Br.)

THAILAND

FRENCH INDO-CHINA

South China Sea

9 Jan 1945

Corregidor May 1942

Manila

PHILIPPINES (U.S.)

Pacific Ocean

Mariana Is. (Japan)

Saipan

Tinian

15 June 1944

Bangkok

CAMBODIA

VIETNAM

Mekong

15 Dec 1945

Leyte

20 Nov 1944

Guam (U.S.)

21 July 1944

Phnom Penh

Saigon

Yap

Caroline Is. (Japan)

Kota Baharu

10 June 1945

MALAYA (Br.)

BRUNEI (Br.)

NORTH BORNEO (Br.)

Palau Is.

Kuala Lumpur

1 May 1945

SARAWAK (Br.)

Singapore

Sumatra

Borneo

15 Sept 1944

Morotai

Halmahera

22 April 1944

Hollandia

New Guinea

Celebes

NETHERLANDS INDIES

Seram

PAPUA

Indian Ocean

Batavia

Java

Timor (Port.)

Arafura Sea

Darwin

AUSTRALIA

Port Moresby

© Creative Cartography Ltd © The Hamlyn Group

The emergence of the modern world III

The Second World War

79 The Far East 1931-45
With the invasion of Manchuria in 1931 Japan, increasingly under the domination of its military leaders, and badly affected by the Depression, embarked upon a programme of military expansion designed to secure its domination of Asia and especially to eliminate western economic influence. The Far East consequently became a major theatre of the Second World War.

THE SECOND World War was more truly a global conflict than the first. In a sense it consisted of three wars, intertwined but distinct: the Japanese attempt to build an east Asian empire which brought her into conflict with China and the western powers which had interests in the area; the German ambition to dominate continental Europe (coupled with the Italian desire to render the Mediterranean an Italian lake) which led to war with Britain and France; and the German attack on the Soviet Union which made Russia the ally of Britain and the USA.

The roots of the Far Eastern war lay in the aim of the Japanese militarists to establish a 'New Order in East Asia'—a sphere of Japanese paramountcy in which western interests would be eliminated, and economic resources exploited to Japan's exclusive benefit. The invasion of Manchuria in 1931 marked the beginning of the descent to war (*Map 79*). The League of Nations was a broken reed, unable to compel Japan to withdraw from Manchuria—although Japan withdrew from the League. A puppet state called Manchukuo was erected under the nominal suzerainty of the last Chinese emperor, in reality under the supervision of Tokyo. Japan's 20-year alliance with Britain had been permitted to lapse in 1922, and in 1936 Japan's new diplomatic alignment was sealed by the Anti-Comintern Pact with Nazi Germany.

The Japanese invasion of China in 1937 is sometimes held to mark the real beginning of the Second World War. However, the British Empire and the USA were not at this stage engaged, and Japan did not declare war on Britain upon the outbreak of the European war in September 1939, nor on the USSR after Hitler's attack in mid-1941. Nevertheless further Japanese incursions in China and French Indo-China provoked an American, British, and Dutch economic embargo which led to the fatal decision in December 1941 to attack the US naval base at Pearl Harbor (in Hawaii), thus drawing the USA into both the Pacific and the European wars.

The war in Europe also arose out of the bid for imperial aggrandisement of an authoritarian régime. Hitler's Nazi movement had cultivated the myth of the 'stab in the back' (the notion that Germany had not been militarily defeated by the Allies in 1918 but had been the victim of internal conspiracy by socialists and Jews). The Nazis had played on the widespread resentment in Germany of the punitive impositions of the Versailles Treaty. Massive rearmament in breach of the treaty was accompanied by the demand for *lebensraum* ('living-space'), revision of borders, and the inclusion within the fatherland of the substantial German minorities outside the Third Reich (*Map 77*). The remilitarisation of the Rhineland (in further breach of the treaty) in March 1936 failed to evoke an effective response from Britain and France. In late 1936 Hitler and Mussolini allied in the so-called 'Rome-Berlin Axis'. Meanwhile Italian forces attacked the ancient and backward empire of Abyssinia (Ethiopia), providing a further demonstration of the ineffectualness of the League. Both Italy and Germany sent forces to aid the fascists in the Spanish Civil War, which was seen as an ideological and military testing-ground between 1936 and 1939. Russia sent some aid to the Spanish Republican government, but France (although ruled by a left-wing 'Popular Front' government) and Britain enunciated the doctrine of 'non-intervention', which effectively ensured a fascist victory.

The 'appeasement' policy of the democracies was the product of a profound horror of war on the part of a generation traumatised by the nightmare of 1914-18, compounded by the isolationism of the USA, the slowness to rearm of Britain, and the deep internal divisions in France. Moreover, the suggestion of an alliance with Bolshevik Russia was anathema to many conservatives. Hitler's annexation of Austria in 1938 (the *Anschluss*), and his demand for territorial concessions from Czechoslovakia brought matters to a head. At the Munich conference in September 1938, Britain and France avoided war by conceding Hitler's demands and permitting the emasculation of Czechoslovakia. Six months later the rump of Czechoslovakia was occupied by Germany, and Hitler turned his attention east towards Poland. Undeterred by a British guarantee to Poland, Hitler demanded the redress of various grievances concerning Danzig and the Polish corridor (Poland's link with the Baltic coast). In August 1939 he scored a diplomatic coup with the surprise conclusion of the Nazi-Soviet pact, under which Germany and Russia secretly agreed to a renewed partition of Poland. This was a *carte blanche* for the German attack on Poland on 1 September 1939, which induced the British empire and France to declare war on Germany.

Germany conquered western Poland in a fortnight, and the USSR then occupied the eastern portion and later took the opportunity to attack Finland and swallow the Baltic republics of Latvia, Lithuania, and Estonia (*Map 81*). After September 1939 a period known as the 'phoney war' ensued, in which little fighting occurred and there was even the whisper of a negotiated peace. But in May 1940 Germany attacked the Low Countries and France, and in a spectacular seven-week 'Blitzkrieg' won a smashing victory which made her the dominant power in Europe, and attracted Italy into the war as a junior ally eager to share the spoils.

Britain now stood alone under the inspiring leadership of Churchill, Prime Minister from May 1940. In the aerial 'Battle of Britain' the Royal Air Force prevented the Luftwaffe from gaining mastery of the skies, and thereby thwarted Hitler's cross-Channel invasion plans. Meanwhile the American President Roosevelt, although conscious of what was still a strongly isolationist mood in Congress and among public opinion, nudged the USA closer to war with the 'Lend-Lease' agreement, by which the USA agreed to 'lend' Britain fifty surplus destroyers in return for long-term 'leases' on bases in the Caribbean and western Atlantic (*Map 85*).

In April 1941 Germany moved into Yugoslavia and Greece in a campaign which, although it inflicted further painful humiliations on Hitler's enemies, delayed (and thereby gravely imperilled) his most ambitious, and ultimately fatal, gamble—the attack on the Soviet Union on 22 June 1941. This turned Stalin into the involuntary ally of Churchill and Roosevelt and inaugurated the critical phase of the war.

Even more than the First World War this was 'total war'—more extensive in its scope, more intensive in its impact, producing breathtakingly rapid innovations in military technique, scientific invention, and economic and social organisation. Unlike its predecessor the Second World War was pre-eminently a war of movement in which the characteristic forms of locomotion were not infantry or cavalry but motorised armour and warplanes. Warfare in East Asia and Africa still provided some scope for human ingenuity in 'guerrilla' campaigns

The Second World War

with only limited mechanisation, but in general the capability to invent, construct, deploy and operate machines and sophisticated instruments became the determining element in the war. Britain and the USA in particular gained the edge in scientific warfare, most notably with their 'Manhattan Project' for the manufacture of the atomic bomb (in which they were greatly aided by intellectual emigrants from Nazi Europe).

Remarkably, in spite of their authoritarian régimes, the Axis powers were less successful in gearing their economies to the requirements of total war. Germany sought to exploit the resources of occupied Europe to the full, but her ruthless 'New Order' in Europe did not succeed in creating a coherently integrated continental war economy. Even Germany attained her full productive capacity only in 1944. The Japanese 'Co-Prosperity Sphere' in East Asia (*Map 79*) embittered occupied populations and failed to produce vitally needed goods: by early 1943 Japan was losing ten times as much shipping sunk as was being replaced by new building. In contrast the Allies not only succeeded in concentrating their productive efforts more intensively and rationally, but also pooled their (potentially far greater) resources in what was, particularly in the case of Britain and the USA, very intimate co-ordination. Indeed, although the Russians stood somewhat apart, the co-operation of the Allies in every sphere – economic, military, and diplomatic – contrasted tellingly with the wary suspiciousness of one another with which the Axis powers fought their separate wars. Beyond the battlefield, the factory, and the laboratory, the arena of conflict extended into men's minds. This was an ideological struggle in which the wireless, the printed word, and the cinema were potent weapons.

If the war stimulated sophisticated technological and scientific advances, it also discredited the outlook, hitherto widespread, which equated the material civilisation of the white races with moral superiority. For the war was conducted with a ruthless ferocity and disregard of humane values which dwarfed the horrors of all previous conflicts. Civilian populations were drawn into the struggle as never before. German, Japanese, and Russian treatment of prisoners-of-war was often brutal. Terror bombing of cities, a tactic initiated by Germany but adopted also by the Allies, left hundreds of thousands of dead. The age-old distinction between combatants and civilians was blurred, especially in those areas of occupied Europe where anti-Nazi resistance movements sought to conduct guerrilla warfare, which in some areas developed into internecine conflict between resistance forces and 'collaborators' or between communists and anti-communists.

Inspired by Hitler's obsessive anti-semitism, the Nazis (often, particularly in eastern Europe, with the active support of local populations) gathered together the Jews of Europe in 'ghettos' or forced-labour concentration camps (*see Map 80*). Hundreds of thousands of Jews were murdered during the early years of the war by special killing squads ('Einsatzgruppen') or by other military and para-military units. Later special mass murder

centres were established in eastern Europe, such as the Auschwitz camp, to which millions of Jews and others were deported, killed in gas chambers, and cremated. Resistance, such as the revolt of the Jews in the Warsaw Ghetto in 1943, was hopeless. Nor did the Allies take effective action to admit significant numbers of refugees from the holocaust or seek to blunt its impact.

In spite of initial German and Japanese successes, the tide of the war had begun to turn by early 1943. In June 1942 American air and naval forces in the central Pacific won an important victory over the Japanese in the Battle of Midway Island, which for the first time threw the Japanese on to the defensive (*Map 79*). In November 1942 British forces defeated a German army at el Alamein in Egypt, thereby preventing German capture of the Suez Canal, vital to British imperial communications (*Map 81*). Still more significant was the dramatic Russian stand in defence of Stalingrad, where in February 1943 large German armies capitulated, decisively halting the German advance into the USSR.

Thenceforth the stubborn resistance of the Axis powers was slowly ground down. The first to collapse was Italy where in mid-1943 Mussolini was overthrown and replaced by a government which surrendered to the Allies. However, before the Allied forces in southern Italy could capitalise fully on this success, the Germans had occupied the northern half of the peninsula whence they were dislodged only after long and gruelling battles in 1944 and 1945. The crucial battles were fought elsewhere. During 1944 the Red Army steadily pressed the Germans back on the eastern front while demanding that the western allies open a 'second front' in north-west Europe. After some delays this was at last secured on 6 June 1944 ('D-Day'), when American and British troops landed in Normandy. By late 1944 nearly the whole of France had been liberated, although even now German resistance was such that in December 1944 a surprise German offensive in the Ardennes achieved temporary success. But this was soon reversed, and by early 1945 the Allies in the west were advancing into Germany on a broad front. In late April they met the Russians at the Elbe, and by 8 May were able to celebrate V-E (Victory in Europe) Day.

Japan now faced certain defeat, but she continued to defy her enemies even after Germany's collapse. Japanese surrender on 14 August 1945 came only after the USA had dropped atomic bombs on Hiroshima and Nagasaki causing huge and hideous casualties. The world war thus terminated, but the mushroom cloud of Hiroshima cast a shadow over the moral quality of the victory, and darkened the prospects of post-war international harmony, perhaps even of long-term human survival.

Further reading: B. Liddell Hart, *The Second World War* (Cassell, 1970; Pan, 1972); G. Wright, *The Ordeal of Total War* (Harper & Row, 1968; p.b.); W. L. S. Churchill, *The Second World War* (Cassell, 1945-54); A. Bullock, *Hitler: a Study in Tyranny* (Odhams, 1956; Penguin, 1969); H. Feis, *Churchill, Roosevelt, Stalin* (Oxford University Press, 1957).

80 Fascist Europe
The violent authoritarian movements which, assisted by economic recession and resentment of the Versailles settlement, seized power in much of inter-war Europe, shared an aggressive nationalism and brutal hostility to minorities. These reached a peak in Nazi Germany.

81 The Second World War in Europe
The second great war of the century was shaped this time by the rapid movement of both land and air forces, with correspondingly widespread devastation. The European powers exhausted one another and domination passed to the USA and Russia, whose intervention had decided the outcome of the war.

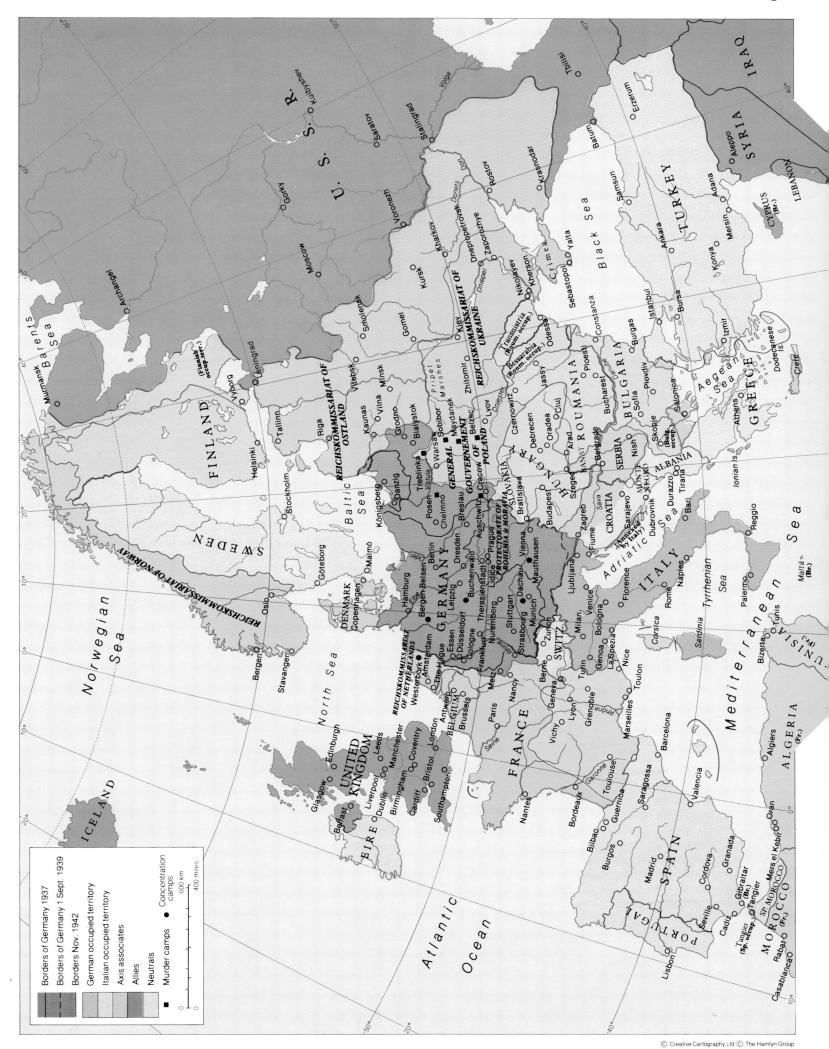

Atlantic Ocean

To North America

To Murmansk and Archangel

UNITED KINGDOM

EIRE

Glasgow
Aberdeen
Edinburgh
Belfast
Newcastle
Dublin
Manchester
Leeds
Liverpool
Hull
Sheffield
Birmingham
Norwich
Coventry
Swansea
Cardiff
London
Southampton
Plymouth
Exeter
Dover

North Sea

SWEDEN
Stockholm
Göteborg
Copenhagen
Peenemünde

Skagerrak
9-4-40
DENMARK
Kiel
9-4-40
Lübeck
Hamburg

Kattegat

Bremerhaven
Bremen
Hanover
Potsdam
Berlin
Posen
GERMANY
1-9-39
Leipzig
Dresden
Breslau

British landings in Norway April 1940

English Channel
6-6-44
Cherbourg
Dieppe
Le Havre
Dunkirk
Calais
Boulogne
Lille
Amiens
Rouen
Caen
Seine
NETHERLANDS
Amsterdam
Arnhem
Rotterdam
Antwerp
Brussels
BELGIUM
Essen
Düsseldorf
Cologne
Frankfurt
10-5-40
Schweinfurt
May 1945
Lidice
Prague
CZECHOSL

Late June 1944
Brest
Paris
11-6-40
Reims
Ardennes
Metz
10-5-40
Karlsruhe
Mannheim
Nuremburg
Stuttgart
Brno
Bratislava

Le Mans
Alençon
Angers
Nantes
Troyes
Orléans
Nancy
Dec-1944
Strasbourg
Mulhouse
Munich
Vienna
Sopron
6-4-41
Graz

FRANCE
Dijon
Berne
Innsbruck
Drava
Danube

Poitiers
Vichy
22-6-40
Lyon
SWITZ
ALPS
Bolzano
Ljubljana
Trieste
Zagreb

Bay of Biscay
Bordeaux
Grenoble
Rhône
The
Milan
Turin
11-6-40
Genoa
Po
Venice
Bologna
YUGOS
Sarajevo

Bilbao
Oporto
Douro
Toulouse
Marseille
Nice
La Spezia
December 1944
Ancona
Adriatic Sea
Vis
Dubrovnik

PORTUGAL
Madrid
SPAIN
Tagus
Guadiana
Pyrenees

Lisbon
Barcelona
Corsica
Ajaccio
late June 1944
 App
Rome
Monte Cassino
Anzio
Caserta
Naples
ITALY
Dec. 1943
Foggia
Bari
Brindisi
Taranto

15-8-44
Balearic Is. (Sp.)
Sardinia
Tyrrhenian Sea
Cagliari
22-1-44
9-9-43
Salerno

Mediterranean Sea

Seville
Guadalquivir
Malaga
Gibraltar (Br.)
Tangier

Palermo
Messina
Reggio
3-9-43
Sicily
Catania
Syracuse
9-9-43
Ionia

8-11-42
Rabat
SP. MOROCCO
Fez
Casablanca
MOROCCO (France)

8-11-42
Oran
Algiers
Constantine
Bizerta
Tunis
TUNISIA
10-7-43
Pantelleria
Malta (Br.)

ALGERIA (France)

Atlas Mts.
Sahara
November 1942
LIBYA
Tripoli

March 1941

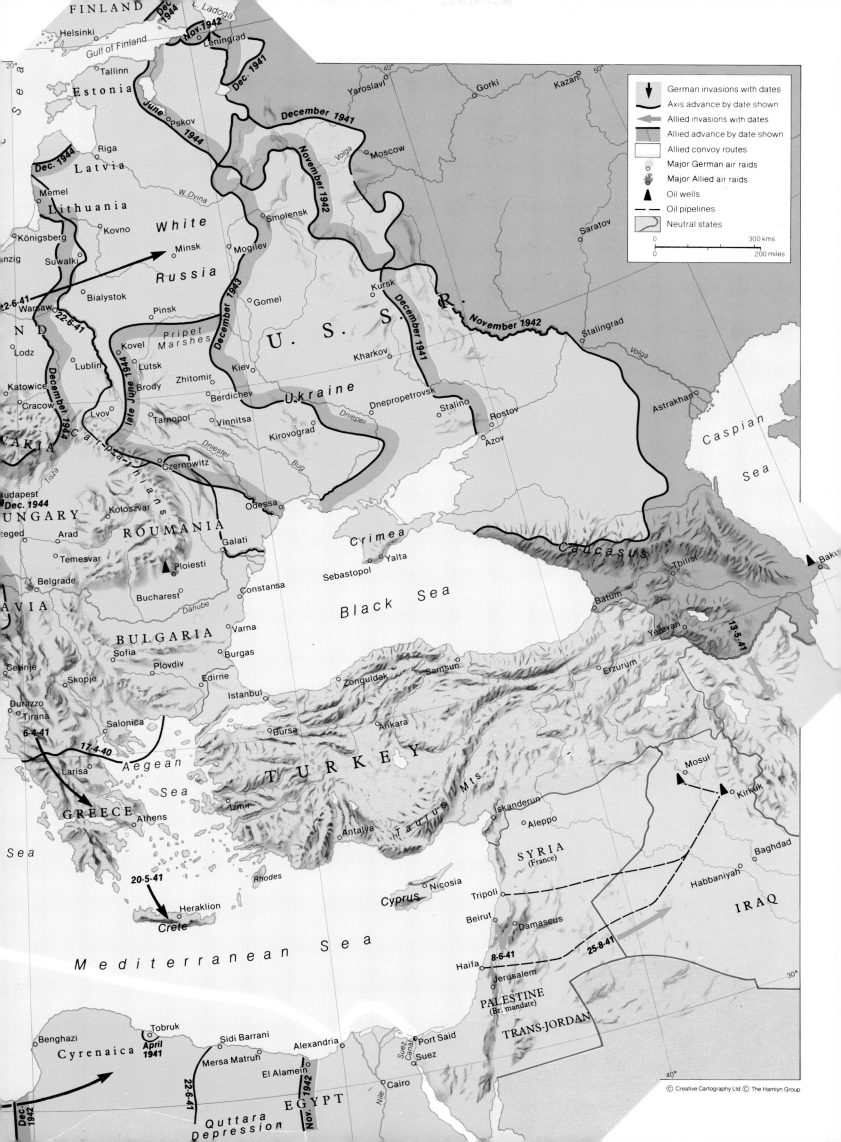

FINLAND

Helsinki
Gulf of Finland
Tallinn
Estonia
Riga
Latvia
Memel
Königsberg
Lithuania
Suwalki
Warsaw
Lodz
Lublin
Katowice
Cracow
VAKIA

Dec. 1944
Nov. 1942
L. Ladoga
Leningrad
Dec. 1941
Pskov
June 1944
December 1941
White
Russia
Minsk
Bialystok
Pinsk
Pripet Marshes
Kovel
Lutsk
Brody
Lvov
Tarnopol
Czernowitz

Yaroslavl
Gorki
Kazan
Moscow
Volga
Smolensk
Mogilev
December 1943
Gomel
Kursk
November 1942
Kiev
Zhitomir
Berdichev
Vinnitsa
Kirovograd
Dnieper
Dnepropetrovsk
Stalino
U. S. S. R.
December 1941
November 1942
Saratov
Stalingrad
Volga
Astrakhan
Kharkov
Rostov
Azov
Caspian Sea

Budapest
Dec. 1944
HUNGARY
Szeged
Arad
Temesvar
Belgrade
AVIA
Cetinje
Durazzo
Tirana
6-4-41
17-4-40
Larisa
GREECE
Athens

ROUMANIA
Galati
Bucharest
Danube
BULGARIA
Sofia
Plovdiv
Varna
Burgas
Edirne
Skopje
Aegean Sea
Izmir
Rhodes
20-5-41
Heraklion
Crete

Czernowitz
Dniester
Bug
Odessa
Crimea
Sebastopol
Yalta
Constansa
Black Sea
Caucasus
Batum
Tbilisi
Yerevan
Erzurum
13-5-41
Baku

Zonguldak
Samsun
Istanbul
Bursa
Ankara
TURKEY
Taurus Mts
Antalya
Aleppo
Iskanderun
Mediterranean Sea
Nicosia
Cyprus
Tripoli
Beirut
Damascus
Haifa
8-6-41
Jerusalem
25-8-41
SYRIA (France)
Mosul
Kirkuk
Baghdad
Habbaniyah
IRAQ

PALESTINE (Br. mandate)
TRANS-JORDAN

Benghazi
Cyrenaica
Tobruk
April 1941
Sidi Barrani
Alexandria
Mersa Matruh
El Alamein
22-6-41
Nov. 1942
Dec. 1942
EGYPT
Quttara Depression
Suez Canal
Port Said
Suez
Nile
Cairo

22-6-41
December 1944
Carpathians
late June 1944

Legend

- German invasions with dates
- Axis advance by date shown
- Allied invasions with dates
- Allied advance by date shown
- Allied convoy routes
- Major German air raids
- Major Allied air raids
- Oil wells
- Oil pipelines
- Neutral states

0 — 300 kms
0 — 200 miles

© Creative Cartography Ltd © The Hamlyn Group

Barents Sea

Arctic Circle

Norwegian Sea

ICELAND
Reykjavik

Faeroe Is.

Atlantic Ocean

N O R W A Y
Trondheim

Bergen

Oslo

Stavanger

S W E D E N

Göteborg

Stockholm

Uppsala

Gulf of Bothnia

FINLAND

Helsinki

Gulf of Finland

from Finland 1945

Murmansk

White Sea

Archangel

L. Onega

L. Ladoga

Vyborg (Viipuri)

Leningrad

1945

1945

UNITED KINGDOM
Glasgow
Aberdeen
Edinburgh
Newcastle
Belfast
IRELAND
Dublin
Liverpool
Leeds
Manchester
Sheffield
Birmingham
Cardiff
London
Bristol

1973

1973

North Sea

Århus

Copenhagen
Malmö

DENMARK
1973
Kiel
Rostock

Hamburg
Lübeck
Bremen
NETHERLANDS
Amsterdam
The Hague
Rotterdam
Hanover
EAST

WEST
GERMANY

Szcecin (Stettin)

from Germany 1945-

Berlin
Potsdam

Gdynia
Gdansk (Danzig)
93%

(East Prussia) 94%
from Germany 1945
to Poland 1945

Kaliningrad (Königsberg)

Estonia to U.S.S.R. 1940-45
Tallinn

Latvia to U.S.S.R. 1940-45
Riga

Lithuania to U.S.S.R. 1940-45
Kaunas

Vilnius

Minsk

from Germany 1945

Moscow

Smolensk

U. S. S. R.

Baltic Sea

1958

BELGIUM
Antwerp
Essen
Lille
Brussels
1958
Rouen

Dortmund
Cologne
Düsseldorf
Bonn

Leipzig
Dresden
Frankfurt

Prague

GERMANY
Mannheim
LUX. 1958
Fr. Prot. 1945-57

Wrocław (Breslau)
57%

POLAND
99%

Poznan

Warsaw

Lodz

Lublin

Kraków

from Poland 1945

Białystok
1947

from Poland 1945

Kiev

Kharkov

FRANCE
Paris
Nancy
Strasbourg

1958

Karlsruhe
Stuttgart
Nuremberg
Munich

Linz

CZECHOSLOVAKIA
1948
Brno
Bratislava

from Czech 1945

Lvov (Lemberg)

Chernovtsy (Czernowitz)

from Rumania 1940-44

Jasy
Kishinev

Sea of Azov

Nantes

Bay of Biscay

Bordeaux

San Sebastian

Bilbao

SPAIN

Madrid

1958

Berne
SWITZ.
Geneva
Lyon

Lausanne

Innsbruck

AUSTRIA

Zurich

Milan

Venice
Turin

Ljubljana

Zagreb

Vienna
Budapest

HUNGARY

from Hungary 1945

from Hungary 1945

Debrecen

Cluj (Kolozsvár)

Timisoara (Temesvár)

RUMANIA

1947

Bucharest

Sebastopol

Crimea

Yalta

Odessa

Constantsa

Black Sea

1947

Grenoble

Toulouse

Marseille

Nice

MONACO

Genoa
Bologna

Florence

from Italy 1945-
Trieste

Rijeka (Fiume)

Split

Belgrade

Sarajevo

YUGOSLAVIA

1945

ANDORRA
Saragossa

Barcelona

Corsica

Rome

ITALY
1958

Naples

Adriatic Sea

Tirana

ALBANIA
1945

Sofia

BULGARIA
1945

Istanbul

Ankara

TURKEY

PORTUGAL
Lisbon
Séville
Malaga

Valencia

Gibraltar (Br)

Balearic Is.

Sardinia

Tyrrhenian Sea

Ionian Sea

GREECE
1981

Thessaloniki

Aegean Sea

Izmir (Smyrna)

Palermo

Reggio
Sicily

Athens

Crete

Turkish occ. 1974
Nicosia
CYPRUS

MALTA

Mediterranean Sea

Pre-war boundaries

National boundaries 1978

1947 Date of communist takeover

1958 Date of accession to EEC

98% Percentage of Germans in pre-war population

Areas occupied 1945-55:

American zone

British zone

French zone

Russian zone

Berlin: Four-power control since 1945
Vienna: Four-power occupation, 1945-55
Trieste: British and American occupation, 1945-54

© Creative Cartography Ltd © The Hamlyn Group

The emergence of the modern world IV

The post-war world

EVEN BEFORE the end of the Second World War the contours of the new pattern of international relations were beginning to emerge. Of the five 'great powers' in the victorious wartime coalition, three had been disastrously weakened and two immeasurably strengthened by the years of struggle. The claim of France to 'great power' status, insistently advanced by the majestic figure of General De Gaulle, was barely conceded by her allies, and accorded ill with France's straitened condition after the trauma of Nazi occupation. China's membership of the 'great power' club was thrown into question as the war to eject the Japanese invader melted into a civil war in which the anti-Communist *Kuomintang* government's grip on power became ever more tenuous (*see Map 86*). Britain was economically exhausted by the war, and its post-war Labour government, preoccupied with social reform at home, was compelled to recognise that Britain now cut a much-reduced figure on the diplomatic stage. By contrast the USA and the USSR had emerged by 1945 as the unquestioned 'super-powers' of the post-war era. Of the two the USA was by far the more powerful. Her prodigious wartime economic growth rendered her by 1945 the producer of over half the world's manufactured goods. Moreover she possessed nuclear weapons, whereas the USSR detonated its first atomic bomb only in 1949.

Mutual suspicions as to post-war ambitions had been evident at the 'big three' wartime conferences of the USA, USSR, and Britain which were held at Tehran in 1943, Yalta in February 1945, and Potsdam in July 1945. The severe strains between the USSR and the western allies had surfaced in mid-1944, particularly over the Russian refusal to allow adequate aid to be given to the anti-Nazi rising of the (anti-communist) Polish underground movement in Warsaw. At the end of the war communist and western forces confronted one another in a great arc stretching from central Europe through the middle east to east Asia (*Map 84*). The United Nations, successor to the now-defunct League of Nations, was established at the San Francisco Conference in mid-1945, with the primary aim of preserving world peace. The UN succeeded, unlike the League, in securing the adhesion of nearly all independent states, but beyond this its political achievements were slight. It soon became apparent that world politics would henceforth be dominated by the east-west rivalry for power, influence, and prestige, a contest dubbed after 1947 the 'cold war'.

The 'iron curtain' which descended across Europe generally followed the lines secured by Russian and western forces at the end of the war (*Map 81*). Determined to establish firm buffers against any possible threat to the USSR, Stalin annexed large territories from Finland, East Prussia, Poland, Czechoslovakia, and Roumania. In Poland, Roumania, Bulgaria, and Hungary non-communist elements were squeezed out of all effective positions of power and communist-dominated 'puppet' régimes took office under Russian supervision. In Czechoslovakia in February 1948 democratic politicians were eliminated and a communist-directed 'coalition' government was installed in power. Only in Yugoslavia, where the resistance forces headed by Josip Broz (Tito) assumed power, was a communist government successful in maintaining independence from Moscow. In Greece a bitter civil war broke out late in 1944 between communist and anti-communist forces. British troops supported the anti-communists, while Stalin, faithful to commitments he had made to Churchill in October 1944,

refrained from intervention. After renewed fighting in 1947-9 the pro-western groups achieved victory.

In most of western Europe, liberated by the western allies, democratic governments in the immediate aftermath of the war found themselves heavily dependent on American military protection and economic aid. The Marshall Plan, inaugurated by the US Secretary of State, George Marshall, in June 1947, channelled $17,000 million-worth of American economic assistance to the war-ravaged economies of western Europe and stimulated their rapid recovery. Under Russian influence, however, the east European states rejected American aid. In 1949 most west European states joined the USA in the North Atlantic Treaty Organisation (NATO), an alliance formed with the aim of 'containing' the Soviet Union. The Warsaw Pact of 1955 formalised the military alliance of the USSR with its east European satellites, whose economies were subordinated to Russian interests.

The focus of the cold war in Europe was on Berlin and the fate of Germany. In its old form the German problem was solved in the aftermath of the war. Over thirteen million Germans were expelled from eastern Europe (*see Map 83*), the majority moving to western Germany in what was the greatest European population movement of the century. Poland shifted west, being compensated for her eastern losses to the USSR by western gains at the expense of Germany (*see Map 82*). Germany, shorn of these lands and of East Prussia, was divided into four occupation zones. In 1949 the American, British, and French zones united to form the Federal German Republic which was granted full independence in 1955. In the Russian-occupied eastern zone the communist German Democratic Republic (GDR) was established. A four-power occupation administration ruled Berlin, with the three western zones now an island within East Germany, an unstable arrangement which gave rise to three major international crises. In 1948-9 a western airlift defeated a Russian land blockade of West Berlin. Ten years later a further crisis was precipitated by a Russian ultimatum (rejected by the western powers) that western forces leave West Berlin. The third Berlin crisis came in August 1961 when the East German government, alarmed at the huge exodus of its citizens to the west, erected a wall separating East from West Berlin. Meanwhile the partition of Germany congealed into permanence, with the GDR absorbed into the Soviet orbit, while the Federal Republic, led by Chancellor Konrad Adenauer, pursued a resolutely pro-western course. After severe economic tribulations in the late 1940s both German states made dramatic recoveries from the 1950s onwards to emerge once again among the world's foremost industrial nations.

Like its former ally, Japan was occupied at the end of the war and compelled to absorb millions of its nationals from its former imperial possessions. The American occupation régime stripped Japan of her colonies and of her armed strength. Under American tutelage Japan was transformed into a liberal parliamentary state without its previous expansionist ambitions. After regaining independence in 1952 Japanese foreign policy remained firmly pro-American, and she (like Germany) experienced an 'economic miracle' with an average annual growth of ten per cent in gross national product between 1953 and 1965. By the late 1960s Japan had overtaken West Germany to become (after the USA and the USSR) the world's third largest economy (*Map 88*).

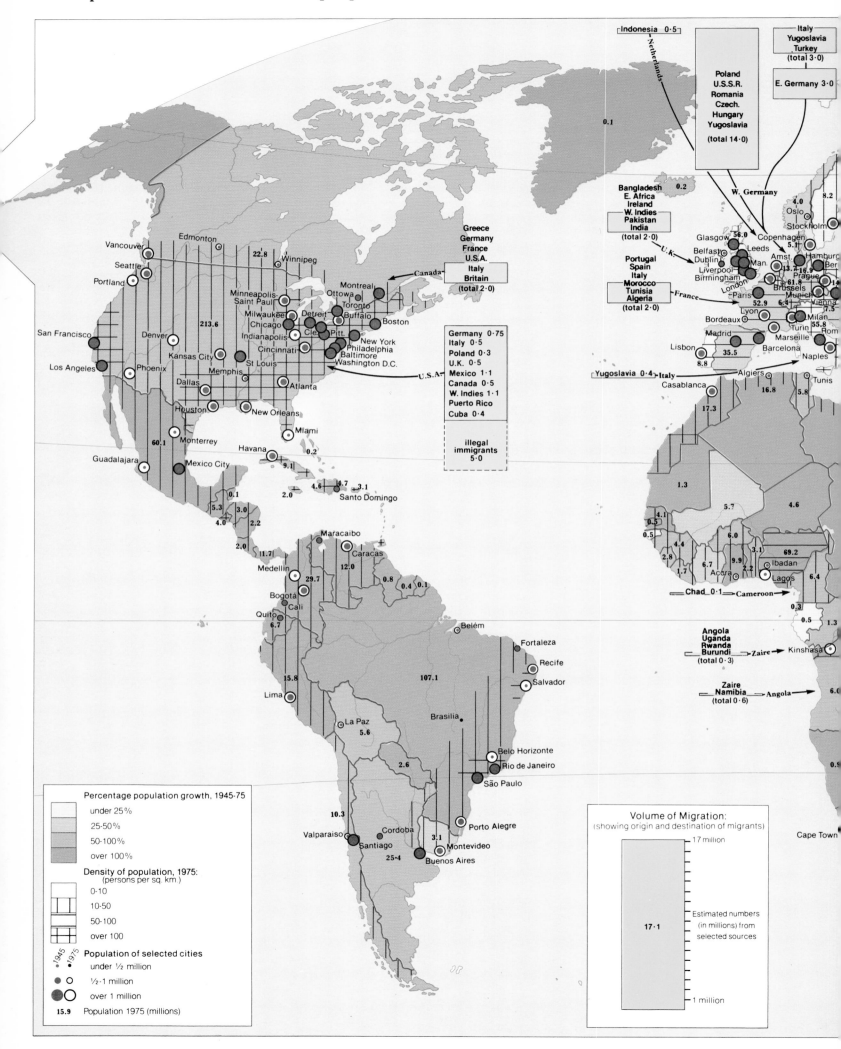

Indonesia 0·5

Netherlands

Italy
Yugoslavia
Turkey
(total 3·0)

E. Germany 3·0

Poland
U.S.S.R.
Romania
Czech.
Hungary
Yugoslavia
(total 14·0)

0.1

0.2

W. Germany

Bangladesh
E. Africa
Ireland
W. Indies
Pakistan
India
(total 2·0)

Portugal
Spain
Morocco
Tunisia
Algeria
(total 2·0)

4.0   8.2

Oslo

Stockholm

5.1

Glasgow   56.0   Copenhagen
U.K.
Belfast   Leeds   Hamburg
Dublin   Man.   13.7 16.9 Ber
Liverpool   Amst.   Prague
Birmingham   61.8
London Paris Brussels Munich
France   52.9   6.4   Vienna
Lyon   7.5
Bordeaux   Milan 55.8
Madrid   Turin   Rom
35.5   Marseille
Lisbon   Barcelona
8.8   Naples

Yugoslavia 0·4 → Italy → Italy

Casablanca   Algiers   Tunis

16.8   5.8

17.3

1.3

5.7   4.6

4.1
0.5
0.5   2.8   4.4   6.0   3.1   69.2
1.7   6.7   9.9   2.2   Ibadan
Acora   Lagos   6.4

Chad 0·1 → Cameroon

0.3
0.5   1.3

Angola
Uganda
Rwanda
Burundi
(total 0·3) → Zaire → Kinshasa

Zaire
Namibia → Angola → 6.0
(total 0·6)

0.9

Cape Town

Greece
Germany
France
U.S.A.
Italy
Britain
(total 2·0)

← Canada

Germany 0·75
Italy 0·5
Poland 0·3
U.K. 0·5
Mexico 1·1
Canada 0·5
W. Indies 1·1
Puerto Rico
Cuba 0·4

illegal
immigrants
5·0

U.S.A →

Edmonton
Vancouver
Seattle   22.8   Winnipeg
Portland   Montreal
Minneapolis-   Ottawa
Saint Paul   Toronto   Boston
213.6   Milwaukee Detroit Buffalo
Chicago   Cle. Pitt.
San Francisco   Denver   Indianapolis   New York
Kansas City   Cincinnati   Philadelphia
St Louis   Baltimore
Los Angeles   Washington D.C.
Phoenix   Memphis
Dallas   Atlanta
Houston
60.1   New Orleans
Monterrey
Guadalajara   Havana   Miami
Mexico City   0.2
0.1   9.1
5.3   3.0   2.0   4.6 4.7 3.1
4.0   2.2   Santo Domingo
2.0
[1.7]   Maracaibo
Medellin   12.0   Caracas
29.7   0.8 0.4 0.1
Bogotá
Cali
Quito
6.7
15.8   Belém
Lima   Fortaleza
107.1   Recife
La Paz
5.6   Salvador
Brasilia
2.6   Belo Horizonte
Rio de Janeiro
São Paulo
10.3   Porto Alegre
Valparaiso   Cordoba
Santiago   3.1   Montevideo
25·4   Buenos Aires

Percentage population growth, 1945-75

under 25%

25-50%

50-100%

over 100%

Density of population, 1975:
(persons per sq. km.)

0-10

10-50

50-100

over 100

Population of selected cities

1945 1975
under ½ million

½-1 million

over 1 million

15.9 Population 1975 (millions)

Volume of Migration:
(showing origin and destination of migrants)

17 million

17·1   Estimated numbers
(in millions) from
selected sources

1 million

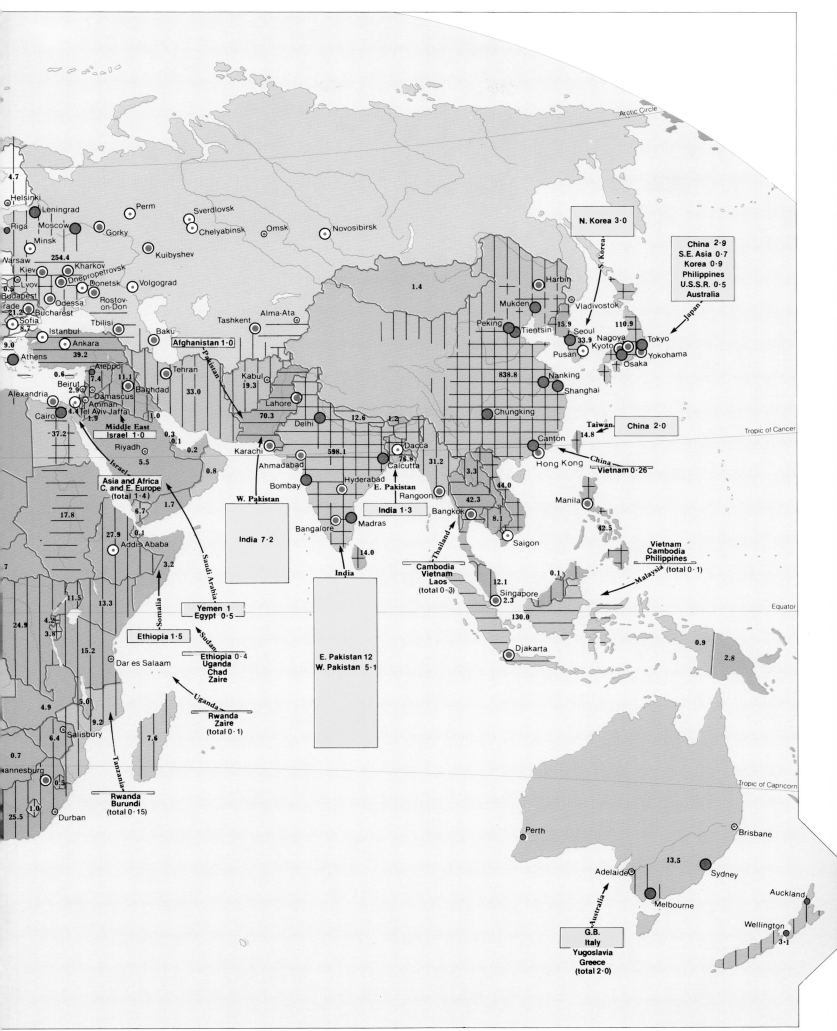

Arctic Circle

Helsinki 4.7

Leningrad
Perm
Riga
Moscow
Minsk
254.4
Warsaw
Kiev
Lvov
0.5
Dnepropetrovsk
Budapest
Donetsk
Odessa
21.2
Bucharest
Rostov-on-Don
Sofia
8.7
Istanbul
Tbilisi
9.0
Ankara
39.2
Athens

Sverdlovsk
Chelyabinsk
Gorky
Omsk
Novosibirsk
Kuibyshev
Volgograd

Baku
1.4

Afghanistan 1·0

Aleppo
0.6
7.4
Beirut
11.1
2.9
Damascus
Baghdad
Amman
4.4 Tel Aviv-Jaffa
1.9
1.0
Middle East
Israel 1·0
0.3
0.1
0.2

Alexandria
Cairo
–37.2
Riyadh
5.5

Asia and Africa
C. and E. Europe
(total 1·4)
1.7
6.7
0.8
17.8
27.9
0.1
Addis Ababa

Tehran
33.0

Tashkent
Alma-Ata

Kabul
19.3
Lahore
70.3

Karachi
Ahmadabad
Bombay

Delhi
12.6
598.1

1.2
76.8
Dacca
Calcutta

W. Pakistan

India 7·2

Hyderabad
Bangalore
Madras
14.0

India

Harbin
Mukden
Vladivostok
15.9
Peking
Tientsin
Seoul
33.9
838.8
Pusan
Kyoto
Nanking
Shanghai
Chungking
Canton
Hong Kong

N. Korea 3·0

China 2·9
S.E. Asia 0·7
Korea 0·9
Philippines
U.S.S.R. 0·5
Australia

Japan
110.9
Nagoya
Tokyo
Osaka
Yokohama

Tropic of Cancer

Taiwan
14.8
China 2·0

China
Vietnam 0·26

31.2
Rangoon
E. Pakistan
India 1·3
3.3
44.0
Bangkok
42.3
8.1
Saigon

Manila
42.5

Cambodia
Vietnam
Laos
(total 0·3)

Vietnam
Cambodia
Philippines
Malaysia (total 0·1)

3.2
Saudi Arabia
Israel
Sudan
Yemen 1
Egypt 0·5
Ethiopia 1·5
11.5
13.3
15.2
4.2
4.9
3.8
24.9
Somalia
Dar es Salaam

Ethiopia 0·4
Uganda
Chad
Zaire

Uganda
Rwanda
Zaire
(total 0·1)

E. Pakistan 12
W. Pakistan 5·1

12.1
Singapore
2.3
130.0
0.1

Djakarta

Equator

0.9
2.8

7
5.0
11.5
9.2
6.4
7.6
0.7
Salisbury
0.5
Johannesburg
1.0
25.5
Durban

Tanzania
Rwanda
Burundi
(total 0·15)

Tropic of Capricorn

Perth
Brisbane

13.5
Sydney

Adelaide
Australia
Melbourne

Auckland

Wellington
3·1

G.B.
Italy
Yugoslavia
Greece
(total 2·0)

© Creative Cartography Ltd © The Hamlyn Group

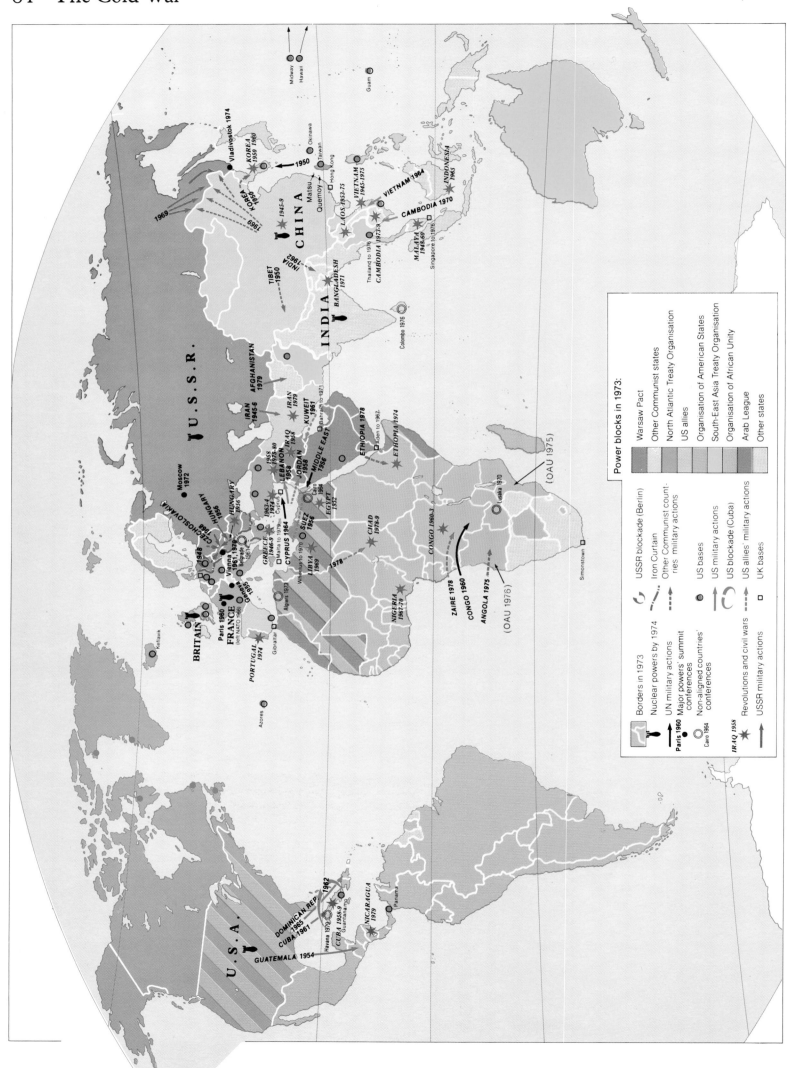

Midway
Hawaii
Guam

Vladivostok 1974
KOREA 1950 1960
KOREA 1950
1969
1969
1950
Okinawa
Taiwan
Quemoy
Hong Kong
Matsu
1945-9
CHINA
TIBET 1950
INDIA 1962
Moscow 1972
BANGLADESH 1971
LAOS 1953-75
VIETNAM 1945-1975
VIETNAM 1964
CAMBODIA 1970
INDONESIA 1965
Thailand to 1976
CAMBODIA 1973-9
MALAYA 1948-60
Singapore to 1976
Colombo 1976

U.S.S.R.
AFGHANISTAN 1979
IRAN 1945-6
IRAN 1979
KUWEIT 1961
Bahrain to 1971
ETHIOPIA 1978
Aden to 1967
ETHIOPIA 1974

CZECHOSLOVAKIA 1968
HUNGARY 1956
HUNGARY 1956
Vienna 1961, 1979
Belgrade 1961
Geneva 1955
1948
1958 1975-80
IRAQ 1958
LEBANON 1958
JORDAN 1958
MIDDLE EAST 1956
Cairo 1952
EGYPT 1956
SUEZ 1956
CONGO 1960-3
Lusaka 1970
(OAU 1975)
1963-4 1974
GREECE 1946-9
CYPRUS 1964
Malta to 1979
Cyprus
LIBYA 1969
Wheelus to 1967
CHAD 1978-9
CONGO 1960
ZAIRE 1978
ANGOLA 1975
(OAU 1976)
Algiers 1973
NIGERIA 1967-70
Keflavik
BRITAIN
Paris 1960
FRANCE (left NATO 1966)
PORTUGAL 1974
Gibraltar
Simonstown

Azores

U.S.A.
DOMINICAN REP. 1965
CUBA 1961
CUBA 1958-9
Havana 1979
Guantanamo
NICARAGUA 1979
GUATEMALA 1954
Panama
1962

Power blocks in 1973:
- Warsaw Pact
- Other Communist states
- North Atlantic Treaty Organisation
- US allies
- Organisation of American States
- South-East Asia Treaty Organisation
- Organisation of African Unity
- Arab League
- Other states

- ↻ USSR blockade (Berlin)
- / Iron Curtain
- ↑ Other Communist countries' military actions
- Borders in 1973
- ● US bases
- US military actions
- Nuclear powers by 1974
- UN military actions
- **Paris 1960** Major powers' summit conferences
- US blockade (Cuba)
- Cairo 1964 Non-aligned countries' conferences
- US allies' military actions
- □ UK bases
- *IRAQ 1958* Revolutions and civil wars
- ↑ USSR military actions

84 The Cold War
The mutual distrust of the USA and USSR divided much of the post-war world into opposing camps in a series of occupations and military alliances, and produced a succession of confrontations when war seemed imminent. There was some relaxation after the Cuba crisis of 1963, when the 'super-powers' began to seek a degree of diplomatic and economic co-operation with each other.

Although the Russo-American rivalry in east Asia never produced direct fighting between the super-powers, the cold war in this area was punctuated by a series of bitter localised wars. The Chinese civil war ended in 1949 in total victory for the communist forces headed by Mao Tse Tung (*Map 86*). The rump of the anti-communist armies withdrew to the island of Formosa (Taiwan) where they remained under American protection. In 1950 the invasion of pro-western South Korea by communist North Korea provoked American armed intervention. The American forces were joined by small contingents from their allies, while Chinese troops came to the aid of the North Koreans. The war swung back and forth until it ground to a halt along the original partition line of the 38th parallel in 1953. The 'loss of China', as it was seen in the USA, helped to engender a profound anti-communist reaction among Americans, culminating in the hysteria of 'McCarthyism' (so-called after the most prominent anti-communist demagogue, Senator Joseph McCarthy) in the early 1950s. However, in spite of reverses, the USA remained determined to maintain its influence in east Asia, and in 1954 formed the South-East Asia Treaty Organization (SEATO) with Britain, France, and several Asian states (*Map 84*).

The cold war reached its climax in the late 1950s and early 1960s as both super-powers developed hydrogen bombs and inter-continental missile delivery systems. The poisoning of the atmosphere by above-ground nuclear tests, the building-up of vast arsenals of hydrogen bombs capable of destroying nearly all human beings, and the danger of nuclear 'proliferation' to smaller powers cast over the world a shadow of prospective self-immolation. For one week in late October 1962 the world seemed to shudder on the brink of nuclear catastrophe as a result of a Russo-American conflict over Cuba. The USSR had sought to install offensive missiles armed with nuclear warheads on Cuba, where a revolutionary movement headed by Fidel Castro had in 1959 ousted a pro-American dictatorship. The American President, John F. Kennedy, blockaded the island and demanded the removal of the missiles. The crisis ended when the Russian leader, Nikita Khrushchev, yielded to the American demands (*see Map 85*).

With the resolution of the Cuban crisis the cold war gradually eased, giving way to a period of 'detente', while new powers challenged and steadily eroded the predominance of the super-powers in the international system, heralding the end of the 'bi-polar' era.

In western Europe renewed economic strength and moves towards economic integration provided a basis for foreign policies more independent of the USA. In 1951 France, Germany, Italy and the Benelux countries formed the European Coal and Steel Community, and by the Treaty of Rome in 1957 they agreed to the creation of a European Economic Community (EEC) involving an unprecedented measure of economic integration between major sovereign states (*Map 82*). The EEC enjoyed spectacular growth in production and trade in the 1960s. Britain joined the Community, after two unsuccessful attempts, in 1972, at the same time as Ireland and Denmark, and by the end of the decade preparations were in hand for Greece, Portugal and Spain, having rid themselves of dictatorships, to become members. The EEC and Japan developed by the late 1960s into powerful competitors with the USA in the capitalist world.

In the communist world too the overwhelming dominance of the super-power diminished. The death of Stalin in 1953 had excited hopes of democratisation in eastern Europe. However, although a short-lived liberalising 'thaw' took place in Russia, Stalin's successors sought to maintain a firm grip on power over other communist states. In November 1956 Russian troops crushed a brief attempt by Hungary to withdraw from the Warsaw Pact. In August 1968 the USSR again used armed strength to destroy the democratic reforms which had been introduced by the Czechoslovak communists headed by Alexander Dubček. Nevertheless there was an easing of the atmosphere in eastern Europe as the grim Stalin years gave way to a period of relative economic prosperity. Yugoslavia maintained its independence of Moscow, and during the 1960s Roumania too assertively emphasised its national independence. Soviet power was further challenged in the ideological domain by the increased tendency of west European communist parties (most notably the Italian and French) to defy directives from Moscow.

The most striking challenge to the USSR came, however, from China which from 1960 onwards engaged in a virulent ideological conflict with the USSR, whose leaders were denounced by Mao Tse Tung as 'revisionists'. Ideological warfare intensified between 1966 and 1969 during the period of internal upheaval in China known as the 'cultural revolution'. That the conflict was a serious threat to world peace became clear with the development of armed skirmishes along the disputed Russo-Chinese border and with the emergence of China as a nuclear power in the late 1960s.

As the Sino-Soviet conflict deepened the USSR and later China moved into a period of cautious 'détente' with the western powers. In 1963 the USA, USSR, and UK (but not France or China) signed a partial nuclear test ban treaty. The persistent irritant of the German question moved towards a solution after 1969, a process facilitated by the conciliatory 'Ostpolitik' of the socialist West German Chancellor, Willy Brandt. In 1972 and 1979 the two super-powers signed agreements on the limitation of strategic weapons. From the early 1970s China too moderated her hostility to the western powers, re-opening relations with the USA and seeking closer links with western Europe. The Sino-Soviet conflict was perhaps the most important single factor disturbing the precarious international equilibrium of the post-war period. While it helped to produce 'détente' it also helped to ensure that the end of the 'cold war' did not effect a major relaxation of international tension.

A Fontaine, *A History of the Cold War* (Secker and Warburg, 1968-70); W. Laqueur, *Europe Since Hitler* (Weidenfeld and Nicolson, 1970); A. Nove, *Stalinism and After* (Allen & Unwin, 1975); C. P. Fitzgerald, *The Birth of Communist China* (Penguin, 1964); D. S. Zagorin, *The Sino-Soviet Conflict* (Princeton 1962; Octagon, 1979); Sir J. Wheeler-Bennett and A. Nicholls, *The Semblance of Peace* (Macmillan, 1972).

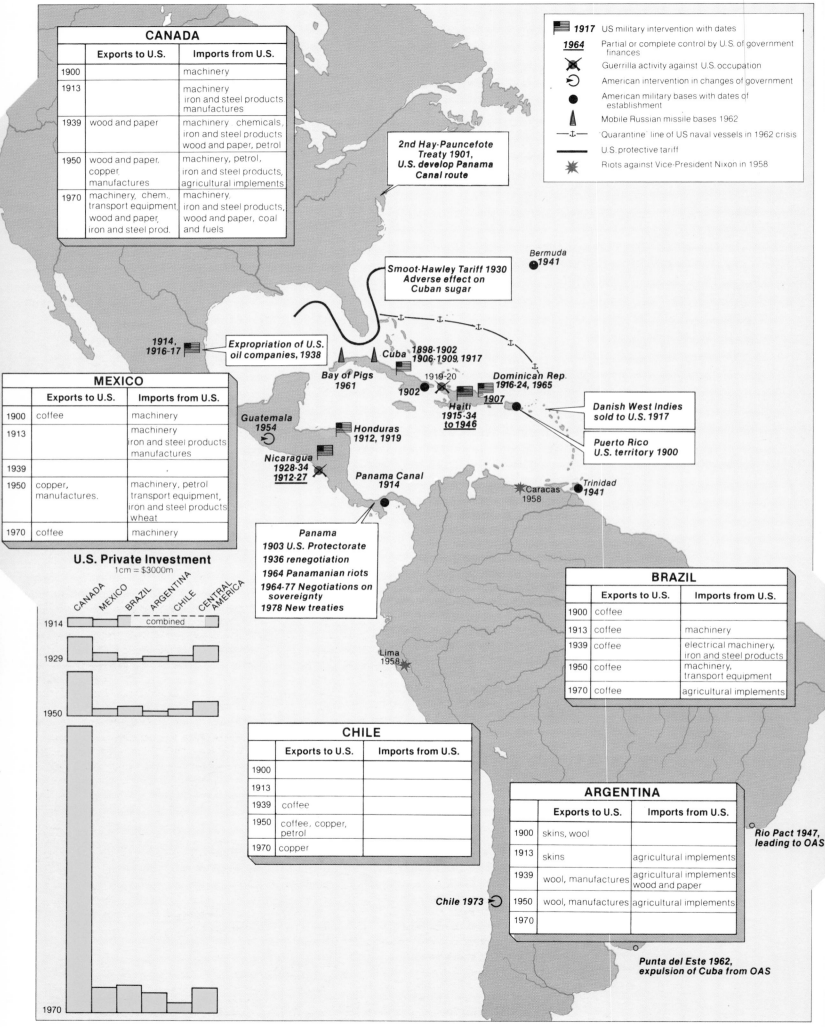

CANADA

	Exports to U.S.	Imports from U.S.
1900		machinery
1913		machinery iron and steel products manufactures
1939	wood and paper	machinery chemicals, iron and steel products wood and paper, petrol
1950	wood and paper, copper, manufactures	machinery, petrol, iron and steel products, agricultural implements
1970	machinery, chem., transport equipment, wood and paper, iron and steel prod.	machinery, iron and steel products, wood and paper, coal and fuels

US military intervention with dates *1917*

1964 Partial or complete control by U.S. of government finances

Guerrilla activity against U.S. occupation

American intervention in changes of government

American military bases with dates of establishment

Mobile Russian missile bases 1962

'Quarantine' line of US naval vessels in 1962 crisis

U.S. protective tariff

Riots against Vice-President Nixon in 1958

2nd Hay-Pauncefote Treaty 1901, U.S. develop Panama Canal route

Bermuda ●1941

Smoot-Hawley Tariff 1930 Adverse effect on Cuban sugar

1914, 1916-17

Expropriation of U.S. oil companies, 1938

Cuba **1898-1902 1906-1909, 1917**

Bay of Pigs 1961

1919-20

1902

Dominican Rep. **1916-24, 1965**

Haiti **1915-34 to 1946**

1907

Danish West Indies sold to U.S. 1917

Puerto Rico U.S. territory 1900

Guatemala 1954

Honduras 1912, 1919

Nicaragua 1928-34 1912-27

Panama Canal 1914

Caracas 1958

Trinidad 1941

MEXICO

	Exports to U.S.	Imports from U.S.
1900	coffee	machinery
1913		machinery iron and steel products manufactures
1939		
1950	copper, manufactures.	machinery, petrol transport equipment, iron and steel products wheat
1970	coffee	machinery

U.S. Private Investment
1cm = $3000m

CANADA MEXICO BRAZIL ARGENTINA CHILE CENTRAL AMERICA

1914 combined

1929

1950

1970

Panama
1903 U.S. Protectorate
1936 renegotiation
1964 Panamanian riots
1964-77 Negotiations on sovereignty
1978 New treaties

Lima 1958

BRAZIL

	Exports to U.S.	Imports from U.S.
1900	coffee	
1913	coffee	machinery
1939	coffee	electrical machinery, iron and steel products
1950	coffee	machinery, transport equipment
1970	coffee	agricultural implements

CHILE

	Exports to U.S.	Imports from U.S.
1900		
1913		
1939	coffee	
1950	coffee, copper, petrol	
1970	copper	

ARGENTINA

	Exports to U.S.	Imports from U.S.
1900	skins, wool	
1913	skins	agricultural implements
1939	wool, manufactures	agricultural implements wood and paper
1950	wool, manufactures	agricultural implements
1970		

Rio Pact 1947, leading to OAS

Chile 1973

Punta del Este 1962, expulsion of Cuba from OAS

AT THE CLOSE of the Second World War China was a victorious ally of the United States, and Japan a defeated enemy. But within four years China had fallen to a Communist revolution (*see Map 86*) and Japan had become an essential partner in America's anti-Communist strategy. Japan's former colony Korea had been divided between American and Soviet zones, while Formosa and Okinawa became bases for United States forces.

Initially America's occupation of Japan sought to weaken and pacify a potential enemy but desire for trade and fear of Communist subversion soon produced policies which aimed at economic recovery. In contrast the inauguration of the People's Republic of China in October 1949 created a government which criticised American imperialism, occupied Tibet, and looked to the Soviet Union for political and military support. In June 1950 pro-Soviet North Korean forces invaded the pro-American South, and United States and Chinese forces soon intervened. Tension between Washington and Peking was heightened and their embittered relations further increased Japan's military importance. America permitted the beginnings of Japanese re-armament and in 1951 many non-Communist powers signed a peace treaty with Japan, while the United States signed a security treaty which provided impressive military protection. In April 1952 Japan's political independence was restored.

Japan's economic recovery continued throughout the 1950s and by 1956 her standard of living surpassed that of the pre-war years. Some Japanese resented their country's dependence on the United States and others feared that they might be drawn into a war between the great powers, but government and industry believed that only the United States could provide the markets and protection which were necessary for continued prosperity. In contrast the Soviet Union refused to restore territories which she had seized from Japan in 1945.

For China problems of reconstruction, modernisation and agricultural improvement were immense but the Communist government soon succeeded in achieving a greater degree of order and stability than there had been for more than a century. The Soviet Union assisted the new régime in many industrial and agricultural projects, but Chinese leaders came to dislike their dependence on a single ally. By 1960 China's more revolutionary ideology, her desire for prestige and her more militant foreign policy led to worsening relations with the Soviet Union. Although some observers were aware of these new tensions, events within China and Indo-China often dominated thinking in Tokyo and Peking. During the history of the People's Republic domestic policies underwent drastic changes of style and direction as leaders sought to combine economic progress with revolutionary enthusiasm. These dramatic fluctuations reached their peak in the 'Cultural Revolution', which began in 1966. This nationwide movement combined social turmoil and revolutionary ardour, and made China appear a potentially aggressive power. In these same years America's involvement in the Vietnam War stimulated Russian and Chinese help for Hanoi and temporarily concealed the depth of hostility between Moscow and Peking.

By 1972 the Cultural Revolution and the Vietnam War had diminished in intensity, and China's fear of the Soviet Union led her to pursue international policies of a strategic rather than an ideological character. She began secret negotiations with the United States, and opened diplomatic contacts with Japan. China now formally forgave Japan for her aggression in the 1930s (*Map 79*), and trade between them rapidly increased. This improvement in relations between Peking and Tokyo soon received further encouragement from events in America and the Middle East. America's failure in Vietnam led her to reduce her military presence in East Asia, while the enormous successes of Japanese goods in the American market led to a bitter dispute over textile imports and fears that the United States might seek to restrict the flow of Japanese products into her domestic market. America's more reticent role in the Far East led to the return of Okinawa to Japanese administration in 1972, but this was less important than Japan's nervousness of the dependability of America's markets and military protection. In 1973 the increased price and diminished supplies of oil which followed the Arab-Israeli war threatened Japan's economy and led her to seek alternative markets and oil in China and South East Asia (*see Map 88*).

At the same time China felt increasingly insecure in her relations with the Soviet Union, and the death of Mao Tse Tung in 1976 and the removal of the radical 'gang of four' in 1977 made it easier for China's leaders to replace policies based upon ideology by a new emphasis on the Four Modernisations which aimed to increase China's economic wellbeing and ability to defend herself against the Soviet Union. By 1978 Japan's need for markets and China's for modern technology had produced a commercial agreement for immense increases in trade and Japanese help in the development of Chinese industry and the exploitation of her natural resources. Perhaps surprisingly Soviet policy in East Asia showed little sign of major changes in the closing years of the 1970s. She, like China, attempted to secure Japanese help in the development of the natural resources of her Far Eastern territories (*see Map 71*), but Japanese officials and businessmen feared the reliability of Soviet undertakings and feared that Russia might draw them into its dispute with Peking. Indeed while Japan's relations with China had undergone a diplomatic revolution, those with the Soviet Union appeared frozen in the pattern of the post-war world. Not only did the Soviet Union take a particularly severe attitude in fishery negotiations, but her refusal to return four small islands – Habomai, Shikotan, Kunashiri and Edorofu – contrasted dramatically with American concessions on territorial issues.

By 1980 the mutual interests of China and Japan had produced a cordiality in relations between Peking and Tokyo that was almost without precedent in the 20th century. Japan feared the growing power of the Soviet navy and China the growth of Soviet influence in Vietnam. In consequence while Japan sought to avoid provocative statements which might threaten her worldwide commercial interests she joined China in her hostility to North Vietnam and in criticism of Soviet policy.

Despite the immense changes in East Asia in the 1970s political conditions in Korea remained unstable and unchanged. This peninsula remained divided between two small hostile régimes whose large armed forces often seemed in danger of turning a small incident into a war between the great powers.

Further reading: J. Chesneaux, *China: The People's Republic 1949-76* (Harvester, 1979); Masataka Kosaka, *100 Million Japanese: the post-war Experience* (Kodansha, Tokyo, 1972); L. Olsen, *Japan in Post-War Asia* (Pall Mall, 1970); W. Mendl, *Issues in Japan's China Policy* (Macmillan, 1979).

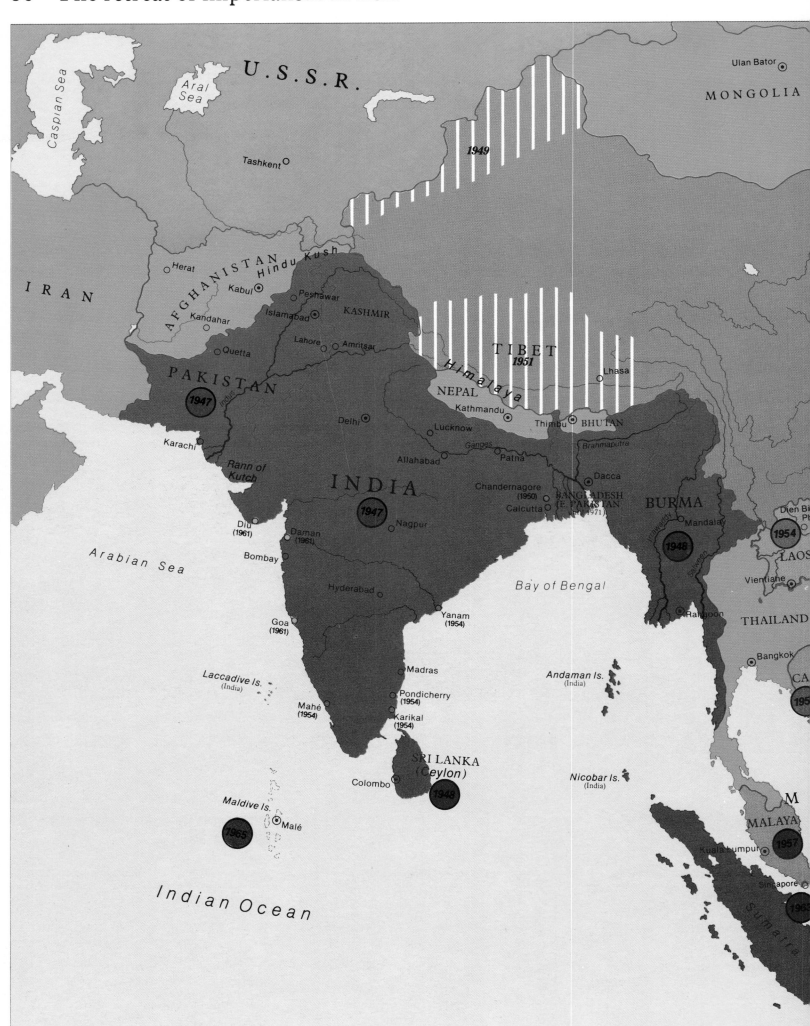

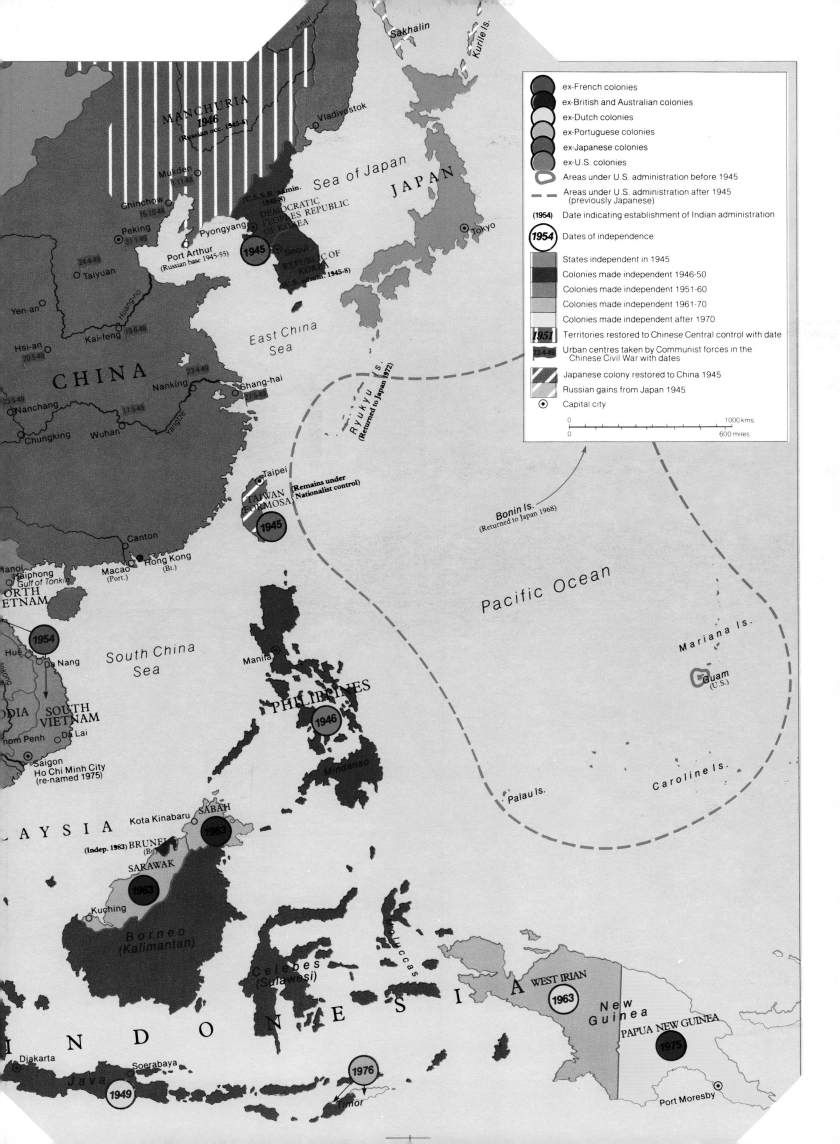

MANCHURIA
1946
(Russian occ. 1945-6)

Mukden
1.11.48

Chinchow
15.10.48

Peking
31.1.49

Port Arthur
(Russian base 1945-55)

24.4.49

Taiyuan

Yen-an

Hsi-an
20.5.49

Kai-feng
19.6.48

Huang-ho

CHINA

Nanking
23.4.49

Nanchang
23.5.49

Shang-hai
17.5.49

Wuhan

Chungking

Yangtze

Sea of Japan

JAPAN

Vladivostok

Sakhalin

Kurile Is.

Amur

DEMOCRATIC
PEOPLES REPUBLIC
OF KOREA
(U.S.S.R. admin. 1945-8)

Pyongyang

1945

Seoul
REPUBLIC OF
KOREA
(U.S. admin. 1945-8)

Tokyo

East China
Sea

Ryukyu Is.
(Returned to Japan 1972)

Taipei

TAIWAN
(FORMOSA)
1945
(Remains under
Nationalist control)

Canton

Macao
(Port.)

Hong Kong
(Br.)

Hanoi
Haiphong
Gulf of Tonkin

NORTH
VIETNAM

1954

Hué
Da Nang

CAMBODIA

SOUTH
VIETNAM

Phnom Penh
Da Lai

Saigon
Ho Chi Minh City
(re-named 1975)

South China
Sea

Manila

PHILIPPINES

1946

Mindanao

Pacific Ocean

Bonin Is.
(Returned to Japan 1968)

Mariana Is.

Guam
(U.S.)

Palau Is.

Caroline Is.

MALAYSIA
Kota Kinabaru

SABAH
1963

(Indep. 1983) BRUNEI
(Br.)

SARAWAK
1963

Kuching

Borneo
(Kalimantan)

Celebes
(Sulawesi)

Moluccas

INDONESIA

WEST IRIAN
1963

New
Guinea

PAPUA NEW GUINEA
1975

Djakarta

Soerabaya

Java

1949

1976

Timor

Port Moresby

The emergence of the modern world VI

Contemporary society

CONTEMPORARY HISTORY is dominated by the heightened competition of a rapidly growing population for control of the Earth's territory and resources (*see Map 88*). In Asia and Africa a series of local and regional power struggles occurred in the wake of the collapse of European imperialism after the Second World War. The inability of nearly all post-colonial states to conquer endemic poverty, famine, and over-population exacerbated the enduring ethnic, religious, and economic differences within and between many of the new states. In the decolonised 'third world' (as in inter-war Europe) independence seemed to increase rather than to diminish human aggression, particularly in the form of national conflicts, giving rise to vast refugee movements (*see Map 83*), mass murder of civilian populations, torture, terrorism, economic warfare, and a descent in the 1970s into severe economic crisis.

The greatest imperial power in history was also among the most short-lived. The British Empire had reached its territorial apogee in the aftermath of the First World War (*Map 67*). The retreat began almost immediately. In 1931 the Statute of Westminster acknowledged the independence as 'dominions' within the British Commonwealth of Canada, Australia, New Zealand, South Africa, and the Irish Free State. However, these were all countries dominated by peoples of European origin. Claims to independence by non-Europeans, most notably the demands of the Indian nationalist movement headed by Mahatma Gandhi, were resisted by imperial governments during the inter-war period.

The Second World War, which shattered the prestige and economies of many of the imperial powers, and which helped, especially in east Asia and the middle east, to stimulate anti-colonial nationalisms, forced the pace of European withdrawal from Asia and Africa. In 1947 Britain accorded independence to India. However, upon the British withdrawal the sub-continent split into two sovereign states. The smaller, Muslim state of Pakistan was formed out of north-western India and east Bengal, the two portions of the new country being separated by a thousand miles of territory belonging to the larger, secular state of India (*Map 86*). The partition was accompanied by massive bloodshed in communal riots and by huge movements in population. Pakistan initially pursued a pro-American foreign policy, while India, under the leadership of Gandhi's disciple, Jawaharlal Nehru, followed a 'neutralist' course between the two power blocs. A military government took power in Pakistan in 1958, whereas India was one of the few post-colonial states to preserve parliamentary democracy. The two states disputed possession of the province of Kashmir, predominantly Muslim in population but occupied by India. For this and other reasons relations between the two remained sour. In 1965 they fought an inconclusive war. In 1971 a fierce civil war in Pakistan produced a further Indo-Pakistani conflict in which India won a decisive victory. East Pakistan, under Indian protection, became the new, independent state of Bangladesh.

The British withdrawal from India marked the start of a general European evacuation of South Asia. In 1948 the British left Burma. In 1949, after some years of fighting, the Dutch recognised the independence of Indonesia. In 1957 Britain granted independence to Malaya, although the naval base at Singapore was retained until 1971. The most humiliating colonial ejection from the area was that of France from Indo-China after its defeat at Dien Bien Phu in 1954. The independent states of Cambodia, Laos, and Vietnam were formed, the latter partitioned at the 17th parallel between a communist north and a non-communist south. American efforts in the 1960s to shore up the South Vietnamese régime against communist revolution, aided by attack from the north, gave rise to a murderous war involving, at its peak in 1968, over half a million American troops. The Vietnam war produced severe internal unrest in the USA which led to a gradual American military withdrawal, completed by 1973. By 1975 communist forces had ousted the South Vietnamese régime, and shortly afterwards Laos and Cambodia fell to communist guerrillas. In Cambodia the victorious revolutionaries enacted a ruthless 'pastoralisation' of the cities resulting in millions of deaths and the destruction of the country's economy and social organisation. In 1977 internecine warfare between the Cambodian and Vietnamese communists erupted, expanding into a full-scale war in which Vietnam, although opposed by China, occupied most of Cambodia and installed a new government of its own choosing. The almost continuous warfare and turmoil in much of Indo-China for more than thirty years led to widespread famine, vast refugee movements, and terrible suffering.

In the Middle East, as in South Asia, British and French power collapsed after the Second World War, although here the two countries made a more determined stand, alive to the economic importance of the area, which was now thought to contain the world's largest deposits of petroleum, and to the strategic significance of the Suez Canal. France was compelled, under British pressure, to withdraw from Syria and Lebanon.

In 1948 Britain abandoned Palestine, where a bitter civil war had broken out between Arabs and Jews. The latter established the State of Israel and defeated an invasion by the neighbouring Arab states. A part of Palestine west of the River Jordan (the 'West Bank') was incorporated into the Kingdom of Jordan (*see Map 87*). The bulk of the Arab population of Palestine fled into neighbouring countries, and nursed the ambition of overthrowing Israel and returning to their homes. Tension between the Arab states and Israel remained acute and there were frequent border skirmishes. In 1956 the simmering conflict exploded into war between Israel and Egypt in which Britain and France supported Israel. Britain's military intervention was the result of concern about the security of the Suez Canal, following its nationalisation by the Egyptian military régime headed by Gamal Abdel Nasser. France joined the invasion of Egypt primarily because of her determination to eliminate Egyptian backing for the anti-French nationalist revolution in Algeria. Although Israel won a military victory, the Suez affair ended in the humiliation of Britain and France which, lacking even the support of their American ally, were forced to withdraw their troops from Egypt. Suez was held to be definite proof that the age of European imperialism was past, and the break-up of the colonial empires now accelerated.

During the following decade most of the European colonies achieved independence. France had already recognised the independence of Morocco and Tunisia in early 1956, but she clung doggedly to Algeria in spite of an increasingly bloody war there which led in 1958 to the collapse of the Fourth French Republic and the return to power of General De Gaulle as President. De Gaulle consolidated the institutions of the Fifth Republic in a

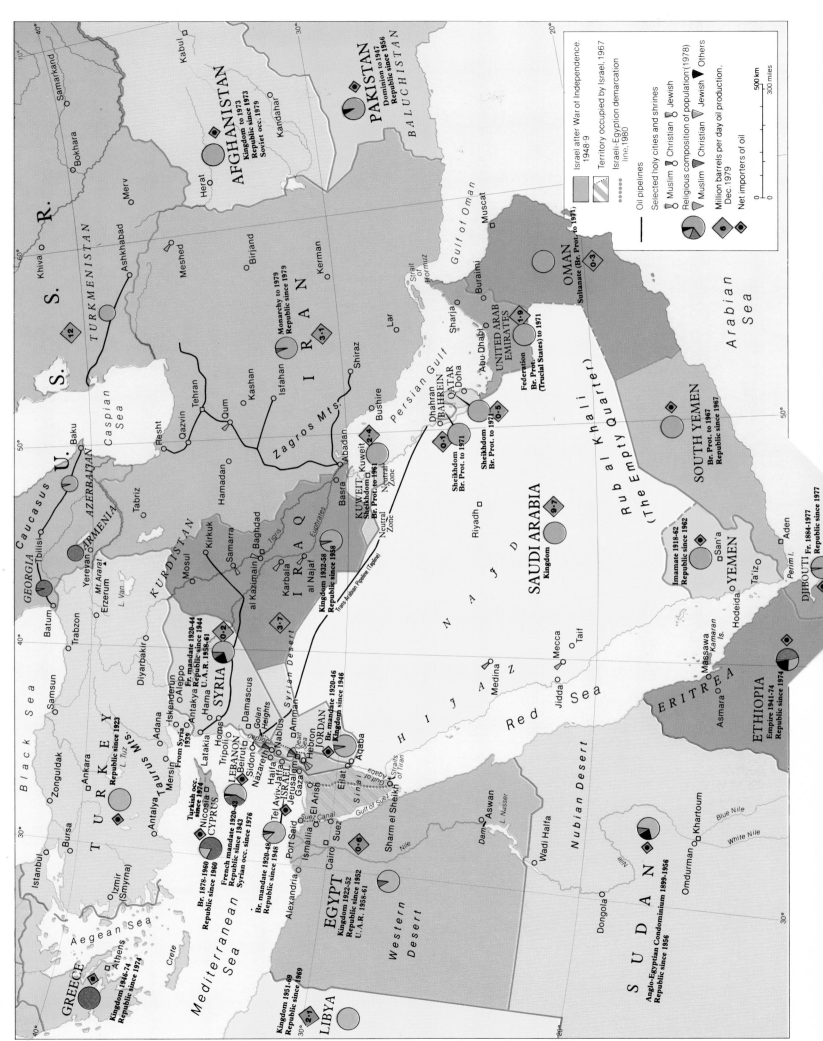

Israel after War of Independence, 1948-9

Territory occupied by Israel, 1967

Israeli-Egyptian demarcation line, 1980

Oil pipelines

Selected holy cities and shrines

Muslim   Christian   Jewish

Religious composition of population (1978)
Muslim   Christian   Jewish   Others

Million barrels per day oil production, Dec. 1979

Net importers of oil

500 km
300 miles

© Creative Cartography Ltd © The Hamlyn Group

AFGHANISTAN
Kingdom to 1973
Republic since 1973
Soviet occ. 1979

PAKISTAN
Dominion to 1947
Republic since 1956
Republic since 1971

BALUCHISTAN

I R A N
Monarchy to 1979
Republic since 1979
3·1

T U R K M E N I S T A N
1·2

S. S. R.

U. S.

GEORGIA

AZERBAIJAN

ARMENIA

Caucasus Mts.

Caspian Sea

T U R K E Y
Republic since 1923

Zagros Mts.

K U R D I S T A N

S Y R I A
Fr. mandate 1920-44
Antakya Republic since 1944
Antakya U.A.R. 1958-61
0·2

I R A Q
Kingdom 1932-58
Republic since 1958
3·7

LEBANON
French mandate 1920-43
Republic since 1943
Syrian occ. since 1976

CYPRUS
Br. 1878-1960
Republic since 1960
Turkish occ. since 1974

ISRAEL
Br. mandate 1920-48
Republic since 1948

JORDAN
Br. mandate 1920-46
Kingdom since 1946

EGYPT
Kingdom 1922-52
Republic since 1952
U.A.R. 1958-61
0·6

GREECE
Kingdom 1946-74
Republic since 1974

LIBYA
Kingdom 1951-69
Republic since 1969
2·1

KUWEIT
Sheikhdom
Br. Prot. to 1961
2·4

Neutral Zone

Trans Arabian Pipeline (Tapline)

BAHREIN
Sheikhdom
Br. Prot. to 1971
0·1

QATAR
Sheikhdom
Br. Prot. to 1971
0·5

UNITED ARAB EMIRATES
Federation
Br. Prot.
(Trucial States) to 1971
1·9

OMAN
Sultanate (Br. Prot. to 1971)
0·3

Gulf of Oman

Strait of Hormuz

Persian Gulf

N A J D

SAUDI ARABIA
Kingdom
9·7

R u b   a l   K h a l i
(The Empty Quarter)

H I J A Z

Arabian Sea

SOUTH YEMEN
Br. Prot. to 1967
Republic since 1967

YEMEN
Imamate 1918-62
Republic since 1962

DJIBOUTI
Fr. 1884-1977
Republic since 1977

ERITREA

ETHIOPIA
Empire 1941-74
Republic since 1974

Red Sea

S U D A N
Anglo-Egyptian Condominium 1899-1956
Republic since 1956

Nubian Desert

Western Desert

Mediterranean Sea

Aegean Sea

Black Sea

Cities and labels:
Samarkand, Kabul, Bokhara, Kandahar, Herat, Merv, Meshed, Birjand, Kerman, Ashkhabad, Khiva, Baku, Kashan, Istahan, Qum, Shiraz, Lar, Tehran, Qazvin, Resht, Tabriz, Hamadan, Yerevan, Mt. Ararat, Erzerum, L. Van, Tbilisi, Batum, Trabzon, Zonguldak, Samsun, Bursa, Istanbul, Izmir (Smyrna), Ankara, Antalya, Adana, Mersin, Iskenderun, Aleppo, Diyarbakir, Mosul, Kirkuk, Samarra, Baghdad, al Kazimain, Karbala, al Najaf, Basra, Abadan, Bushire, Dhahran, Doha, Abu-Dhabi, Sharja, Buraimi, Muscat, Riyadh, Mecca, Taif, Medina, Jidda, Aswan, L. Nasser, Wadi Halfa, Dongola, Omdurman, Khartoum, Blue Nile, White Nile, Nile, Asmara, Massawa, Kamaran Is., Perim I., Aden, Ta'iz, San'a, Hodeida, Homs, Hama, Tripoli, Latakia, Beirut, Damascus, Sidon, Golan Heights, Amman, Nablus, Nazareth, Haifa, Jaffa, Tel Aviv, Jerusalem, Hebron, Gaza, El Arish, Port Said, Ismailia, Alexandria, Cairo, Suez, Sharm el Sheikh, Eilat, Aqaba, Dead Sea, Jordan R., Syrian Desert, Euphrates, Tigris, Nicosia, Athens, Crete, Gulf of Aqaba, Straits of Tiran, Gulf of Suez, Suez Canal, Sinai, From Syria 1939, Antalya, Taurus Mts., Tuz, Mt. Ararat

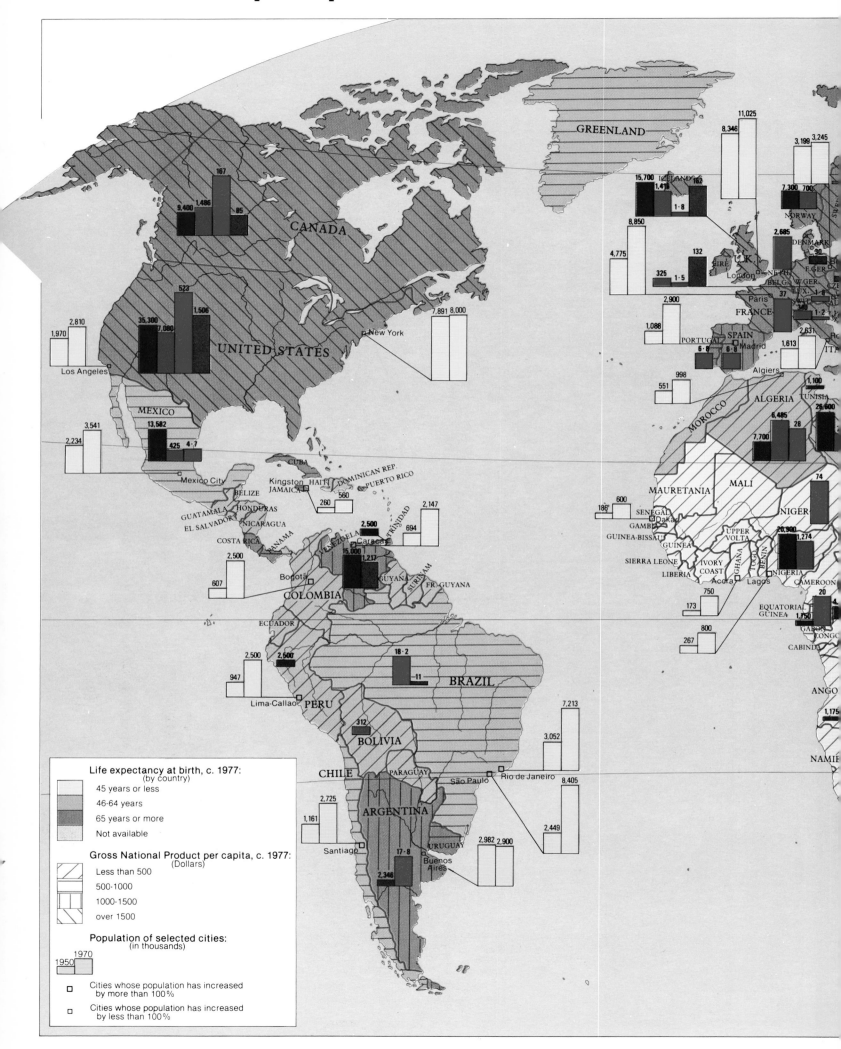

GREENLAND

CANADA

167
9,400　1,486
85

523
1,506
35,300
7,080

1,970　2,810

Los Angeles

UNITED STATES

New York
7,891　8,000

MEXICO

13,582
425　4·7

2,234　3,541

Mexico City

CUBA

DOMINICAN REP.
Kingston　HAITI
JAMAICA　PUERTO RICO

BELIZE
GUATAMALA　HONDURAS
EL SALVADOR　NICARAGUA
COSTA RICA　PANAMA

260　560

2,147

694

2,500
VENEZUELA
Caracas　TRINIDAD
15,000
1,217

2,500
607

Bogotá

GUYANA
SURINAM
FR. GUYANA

COLOMBIA

ECUADOR

2,500　2,600

947

Lima-Callao　PERU

18·2
11

BRAZIL

312

BOLIVIA

CHILE　PARAGUAY

São Paulo　Rio de Janeiro

7,213

3,052

8,405

2,449

2,725

1,161

ARGENTINA

Santiago

17·8

2,346

URUGUAY
2,982　2,900
Buenos
Aires

8,346

11,025

3,199　3,245

15,700　ICELAND
1,416　162
1·8

7,300　700

NORWAY

8,850

4,775

325　1·5

132

2,685

DENMARK
30

IRE.　U.K.
London　NETH.
BELG.　W.GER.
LUX.
Paris　SWIT.
FRANCE

E.GER.

37

2,900

1,088

PORTUGAL　SPAIN
6·8　6·8　Madrid

551　998

Algiers

MOROCCO　ALGERIA
6,485

7,700

2,631

ITA.

1,613

1,100
TUNISIA
26,600
28

MAURETANIA　MALI

74

186　600
SENEGAL　Dakar
GAMBIA
GUINEA-BISSAU

NIGER
20,900
1,274

GUINEA
SIERRA LEONE
LIBERIA

UPPER
VOLTA
IVORY
COAST　GHANA
Accra　Lagos

TOGO
BENIN
NIGERIA

CAMEROON

750
173

20
EQUATORIAL
GUINEA　1,750
GABON
CONGO
CABINDA

ANGOLA

1,175

800
267

NAMIBIA

Life expectancy at birth, c. 1977:
(by country)
45 years or less
46-64 years
65 years or more
Not available

Gross National Product per capita, c. 1977:
(Dollars)
Less than 500
500-1000
1000-1500
over 1500

Population of selected cities:
(in thousands)

1970
1950

□ Cities whose population has increased
by more than 100%

□ Cities whose population has increased
by less than 100%

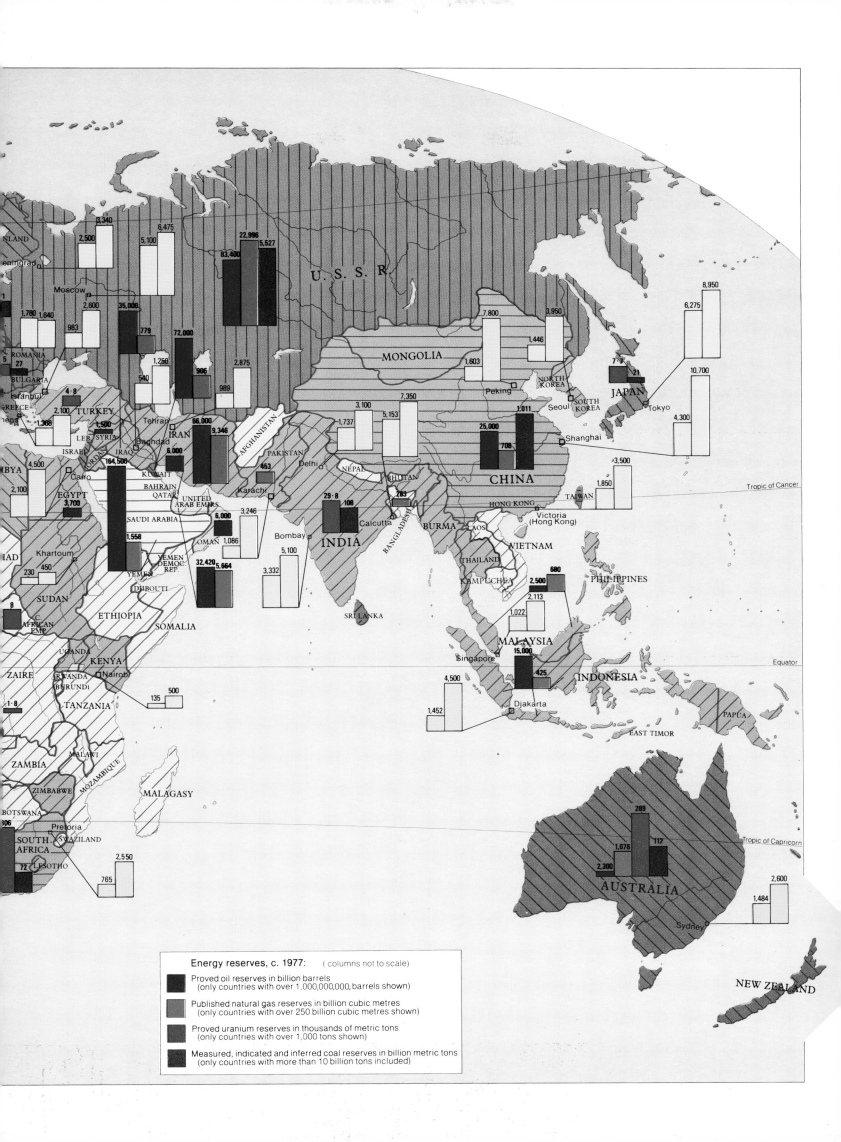

Energy reserves, c. 1977: (columns not to scale)

Proved oil reserves in billion barrels
(only countries with over 1,000,000,000 barrels shown)

Published natural gas reserves in billion cubic metres
(only countries with over 250 billion cubic metres shown)

Proved uranium reserves in thousands of metric tons
(only countries with over 1,000 tons shown)

Measured, indicated and inferred coal reserves in billion metric tons
(only countries with more than 10 billion tons included)

Contemporary society

presidential régime, and in 1962 he finally granted independence to Algeria. Meanwhile most of the British and French possessions in west and east Africa had shaken off colonial rule with relatively little bloodshed (*Map 74*). However, in the Belgian Congo chaos followed the sudden Belgian withdrawal in 1960. An attempt, backed by powerful western economic interests, was made to form an independent state in the mineral-rich Katanga province. Order was eventually restored by an international force dispatched by the United Nations. A civil war erupted also in Nigeria in 1966, ending in 1970 with victory for the central government over the army of the secessionist eastern region, 'Biafra'.

By the late 1960s European rule had been eliminated from nearly all Africa. In the 1970s even the white bastions of Angola, Mozambique, Rhodesia and South Africa were shaken. Portugal, which had held coastal areas of Angola and Mozambique for more than three centuries (*compare Map 36*), engaged in an increasingly costly struggle during the 1960s and early 1970s to repress anti-colonial nationalist movements. As in France in 1958 colonial warfare led to political upheaval at home. In 1974 a military junta carried out a peaceful 'revolution of flowers'. The new democratic government speedily conceded independence to Portugal's colonies, although in Angola the anti-colonial struggle was merely transformed into a fierce civil war between rival factions. Rhodesia (formerly Southern Rhodesia), ruled by a small white élite comprising under five per cent of its population, had issued a 'unilateral declaration of independence' in November 1965. For more than a decade the Rhodesian whites succeeded in defying United Nations economic sanctions and maintained their oligarchic society intact. But by 1979 the fall of Portuguese colonialism and the rise of African nationalist guerrilla movements operating from Mozambique and Zambia had compelled the Rhodesian régime to concede black majority rule.

South Africa, the richest country on the continent, with the highest proportion of whites among its population, remained under white control. From 1948 it was ruled by the Afrikaner (Dutch-origin whites) Nationalist Party which pursued the policy of *apartheid* or 'separate development'. This sought to maintain white supremacy by the enactment of discriminatory repressive laws directed against the black majority of the population and by racial segregation. Certain areas (amounting to a total of thirteen per cent of the land area of the country) were to be set aside as independent black-ruled 'Bantustans'. The first two such areas to be granted independence were the Transkei and Bophuthatswana but neither secured international recognition. In 1960 a massacre of Africans at Sharpeville aroused worldwide protest which culminated in a South African decision to leave the British Commonwealth. Severe rioting (with over 200 deaths) at Soweto township near Johannesburg in 1976 heightened international criticism. By the late 1970s South Africa found herself increasingly isolated, but in spite of external hostility and internal unrest the Nationalists, bolstered by powerful armed forces and by the country's large deposits of gold, diamonds, and other precious minerals, remained firmly in power.

Of all the post-colonial conflicts it was that in the Middle East which had the most enduring and profound disruptive effects on the international system. In 1967 a further war between Israel and her Arab neighbours, Egypt, Jordan, and Syria, resulted in a decisive victory for the Israelis within six days. Israel occupied large areas of Arab territory and refused to withdraw unless the Arab states made peace with her. A six-year impasse was broken in 1973 by the outbreak of a further war between Israel and an Egyptian-Syrian alliance. Although Israel again won militarily, she found herself gravely weakened politically by initial Arab military successes and under pressure from the USA (on which Israel was heavily dependent for economic aid and arms supplies) to reach an accommodation with her enemies. Indefatigable 'shuttle' diplomacy by the US Secretary of State, Henry Kissinger, secured limited 'disengagement' accords between Israel and Egypt in 1974 and 1975 and Israel and Syria in 1974. In 1977, in a startling *volte-face*, President Sadat of Egypt visited Israel and addressed the Israeli parliament in Jerusalem, announcing Egyptian readiness to live at peace with Israel. After negotiations in which the USA acted as a mediator, an Israeli-Egyptian peace treaty was signed in 1979. The treaty provided for Israeli withdrawal in stages from the Sinai peninsula. However, the treaty was denounced by other Arab states as a betrayal of the cause of the Palestinian Arabs, and opposition to the treaty was given added weight by the threat of the so-called 'oil weapon'.

In 1960 the major oil-producing states (particularly Saudi Arabia and Iran) formed a cartel known as the Organization of Petroleum Exporting Countries (OPEC). The economic boom of the late 1960s and early 1970s created a great increase in demand for oil which enabled OPEC to demand vast price increases (*Map 88*). The 1973 war, while it did not initiate the price rise, accelerated it, and the price increases were accompanied by threats of an oil boycott of countries sympathetic to Israel. The USA, which used more oil per head of population than any other major state, had lost its previous self-sufficiency in oil production by the early 1970s and swiftly became dependent on large oil imports after 1973. Revolution in Iran in 1979, in which the pro-American Shah was ousted by Islamic nationalists, raised fears in the USA of an impending shortage of energy needed for continued economic growth.

The dramatic oil price rises of the 1970s were one of the major causes of the world-wide recession after 1974. This, the worst 'slump' since the 1930s, produced widespread unemployment, high levels of inflation, rocketing interest rates, wildly fluctuating currency values, and a halt to the rapid economic growth of the post-war period. Above all, the recession increased pressures everywhere towards economic nationalism representing perhaps the gravest threat to international peace since the Second World War. In what was now a global market, if not yet in any real sense an international community, man faced anew, though with no great certainty of solution, the fundamental questions of survival and social organisation with which he had grappled since the dawn of civilised life on earth.

G. Barraclough, *An Introduction to Contemporary History* (Penguin, 1967); H. Grimal, *Decolonisation: The British, French, Dutch and Belgian Empires, 1919-63* (Routledge & Kegan Paul, 1978); V. P. Menon, *The Transfer of Power in India* (Longman, 1957); H. Thomas, *The Suez Affair* (Weidenfeld and Nicolson, 1976); G. Lewy, *America in Vietnam* (Oxford University Press, New York, 1978); Alistair Horne, *A Savage War of Peace: Algeria, 1954-1962* (Macmillan, 1977; Penguin, 1979).

THE SEARCH FOR ADVENTURE, wealth, and freedom has inspired those coming to America since the discovery of the New World. The Spaniard Cortez, confessing to a "sickness of the soul only gold could cure," exemplified the early explorer who set out to claim land and gold for his king and riches for himself. But Great Britain soon discovered that true wealth lay in the land itself, and in North America chose colonization as the road to political and economic power.

The maps that follow chronicle the remarkable development of Britain's one-time colony—the United States. Covering eight historical periods from 1700 to 1970, the maps illustrate the country's foundation and expansion westward, its richly varied population, and three major conflicts—the Revolutionary and Civil wars and World War II. The maps portray these developments in a vivid, colorful style, depicting often overlapping events, such as the construction of transcontinental railways and the rise and fall of the great cattle empires. Short summaries accompanying each map provide more detailed information of each historical period. A series of tables at the end of this section list the entry of the states into the union, the flow of immigrants by nationality, and recent shifts in regional population.

From the beginning, the vastness of the continent challenged the imaginations of early settlers. The new land offered not only abundant natural resources but the opportunity to experiment with various social, religious, and political ideals. Freed from traditional European constraints, Americans rapidly created an economy and industry that outstripped the combined production of Europe. These successes built into the national character expectations for a continually rising standard of living and unlimited opportunity.

But the nation's growth was not always a steady progress forward. Native American Indians and other racial minorities have long struggled for an equal place in American society. And as far back as the early 1800s, some people felt the nation's emphasis on commercial development meant neglecting the long-term consequences of uncontrolled growth. Finally, the legacy of World War II—that America would enjoy continued political and economic expansion—left the country somewhat unprepared for the problems that emerged only a few decades later. The energy crisis, worldwide inflation and instability now challenge the United States on several fronts at once.

Yet the maps show the development of a confident and energetic people. Perhaps the national experience of taming a continent, creating a vast industry, and absorbing millions of newcomers into the culture may prove to be adequate preparation for meeting the problems of today. It has seemed, in the past, that the nation is never more resourceful than when facing a difficult challenge.

The American Colonies, 1700

THE FABULOUS WEALTH discovered by Spain in Central and South America touched off a race among other nations—chiefly France and England—to share in the riches of the New World. By the early 1600s, French holdings in North America reached from the Appalachian Mountains to the western plains and north beyond the Great Lakes; while Spain claimed the south and southwest regions. As the map on the following page shows, Great Britain possessed only a narrow strip along the Atlantic seaboard and a small area in the northwest.

Dreams of finding easy treasure faded; England and France began to realize the commercial and military value of colonizing these lands. Except for the settlements at Québec, Trois-Rivières, and Montréal, however, few people immigrated to the French regions. In contrast, America fired the imaginations of the English people. Even so, the early settlers of Jamestown and similar camps barely survived the "starving times," when disease and lack of food decimated the small population. The settlements slowly began to prosper as more immigrants arrived, bringing with them a complex array of religious, social, and political beliefs.

Most of the settlements were clustered near waterways and along the sea coast, leaving large inland areas virtually uninhabited. Provincetown, Plymouth, Philadelphia, and the Chesapeake settlements—founded as religious communities—became thriving commercial centers by the late 1600s. Boston and New York prospered as port cities, and towns scattered along the coast benefited from a growing fishing industry. The rich farmlands of Maryland, Virginia, and the Carolinas proved ideal for valuable cash crops such as cotton and tobacco. As the transplanted European population grew, native Indian tribes were forced out of coastal areas and pushed further west. By 1700, the colonies were loosely organized into eleven provinces. The population, with its unusual social, political, and religious makeup, was already markedly different from any society in Europe.

England was clearly winning the race to settle and develop its colonies. With the eventual defeat of France in the French and Indian War (1754-63), Great Britain became the dominant power in North America.

Independence, 1775-1783

TO MANY HISTORIANS, the Revolutionary War remains the single most important event in American history, instilling in the people a sense of their nation's special destiny. The war arose from conflicts between a diverse, fiercely independent colonial population and a British government determined to tighten its control over King George's colonies. Americans viewed the revenue acts passed to subsidize Britain's colonial army as a threat to their political and economic freedoms. Mounting hostility finally erupted in the Boston Massacre of 1770. By 1775, colonial resistance had become armed rebellion. The following map depicts the major battles and strategies of the war.

Expecting easy victories at Lexington, Concord, and Bunker Hill, the British, instead, suffered heavy losses defeating the Yankee militia. Action in the western regions remained indecisive for both sides. By July, 1776, Britain was mounting a full-scale military effort to end the rebellion. Though well equipped and trained, the British army often had to deal with a largely hostile population and fight in wilderness terrain. In contrast, the Americans, outnumbered and poorly equipped, were fighting for their own land.

The British sought to divide the colonies by isolating New England. They defeated George Washington's Continental Army at Long Island and New York; but at the end of 1776, Continental troops had captured Princeton and Trenton. The American victory at Saratoga in October, 1777, dealt a final blow to Britain's northern strategy. And by the following year, France had allied itself with the American cause.

From 1778 onward, Britain concentrated on the South and the sea coast. British Commander Cornwallis captured Savannah, Charleston, and Camden, but could not secure the countryside. American irregular forces continually harassed the British army until it withdrew to the coast. Finally, in October, 1781, Cornwallis surrendered his entire command to Washington and Rochambeau, Commander of the French forces dispatched to aid Americans, at Yorktown.

The peace treaty of 1783 recognized American independence and more than doubled the size of the former territory. The victorious Americans believed that their emerging nation was destined to lead the world toward liberty.

The American Colonies, 1700

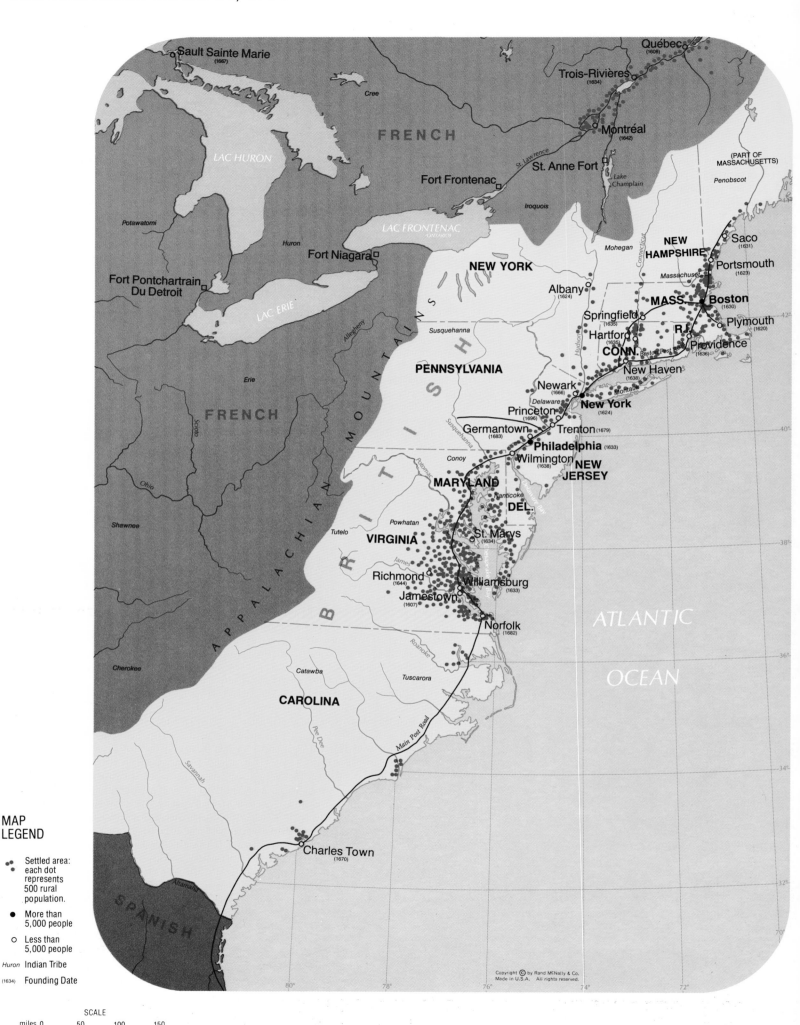

MAP
LEGEND

```
•••  Settled area:
•     each dot
      represents
      500 rural
      population.

•     More than
      5,000 people

○     Less than
      5,000 people

Huron  Indian Tribe

(1634)  Founding Date
```

SCALE

miles 0   50   100   150

kilometers 0 50 100 150 200

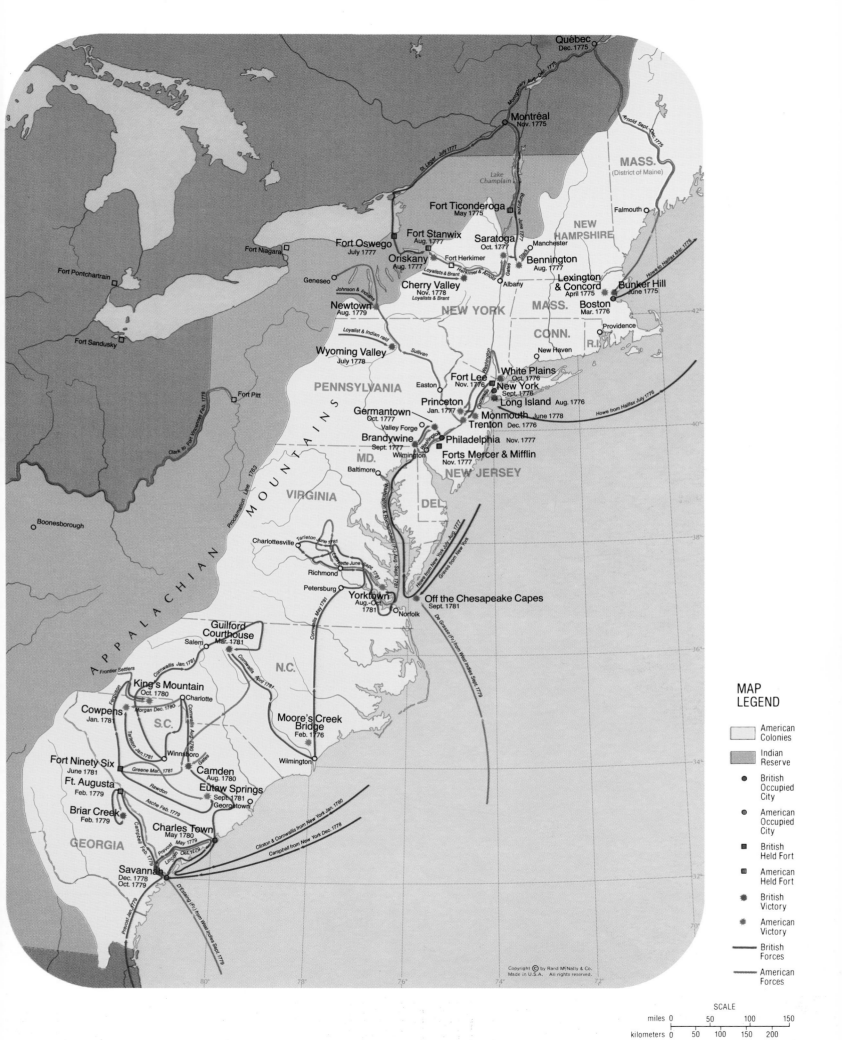

Québec
Dec. 1775

Montréal
Nov. 1775

MASS.
(District of Maine)

NEW
HAMPSHIRE

Falmouth

Fort Ticonderoga
May 1775

*Lake
Champlain*

Fort Oswego
July 1777

Fort Stanwix
Aug. 1777

Saratoga
Oct. 1777

Manchester

Fort Niagara

Oriskany
Aug. 1777

Fort Herkimer

Bennington
Aug. 1777

Lexington
& Concord
April 1775

Bunker Hill
June 1775

Fort Pontchartrain

Geneseo

Johnson & Indians

Cherry Valley
Nov. 1778
Loyalists & Brant

Albany

NEW YORK

MASS.

Boston
Mar. 1776

Loyalists & Brant

Herkimer & Arnold

Gates

CONN.

Providence

Fort Sandusky

Newtown
Aug. 1779

R.I.

New Haven

Loyalist & Indian raid

Wyoming Valley
July 1778

Sullivan

White Plains
Oct. 1776

PENNSYLVANIA

Fort Pitt

Easton

Fort Lee
Nov. 1776

New York
Sept. 1776

Long Island Aug. 1776

Howe from Halifax July 1776

Princeton
Jan. 1777

Germantown
Oct. 1777

Monmouth June 1778

Valley Forge

Trenton
Dec. 1776

Brandywine
Sept. 1777

Philadelphia
Nov. 1777

Wilmington

Forts Mercer & Mifflin
Nov. 1777

MD.

NEW JERSEY

Baltimore

VIRGINIA

DEL.

Clark to Fort Vincennes Feb. 1778

Proclamation Line 1763

Boonesborough

Charlottesville

Tarleton June 1781

Howe from New York July-Aug. 1777

Richmond

Lafayette June-Sept. 1781

Petersburg

Yorktown
Aug.-Oct.
1781

Off the Chesapeake Capes
Sept. 1781

Washington & Rochambeau (Fr.) Aug.-Sept. 1781

Graves from New York

Norfolk

De Grasse (Fr.) from West Indies Sept. 1781

Guilford
Courthouse
Mar. 1781

Cornwallis May 1781

Salem

Cornwallis Jan. 1781

N.C.

Cornwallis April 1781

Frontier Settlers

King's Mountain
Oct. 1780

Charlotte

Ferguson

Cowpens
Jan. 1781

Morgan Dec. 1780

Moore's Creek
Bridge
Feb. 1776

S.C.

Cornwallis Aug. 1780

Wilmington

Fort Ninety Six
June 1781

Tarleton Jan. 1781

Winnsboro

Gates

Ft. Augusta
Feb. 1779

Greene Mar. 1781

Camden
Aug. 1780

Rawdon

Eutaw Springs
Sept. 1781

Georgetown

Briar Creek
Feb. 1779

Asche Feb. 1779

GEORGIA

Campbell Feb. 1779

Charles Town
May 1780
May 1779

Clinton & Cornwallis from New York Jan. 1780

Prevost May 1779

Campbell from New York Dec. 1778

Savannah
Dec. 1778
Oct. 1779

Lincoln Oct. 1779

Prevost Jan. 1779

D'Estaing (Fr.) from West Indies Sept. 1779

APPALACHIAN MOUNTAINS

MAP
LEGEND

American
Colonies

Indian
Reserve

● British
Occupied
City

● American
Occupied
City

■ British
Held Fort

■ American
Held Fort

✳ British
Victory

✳ American
Victory

— British
Forces

— American
Forces

*Copyright © by Rand McNally & Co.
Made in U.S.A. All rights reserved.*

SCALE

miles 0   50   100   150

kilometers 0   50   100   150   200

Westward Expansion, 1803-1860

THE RALLYING CRY of "Manifest destiny!" reflected the American belief that providence itself had granted the United States exclusive right to settle North America. The country's rapidly expanding population and commercial development, the flood of European immigrants, and a growing transportation system all played a part in the first great western migration.

In 1803, Thomas Jefferson, deeply concerned about European influence on the continent, made the bold step of purchasing the Louisiana Territory from France—in one stroke doubling the nation's size. Early explorers such as Zebulon Pike and Meriwether Lewis and William Clark brought back glowing reports of the territory's rich land and abundant fur trade. In 1819, Spain ceded the remainder of Florida to the Republic. For many people in the crowded eastern states, including hundreds of Irish and German immigrants, the new lands represented opportunities for a better life. Soon a complex network of turnpikes, canal and river systems, and railroads carried settlers into the Mississippi Valley and parts of Texas, and opened the lands to eastern markets.

As the Louisiana Territory became more densely settled, pioneers began to push beyond the formal borders of the country. By the early 1840s, the St. Joseph, Missouri rail line served as a starting point for wagon trains heading west over the Oregon, Santa Fe, Fremont, and California trails. Mexico, attempting to stop the flow of settlers into its lands, soon found itself at war with the Americans, losing Texas in 1836 and its vast southwestern territories in 1848. The Gadsden Purchase of 1853 completed America's southernmost border. In the Pacific Northwest, early explorers and settlers had strengthened American claims to the Oregon Territory, held jointly with Great Britain. The two countries agreed in 1848 to divide the land at the 49th parallel. As more settlers poured into these territories, native Indian tribes were forced off their lands and eventually moved to reservations.

In little over half a century, America had fulfilled its manifest destiny on the continent. Seventeen new states had joined the Republic, eight of them west of the Mississippi. Only the deepening conflict over slavery seemed to dim the nation's brilliant future.

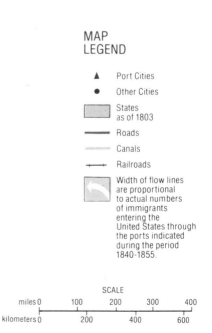

MAP LEGEND

▲ Port Cities

● Other Cities

▨ States as of 1803

━━━ Roads

┄┄┄ Canals

┼┼┼ Railroads

◀ Width of flow lines are proportional to actual numbers of immigrants entering the United States through the ports indicated during the period 1840-1855.

SCALE

| miles | 0 | 100 | 200 | 300 | 400 |
| kilometers | 0 | 200 | 400 | 600 | |

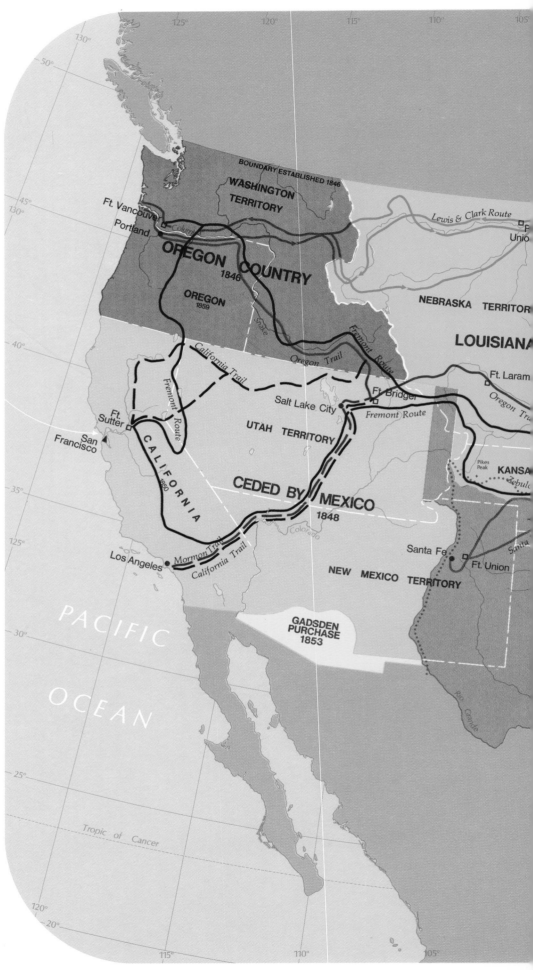

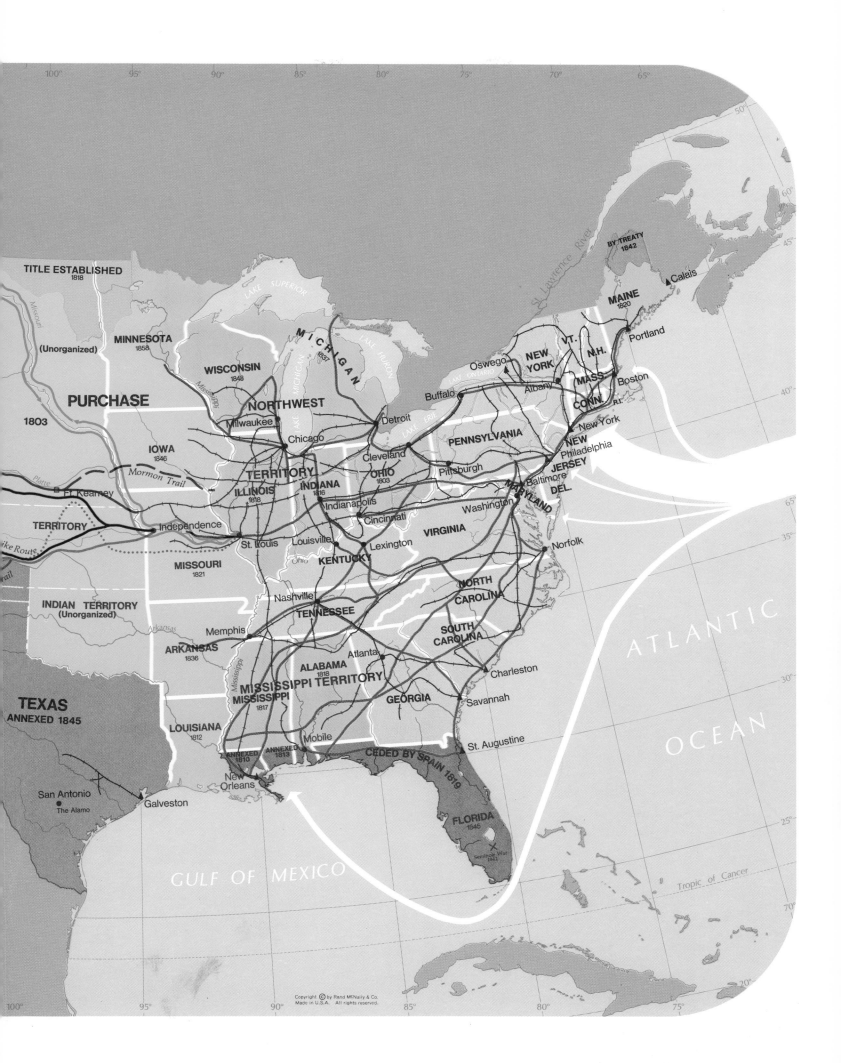

TITLE ESTABLISHED
1818

PURCHASE

1803

MINNESOTA
1858

(Unorganized)

WISCONSIN
1848

LAKE SUPERIOR

MICHIGAN
1837

LAKE HURON

LAKE MICHIGAN

BY TREATY
1842

MAINE
1820

Calais

St. Lawrence River

Portland

NORTHWEST

Milwaukee

Chicago

Detroit

LAKE ERIE

Oswego

NEW
YORK

VT.

N.H.

Buffalo

Albany

MASS.

CONN.

Boston

R.I.

IOWA
1846

Mormon Trail

TERRITORY

ILLINOIS
1818

INDIANA
1816

Cleveland

OHIO
1803

PENNSYLVANIA

Pittsburgh

New York

NEW

JERSEY

Philadelphia

DEL.

Ft. Kearney

Platte

Indianapolis

Baltimore

TERRITORY

Independence

St. Louis

Cincinnati

Louisville

Lexington

Washington

MARYLAND

Pike Route

VIRGINIA

Norfolk

MISSOURI
1821

Ohio

KENTUCKY

INDIAN TERRITORY
(Unorganized)

Arkansas

NORTH
CAROLINA

Nashville

TENNESSEE

Memphis

ARKANSAS
1836

Atlanta

SOUTH
CAROLINA

TEXAS

ANNEXED 1845

Mississippi

MISSISSIPPI TERRITORY

MISSISSIPPI
1817

ALABAMA
1818

GEORGIA

Charleston

Savannah

LOUISIANA
1812

Mobile

CEDED BY SPAIN 1819

St. Augustine

ATLANTIC

San Antonio

The Alamo

Galveston

ANNEXED
1810

ANNEXED
1813

New
Orleans

OCEAN

FLORIDA
1845

GULF OF MEXICO

Seminole War
1842

Tropic of Cancer

The Civil War, 1861-1865

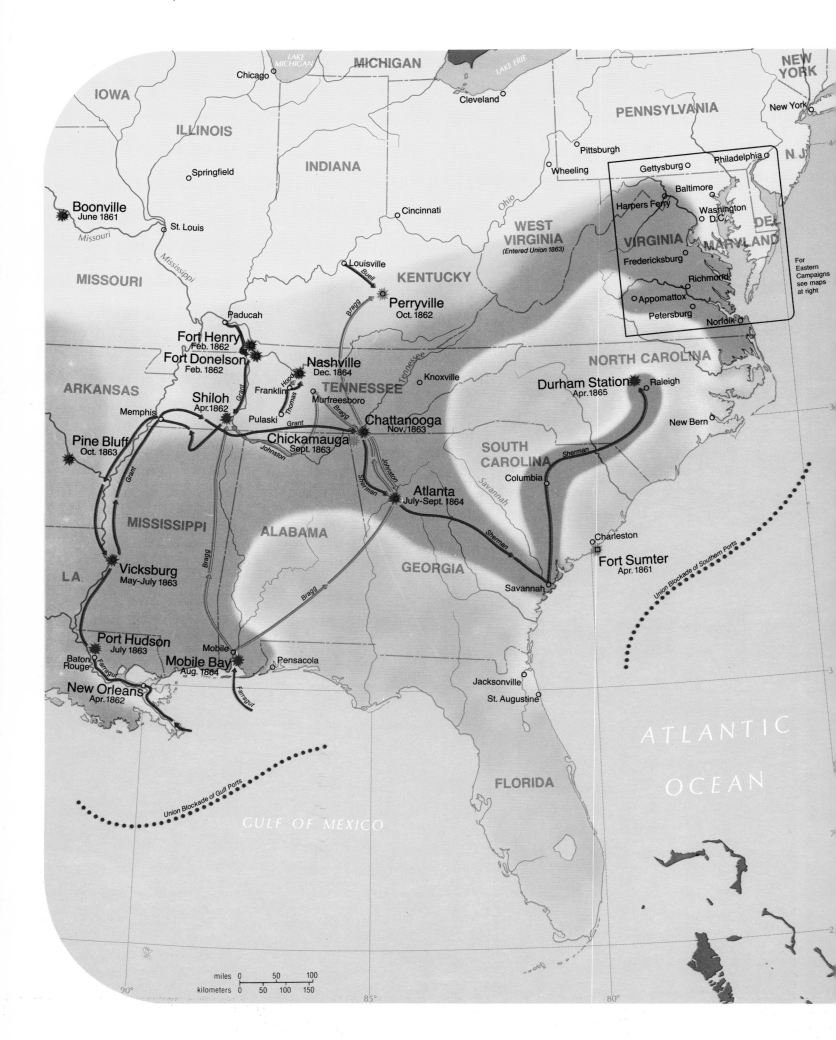

MICHIGAN

IOWA

ILLINOIS

INDIANA

Chicago

LAKE MICHIGAN

LAKE ERIE

Cleveland

NEW YORK

New York

PENNSYLVANIA

Springfield

Pittsburgh

Wheeling

N.J.

Gettysburg

Philadelphia

Cincinnati

WEST VIRGINIA
(Entered Union 1863)

Harpers Ferry

Baltimore

Washington D.C.

DEL.

Boonville
June 1861

St. Louis

Ohio

VIRGINIA

MARYLAND

Missouri

Louisville

Buell

KENTUCKY

Fredericksburg

Richmond

For Eastern Campaigns see maps at right

MISSOURI

Bragg

Perryville
Oct. 1862

Appomattox

Petersburg

Norfolk

Paducah

Fort Henry
Feb. 1862

Fort Donelson
Feb. 1862

Nashville
Dec. 1864

Tennessee

Knoxville

NORTH CAROLINA

ARKANSAS

Franklin

Hood

TENNESSEE

Durham Station
Apr. 1865

Raleigh

Shiloh
Apr. 1862

Thomas

Murfreesboro

Grant

Memphis

Pulaski

Bragg

Grant

Chattanooga
Nov. 1863

New Bern

Chickamauga
Sept. 1863

Johnston

SOUTH CAROLINA

Pine Bluff
Oct. 1863

Sherman

Columbia

Savannah

Grant

Johnston

Sherman

MISSISSIPPI

Atlanta
July-Sept. 1864

ALABAMA

Bragg

GEORGIA

Sherman

Charleston

Fort Sumter
Apr. 1861

Union Blockade of Southern Ports

Vicksburg
May-July 1863

LA.

Bragg

Savannah

Port Hudson
July 1863

Baton Rouge

Farragut

Mobile

Pensacola

Mobile Bay
Aug. 1864

New Orleans
Apr. 1862

Farragut

ATLANTIC

OCEAN

Jacksonville

St. Augustine

FLORIDA

Union Blockade of Gulf Ports

GULF OF MEXICO

miles 0 50 100

kilometers 0 50 100 150

90°

85°

80°

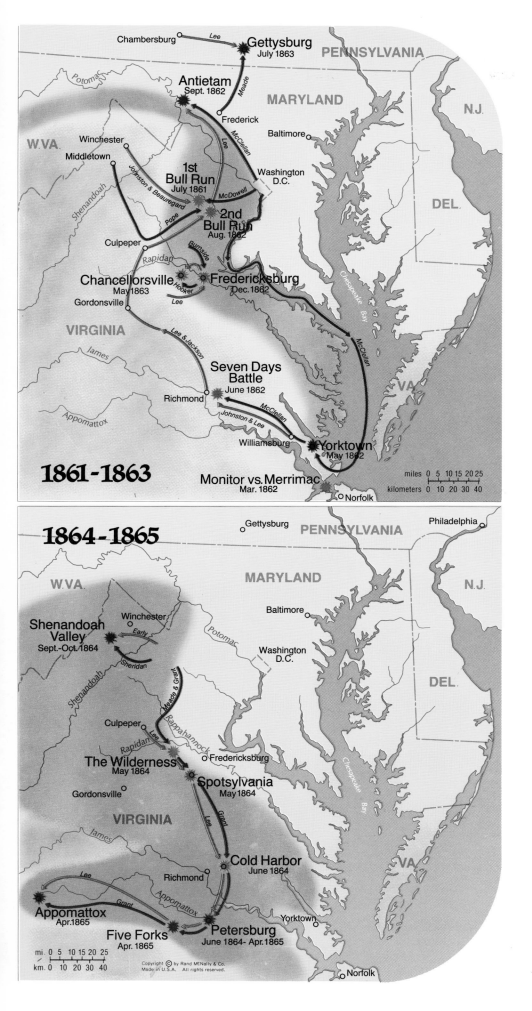

1861-1863

Chambersburg — Lee — **Gettysburg** July 1863

PENNSYLVANIA

Antietam Sept. 1862

MARYLAND

Frederick

Baltimore

N.J.

W.VA.

Winchester

Middletown

Potomac

DEL.

Washington D.C.

1st Bull Run July 1861

McDowell

2nd Bull Run Aug. 1862

Culpeper

Pope

Rapidan

Burnside

Chancellorsville May 1863

Hooker

Fredericksburg Dec. 1862

Gordonsville

Lee

VIRGINIA

James

Seven Days Battle June 1862

Richmond

Johnston & Lee

McClellan

Appomattox

Williamsburg

Yorktown May 1862

Monitor vs. Merrimac Mar. 1862

Norfolk

Chesapeake Bay

VA.

miles 0 5 10 15 20 25
kilometers 0 10 20 30 40

1864-1865

Gettysburg

PENNSYLVANIA

Philadelphia

W.VA.

MARYLAND

N.J.

Baltimore

Shenandoah Valley Sept.-Oct. 1864

Winchester

Early

Potomac

Sheridan

Washington D.C.

DEL.

Shenandoah

Meade & Grant

Culpeper

Rappahannock

Lee

Rapidan

Fredericksburg

The Wilderness May 1864

Spotsylvania May 1864

Gordonsville

Lee

Grant

VIRGINIA

James

Chesapeake Bay

Cold Harbor June 1864

Richmond

Appomattox

VA.

Appomattox Apr. 1865

Lee

Grant

Yorktown

Five Forks Apr. 1865

Petersburg June 1864- Apr. 1865

Norfolk

mi. 0 5 10 15 20 25
km. 0 10 20 30 40

Copyright © by Rand McNally & Co.
Made in U.S.A. All rights reserved.

BY THE 1860 PRESIDENTIAL ELECTION, it was clear that compromise on the issue of slavery could no longer hold the nation together. While the North vehemently denounced slave holding, the South as passionately defended its way of life against a "despotic" federal authority. Soon after Abraham Lincoln was elected president, the South seceded from the union and chose Jefferson Davis to head a new government in Richmond, Virginia. By May, 1861, the United States and the Confederacy were at war.

Both sides expected a quick end to the conflict. But after the decisive Confederate victory at Bull Run in July, the war bogged down. Not until early 1862 did the Union army, under George Brinton McClellen and Ulysses S. Grant, take the offensive, winning in the west at Fort Henry, Fort Donelson, and Shiloh. McClellen's subsequent move against Richmond, though supported by the Navy, was stopped by Confederate forces under the command of Robert E. Lee in the Seven Days battle. With the Union offensive stalled, Lee and Pope launched a Confederate invasion of the North, reaching Antietam before being pushed back into Virginia. But the Union losses at Fredericksburg and Chancellorsville encouraged Lee to attempt a second invasion. In July, 1863, he was defeated at Gettysburg in the most decisive battle of the war. That same month, Grant captured Vicksburg, and joining William Tecumseh Sherman, Commander of the Tennessee troops, went on to win at Chattanooga, driving the Confederate troops back into Georgia.

By 1864, the North's economic superiority and the Union naval blockade had become critical factors in the war. In May of that year, Grant and George Meade, Commander of the Army of the Potomac, made the final march on Richmond. Although defeated by Lee in the battle of the Wilderness, and again at Spotsylvania and Cold Harbor, Grant's well-supplied troops continued to press toward Richmond and Petersburg. In a coordinated effort, Sherman began his march to the sea, capturing Atlanta, Savannah, and Columbia before turning north to Raleigh. On April 9, 1865, Lee finally surrendered to Grant at Appomattox Court House: The Union had been preserved.

When the war ended, the nation had undergone profound changes. The Emancipation Proclamation had abolished slavery; the South's agricultural economy lay in ruins. But the conflict had awakened the industrial might of the North. If one way of life had been lost, another was already rising to take its place.

MAP LEGEND

Union

Union Penetration of Confederate Area 1862-1865

Confederate

Union Victory

Confederate Victory

Battle Indecisive

Union Forces

Confederate Forces

Western Frontiers, 1860-1890

THE FINAL SETTLEMENT of the West involved the greatest movement of people in the nation's history. In only 30 years—one generation after the Civil War—the "Great American Desert" had been transformed into the mineral and agricultural empire of the Republic.

The railroad boom of this era soon opened the plains and mountain-desert regions to settlement. Between 1869 and 1884, four transcontinental railways were built; along with the overland stage, they linked the industrial East to the West. In a few years, the railroads were shipping cattle and grain east, carrying mail and payrolls, helping to supply the frontier army, and bringing settlers, many of them immigrants, into western territories.

The first wave of settlers were miners. In the 1860s and '70s, gold and silver strikes in the Black Hills, Nevada, Colorado, Arizona, and Montana brought thousands of prospectors swarming into Indian lands. Inevitably, war broke out with tribes in the north and southwest. Although the Indians won isolated battles—the most famous at Little Big Horn—they could not prevail against the army's superior weapons. By 1887, the Indians and buffalo were gone from the open range.

Ranchers and farmers soon followed in the miners' wake. From the mid-1860s to the late 1880s, a vast cattle empire dominated Texas, Wyoming, and Montana. Cattle drives up the Chisholm and Sedalia trails helped inspire the romance of the cowboy, a figure that, like the notorious western outlaw, quickly passed into American legend. But the open range was short-lived. Sheepherders soon challenged the ranchers, and farmers began fencing off grazing land and planting crops in the semiarid soil. In the end, windmills and barbed wire tamed the West as effectively as the railroads and Colt repeating revolver.

By 1890, an almost continuous line of settlement stretched from the Midwest to the Pacific, and population in the territories had soared. The "frontier" had all but disappeared. Ten new states joined the Union, bringing with them the regional flavor of the West. Only the great waves of immigration in the early 1900s would compare with the extensive migration of this era.

MAP LEGEND

▨	Settled by 1890
▨	Indian Reservations 1880
—+—+—	Railroads
———	Trails West
———	Buffalo Herds 1870
– – –	Cattle Trails
✕	Mining
✸	Indian Battle
✸	Incident of Violence
1867	Dates of Admission

SCALE

miles	0	50	100	150	200	250
kilometers	0	100	200	300	400	

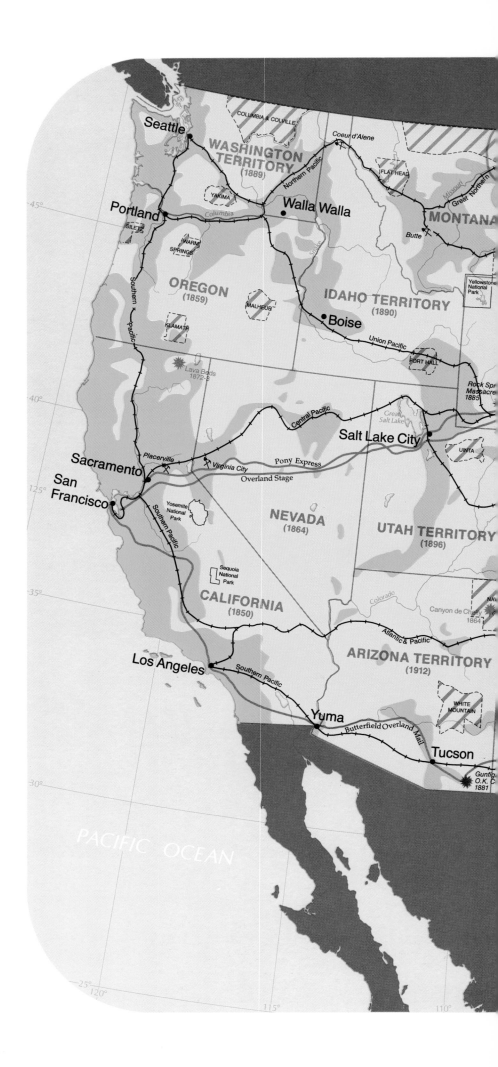

GROS VENTRE & BLACKFEET

r Paw
untain

TERRITORY
89)

Little Big Horn
1876

CROW

Johnson
County Invasion
Circa, 1890

Dull Knife
1876

RIVER
&
OSHONE

WYOMING
TERRITORY
(1890)

Creek
1879

Laramie

Cheyenne

Denver

Leadville

COLORADO
(1876)

Durango

Santa Fe

NEW MEXICO
TERRITORY
(1912)

Billy the Kid Killed
July 14, 1881

Lincoln County War
1875-1881

FORT
STANTON

El Paso

Lower
Emigrant

Southern
Pacific
Trail

Rio Grande

BERTHOLD

NORTH
DAKOTA
(Part of Dakota Territory until 1889)

DEVILS LAKE

RED LAKE

LAKE SUPERIOR

Northern Pacific

LAKE HURON

Northern Pacific

Bismarck

LAKE
TRAVERSE

MINNESOTA

Great Northern

St. Paul

Minneapolis

End of James-Younger Gang
Northfield September 7, 1876

SOUTH
DAKOTA
(Part of Dakota Territory until 1889)

SIOUX

Deadwood

Wounded
Knee 1890

Younger Brothers Captured
Madelia September 11, 1876

WISCONSIN

MICHIGAN

LAKE MICHIGAN

IOWA

Chicago

LAKE ERIE

Cleveland

NEBRASKA
(1867)

Des Moines

OHIO

Union Pacific

Ogallala

Omaha

James-Younger
First Train Robbery
July 21, 1873

ILLINOIS

INDIANA

Platte

Pony Express

Overland Stage

St. Joseph

Cincinnati

Jesse James
First Bank Robbery
February 14, 1866

W.V.

Union Pacific

Salina

Abilene

St. Louis

KANSAS
(1861)

Sedalia

James Brothers
Train Robbery
Oct. 3, 1879

KENTUCKY

VA.

Sand Creek
1864

MISSOURI

Dodge City

Wichita

Coffeyville

TENNESSEE

N.C.

Adobe Walls 1874

CHEYENNE

CHEROKEE

ARKANSAS

Chattanooga

S.C.

INDIAN TERRITORY
(OKLAHOMA 1907)

CREEK

Judge Parkers
Federal Court

GEORGIA

Santa Fe   Ft. Smith

ARRAPAHOE

CHICKASAW

APACHE

CHOCTAW

ALABAMA

Western Trail

Dallas

Fort Worth

Chisholm Trail

Sedalia Trail

LOUISIANA

MISSISSIPPI

Mobile

FLORIDA

Overland Mail

Butterfield

Lake
Pontchartrain

Pecos Trail

TEXAS

Houston

New Orleans

Judge Roy Bean

San Antonio

Butterfield Overland Mail

Illinois Central

Mississippi

Ohio

95°   90°   85°

Immigration's Impact, 1910

FOR THE FIRST ONE HUNDRED YEARS of its history, the United States opened its doors to all nationalities. Often war, famine, or oppression drove millions of people from their homelands to American shores. The accompanying map depicts where these immigrants and the children of mixed or foreign parentage had settled by 1910.

European immigrants who arrived before, and two decades after, the Civil War, came primarily from England and Ireland, Scandinavia, and Germany. While the Irish tended to remain in the eastern cities, other immigrants seized the chance to journey westward to Oregon, then later to the northern plains states and parts of Texas and California. Many were skilled farmers and artisans, and blended quickly into the mainstream of American life. By the early 1900s, however, the character of immigration had changed considerably. Conditions in eastern and southern Europe led over eight million people to make the arduous journey across the Atlantic. Most of these immigrants, illiterate and unskilled, crowded into the poorer sections of industrial cities such as New York, Boston, and Chicago, creating ethnic communities that insulated them from the language and customs of their new country. Yet they answered industry's insatiable demand for labor, and filled the factories, mines, textile and steel mills, stockyards and railroads, helping to build the industrial might of the nation.

On the West Coast, the Chinese and Japanese did not fare as well. Their numbers alarmed American workers, and in 1882, the first in a series of immigration laws was passed, restricting the entry of Asians into the United States. Mexicans and Latin Americans entering California and the southwestern states often encountered the same resistance and hostility.

In contrast, since the South lacked both heavy industry and available land, immigrants tended to bypass this region in favor of the North and West. Also, restrictive state immigration laws made it difficult for the foreign-born to settle in the South.

The constant stream of newcomers helped create a rich and varied culture in America, making it truly a "nation of nations." Immigrants, and the children of immigrants, contributed immeasurably to the country's industry, science, and arts, and in two world wars, served their new country with distinction.

MAP LEGEND

Immigrants

Foreign born whites and children of foreign or mixed parentage; by counties.

Source: U.S. Decennial Census, 1910

- Less Than 10%
- 10% To 25%
- 25% To 50%
- 50% To 75%
- 75% & Over

MONTANA 94,713 Total Foreign born population in 1910

SCALE

miles 0 — 100 — 200 — 300 — 400

kilometers 0 — 200 — 400 — 600

NORTH DAKOTA
156,654

MINNESOTA
543,595

SOUTH DAKOTA
100,790

Minneapolis

WISCONSIN
512,865

Milwaukee

MICHIGAN
591,650

LAKE SUPERIOR

LAKE HURON

LAKE MICHIGAN

Detroit

LAKE ONTARIO

LAKE ERIE

MAINE
110,562

VT.
49,921

N.H.
96,667

Boston

NEW YORK
2,748,011

MASS.
1,059,245

CONN.
329,874

R.I.
179,141

Buffalo

NEBRASKA
176,662

IOWA
273,765

Chicago

ILLINOIS
1,205,314

INDIANA
159,663

Cleveland

OHIO
598,374

PENNSYLVANIA
1,442,374

Pittsburgh

Newark

New York

N.J.
590,788

Philadelphia

Baltimore

DEL.
17,492

Missouri

Kansas
City

St. Louis

MISSOURI
229,779

Cincinnati

Ohio

WEST
VIRGINIA
57,218

Washington
D.C.
24,902

MARYLAND
104,943

KANSAS
135,450

KENTUCKY
40,162

VIRGINIA
27,057

Nashville

NORTH CAROLINA
6,092

OKLAHOMA
40,442

ARKANSAS
17,046

TENNESSEE
18,607

Atlanta

SOUTH
CAROLINA
6,179

Mississippi

TEXAS
241,938

MISSISSIPPI
9,770

ALABAMA
19,286

GEORGIA
15,477

LOUISIANA
52,766

New Orleans

Jacksonville

FLORIDA
40,633

San Antonio

ATLANTIC

OCEAN

GULF OF MEXICO

Tropic of Cancer

The U.S. in World War II, 1941-1945

MAP LEGEND

Allied Powers
Axis Powers
Axis Controlled Areas
Neutral Nations
Battles
Allied Advances

THE UNITED STATES entered World War II almost totally unprepared to fight on the two fronts of Europe and the Pacific. Yet its vast industrial capacity proved to be a decisive factor in the Allied victory, and eventually thrust America into a position of world leadership. Early in the war, however, the Axis alliance seemed invincible.

By 1942, Germany had swept through most of Europe, isolated Great Britain, and launched an invasion of Russia. In North Africa, Rommel, Commander of German forces, threatened the vital Suez Canal. Russian leader, Joseph Stalin desperately called for a "second front" in Europe to relieve his hard-pressed troops, but the Allies were unprepared to invade the continent. Instead, in November, 1942, Dwight D. Eisenhower, U.S. General and Allied Supreme commander in North Africa, led a coordinated attack on Morocco and Algeria, and by May of the next year had driven the Axis powers out of North Africa. Bolstered by American material, Soviet troops regained the offensive in the 1942-43 winter war and began forcing the Germans back toward Berlin. Finally, after an ill-advised invasion of Sicily, the Allies landed on the beaches of Normandy and southern France in June, 1944. Caught between advancing Russian and Allied troops, Ger-

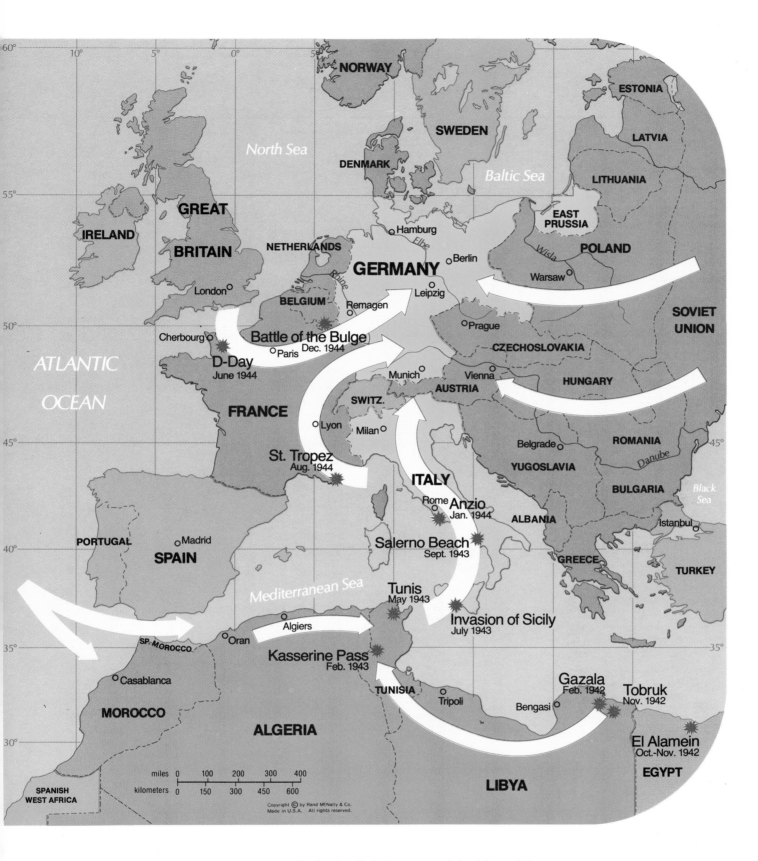

North Sea

Baltic Sea

NORWAY

SWEDEN

ESTONIA

LATVIA

LITHUANIA

DENMARK

EAST
PRUSSIA

POLAND

SOVIET
UNION

GREAT
BRITAIN

IRELAND

NETHERLANDS

○Hamburg

○Berlin

Warsaw○

Elbe

Wisla

GERMANY

○Leipzig

BELGIUM

London○

Remagen

Battle of the Bulge
Dec. 1944

○Prague

CZECHOSLOVAKIA

Cherbourg○

Paris○

D-Day
June 1944

Munich○

Vienna○

AUSTRIA

HUNGARY

ATLANTIC

OCEAN

FRANCE

SWITZ.

○Lyon

Milan○

Belgrade○

ROMANIA

Danube

St. Tropez
Aug. 1944

ITALY

YUGOSLAVIA

BULGARIA

Black
Sea

PORTUGAL

Madrid○

SPAIN

Rome○ Anzio
Jan. 1944

ALBANIA

Istanbul○

Salerno Beach
Sept. 1943

GREECE

TURKEY

Mediterranean Sea

Tunis
May 1943

Algiers○

SP. MOROCCO

Oran○

Invasion of Sicily
July 1943

Kasserine Pass
Feb. 1943

Casablanca○

TUNISIA

Tripoli○

Bengasi○

Gazala
Feb. 1942

Tobruk
Nov. 1942

MOROCCO

ALGERIA

LIBYA

El Alamein
Oct.-Nov. 1942

EGYPT

SPANISH
WEST AFRICA

miles 0   100   200   300   400
kilometers 0   150   300   450   600

many surrendered on May 7, 1945.

In the early months of the Pacific war, Japan had quickly overrun Manchuria, Southeast Asia, Singapore, and Indonesia and gained control of the seas. But by 1942, Allied forces had defeated the Japanese navy at Coral Sea, Midway, and Solomon Islands, and in 1944, destroyed the remaining fleet at Leyte Gulf. Douglas MacArthur, Commander of the U.S. Forces in the Far East, liberated the Philippines in October of that year and, with Chester Nimitz, Commander of the U.S. Pacific Fleet, launched a two-pronged attack toward Japan. Capturing one island after another, American forces were soon poised to invade the Japanese mainland. Instead, in early August, 1945, the first atomic bombs were exploded over Hiroshima and Nagasaki. Japan surrendered on August 14.

The war had profoundly changed the world. The United States and Russia now faced one another as rival superpowers over a divided Europe, and the spectre of the atom bomb haunted the world. As people returned to peacetime, it was hoped that the newly chartered United Nations would provide a forum for all nations to seek peaceful solutions to world problems and to begin to build a more lasting peace throughout the world.

A Nation on the Move, 1940-1970

WHENEVER OPPORTUNITY HAS DIMINISHED in one region, Americans have pulled out and moved on—traditionally to the West and North where jobs or land seemed more plentiful. In the last two decades, however, more people have been migrating to the suburbs of major cities and to the West and South in search of greater opportunities. The accompanying map reflects some of these regional changes for the period 1940 to 1970.

Until the late 1950s, the "industrial belt"—stretching from the Northeast to St. Louis—continued to attract businesses and labor. Thousands of blacks from the South and whites from Appalachia migrated North to the great cities, while inner-city whites moved to the rapidly growing suburbs. By the late 1950s and early 1960s, many light industries were also leaving the inner city not only for the suburbs but for the "Sunbelt" of the West and South where labor and energy costs were lower and tax incentives more attractive. In addition, a growing aerospace and electronics industry drew a large, highly skilled work force to Florida, Texas, and California. As a result, though the suburbs continued their explosive growth, the inner-city areas of most northern cities began losing population as steadily as the South and West were gaining it.

Changing American lifestyles also contributed to the exodus to warmer climates. The ecology movement of the 1960s encouraged people to escape from crowded industrial areas to less developed sections in the Southwest and Pacific states. In contrast, rural areas—particularly the drier western states—were losing population as people sought employment in cities and the new industrial regions. More retired people looked to the "sunbelt" as a place to enjoy their later years. Soon retirement and leisure communities were springing up in Florida, Arizona, and California, turning swampland and desert into "model cities."

By 1970, the restless search for a better life had broken down old regional ties and created new communities and industrial areas in the South and West. Not only were lifestyles changing, there was a shift from heavy industry and manufacturing to light industry and service-oriented businesses. Cities in the northern regions—built by the old industries—struggled to regain their vitality. As the shift in population continues, it remains to be seen what type of society will emerge from this latest American migration.

MAP LEGEND

Population Increased 1940-1970

Population Decreased 1940-1970

Population Increased and Decreased 1940-1970

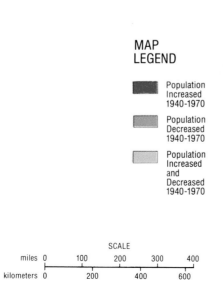

SCALE

| miles | 0 | 100 | 200 | 300 | 400 |

| kilometers | 0 | 200 | 400 | 600 |

U.S. Historical Tables

The tables below reflect three major movements in American history—the filling out of the nation's boundaries, the flow of immigrants entering the United States, and the latest trends in population shifts. These figures depict a nation in a state of constant change and development.

THE EXPANDING NATION

State	Date Admitted	No.	State	Date Admitted	No.	State	Date Admitted	No.
Alabama	Dec. 14, 1819	22	Louisiana	April 30, 1812	18	Ohio	March 1, 1803	17
Alaska	Jan 3, 1959	49	Maine	March 15, 1820	23	Oklahoma	Nov. 16, 1907	46
Arizona	Feb. 24, 1912	48	Maryland	April 28, 1788	7	Oregon	Feb. 14, 1859	33
Arkansas	June 15, 1836	25	Massachusetts	Feb. 6, 1788	6	Pennsylvania	Dec. 12, 1787	2
California	Sept. 9, 1850	31	Michigan	Jan. 26, 1837	26	Rhode Island	May 29, 1790	13
Colorado	Aug. 1, 1876	38	Minnesota	May 11, 1858	32	South Carolina	May 23, 1788	8
Connecticut	Jan. 9, 1788	5	Mississippi	Dec. 10, 1817	20	South Dakota	Nov. 2, 1889	40
Delaware	Dec. 7, 1787	1	Missouri	Aug. 10, 1821	24	Tennessee	June 1, 1796	16
Florida	March 3, 1845	27	Montana	Nov. 8, 1889	41	Texas	Dec. 29, 1845	28
Georgia	Jan. 2, 1788	4	Nebraska	March 1, 1867	37	Utah	Jan. 4, 1896	45
Hawaii	Aug. 21, 1959	50	Nevada	Oct. 31, 1864	36	Vermont	March 4, 1791	14
Idaho	July 3, 1890	43	New Hampshire	June 21, 1788	9	Virginia	June 25, 1788	10
Illinois	Dec. 3, 1818	21	New Jersey	Dec. 18, 1787	3	Washington	Nov. 11, 1889	42
Indiana	Dec. 11, 1816	19	New Mexico	Jan. 6, 1912	47	West Virginia	June 20, 1863	35
Iowa	Dec. 28, 1846	29	New York	July 26, 1788	11	Wisconsin	May 29, 1848	30
Kansas	Jan. 29, 1861	34	North Carolina	Nov. 21, 1789	12	Wyoming	July 10, 1890	44
Kentucky	June 1, 1792	15	North Dakota	Nov. 2, 1889	39			

A NATION OF IMMIGRANTS: 1851-1950

Region	1851-60	1861-70	1871-80	1881-90	1891-1900	1901-10	1911-20	1921-30	1931-40	1941-50
Europe—Northern and Western England, Scotland, Ireland, Germany, Denmark, Norway, Sweden, Finland, Netherlands, Belgium, Switzerland, France	2,431,336	2,031,642	2,070,373	3,778,633	1,643,492	1,910,035	906,730	1,127,194	1,850,078	242,178
Europe—Southern and Eastern Italy, Poland, Bulgaria, Austria-Hungary, Greece, Rumania, Yugoslavia, Portugal, Spain, U.S.S.R., Turkey, Czechoslovakia	21,319	33,491	200,888	957,731	1,915,204	6,186,036	3,370,259	1,154,883	135,751	125,307
Asia China, Japan	41,455	64,487	123,350	63,981	40,741	150,402	105,115	63,369	6,876	18,264
America Canada, Mexico, Latin America, West Indies	74,720	166,607	404,044	426,967	38,972	361,888	1,143,671	1,516,716	160,037	354,804
Other Countries Australia, New Zealand, Pacific Islands, and African countries	29,379	17,969	12,062	14,220	18,378	53,915	21,870	15,012	4,761	26,609

REGIONAL TRENDS IN POPULATION: 1960 to 1990

Region	1960	1970	1980	1990	Per Cent Change		
					1960-70	1970-80	(Projected) 1980-90
Northeast Maine, New Hampshire, New York, New Jersey, Vermont, Rhode Island, Massachusetts, Connecticut, Pennsylvania	44,678,000	49,061,000	49,137,000	49,314,000	9.8%	.2%	.4%
North Central Ohio, Indiana, Illinois, Michigan, Wisconsin, Minnesota, Iowa, Missouri, North Dakota, South Dakota, Nebraska, Kansas	51,619,000	56,590,000	58,854,000	61,224,000	9.6	4.0	4.0
South Delaware, Maryland, Virginia, District of Columbia, West Virginia, North Carolina, South Carolina, Georgia, Kentucky, Florida, Tennessee, Alabama, Mississippi, Arkansas, Louisiana, Oklahoma, Texas	54,973,000	62,813,000	75,349,000	91,065,000	14.3	20.0	20.9
West Montana, Idaho, Wyoming, Colorado, New Mexico, Arizona, Utah, Nevada, Washington, Oregon, California, Hawaii, Alaska	28,053,000	34,838,000	43,165,000	53,826,000	24.2	23.9	24.7

Index of alternative place names

There has been no attempt to standardise the spelling of place names in this Atlas. Many places have changed their names in the course of history; many different forms of transcription or romanisation have been used for oriental names; and many places, especially the best-known ones, are more familiar to English-speaking readers in their modern, Anglicised form than in the vernacular which may be more common for their less-well-known neighbours. The maps in this Atlas reflect this diversity. Rather than attempt to impose any rule of thumb – such as modern internationally-accepted spellings – the editor has asked the contributors to use the spellings and forms which students in their particular fields are most likely to encounter in their reading on the subject. Thus two maps of the same area, separated in date by two or three hundred years, may show minor differences. Sometimes, also, local forms are shown, sometimes Anglicised ones. It is hoped that these differences will be aids to general clarity rather than confusion.

The list that follows is intended to be a guide to the major places that have changed their names significantly over the centuries. Minor variations, modernisations or Anglicisations have been ignored; but where cultural, political or linguistic developments have given rise to entirely new names, these are listed below. The modern forms, given in bold type, are those to be found in *The Times Atlas of the World* (6th ed., 1980); the variants are mostly to be found on the maps in the present volume. The main entry for each place is listed under its modern spelling with its variants in roughly chronological order; a major (though not necessarily the only) map reference has also been given.

Only town names, sites of battles, archaeological sites and some rivers have been included in this list. The names of regions and countries, which have changed in both name and area too much to be included in a list of this kind, are to be found in the main index.

Aachen (West Germany) – Aquisgranum, Aix-la-Chapelle 22
Abarshahr *see* Neyshabur
Abila (Syria) – Seleuceia 9
Aboba *see* Pliska
Abrotonum *see* Sabratah
Abydus *see* Canakkale
Acre *see* 'Akko
Adalia *see* Antalya
Adana (Turkey) – Antiocheia 9
Adrianople *see* Edirne
Aela *see* Aqaba
Aelia Capitolina *see* Jerusalem
Afamiyah (Syria) – Apamea 26
Agedincum *see* Sens
Agram *see* Zagreb
Agrigento (Sicily) – Agrigentum, Acragas 8
Ahvaz (Iran) – Ahwaz 27
Aix-en-Provence – Aquae, Aquae Sextiae 25
Aix-la-Chapelle *see* Aachen
Ajodhan *see* Pakpattan
Akhtiar *see* Sebastopol
'Akko (Israel) – Acre, Ptolemais, St Jean d'Acre 26
Akşehir (Turkey) – Philomelium 19, 26
Alaşehir (Turkey) – Philadelphia 26
Alba Julia (Romania) – Apulum, Gyulafehérvár, Karlsburg 13
Albany (New York, USA) – Fort Orange 38
Albertville *see* Kalémié
Aleppo (Syria) – Beroea, Halab 87
Alexandretta *see* Iskenderun
Alexandria *see* Arbil, Ghazni, Herat
Alexandria (Egypt) – El Iskandariya 19
Alexandria in Arachosia *see* Kandahar
Alexandria Troas *see* Eski Stambul
Alexandrov (USSR) – Alexandrovskaya Sloboda 43
Al-Faramah *see* Pelusium
Algiers (Algeria) – Icosium, Alger 74
Al-Hillah (Iraq) – Kufa, Kafa 27
Aligarh (Rajasthan, India) – Koil 29
Al Khal *see* Hebron
Allahabad (Uttar Pradesh, India) – Prayāga 65
Allenstein *see* Olsztyn
Alma-Ata (Kazakhstan, USSR) – Vernyy 71
Al Quds *see* Jerusalem
Amasra (Turkey) – Amastris 19
Ambiani *see* Amiens
Ambon (Moluccas) – Amboina 39
Amfissa (Greece) – Salona 26
Amga (USSR) – Amginsk 70
Amid, Amida *see* Diyarbakir

Amiens (France) – Samarobriva, Ambian 25
Amisea *see* Amasya
Amisus *see* Samsun
Amman (Jordan) – Philadelphia 87
Ammochostos *see* Famagusta
Amphipolis *see* Thapsacus
Amselfeld *see* Kosovo
Anazarbus *see* Dijhan
Anas, R *see* Guadiana, R
Ancyra *see* Ankara
An-i *see* Ho-tung
Ankara (Turkey) – Ancyra 87
'Annaba (Algeria) – Hippo Regius, Bône 17
Anping (Taiwan) – Anpeijo 39
Antakya (Turkey) – Antiochia, Antioch 26
Antalya (Turkey) – Attalia, Adalia 26
Antibes (France) – Antipolis
Antietam *see* Sharpsburg
Antiocheia *see* Adana, Antakya, Gerasa, Mallus, Mary, Nusaybin, Tarsus Cayi
Antiocheia-Edessa *see* Urfa
Antiochia in Pisidia *see* Yalvaç
Antipolis *see* Antibes
Apamea *see* Afamiyah, Celaenae, Kala'at el Medik, Mudanya
Aparri (Philippines) – Kagayan 39
Apulum *see* Alba Julia
Aqaba (Jordan) – Aela 87
Aquae, Aquae Sextiae *see* Aix-en-Provence
Aquileia *see* Cividale del Friuli
Aquincum *see* Budapest
Aquisgranum *see* Aachen
Aradus (Syria) – Arvad, Ruad, Rowad 26
Arausio *see* Orange
Arbil (Iraq) – Arbela, Alexandria 6
Archangel *see* Arkhangelsk
Arelate *see* Arles
Argentoratum *see* Strasbourg
Ariha *see* Jericho
Ariminum *see* Rimini
Arkhangelsk (USSR) – Archangel 70
Arles (France) – Arelate 25
Arsinoe *see* Patara
Artashat (Armenia, USSR) – Artazata 13
Arvad *see* Aradus
Ashdod (Israel) – Azotus 9
Ash Sham *see* Damascus
Ashur *see* Sharqat
Ashqelon (Israel) – Ascalon, Ashkelon, Tel Ashqelon 26
Asido *see* Medina Sidonia
Atri (Italy) – Hadria 8
Attalia *see* Antalya

Augsburg (West Germany) – Augusta Vindelicorum 28
Augst (Switzerland) – Augusta Rauricorrum 8
Augusta Taurinorum *see* Turin
Augusta Treverorum *see* Trier
Augusta Vindelicorum *see* Augsburg
Auschwitz *see* Oświęcim
Auximium *see* Osimo
Avaricum *see* Bourges
Avignon (France) – Avenio 54
Avlona *see* Vlore
Aylah *see* Elat
Azotus *see* Ashdod

Baalbek (Lebanon) – Heliopolis 8
Bactria *see* Balkh
Baeterrae *see* Béziers
Bagrationovsk (USSR) – Eylan
Baile Atha Cliath *see* Dublin
Balchik (Bulgaria) – Dionysiopolis 18
Balkh (Afghanistan) – Bactria 27
Bambyce *see* Membij
Bandar Abbas (Iran) – Gombroon
Bangkok (Thailand) – Krung Thep 86
Banjul (The Gambia) – Bathurst 74
Banten (Java, Indonesia) – Bantam 39
Bardaa *see* Dashkesan
Barygaza *see* Bharuch
Batavia *see* Djakarta
Bathurst *see* Banjul
Bayonne (France) – Lapurdum 54
Beç *see* Vienna
Beijing (China) – Khanbalik, Peking 40
Beirūt (Lebanon) – Berytus, Laodiceia 87
Beja (Portugal) – Pax Iulia 8
Bejaïa (Algeria) – Bougie 28
Belgrade *see* Beograd
Belkis (Turkey) – Cyzicus 14
Belostok *see* Bialystok
Belvoir (Israel) – Kaukab 26
Benares *see* Varanasi
Beograd (Yugoslavia) – Singidunum, Belgrade 63
Berenice (Egypt) – Berghāzi
Bergama (Pergamum) 8
Bergen *see* Mons
Berghāzi *see* Berenice
Berroea *see* Aleppo, Stara Zagora
Berytus *see* Beirūt
Beseire (Iraq) – Ciresium 14
Béziers (France) – Baeterrae 16
Bharuch (Gujarat, India) – Barygaza, Broach 65
Bialystok (Poland) – Belostok 77
Bishapur *see* Shapur
Bitola (Yugoslavia) – Monastir 63
Bituriges *see* Bourges
Bizerte (Tunisia) – Hippo Zarytus, Bizerta
Boğazköy (Turkey) – Hattusha, Hattushash, Pteria 4
Bologna (Italy) – Bononia, Felsina 32
Bône *see* Annaba
Bononia *see* Bologna, Boulogne, Vidin
Bor (Turkey) – Tyana 19, 26
Bordeaux (France) – Burdigala 13, 16
Borysthenes, R *see* Dnepr/Dnieper, R
Bosporus *see* Kerč
Bougie *see* Bejaïa
Boulogne (France) – Bononia, Gesoriacum 16
Bourges (France) – Avaricum, Bituriges 16
Braga (Portugal) – Bracara 16
Brasov (Romania) – Koronstadt 52
Bratislava (Czechoslovakia) – Pressburg 77
Braunschweig (West Germany) – Brunswick 52
Brecia *see* Wroclaw
Breslau *see* Wroclaw
Bressanone (Italy) – Brixen 32
Brindisi (Italy) – Brundisium 62
Brixen *see* Bressanone
Brno (Czechoslovakia) – Brünn 77
Broach *see* Baruch
Brundisium *see* Brindisi

Brünn *see* Brno
Brunswick *see* Braunschweig
Budapest (Hungary) – Aquincum 77
Buffavento (Cyprus) – Koützivendi 21
Bulandshahr (Uttar Pradesh, India) – Baran 29
Burdigala *see* Bourdeaux
Byblos *see* Jubail
Byzantium *see* Istanbul

Cádiz (Spain) – Gades 33
Caerleon (Wales) – Isca 13, 16
Caernarvon (Wales) – Segontia 25
Caesaraugusta *see* Zaragoza
Caesarea *see* Cherchell, Viayspri
Caesarodunum *see* Tours
Cairo (Egypt) – Fustat 19
Calah *see* Nimrud
Calicut (Kerala, India) – Kozhikode 29
Callinicium *see* Raqqa
Camulodunum *see* Colchester
Canakkale (Turkey) – Abydus 26
Canakkale Boğazi *see* Dardanelles
Candia *see* Iraklion
Canterbury (England) – Cantuaria 25
Canton *see* Guangzhou
Cantuaria *see* Canterbury
Carrhae (Turkey) – Haran, Altinbasak 8
Cartagena (Spain) – Carthago Nova 33
Carthago Nova *see* Cartagena
Castabala (Turkey) – Hierapolis 9
Castra Regina *see* Regensburg
Cawnpore *see* Kanpur
Celaenae (Iran) – Apamea 9
Cenabum *see* Orléans
Cenevo *see* Cherven
Cerigo *see* Kythira
Cernauti *see* Chernovtsy
Ceuta (North Africa) – Sebta, Septem 27
Chalcedon *see* Kadikoy, Usküdar
Chalcis (Greece) – Negroponte 26
Ch'ang-an *see* Xian
Chemnitz *see* Karl-Marx-Stadt
Cherchell (Algeria) – Caesarea 17
Chernovtsy (Ukraine, USSR) – Cernauti, Czernowitz 76
Cherven (USSR) – Cenevo 19
Chester (England) – Deva 25
Chittaurgarh (Rajasthan, India) – Chitor 29
Chiu-yuan (North China) – Wu-yuan 13
Chu (North China) – Tzu-ch'uan 13
Chü-yen *see* Hsi-hai
Circesium *see* Beseire
Cirta *see* Constantine
Citium *see* Larnaka
Cividale del Friuli (Italy) – Aquileia 32
Claudiopolis *see* Bolu, Mut
Cluj (Romania) – Klausenburg, Kolozsvár 81
Colchester (England) – Camulodunum 8
Cologne *see* Köln
Colonia Agrippina *see* Köln
Constanta (Romania) – Tomi 77
Constantia *see* Famagusta
Constantine (Algeria) – Cirta 8
Constantinople, Constantinopolis *see* Istanbul
Corcyra *see* Corfu
Córdoba (Spain) – Córdova, Karmona 33
Corfu (Greece) – Corcyra, Kerkira 63
Cracow *see* Kraków
Crocodilopolis *see* Patara
Crown Point (Quebec) – Fort St Frédéric
Ctesiphon *see* Madain
Cuddalore *see* Fort St David
Cursat *see* Quseir, El
Cyrene *see* Shahhat
Czernowitz *see* Chernovtsy

Dabiq *see* Kilis
Dagon *see* Rangoon

Dakar (Senegal) – Goree 50
Damascus (Syria) – Ash Sham, Dimashq 87
Damietta *see* Dumyât
Da Nang (Vietnam) – Suran, Tourane 39
Danube, R – Danuvius, Ister, R
Danzig *see* Gdansk
Dara *see* Mardin
Dardanelles (Turkey) – Hellespont, Canakkale Boğazi
Daśapura *see* Mandasore
Dashkesan (Azerblaijan, USSR) – Bardaa 27
Denizli (Turkey) – Laodicea 18
Detroit (Michigan, USA) – Fort Pontchartrain 69
Deva *see* Chester
Dijhan (Turkey) – Anazarbus 16
Dimashq *see* Damascus
Dionysiopolis *see* Balchik
Diyarbakir (Turkey) – Amida, Amid 16, 17, 19
Djakarta (Java, Indonesia) – Batavia, Sunda Kalapa, Jakarta 39, 50, 73
Dnepr/Dnieper, R (USSR) – Borysthenes, R
Dnepropetrovsk (Ukraine, USSR) – Yekaterinoslav, Ekaterinoslav 81
Dnestr, R (USSR) – Tgras, R
Donetsk (Ukraine, USSR) – Stalino, Yuzovka 83
Dorpat *see* Tartu
Dorylaeum *see* Eskisehir
Dorystolum *see* Silistra
Dover (England) – Dubris 25
Dovin (Armenia, SSR) – Dvin 18
Dublin (Irish Republic) – Baile Atha Cliath 25
Dubrovnik (Yugoslavia) – Ragusa 28
Dumyât (Egypt) – Damietta 28
Dura-Europus *see* Qalat es-Salihiya
Durius, R *see* Douro, R
Durocortorum *see* Reims
Dürres (Albania) – Epidamnus, Dyrrachium, Durazzo 77
Dushanbe (USSR) – Stalinabad
Dvin *see* Dovin
Dyrrachium *see* Dürres

Eboracum *see* York
Ebro, R (Spain) – Iberus, R
Eburacum *see* York
Ebusos *see* Ibiza
Ecbatana *see* Hamadan
Ed Dimas (Tunisia) – Thapsus 8
Edessa *see* Urfa
Edirne (Turkey) – Adrianople, Hadrianopolis 77
Edo *see* Tokyo
Elat (Israel) – Eilat, Aylah 87
Elblag (Poland) – Elbing 34
El Faiyum (Egypt) – Fayyum 27
Elisabethville *see* Lubumbashi 66
El Iskandariya *see* Alexandria
El Manshah (Libya) – Ptolemais, Barka, El Marj 17
Elmina (Ghana) – Saõ Horge da Mina
Elne *see* Perpignan
Emerita *see* Mérida
Emesa *see* Homs
Emona *see* Ljubljana
Epidauros, Epidavros (Greece) – Zaptat 7
Erech (Iraq) – Uruk 3
Eregli *see* Marmaraeglisi
Ermenek (Turkey) – Germanicopolis 19
Erzurum (Turkey) – Theodosiopolis, Qaliqala 17
Eshnunna *see* Tell Asmar
Eskisehir (Turkey) – Dorylaeum 17
Eski Stambul (Turkey) – Alexandria Troas 8
Esztergom (Hungary) – Gran 34
Étaples (France) – Quentovic 24
Europus *see* Shahr Rey
Eusebeia *see* Kayseri
Eylan *see* Bagrationovsk
Ezo *see* Hokkaido

183

Recife (Brazil)–Pernambuco 59
Red Sea–Sinus Arabicus
Regensburg (West Germany)–Castra Regina, Ratisbon 23
Reims (France)–Durocortorum, Rheims 49
Réka Dévnja (Bulgaria)–Marcianopolis 14
Reval *see* Tallinn
Rhaedestus *see* Tekirdag
Rhagae *see* Shahr Rey
Rheims *see* Reims
Rijeka (Yugoslavia)–Fiume 82
Rimini (Italy)–Ariminum 8
Rouen (France)–Rotomagus 49
Rowad *see* Aradus
Ruad *see* Aradus
Ryojun *see* Lushun

Sabratah (Libya)–Abrotonum 17
Sadowa *see* Hradec Králové
Saida (Syria)–Sidon 5
Saigon *see* Ho Chi Minh City
St Albans (England)–Verulamium 8
St Jean d'Acre *see* 'Akko
Sakhalin (USSR)–Karafuto 73
Salamis *see* Famagusta
Salekhard (USSR)–Obdorsk 71
Salona *see* Amfissa
Salonae *see* Split
Salonica *see* Thessaloniki
Samarkand (USSR)–Maracanda 70
Samarobriva *see* Amiens
Samsat (Turkey)–Samosata 12
Samsun (Turkey)–Amisus 18
Santa Isabel *see* Malabo
Santarem (Portugal)–Scallabis 8
Santiponce (Spain)–Italica 8
Santorini *see* Thira
Saragossa *see* Zaragoza
Sardica *see* Sofia
Scallabis *see* Santarem
Scodra *see* Shkoder
Scupi *see* Skopje
Scutari *see* Shkoder
Sebastea *see* Sivas
Sebastopol (USSR)–Chersonesus, Cherson, Kherson, Akhtiar, Sevastopol 21
Sebastopolis *see* Sukkhumi

Sebta *see* Ceuta
Segontia *see* Caernarvon
Seleucia *see* Abila, Mopsuestia, Silifke, Susa, Tell Umar
Sens (France)–Agedincum 14
Septum *see* Ceuta
Serdica *see* Sofia
Seville (Spain)–Hispalis 33
Shahhat (Libya)–Cyrene 8
Shahr Rey (nr Tehran, Iran)–Rhagae, Europus, Rayy 31
Shapur (Iran)–Bishapur 15
Sharpsburg (USA)–Antietam
Sharqat (Iraq)–Ashur
Shaubak (Jordan)–Montreal 26
Shenyang (China)–Feng-t'ien, Mukden 73
Shkoder (Albania)–Scodra, Scutari 63
Sian *see* Xi'an
Sibiu (Romania)–Hermanstadt 52
Sidon *see* Saida
Silifke (Turkey)–Seleucia 17
Silistra (Bulgaria)–Dorystolum 18
Silvan (Turkey)–Martyropolis, Maiyafariqin 18
Singidunum *see* Beograd
Sinus Arabicus *see* Red Sea
Sion (Switzerland)–Sitten 23
Siraf *see* Taheri
Sirmium *see* Sremska Mitrovica
Sitten *see* Sion
Sivas (Turkey)–Sebastea 17
Skopje (Yugoslavia)–Justiniana Prima, Scupi, Usküb 63
Smederevo (Yugoslavia)–Viminiacum 17
Smyrna *see* Izmir
Sofia (Bulgaria)–Sardica, Serdica 17
Somara *see* Kuybyshev
Souk Ahras (Algeria)–Thagaste 17
Sousse (Tunisia)–Hadrumetum 17
Spalato *see* Split
Split (Yugoslavia)–Salonae, Spalato 8
Squillace (Italy)–Vivarium 17
Sremska Mitrovica (Yugoslavia)–Sirmium 14
Stabrok *see* Georgetown
Stäklu *see* Svishlov
Stalinabad *see* Dushanbe

Stalingrad *see* Volgograd
Stanleyville *see* Kisangani
Stara Zagora (Bulgaria)–Berroea 18
Stettin *see* Szczecin
Strasbourg (France)–Argentoratum, Strassburg 54
Sukhumi (USSR)–Sebastopolis 17
Sunda Kalapa *see* Djakarta
Sur (Lebanon)–Tyre 26
Suran *see* Da Nang
Susa (Iran)–Seleucia 9
Svenska Mitrovica (Yugoslavia)–Sirmium 12
Svishtov (Bulgaria)–Stäklen, Novae 17
Szczecin (Poland)–Stettin 35

Tacape *see* Gabes
Taheri (Iran)–Siraf 15
Taiwan–Formosa 40
Tallinn (USSR)–Reval 76
Tamsui *see* Tanshui
Tanais, R *see* Don, R
Tangier (Morocco)–Tingis 74
Tanjore *see* Thanjavur
Tanshui (Taiwan)–Tamsui 39
Taranto (Italy)–Tarentum 62
Tarsus Cayi (Turkey)–Antiocheia, Tarsus 8
Tartu (Estonia, USSR)–Dorpat, Yuryev
Tayspun *see* Madain
Tbilisi (USSR)–Tiflis 18
Tebessa (Algeria)–Theveste 14
Tekirdag (Turkey)–Rhaedestus 26
Tell Asmar (Iraq)–Eshnunna
Temesvar *see* Timisoara
Tenochtitlan *see* Mexico City
Terranova di Sibari (Italy)–Thurii 8
Thagaste *see* Souk Ahras
Thang Long *see* Hanoi
Thanjavur (India)–Tanjore 29
Thapsacus (Syria)–Amphipolis 9
Thapsus *see* Ed Dimas
Thebes *see* Karnak
Theodosia *see* Feodosiya
Theodosiopolis *see* Erzerum
Thessaloniki (Greece)–Salonica, Thessalonica 63
Theveste *see* Tebessa

Thira (Greece)–Santorini 26
Thorn *see* Torun
Thuburbo Maius *see* Henchir el Kashat
Thurii *see* Terranova di Sibari
Ticinun *see* Pavia
Tiflis *see* Tbilisi
Tigras, R *see* Dnestr, R
Timisoara (Romania)–Temesvar 82
Tingis *see* Tangier
Tlemcen (Algeria)–Pomaria 17
Tokyo (Japan)–Edo 72
Tomi *see* Constanta
Topinos *see* Xanthi
Torun (Poland)–Thorn 21
Tourane *see* Da Nang
Tours (France)–Turones, Caesarodunum 14
Trabazon *see* Trebizond
Trajeahim *see* Utrecht
Trapezus *see* Trebizond
Trebizond (Turkey)–Trabazon, Trapezus 28
Trier (W Germany)–Treveri, Augusta Treverorum, Treves 61
Tripoli (Libya)–Tarabulus, Oea 27
Troy (Turkey)–Ilium, Troas
Tsaritsyn *see* Volgograd
Tulmaythath (Libya)–Ptolemais 17
Tunnan-fu *see* Kunming
Turda (Romania)–Potaissa 12
Turin (Italy)–Augusta Taurinorum 62
Turones *see* Tours
Tver *see* Kalinin
Tyana *see* Bor
Tyre *see* Sur
Tzu-ch'uan *see* Chu

Urfa (Turkey)–Antiocheia, Edessa, Orrhoe 27
Uruk (Iraq)–Orchoe, Erech 9
Usküb *see* Skopje
Usküdar (Turkey)–Chalcedon 16
Utrecht (Netherlands)–Trajeatum

Varanasi (Uttar Pradesh, India)–Benares, Kasi 16
Varna (Bulgaria)–Odessos 19
Vernyy *see* Alma-Ata

Verulamium *see* St Albans
Vetera *see* Xanten
Viadua, R *see* Oder, R
Vidin (Bulgaria)–Bononia 18
Vienna (Austria)–Vindobona, Beç, Wien 82
Vienne (France)–Vienna 8
Viipuri *see* Vyborg
Viminiacum *see* Smederevo
Vindobona *see* Vienna
Vistula, R *see* Wista, R
Visurgis, R *see* Weser, R
Vivarium *see* Squillace
Vlore (Albania)–Avlona 18
Volgograd (USSR)–Tsaritsyn, Stalingrad 70
Vyborg (USSR)–Viipuri 82

Wahran *see* Oran
Wels (Austria)–Ovilava 12
Weser, R–Visurgis, R
Wien *see* Vienna
Wista, R–Vistula, R
Wroclaw (Poland)–Brecia, Breslau 82
Wu-yuan *see* Chiu-yuan

Xanten (West Germany)–Vetera 12
Xanthi (Greece)–Topinos 17
Xi'an (China)–Chang-an, Feng-yüan, Sian 13

Yalvaç (Turkey)–Antiochia in Pisidia 8
Yekaterinoslav *see* Dnepropetrovsk
Yorgan Ladik (Turkey)–Laodicea Katakekaumene 18
York (England)–Eboracum, Eburacum 14
Ypres *see* Ieper
Yuryev *see* Tartu

Zagreb (Yugoslavia)–Agram 63
Zakinthos *see* Zante
Zante (Greece)–Zakinthos 63
Zara (Yugoslavia)–Iadera 8
Zaragoza (Spain)–Caesaraugusta, Saragossa 33
Zaptat *see* Epidauros

Main index

This index includes the major places, events, peoples and activities to be covered by the text and maps. For the most part individual towns have not been included. References to the map numbers are listed in roman type; references to the text are in *italic* type, and indicate the relevant page numbers.

187

Acknowledgements

It would be quite impossible to list all the sources which have been consulted in the preparation of these maps. Among general works of reference, those much used include:

Atlas zur Geschichte (2 vols., Leipzig 1976).

C. M. Cipolla, ed., *The Fontana Economic History of Europe* (6 vols., London, 1972-   ).

H. C. Darby and H. Fullard, eds., *The New Cambridge Modern History* Vol. XIV, *Atlas* (Cambridge, 1970).

M. Gilbert, *Atlas of American History* (London, Weidenfeld and Nicolson, 1968).

Grosser Historischer Weltatlas, ed. J. Engel (3 vols., Munich 1953-70).

A. Herrmann, *An Historical Atlas of China* (Edinburgh, 1966).

The International Atlas (New York, Rand MacNally, 1974).

H. Jedin, K. S. Latourette and J. Martin, *Atlas zur Kirchengeschichte* (Freiburg, 1970).

H. Kinder and W. Hilgemann, *The Penguin Atlas of World History* (2 vols., London, 1974, 1978).

C. McEvedy and R. Jones, *Atlas of World Population History* (London, Penguin Books, 1978).

W. H. McNeill, *The Rise of the West* (Chicago, Chicago U.P., 1968).

B. R. Mitchell, *European Historical Statistics, 1750-1970* (London, 1975).

W. G. Moore, *The Penguin Encyclopedia of Places* (London, 1971).

Ramsey Muir, *Historical Atlas*, ed. R. F. Treharne and H. Fullard (London, Philip, 1966).

D. E. Pitcher, *An Historical Geography of the Ottoman Empire* (Leiden, 1973).

The New Oxford Atlas (Oxford, 1975).

J. M. Roberts, *The Hutchinson History of the World* (London, 1976).

The Statesman's Yearbook.

The Times Atlas of the World, comprehensive edition (London, 1976).

The United Nations Yearbook.

G. Westermann, *Grosser Atlas zur Weltgeschichte* (Brunswick, 1976).

The Editor and contributors are also grateful to acknowledge specific obligations in respect of the following:

Map 17: 'Frontier of literacy'–P. Riché, *Education and Culture in the Barbarian West* (Engl. trans., Columbia, South Carolina U.P., 1976), pp. 177-183.

Map 21: states of Kievan Russia–G. Vernadsky, *A History of Russia* 2 (New Haven, Yale U.P., 1948), endpaper; use of Glagolitic rite–A. P. Vlasto, *The Entry of the Slavs into Christendom* (Cambridge, Cambridge U.P., 1970), p. 204.

Map 22, 23: itineraries–Carlrichard Bruhl, *Fodrum, Gistum, Servitium Regis* (Köln, Böhlau, 1968), vol. II.

Map 24: Viking graves–D. M. Wilson, 'Scandinavian Settlement in the North and West of the British Isles', *Transactions of the Royal Historical Society* 5th series 26 (1976), pp. 108-9.

Map 26: Latin sees in Frankish Greece–P. Fedelto, *La chiesa Latina in Oriente* (Verona, 1973-76), II: *Hierarchia Latina Orientis, Studi Religiosi*, 3.

Map 28: Pegolotti–J. K. Hyde, *Society and Politics in Medieval Italy* (London, Macmillan, 1973), Map 6.

Map 31: Mongol strategy–O. Lattimore, 'The Geography of Chingis Khan', *Geographical Journal* CXXIX, 1963, 1-7.

Map 36: distribution of peoples–G. W. Hewes, *A Conspectus of the World's Cultures in 1500 A.D.*

Map 37: population figures–P. Chaunu, *Amérique et les Amériques* (Paris, 1964), p. 22. Other estimates differ widely.

Map 40: economic regions–G. William Skinner, ed., *The City in Late Imperial China*, (Stanford, Stanford U.P., 1977), pp. 214-15; couriers–Y. W. Cheng, *Postal Communication in China and its modernisation*, 1860-96 (Cambridge, Mass., Harvard U.P. for East Asian Research Center, 1970), pp. 11, 22.

Map 41: Mughal service élite–M. Athar Ali, 'Towards an interpretation of the Mughal Empire', *Journal of the Royal Asiatic Society*, 1976, No. 1, p. 45.

Map 44: Origins of Hapsburg infantry–G. Parker, *The Army of Flanders and the Spanish Road*, (Cambridge, Cambridge U.P., 1972), p. 28 Fig. iv.

Map 45: iconoclastic riots in Netherlands–G. Parker, *The Dutch Revolt* (London, Allen Lane, 1977), p. 77; dissemination of printing–L. Febvre and H. J. Martin, *L'apparition du livre* (Paris, Albin Michel, 1958), map opposite p. 272.

Map 46: currency–F. Braudel and F. L. Spooner, 'Movements of Prices, 1450-1650' in *Cambridge Economic History of Europe* IV, ed. E. E. Rich and C. H. Wilson (Cambridge, Cambridge U.P., 1967), p. 463; Dutch engineers–J. van Deem, *Dredge, Drain, Reclaim* (The Hague, Nijhoff, 1962).

Map 51: imports of slaves–P. Curtin, *The Atlantic Slave Trade* (Madison, Milwaukee and London, 1969), p. 268.

Map 52: T. Bestermann, ed. *The Complete Works of Voltaire* (Geneva, 57 vols., 1968-   ); P. M. Scholes, ed., *Dr. Charles Burney's Musical Tours in Europe* (London, Oxford U.P., 1969); C. B. Oldham ed., *The Letters of Mozart and his Family* (London, 1938).

Map 54: Great Fear–G. Lefebvre, *The Great Fear of 1789–Rural Panic in Revolutionary France* (Engl. trans. London, New Left Books, 1970), p. 4; town councils–L. A. Hunt, *Revolution and Urban Politics in Provincial France, Troyes and Reims 1786-1790* (Stanford, Stanford U.P., 1978), p. 136; federalist revolts–original material supplied by Paul Hansen (University of California at Berkeley) from his thesis in progress, *The Federalist Revolt of 1793: a Comparative Study of Caen and Limoges*.

Map 55: departmental government–J. Godechot, *Les institutions de la France sous la révolution et l'empire* (Paris, 1968), p. 112.

Map 57: railways in 1848–J. Jouffroy, 'Aperçu du développement du réseau ferré en Europe', *Annales de Géographie* xl (1931), pp. 504-18.